SEGUNDO NIVEL

¡Ya verás!

SECOND EDITION

JOHN R. GUTIÉRREZ
The Pennsylvania State University

HARRY L. ROSSER
Boston College

HH
Heinle & Heinle Publishers
An International Thomson Publishing Company • Boston, MA 02116 U.S.A.

Visit us on the internet http://www.thomson.com/heinle.html

The publication of *¡Ya verás! Segundo nivel* 2/e was directed by the members of the Heinle & Heinle School Publishing Team:

Editorial Director: Beth Kramer
Market Development Director: Pamela Warren
Production Editor: Mary McKeon
Developmental Editor: Regina McCarthy
Publisher/Team Leader: Stanley J. Galek
Director of Production/Team Leader: Elizabeth Holthaus

Also participating in the publication of this text were:

Manufacturing Coordinator: Barbara Stephan
Project Manager: Kristin Swanson
Interior Design: Susan Gerould/Perspectives
Composition: NovoMac Enterprises
Cover Art: Mark Schroder
Cover: Corey McPherson Nash
Photo/Video Specialist: Jonathan Stark

Gutiérrez, John R.
    Ya veras! segundo nivel / John R. Gutiérrez, Harry L. Rosser. — 2nd ed.
       p.   cm.
    Includes index.
    Summary: Continues study of the Spanish language by utilizing everday situations.
    ISBN 0-8384-6177-8
    1. Spanish language—Textbooks for foreign speakers—English.
    [1. Spanish language—Textbooks for foreign speakers—English.]
    I. Rosser, Harry L. II. Title.
    [PC4129.E5G89   1997]
    468.2'421—dc20   95-45122
                                         —CIP
                                           AC

Manufactured in the United States of America.

ISBN 0-8384-6177-8 Student

As you continue your study of Spanish, you will not only discover how much you can already do with the language, but you will also learn to build on what you know. By now, you know how to talk about yourself, your family, and your friends; you can get around towns, use the subway in Madrid, and give directions; you are able to make purchases in a variety of stores; you can talk about the diversity of the Spanish-speaking world, including parts of the United States; and you have learned to use appropriate language in a variety of social interactions.

As you move forward, your cultural knowledge will expand as you take a closer look at parts of the Spanish-speaking world, with its varied customs, traditions, landscapes, and points of interest. You will learn to describe people and things, know how to talk about your residence and be able to get lodging (in a hotel or hostel), interact with others about your leisure-time and vacation activities, and talk about health concerns. *Remember that the most important task ahead of you is NOT to accumulate a large quantity of knowledge about Spanish grammar and vocabulary, but rather to USE what you do know as effectively and creatively as you can.*

Communication in a foreign language means understanding what others say and transmitting your own messages in ways that avoid misunderstandings. As you learn to do this, you will make the kinds of errors that are necessary to language learning. DO NOT BE AFRAID TO MAKE MISTAKES! Instead, try to see errors as positive steps toward effective communication. They don't hold you back; they advance you in your efforts.

¡Ya verás! has been written with your needs in mind. It places you in situations that you (as a young person) might really encounter in a Spanish-speaking environment. Whether you are working with vocabulary or grammar, it leads you from controlled exercises (that show you just how a word or structure is used) to bridging exercises (that allow you to introduce your own personal context into what you are saying or writing) to open-ended exercises (in which you are asked to handle a situation much as you might in actual experience). These situations are intended to give you the freedom to be creative and express yourself without fear or anxiety. They are the real test of what you can DO with the Spanish you have learned.

Learning a language is hard work, but it can also be lots of fun. We hope that you find your experience with *¡Ya verás!* both rewarding and enjoyable.

Acknowledgments

reating a secondary program is a long and complicated process which involves the dedication and hard work of a number of people. First of all, we would like to express our heartfelt thanks to our Editorial Director, Beth Kramer, whose expertise and support were crucial for guiding the project through its realization. We are also grateful to our Developmental Editor, Regina McCarthy, who worked closely with us to facilitate our work each step of the way. Our Production Editor, Mary McKeon, managed the many facets of the process with skill, timeliness, and good humor. Vivian Novo-MacDonald flawlessly handled her typesetting responsibilities. Kristin Swanson was a particularly effective Project Manager and we greatly appreciate her keen eye, poignant comments, and excellent suggestions at every phase of the process. We would like to thank many other people who played a role in the production of the program: Susan Gerould, Mary Lemire, María Silvina Persino, Camilla Ayers, Sharon Inglis, and Esther Marshall.

Our thanks also go to others at Heinle and Heinle who helped make this project possible: Charles Heinle and Stan Galek, for their special interest and support; Vincent DiBlasi and Erek Smith for their marketing and technical knowledge; and Jeannette Bragger and Donald Rice, authors of **On y va!** We also wish to express our appreciation to the people responsible for revising the fine set of supporting materials available with the **¡Ya verás!** program. Many thanks to our Project Manager Esther Marshall, and to Greg Harris, Workbook; Chris McIntyre and Jill Welch, Teacher Edition; Joe Wieczorek, Laboratory Tape Program; Ken Janson, Testing Program; Jeff Morgenstein, Software; and Frank Domínguez, Ana Martínez-Lage and Jeff Morgenstein for creating the excellent *Mundos hispanos* multimedia program.

Finally, a very special word of acknowledgment goes to the authors' children:

— To Mía (age 12) and Stevan (age 9) who are always on their daddy's mind and whose cultural heritage is ever present throughout **¡Ya verás!**

— To Susan, Elizabeth, and Rebecca Rosser, whose enthusiasm and increasing interest in Spanish inspired their father to take part in this endeavor.

John R. Gutiérrez and Harry L. Rosser

The publisher and authors wish to thank the following writers for their contributions to **¡Ya verás!** second edition.

Critical Thinking Skills, Learning Strategies

Jane Harper
Tarrant County Junior College

Madeleine Lively
Tarrant County Junior College

Mary K. Williams
Tarrant County Junior College

Reading Strategies, Aquí leemos

Laura Martin
Cleveland State University

Interdisciplinary Lessons

Jessie Carduner
University of Pittsburgh

Charles Grove
University of Pittsburgh

Paul D. Toth
University of Pittsburgh

The publisher and authors wish to thank the following teachers who pilot-tested the *¡Ya verás!* program. They used the materials with their classes and made invaluable suggestions as our work progressed. Their feedback benefits all who use this final product. We are grateful to each one of them for their dedication and commitment to teaching with the program in a prepublication format.

Nola Baysore
Muncy JHS
Muncy, PA

Barbara Connell
Cape Elizabeth Middle School
Cape Elizabeth, ME

Frank Droney
Susan Digiandomenico
Wellesley Middle School
Wellesley, MA

Michael Dock
Shikellamy HS
Sunbury, PA

Jane Flood Clare
Somers HS
Lincolndale, NY

Nancy McMahon
Somers Middle School
Lincolndale, NY

Rebecca Gurnish
Ellet HS
Akron, OH

Peter Haggerty
Wellesley HS
Wellesley, MA

José M. Díaz
Hunter College HS
New York, NY

Claude Hawkins
Flora Mazzucco
Jerie Milici
Elena Fienga
Bohdan Kodiak
Greenwich HS
Greenwich, CT

Wally Lishkoff
Tomás Travieso
Carver Middle School
Miami, FL

Manuel M. Manderine
Canton McKinley HS
Canton, OH

Grace Angel Marion
South JHS
Lawrence, KS

Jean Barrett
St. Ignatius HS
Cleveland, OH

Gary Osman
McFarland HS
McFarland, WI

Deborah Decker
Honeoye Falls-Lima HS
Honeoye Falls, NY

Carrie Piepho
Arden JHS
Sacramento, CA

Rhonda Barley
Marshall JHS
Marshall, VA

Germana Shirmer
W. Springfield HS
Springfield, VA

John Boehner
Gibson City HS
Gibson City, IL

Margaret J. Hutchison
John H. Linton JHS
Penn Hills, PA

Edward G. Stafford
St. Andrew's-Sewanee School
St. Andrew's, TN

Irene Prendergast
Wayzata East JHS
Plymouth, MN

Tony DeLuca
Cranston West HS
Cranston, RI

Joe Wild-Crea
Wayzata Senior High School
Plymouth, MN

Katy Armagost
Manhattan HS
Manhattan, KS

William Lanza
Osbourn Park HS
Manassas, VA

Linda Kelley
Hopkinton HS
Contoocook, NH

John LeCuyer
Belleville HS West
Belleville, IL

Sue Bell
South Boston HS
Boston, MA

Wayne Murri
Mountain Crest HS
Hyrum, UT

Barbara Flynn
Summerfield Waldorf School
Santa Rosa, CA

The publisher and authors wish to thank the following people who reviewed the manuscript for the second edition of the *¡Ya verás!* program. Their comments were invaluable to the development of this edition.

Georgio Arias, Juan De León, Luís Martínez (McAllen ISD, McAllen, TX); **Katy Armagost** (Mt. Vernon High School, Mt. Vernon, WA); **Yolanda Bejar, Graciela Delgado, Bárbara V. Méndez, Mary Alice Mora** (El Paso ISD, El Paso, TX); **Linda Bigler** (Thomas Jefferson High School, Alexandria, VA); **John Boehner** (Gibson City High School, Gibson City, IL); **Kathleen Carroll** (Edinburgh ISD, Edinburgh, TX); **Louanne Grimes** (Richardson ISD, Richardson, TX); **Greg Harris** (Clay High School, South Bend, IN); **Diane Henderson** (Houston ISD, Houston, TX); **Maydell Jenks** (Katy ISD, Katy, TX); **Bartley Kirst** (Ironwood High School, Glendale, AZ); **Mala Levine** (St. Margaret's Episcopal School, San Juan Capistrano, CA); **Manuel Manderine** (Canton McKinley Sr. High School, Canton, OH); **Laura Martin** (Cleveland State University, Cleveland, OH); **Luís Millán** (Edina High School, Minneapolis, MN); **David Moffett, Karen Petmeckey, Pat Rossett, Nereida Zimic** (Austin ISD, Austin, TX); **Jeff Morgenstein** (Hudson High School, Hudson, FL); **Rosana Pérez, Jody Spoor** (Northside ISD, San Antonio, TX); **Susan Polansky** (Carnegie Mellon University, Pittsburgh, PA); **Alva Salinas** (San Antonio ISD, San Antonio, TX); **Patsy Shafchuk** (Hudson High School, Hudson, FL); **Terry A. Shafer** (Worthington Kilbourne High School, West Worthington, OH); **Courtenay Suárez** (Montwood High School, Socorro ISD, El Paso, TX); **Alvino Téllez, Jr.** (Edgewood ISD, San Antonio, TX); **Kristen Warner** (Piper High School, Sunrise, FL); **Nancy Wrobel** (Champlin Park High School, Champlin, MN)

Middle School Reviewers:

Larry Ling (Hunter College High School, New York, NY); **Susan Malik** (West Springfield High School, Springfield, VA); **Yvette Parks** (Norwood Junior High School, Norwood, MA)

CONTENTS

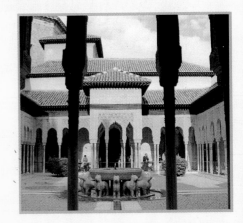

UNIDAD TRES   Nuestro día   206

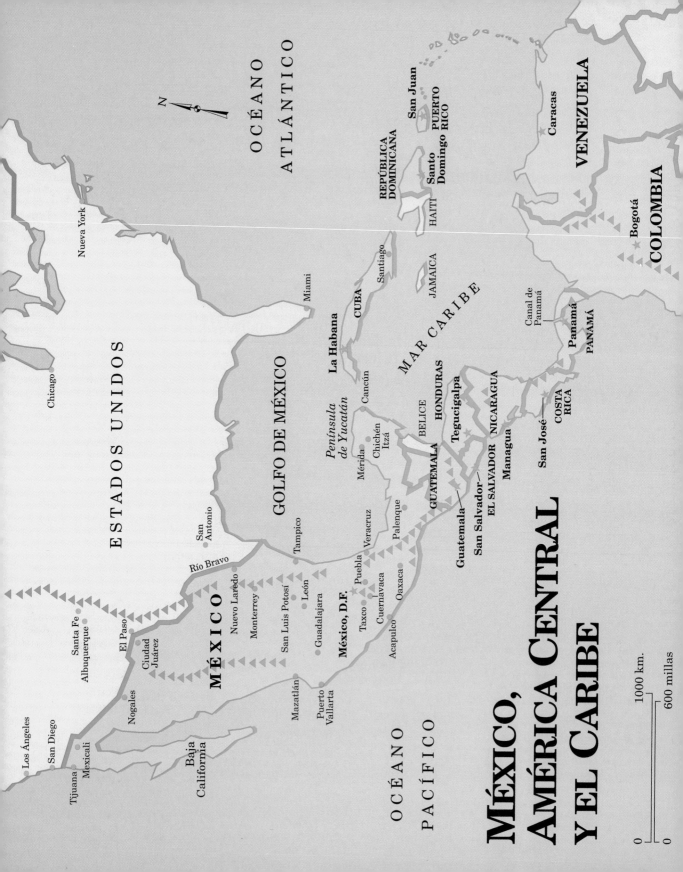

MÉXICO, AMÉRICA CENTRAL Y EL CARIBE

OCÉANO ATLÁNTICO

N

ESTADOS UNIDOS

Nueva York

Chicago

Los Ángeles
San Diego
Tijuana
Mexicali
Nogales

Baja
California

OCÉANO
PACÍFICO

Santa Fe
Albuquerque
El Paso
Ciudad
Juárez

San
Antonio

Río Bravo

Nuevo Laredo
Monterrey
San Luis Potosí
León
Guadalajara

MÉXICO

Mazatlán
Puerto
Vallarta

Tampico

GOLFO DE MÉXICO

Veracruz
Puebla
México, D.F.
Taxco
Cuernavaca
Oaxaca
Acapulco

Palenque

Mérida
Chichén
Itzá

Península
de Yucatán

Cancún

La Habana

CUBA

Miami

Santiago

MAR CARIBE

JAMAICA

BELICE
GUATEMALA
Guatemala
San Salvador
San Salvador
EL SALVADOR
HONDURAS
Tegucigalpa
NICARAGUA
Managua

Costa
RICA
San José

REPÚBLICA
DOMINICANA
Santo
Domingo
HAITÍ

San Juan
PUERTO
RICO

Canal de
Panamá
Panamá
PANAMÁ

Caracas

VENEZUELA

Bogotá
COLOMBIA

0   1000 km.
0   600 millas

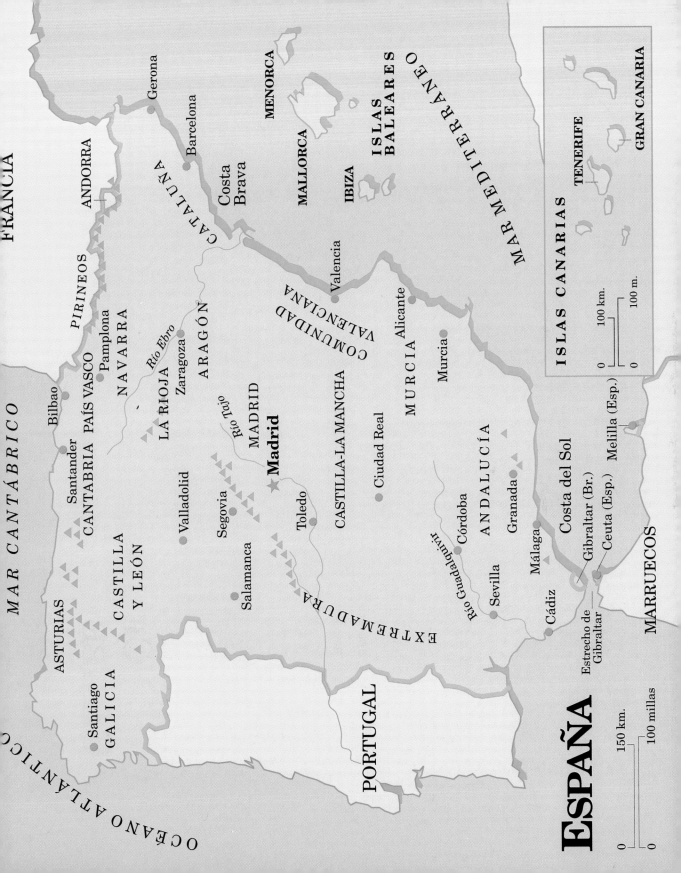

¿QUIÉN SOY YO?

—Hola, ¿qué tal, Teresa?
—Muy bien. ¿Y tú?

Objectives:

》》》 **R**eview words and expressions needed to talk about yourself and your family.

》》》 **R**eview regular verbs ending in **-ar, -er,** and **-ir** and the verbs **ser** and **tener.**

》》》 **P**ractice describing yourself and your family, greeting people, and making introductions.

Strategies:

》》》 **T**aking notes

》》》 **R**eporting

》》》 **D**rawing conclusions

》》》 **E**valuating

》》》 **D**rawing inferences

PRIMERA ETAPA

Yo me llamo...

Yo me llamo María Catarina Gutiérrez. Tengo dieciséis años. Soy española. Vivo en un apartamento en Madrid con mi padre y hermano. Me gustan los deportes de invierno — especialmente el esquí. También me gusta escuchar la radio. Me gusta mucho la música popular norteamericana.

María

Yo me llamo Esteban Méndez. Tengo quince años. Soy mexicano. Mi familia y yo vivimos en Guadalajara, la capital del estado de Jalisco. Tenemos una casa grande en las afueras de la ciudad. Me gusta mucho la música: toco el piano y la trompeta. También me gusta ir al cine con mis amigos.

Esteban

Comprensión

A. *María y Esteban en los Estados Unidos* Imagine that María and Esteban are delegates to an international meeting of young people being held in your region of the United States. You have met them both and would like to introduce them to your teacher. Prepare your introductions of both María and Esteban by answering the following questions: **¿Cómo se llama? ¿Cuál es su nacionalidad? ¿Cuántos años tiene él (ella)? ¿Dónde vive? ¿Con quién? ¿Vive en una casa o en un apartamento? ¿Qué hace en su tiempo libre?** Begin by saying, *"Señora (Señor), quiero presentarle a... Él (Ella) es..."*

R PASO

Regular verbs ending in -ar, -er, and -ir

To conjugate regular **-ar** verbs in the present tense, drop the **-ar** from the infinitive and add the appropriate ending: **-o, -as, -a, -amos, -áis,** or **-an.**

hablar			
yo	habl**o**	nosotros(as)	habl**amos**
tú	habl**as**	vosotros(as)	habl**áis**
él		ellos	
ella	} habl**a**	ellas	} habl**an**
Ud.		Uds.	

B. Replace the words in italics with those in parentheses and make the necessary changes.

1. *Ella* trabaja mucho. (nosotros / yo / él / tú / ellos / vosotros)
2. ¿Habla *él* francés también? (tú / Uds. / ella / ellos / vosotros)
3. *Ellos* viajan todos los años. (ella / nosotras / yo / él / ellas / vosotras)

R PASO

To conjugate regular **-er** verbs in the present tense, drop the **-er** from the infinitive and add the appropriate ending: **-o, -es, -e, -emos, -éis,** or **-en.**

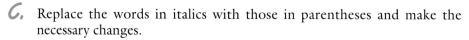

	correr			
yo	corr**o**		nosotros(as)	corr**emos**
tú	corr**es**		vosotros(as)	corr**éis**
él			ellos	
ella	corr**e**		ellas	corr**en**
Ud.			Uds.	

C. Replace the words in italics with those in parentheses and make the necessary changes.

1. *Yo* corro dos millas todos los días. (tú / ella / José y Roberta / nosotros / Uds. / vosotras)
2. *Ella* no bebe leche. (yo / él / Ud. / nosotras / tú / vosotros)
3. ¿Lee *él* el periódico *(newspaper)* todas las mañanas? (tú / Ud. / Uds. / ellos / tu papá / vosotros)

R PASO

To conjugate regular **-ir** verbs in the present tense, drop the **-ir** from the infinitive and add the appropriate ending: **-o, -es, -e, -imos, -ís,** or **-en.**

	escribir			
yo	escrib**o**		nosotros(as)	escrib**imos**
tú	escrib**es**		vosotros(as)	escrib**ís**
él			ellos	
ella	escrib**e**		ellas	escrib**en**
Ud.			Uds.	

D. Replace the words in italics with those in parentheses and make the necessary changes.

1. *Ellos* viven en un apartamento en el centro. (yo / ella / tú / nosotras / Ud. / vosotros)
2. *Él* no asiste a la escuela los sábados. (nosotros / ellos / Uds. / Ud. / tú / vosotras)
3. ¿Escriben *ellas* la composición ahora? (tú / ella / Ud. / Uds. / vosotros)

¿Recuerdan?

1. In order to express in Spanish what activities we like and do not like, the following structure is used:

gustar + *infinitive*

Me gusta estudiar, pero no **me gusta** trabajar.
¿Te gusta cantar o **te gusta** escuchar música?
A Juan le gusta estudiar, pero **a Elena le gusta** hablar por teléfono.
A nosotros nos gusta nadar, pero **a Uds. les gusta** correr.

2. This structure may also be used with singular and plural nouns:

Me gusta la biología, pero no **me gusta** la física.
Te gustan las ciencias, pero no **te gustan** las lenguas.
A Marisol le gusta la música, pero **a Julia le gustan** los deportes.
Nos gustan las clases, pero **a ellos les gustan** los profesores.

3. Remember that **gusta** is used with singular nouns and infinitives and **gustan** is used with plural nouns.

4. The definite articles in Spanish are: **el, la, los,** and **las.** They are often used after the verb **gustar** to indicate a general like or dislike of something:

Sí, me gustan **los** deportes.   No me gustan **las** ciencias.
¿Te gusta **la** historia?   ¿Te gusta **el** fútbol?

Cooperative Learning

Learning Strategies:

Collecting information, taking notes, reporting

Critical Thinking Strategy:

Evaluating

E. Entrevista   Find out about your classmate and his or her family and friends. Begin by preparing a set of at least 12 interview questions based on the expressions you have studied along with those in the **Tarjetas de vocabulario: Para indicar dónde vives** and **Para hablar de tus actividades**, pages 10–11. Sample questions include: **¿Te gusta**

escuchar la radio? ¿Qué tipo de música te gusta? ¿Cantas bien o mal? ¿Dónde trabajan tus padres? ¿Dónde vive tu mejor amigo(a)? ¿Tú y tus amigos, comen en un restaurante de vez en cuando? ¿Qué comida les gusta?

Take notes on your classmate's answers, organizing the information in the following sections: **Mi compañero(a), Sus padres, Su mejor amigo(a), Mi compañero(a) y sus amigos(as).** Be sure to collect information for each of the four sections. Choose the most interesting information from each section to report to the class.

REPASO

The verb *ser* (present tense)

	ser			
yo	**soy**		nosotros(as)	**somos**
tú	**eres**		vosotros(as)	**sois**
él			ellos	
ella	**es**		ellas	**son**
Ud.			Uds.	

1. When **ser** is followed by an adjective (such as a description of nationality), the adjective must agree in gender (masculine or feminine) and number (singular or plural) with the subject of **ser:**

   Él es **mexicano; ellos** son **mexicanos.**
   Ella es **argentina; ellas** son **argentinas.**

2. Remember that **ser** + **de** can be used to express origin.

   Él **es de** México, pero ellas **son de** España.
   Nosotros **somos** de los Estados Unidos, pero tú **eres de** Francia.

F. Replace the words in italics with those in parentheses and make the necessary changes.

1. *Él* es de Argentina. (ella / nosotros / yo / ellos / tú / vosotros)
2. ¿Es *ella* rusa? (él / Uds. / tú / ellos / vosotros)
3. *Ellos* no son de aquí. (ella / yo / Ud. / tú / ellas / vosotros)
4. *Ellas* son españolas, ¿verdad? (Uds. / él / tú / ellos / vosotros)

G. *Los delegados*   At a reception being held as part of the international student congress, you point out some of the delegates, indicate their nationalities, and tell what cities they are from. Follow the model.

   Justo Alarcón / Guadalajara, México
Allí está Justo. Él es mexicano. Es de Guadalajara.

Linda Martín y Claudia González / Buenos Aires, Argentina
Allí están Linda y Claudia. Ellas son argentinas.
Son de Buenos Aires.

1. Inge Schnepf / Munich, Alemania
2. Joel Rini / Roma, Italia
3. Julian Weiss y Ralph Withers / Manchester, Inglaterra
4. Janet Maguire y Lisa Mullins / Boston, los Estados Unidos
5. Rosa Domínguez / México, México
6. Tashi Yokoshura (f.) / Tokio, Japón
7. Anne-Marie Pelliser y Jean Firmin / Ginebra, Suiza
8. Ivan Medchenko / Moscú, Rusia

Situaciones

Saludos y presentaciones

a) En la calle
—Buenos días, señora.
—Buenos días, señor. ¿Cómo está?
—Muy bien, gracias. ¿Y Ud.?
—Bastante bien, gracias. ¿Va Ud. al centro?
—No, yo voy a casa.
—Bien. Hasta luego, señor.
—Hasta luego, señora.

b) En el centro
—¡Hola, María!
—¡Hola, Linda! ¿Qué tal?
—Muy bien. ¿Y tú?
—Así, así. Estoy muy cansada. Mira, quiero presentarte a mi amiga, Isabel.
—Mucho gusto, Isabel.
—Encantada, Linda.
—¿Uds. van al centro?
—Sí. ¿Tú también? ¿Vamos juntas?
—De acuerdo. Vamos.

c) En casa de Juan Pablo

—Mamá, papá, quisiera presentarles al Sr. Lima. Es el padre de Francisco.

—Ah, sí. Buenos días, señor. Mucho gusto en conocerle.

—Igualmente. Francisco me habló mucho de Ud. y de su esposa. Encantado, señora.

—Mucho gusto, señor.

d) En la calle

—¡Martín! ¡Martín!

—¡Hola, Patricio! ¿Qué tal?

—Muy, muy bien. ¿Y tú?

—Muy bien. ¿Vas a la escuela?

—Ahora no. Tengo que hacer un mandado.

—¡Cuídate! Hasta luego.

—De acuerdo. Chao.

¡Aquí te toca a ti!

H. Match the preceding four conversations with the following drawings.

1.

2.

3.

4.

I. Presentaciones y saludos   For each of the following tasks give one greeting or introduction that would be appropriate and another that would be inappropriate. Be prepared to explain your examples.

1. Greet your teacher, whom you have just met while downtown.
2. Introduce a new classmate to your teacher. Imagine that it is the first time they have met.
3. Greet a classmate in the street.
4. Introduce a friend to your parents.
5. Introduce a friend's mother or father to your parents.

Actividad

J. Yo soy...   You are planning to study abroad as a foreign exchange student. You know that you will be introducing yourself to a lot of different people and you want to be able to tell some interesting things about yourself. Drawing upon what you have studied along with ideas from the **Tarjetas de vocabulario** on pages 10–11, put together an introduction telling about (1) who you are, (2) where you are from, (3) your home, (4) your family, (5) your favorite activities, and (6) your likes and dislikes.

Then, working with a partner, take turns introducing yourselves to each other. Take notes on your partner's introduction so that you can introduce him or her to others.

Tarjetas de vocabulario

Para saludar

Buenos días, señor (señora, señorita).
¡Hola!
¿Cómo está? (¿Cómo estás?)
¿Qué tal?
Muy bien, gracias. ¿Y Ud.? (¿Y tú?)

Para identificarte

Yo me llamo…
Mi nombre (apellido) es…

Para despedirte

Cuídate. (Cuídese.) Hasta luego.
Adiós.
Chao.

Para hacer una presentación

Quiero presentarte a… (Quiero presentarle a…).
Quisiera presentarte a… (Quisiera presentarle a…).
Te presento a… (Le presento a…).
Mucho gusto.
Encantado(a).
Igualmente.

Para indicar dónde vives

Yo vivo en… (ciudad o país).
Yo vivo en un apartamento.
una casa.

Para hablar de tus actividades

Me gusta (mucho) bailar.
      cantar.
 ir de compras.
 mirar la televisión.
 nadar.
 pasar tiempo con mis amigos.
 tocar el piano.
    la trompeta. la flauta.
    la guitarra. el violín.
 comprar discos compactos.
 trabajar.

No me gusta descansar.
     viajar.
     esquiar.
     aprender español.
     estudiar.
     correr.
     leer.
     asistir a la escuela.
        a un concierto.

También me gusta el arte.
 la naturaleza. la música clásica.
 la política. el jazz.
 la escultura. la pintura.
 la historia. el rock.
 la literatura. el teatro.

No me gustan las películas.
     los animales.
     las ciencias.
     las matemáticas.
     las lenguas.
     los deportes.

Para hablar de tu origen y tu nacionalidad

Yo soy de… (ciudad o país).
Yo soy alemán (alemana).
    americano(a).   italiano(a).
    chino(a).   japonés (japonesa).
    español(a).   mexicano(a).
    francés (francesa). ruso(a).
    inglés (inglesa).
Yo soy de origen alemán (español, americano, mexicano, argentino, etc.).

SEGUNDA ETAPA

Mi familia

Mi mamá murió hace cinco años. Mi padre, mi hermano y yo vivimos en un apartamento en Madrid. Mi padre tiene cuarenta y cuatro años y trabaja en un banco. Mi hermano tiene ocho años y asiste a la escuela primaria. Yo soy estudiante de la escuela secundaria. Mi padre tiene un coche —es un Seat. Yo tengo una bicicleta. Nosotros tenemos un televisor y un estéreo. También tenemos un perro; se llama Chomsky.

María

Mi padre es abogado. Él trabaja en Guadalajara. Mi mamá no trabaja fuera de casa. Ella cuida a mi hermana que tiene tres años. Mis otras dos hermanas y yo somos estudiantes del Colegio Juárez. Mi hermano tiene veinticinco años y está casado. Él vive en la ciudad de México.

Mis padres tienen dos coches. Yo tengo una motocicleta. En casa nosotros tenemos una computadora y un vídeo. Mis hermanas y yo miramos la televisión todas las noches. También tenemos dos gatos.

Esteban

Comprensión

A. ¿Quiénes son?
Based on the comments made by María and Esteban on page 12, identify the following people or animals. Follow the model.

> **Modelo:** *Es la hermana de Esteban.*

1.   2.   3.

4.   5.   6.

REPASO

The verb *tener* (present tense)

tener			
yo	**tengo**	nosotros(as)	**tenemos**
tú	**tienes**	vosotros(as)	**tenéis**
él		ellos	
ella }	**tiene**	ellas }	**tienen**
Ud.		Uds.	

B. Replace the words in italics with those in parentheses and make the necessary changes.

1. *Ella* tiene un perro y dos gatos. (ellos / nosotros / Uds. / yo / él)
2. ¿Tienen *ellos* un coche? (tú / Ud. / Uds. / ellas / ella / vosotras)
3. *Él* no tiene un hermano. (ella / yo / Ud. / nosotras / ellos / tú)

REPASO

Possessive adjectives

Possessive adjectives in Spanish agree with the object possessed (not with the person who is the possessor). Here are the forms of the possessive adjectives:

Subject	Possessive adjective	English equivalent
yo	**mi, mis**	*my*
tú	**tu, tus**	*your*
él, ella, Ud.	**su, sus**	*his, her, your*
nosotros(as)	**nuestro, nuestra, nuestros, nuestras**	*our*
ellos, ellas, Uds.	**su, sus**	*their, your*

C. Replace the words in italics with those in parentheses and make the necessary changes.

1. Es mi *libro*. (lápiz / cintas / bolígrafo / llaves)
2. ¿Son tus *discos compactos*? (calculadora / amigas / cuadernos / estéreo)
3. Es nuestro *amigo*. (llaves / libros / casa / apartamento)
4. No es su *casa*. (libros / mochilas / cámara / apartamento)

¿Recuerdan?

Question words may be used to ask for specific information. Among the question words you know are:

dónde	¿**Dónde** vive tu amigo?	**quién**	¿**Quién** vive en la casa blanca?
cuántos	¿**Cuántos** libros hay en la mesa?	**qué**	¿**Qué** estudias?
cuántas	¿**Cuántas** muchachas hay en la clase?	**por qué**	¿**Por qué** comes pizza?

D. *La curiosidad*   Work in pairs to find out about each other's families. Interview your partner to find out (1) how many people there are in the family and (2) whether he or she has brothers or sisters. If so, find out (3) their names, (4) their ages, and (5) what sports or activities they like. (6) Ask if the family has a dog or cat. If the answer is yes, find out (7) its name and (8) how old it is. (9) Ask if your partner's parents work. If they do, (10) find out where. As you exchange information, note similarities and differences in your families. Take notes on the information you collect, so that you can report on it later.

Use the following expressions in your interview:
¿Cuántas personas hay en tu familia? ¿Cómo se llama(n)... ? ¿Cuántos años tiene(n)... ? ¿Qué deportes le gustan a tu hermana? ¿Dónde trabaja(n)... ?

Presentaciones

La familia

a) Yo me llamo Cristina Sáenz. Tengo una familia tradicional. Vivo con mis padres y mi hermano Raúl.

b) Me llamo Enrique Cuervo. Mi familia no es tradicional. Hace cinco años que mis padres se divorciaron. Mi madre se casó otra vez y vivo con mi madre, mi padrastro y su hijo.

c) Mi nombre es Pablo González. Soy de una familia grande. Vivo con mis padres. Tengo dos hermanos y cuatro hermanas. Mis abuelos, los padres de mi madre, también viven con nosotros.

d) Mi nombre es Catarina Landa. Soy hija única, es decir, yo no tengo hermanos. Vivo con mis padres.

¡Aquí te toca a ti!

E. *¿La familia de quién?*   Match the preceding four descriptions with the following family portraits.

1.
2.
3.
4.

//.//.//.//.//.//.//.//.//
Cooperative
Learning

Learning Strategies:

Selecting information,
reporting based on per-
sonal knowledge

//.//.//.//.//.//.//.//.//
Learning Strategies:

Interviewing, organiz-
ing information

Actividades

F. Mi amigo(a)   Tell your partner about one of your friends.
(1) Describe his or her family; tell (2) where he or she lives, (3) whether
he or she lives in a house or an apartment. Tell about (4) some of his or
her favorite activities and (5) some favorite possessions. (6) Finally, talk
about what the two of you like to do together.

G. Mi familia   Working with a partner, interview each other to do a
profile of your families. Divide your interview into three sections: (1) First,
find out about the immediate family. Get the names, ages, and relationship to your partner of each member of the household. (2) Next ask
about his or her grandparents, aunts, uncles, cousins. (3) Ask about your
partner's most interesting relatives. Try to find out what makes these relatives particularly interesting. Take notes so that you can give a summary
description of your partner's family.

Tarjetas de vocabulario

Para hablar de tu familia

Yo soy de una familia pequeña.
     grande.
     tradicional.
Yo no soy de una familia tradicional.

Del lado de mi padre (mi madre),
 yo tengo un abuelo.
     una abuela.
     un tío.
     una tía.
     un primo.
     una prima.

Yo tengo padre.   una madrastra
   madre.   *(stepmother).*
   un padrastro un hermano.
   (stepfather). una hermana.

Mi padre (Mi madre) se llama…
Mi hermano(a) está casado(a).
       divorciado(a).
Mi abuelo(a) está muerto(a).
Mi tío y mi tía tienen una hija.
       un hijo.
       no tienen hijos.

Para hablar de tu edad

¿Cuántos años tienes?
Yo tengo… años.

Para hablar de tus posesiones

Cuando voy a la escuela,
 llevo un bolígrafo.
   un borrador. un libro.
   una cartera. una llave.
   un cuaderno. una mochila.
   una calculadora. un portafolio.
   un lápiz.   un sacapuntas.

Voy al centro en coche.
    en bicicleta.
    en motocicleta.

En mi cuarto, yo tengo una alfombra.
    una cama. un estéreo. un radio
    una cinta. una grabadora. despertador
    una cómoda. una máquina una silla.
    una computadora. de escribir. un televisor.
    un disco compacto. una planta. un vídeo.
    un escritorio. un póster.

B

¿ADÓNDE VAMOS?

Puerta de Alcalá, Madrid

Objectives:

>>> **R**eview words and expressions needed to talk about your town or city.

>>> **R**eview formal and informal commands.

>>> **R**eview the verbs **ir, estar, pensar, querer,** and **preferir.**

>>> **P**ractice describing where places are located.

Strategies:

>>> **R**eading a map

>>> **D**escribing spatial relationships

>>> **P**olling

>>> **M**aking associations

>>> **C**omparing and contrasting

PRIMERA ETAPA

Mi ciudad

Yo soy de Madrid, la capital de España. Madrid tiene aproximadamente tres millones de habitantes. Está situada en el centro del país. La parte central de la ciudad es la parte antigua. Allí está la Plaza Mayor, la Iglesia de San Pedro y el Palacio Real. Esta parte antigua está rodeada de barrios residenciales con edificios modernos y avenidas anchas. La avenida más animada es la Gran Vía. Allí hay muchos bancos, tiendas, restaurantes, hoteles, discotecas y cines.

María

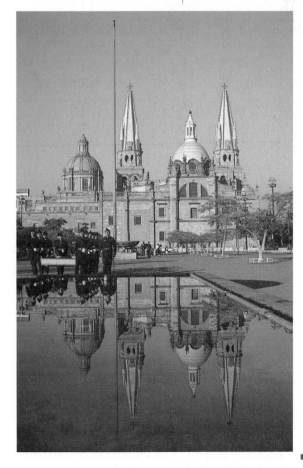

Yo soy de Guadalajara, una ciudad donde viven más de 1.800.000 habitantes. Es la segunda ciudad más grande de México. En el centro de esta linda ciudad hay cuatro plazas que forman una cruz. Éstas son: la Plaza de los Laureles, la Plaza de Armas, la Plaza de los Hijos Ilustres y la Plaza de la Liberación. En el centro de estas plazas está nuestra hermosa catedral. Cerca de aquí también están el Museo Regional de Guadalajara y el Palacio de Gobierno donde hay unos murales que pintó el artista mexicano José Clemente Orozco. Generalmente voy al centro para ir de compras o para visitar a amigos.

19

Comprensión

A. Name three major sights in Madrid and three major sights in Guadalajara. Tell which you would most like to visit. Be able to explain why.

B. Answer the following questions about the city or town where you live.

1. ¿Es tu ciudad (pueblo) grande (bastante grande, pequeña, muy pequeña)?
2. ¿Cuántos habitantes tiene?
3. ¿Está en el norte (el sur, el este, el oeste, el centro) de los Estados Unidos?
4. ¿Está cerca de una ciudad grande? ¿A cuántas millas está de esta ciudad?

C. For each of the following places listed, (1) tell whether or not there is such a place in your city or town; (2) tell whether you like to go there; (3) name an activity that you associate with each place.

Lugares en la ciudad

un hotel	una iglesia	un teatro	una estación de trenes
un restaurante	un estadio	una biblioteca	un aeropuerto
de servicio	una piscina	una tienda de música	un cine
rápido	una escuela	una panadería	una oficina de
un café	un museo	un supermercado	correos

REPASO

The verb *ir* (present tense)

ir			
yo	**voy**	nosotros(as)	**vamos**
tú	**vas**	vosotros(as)	**vais**
él		ellos	
ella	**va**	ellas	**van**
Ud.		Uds.	

The verb **ir** is often used with adverbs such as **siempre, frecuentemente, de vez en cuando, a veces, raramente,** and **nunca.**

¿Recuerdan?

The preposition **a** combines with the article **el** to form **al.** There is no contraction between **a** and the articles **la, las,** and **los.**

Yo voy **al** banco y después voy **a la** tienda de música.
Nosotros vamos **a la** escuela y después vamos **al** centro.

D. *¿Adónde vas?*   From the list in Activity C on page 20, choose four places that you enjoy. Then, following the model, interview at least four of your classmates to find out how often they go to these places. Make a chart like the one below to record their responses.

When you have completed your interviews, assign a value to each response: **nunca = 0, rara vez = 1, de vez en cuando = 2, frecuentemente = 3.** For each place on your list, add up the numbers to see which are most frequented by your classmates.

 Modelo: **Estudiante 1:**   *¿Tú vas frecuentemente al estadio?*
   Estudiante 2:   *Sí, voy al estadio frecuentemente.*   o:
   De vez en cuando voy al estadio.   o:
   No, yo voy rara vez al estadio.   o:
   No, nunca voy al estadio. No me gustan los deportes.

Lugares	Catarina	Roberto	Julia	Antonio
estadio	rara vez	de vez en cuando		
cine	frecuentemente	frecuentemente		
biblioteca	de vez en cuando	frecuentemente		
tienda de música	nunca	rara vez		

E. *¿Y tú?*   For each of the places listed, indicate (1) whether you like to go there, (2) how often you go, and (3) with whom you hope to go next time.

Modelo: a la biblioteca
   Me gusta bastante bien ir a la biblioteca.
   Voy de vez en cuando.
   La próxima vez espero ir con mi madre.

1. al cine
2. al centro
3. al museo
4. a la piscina
5. al aeropuerto
6. al estadio
7. al teatro
8. a la iglesia

Cooperative Learning

Learning Strategies:

Polling, recording information on a chart, tallying results of a poll

Critical Thinking Strategy:

Evaluating

¿Recuerdan?

The phrase **ir + a** + *infinitive* is used to indicate the immediate future—that is, what *is going to happen soon:*

Esta noche yo **voy a hablar** con Linda.
Mis padres **no van a comer** en un restaurante mañana.
El domingo Marirrosa **va a cenar** con nosotros.

Esperar + *infinitive* may also be used to talk about the immediate future:

Yo **espero ir** al centro esta tarde.
Mi amigo y yo **esperamos caminar** al centro mañana.

F. Este fin de semana Miguel is talking to his sister Verónica about what she and her friends are planning to do this weekend. Based on the drawings below and on page 23, give Verónica's answers to her brother's questions.

 Modelo: ¿Va a estudiar Miguel?
No, él va a mirar la tele.

1. ¿Va a jugar al fútbol Jorge?

2. ¿Va a cenar en casa Isabel?

3. ¿Va a jugar al básquetbol Federico?

4. ¿Va a tocar la trompeta Juan?

5. Verónica, ¿vas a trabajar en la computadora?

6. ¿Van a asistir al concierto Micaela y Teresa?

REPASO

The verb *estar* (present tense)

estar

yo	**estoy**	nosotros(as)	**estamos**
tú	**estás**	vosotros(as)	**estáis**
él		ellos	
ella	**está**	ellas	**están**
Ud.		Uds.	

The verb **estar** is used in Spanish to express the location of something or someone.

—¿Dónde **está** Boston?　　　　—¿Dónde **están** Marcos y Elena?
—Boston **está** en Massachusetts.　**—Están** en la biblioteca.

—¿Dónde **está** el restaurante?
—**Está** detrás de la biblioteca.

¿Recuerdan?

The preposition **de** combines with the article **el** to form **del**. There is no contraction between **de** and the articles **la, las,** and **los.**

El hotel está al lado **del** banco.
El restaurante está cerca **de la** iglesia.

//-//-//-//-//-//-//-//-//
Learning Strategies:

Reading a map, describing spatial relationships

G. En Guadalajara
Esteban is trying to help you find your way around Guadalajara. Using the map below, play the role of Esteban and precisely describe the location of the following places.

1. Mercado Libertad
2. Plaza Tapatía
3. Antigua Universidad
4. Parque Morelos

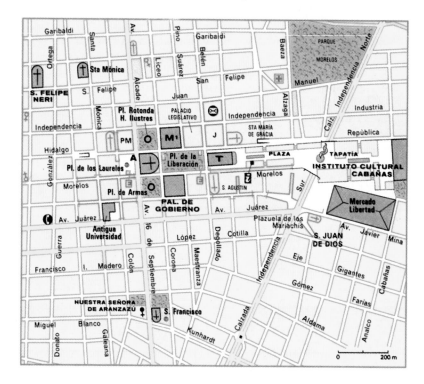

Situaciones

¿Dónde está...?

a) En el centro
—Perdón, señora. ¿Hay un banco cerca de aquí?
—Sí, señor, en la esquina de la Calle Galdós y la Avenida Meléndez.
—Muchas gracias, señora.
—De nada, señor.

b) En la calle
—¿Vas a la fiesta en casa de María esta noche?
—Sí, pero no sé dónde vive. ¿Sabes tú? Su casa está cerca del hospital en la Calle Chapultepec, ¿no?

—Sí, está en la Calle Chapultepec, pero no está cerca del hospital. Tienes
que caminar por la Calle Chapultepec hasta el parque. Su casa está allí,
cerca de la panadería.

c) En la esquina
—Perdón, señor. ¿Está el Hotel Juárez cerca de aquí?
—No, señora. Está al otro lado de la ciudad. Ud. tiene que tomar el
autobús número 28 y bajar en la Plaza Juárez. Allí, al otro lado de la
plaza, está el Hotel Juárez. Hay una estatua del Presidente Juárez
delante del hotel.

d) Delante del banco
—¿Necesita otra cosa?
—Sí. Quisiera comprar un periódico.
—Bueno. Hay un quiosco en la Calle Colón, justo al lado del banco.
—Muy bien. Gracias.

¡Aquí te toca a ti!

H. Match the preceding conversations with the following drawings.

*Critical Thinking
Strategy:*

Drawing conclusions

1.

2.

3.

4.

I. Un peruano en... Work with a partner. One of you will play the role of a Peruvian foreign exchange student who has just arrived in your city or town and who wants tips on places to go. The exchange student begins by making a list of at least four favorite activities. Examples include: **comer pizza, comprar discos compactos, alquilar vídeos, comprar libros, tomar refrescos, correr, ver un partido de fútbol, ver una película.** The exchange student asks where to go for each activity. The other student will think of an appropriate place for each activity and describe where the place is.

Actividades

J. Tu pueblo o ciudad Draw a map of the section of city or town where you live. Show—but don't label—five or six places where you or your family go from time to time and show the streets around them (at least five different streets). Label one of the streets. When you have completed your map, give it to your partner, who will label the streets and places as you describe them. Your partner can ask you if he or she is getting something right (e.g., **¿Cómo eso? / ¿Está aquí el cine Apollo? / ¿Está a la derecha o a la izquierda?**), and you can tell him or her there is a mistake (e.g., **No, el banco está más lejos de la farmacia. / No, la calle Lincoln está en frente de la piscina.**), but don't offer to help by pointing.

K. Otro pueblo o ciudad Choose a town or city other than your own (for example, where you used to live or the town where your grandparents live). Briefly describe this town or city, mentioning (1) population, (2) what part of the state it is located in, (3) whether it is large or small, (4) what the downtown area is like (modern, old, busy), (5) some features that give it its character (buildings, monuments). Use the descriptions of Madrid and Guadalajara given by María and Esteban on page 19 as models.

Tarjetas de vocabulario

Para indicar adonde vas

Yo voy a (al, a la)… frecuentemente.
　　　　　　　　　rara vez.
　　　　　　　　　de vez en cuando.
A veces voy a (al, a la)…
Nunca

Para localizar

Está al final de…　　　　en…
　　　al lado de…　　　　en frente de…
　　　cerca de…　　　　　en la esquina de… y…
　　　delante de…　　　　entre… y…
　　　detrás de…　　　　　lejos de…

Para hablar de tu ciudad

Mi ciudad es (muy, bastante) grande.
　　　　　　　　　　　　　pequeña.
Está situada en el norte de los Estados Unidos.
　　　　　　el sur　　el este
　　　　　　el oeste　el centro
En mi ciudad hay un aeropuerto.　　una farmacia.　　un parque.
　　　　　　　un banco.　　　　una iglesia.　　un restaurante.
　　　　　　　una biblioteca.　　un hospital.　　un estadio.
　　　　　　　una catedral.　　　un hotel.　　　un teatro.
　　　　　　　una discoteca.　　una librería.　　una universidad.
　　　　　　　una escuela.　　　un museo.

SEGUNDA ETAPA

Vamos al centro

Yo vivo cerca de la universidad de Madrid. Cuando quiero ir al centro, generalmente tomo el metro. Es muy fácil. Camino a la estación Moncloa que no está lejos de nuestro apartamento. Normalmente compro un billete de 10 viajes que cuesta 625 pesetas. Entonces tomo la dirección Legazpi y en 15 minutos estoy en Sol. Aquí es donde bajo si voy al Corte Inglés para ir de compras. O si quiero dar un paseo por el Parque del Retiro, cambio de trenes en Sol, dirección Ventas, y bajo en la estación Retiro.

María

Nuestra casa está cerca del Estadio Jalisco en la ciudad de Guadalajara. La escuela donde soy estudiante está en el centro. Para ir allí, tomo un autobús. Tarda media hora para llegar a la escuela. A veces, cuando tiene tiempo, mi papá nos lleva a la escuela en su coche. En esos días, tarda solamente cinco minutos para llegar de nuestra casa a la escuela. Durante el fin de semana, nos gusta dar paseos a pie por la ciudad.

Esteban

Comprensión

A. *¡Vamos en el metro!* You have been staying in Madrid for some time and know the subway system very well. A friend of yours arrives from the U.S. and needs to go to the places listed on pages 29–30. Explain to him or her how to get to these places on the **metro.** Your friend is staying near the **Plaza Castilla** station.

Museo del Prado (Atocha)

Para ir al Museo del Prado, tomas la dirección Portazgo.
Bajas en la estación Atocha.

1. Parque del Retiro   **2.** Plaza de España   **3.** Moncloa

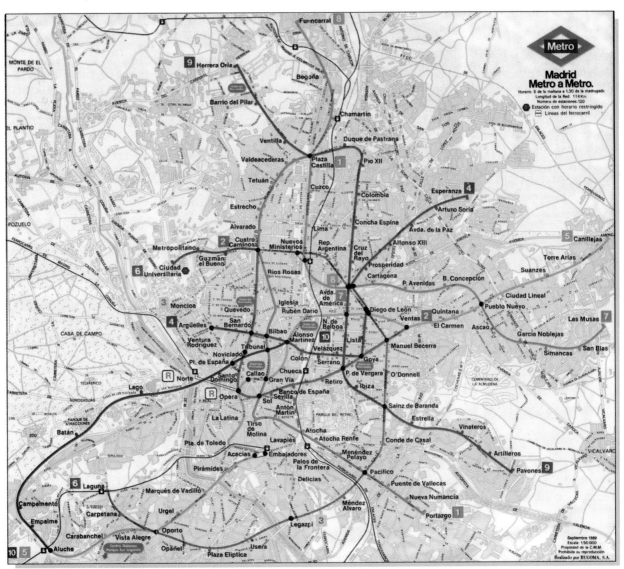

Now a family from Mexico is visiting Madrid. They are interested in seeing some of the sights. Using the map on page 29, explain to this family how to get to the following places. Remember to use **Uds.** when talking to the whole family. They are staying near the **Plaza del Cuzco.**

4. Puerta del Sol   **5.** Ciudad Universitaria

Learning Strategy:

Providing personal information

B. *¿Y tú?* Answer these questions about yourself and your family.

1. ¿Cómo vas a la escuela? ¿Vas a pie? ¿en el coche de tus padres? ¿Vas en tu bicicleta? ¿en el autobús?

2. ¿Tienen tus padres un coche? ¿Qué tipo de coche? ¿Van al trabajo en el coche? Si no van al trabajo en el coche, ¿cómo van?

3. ¿Tienes una bicicleta? ¿Adónde vas en tu bicicleta? ¿a la escuela? ¿al centro?

4. Cuando vas a casa de tus abuelos, ¿cómo vas? ¿a pie? ¿en coche? ¿Vas en tren? ¿en avión?

REPASO

Placing events in time

Days of the week

lunes   martes   miércoles   jueves   viernes   sábado   domingo

Remember that the definite article is often used with the days of the week:

el lunes = Monday, the upcoming Monday
los lunes = on Mondays, indicates a customary action on a specific day of the week

El viernes voy a una fiesta en casa de Jaime.
Los lunes voy a la escuela.

Time of day

Son las dos.

Son las dos y diez.

Son las dos y cuarto.

Son las dos y
media.

Son las tres menos
veinte.

Son las tres
menos cuarto.

Twelve o'clock noon is **mediodía;** twelve o'clock midnight is **medianoche.** To indicate a.m.
and p.m. with other times, add **de la mañana, de la tarde,** or **de la noche.**

C. ¿Dónde está Patricio?   Study the daily schedule of Patricio
Fernández below; then answer the questions.

	lunes	martes	miércoles	jueves	viernes	sábado
9:30–10:25	historia	historia		historia	historia	historia
10:40–11:35	francés	francés	no	el gimnasio	francés	
11:40–12:35	matemáticas	arte	hay	el gimnasio	matemáticas	matemáticas
2:00–2:55	inglés	inglés	clases	inglés	inglés	inglés
3:00–3:55	biología	biología		biología	arte	
4:10–5:05	español	español		español	español	

1. ¿Qué días tiene Patricio su clase de francés?
2. ¿Qué días tiene su clase de matemáticas?
3. ¿Qué clases tiene Patricio por la tarde?
4. ¿A qué hora es su clase de biología?
5. ¿A qué hora es su clase de francés?
6. ¿Dónde está Patricio a las 11:00 de la mañana el jueves?
7. ¿A qué hora llega a la escuela si de costumbre él llega 15 minutos antes de su primera clase?
8. De costumbre, ¿a qué hora almuerza Patricio?

Learning Strategy:

Reading a schedule

31

Cooperative Learning

Learning Strategies:

Providing personal information, active listening, organizing notes on a chart

Critical Thinking Strategy:

Comparing and contrasting

D. *¿Cómo pasas el tiempo?* Working in pairs, take turns describing your typical school day to your partner. Tell about when you arrive at school, your morning classes, when you have lunch, your afternoon classes, what time you leave school, when you get home. As your partner speaks, make a schedule of his or her day. When you have both schedules in hand, compare to see who arrives earlier, has lunch later, etc. Begin your description: **De costumbre, yo llego a la escuela a...**

REPASO

The verbs *querer, pensar, and preferir (present tense)*

yo	**quiero** **pienso** **prefiero**	nosotros(as)	**queremos** **pensamos** **preferimos**
tú	**quieres** **piensas** **prefieres**	vosotros(as)	**queréis** **pensáis** **preferís**
él ella Ud.	**quiere** **piensa** **prefiere**	ellos ellas Uds.	**quieren** **piensan** **prefieren**

Remember that the **e** of the stem of these verbs changes to **ie** in all verb forms except the **nosotros** and **vosotros** forms.

E. Replace the words in italics with those in parentheses and make the necessary changes.

1. *Yo* no quiero ir al centro ahora. (Juan / tú / Elena y Marta / Marirrosa y yo / Uds. / vosotros)
2. ¿Qué prefieren hacer *Uds.* esta noche? (tú / Julián / Éster y Roberto / ellas / Ud. / vosotros)
3. *Ella* no piensa ir a España el año próximo. (nosotros / tú / Marisol / Mari y Esteban / Uds. / vosotras)

Formal commands

1. Formal commands in Spanish are created by dropping the **-o** of the **yo** form of the verb and adding an **-e** or an **-en** for **-ar** verbs and an **-a** or an **-an** for **-er** and **-ir** verbs.

cantar	**comer**	**escribir**
cant**o**	com**o**	escrib**o**
cant**e**	com**a**	escrib**a**
cant**en**	com**an**	escrib**an**

2. Verbs ending in **-car** change the **c** to **qu**. Those ending in **-gar** change the **g** to **gu**. Those ending in **-zar** change the **z** to **c**.

buscar	**llegar**	**cruzar**
bus**c**o	lle**g**o	cru**z**o
bus**que**	lle**gue**	cru**ce**
bus**quen**	lle**guen**	cru**cen**

3. Some other common verbs with irregular formal commands are:

ir	**vaya**	**vayan**
ser	**sea**	**sean**

F. Give both the singular and plural formal command forms for the following verbs.

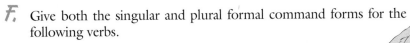

1. estudiar
2. bailar
3. aprender español
4. correr 20 minutos
5. doblar a la izquierda
6. tener paciencia
7. no comer mucho
8. leer todos los días
9. cruzar la calle
10. buscar las llaves

Informal commands

1. The informal command is used to address anyone whom you know well, such as friends and family members, and to address children. Unlike formal commands, the informal command has one form for the affirmative and a different form for the negative.

To form the affirmative informal command, drop the **o** from the **yo** form and add **-a** for **-ar** verbs and **-e** for **-er** and **-ir** verbs.

dobl**o**	→	dobl**a**
corr**o**	→	corr**e**
escrib**o**	→	escrib**e**

2. To form the negative informal command, drop the **o** from the **yo** form and add **-es** for **-ar** verbs and **-as** for **-er** and **-ir** verbs.

dobl**o**	→	no dobl**es**
corr**o**	→	no corr**as**
escrib**o**	→	no escrib**as**

3. In the negative command, verbs that end in **-car** change the **c** to **qu**. Those that end in **-gar** change the **g** to **gu**. Those that end in **-zar** change the **z** to **c**.

buscar	bus**c**o	no bus**ques**
llegar	lle**g**o	no lle**gues**
cruzar	cru**z**o	no cru**ces**

However, none of these verbs change their spellings in the affirmative command:

buscar	bus**c**a
llegar	lle**g**a
cruzar	cru**z**a

4. Other common verbs you know that have irregular informal commands are:

decir	**di**	no **digas**
hacer	**haz**	no **hagas**
ir	**ve**	no **vayas**
poner	**pon**	no **pongas**
salir	**sal**	no **salgas**
ser	**sé**	no **seas**
tener	**ten**	no **tengas**
venir	**ven**	no **vengas**

G. Give familiar affirmative command forms for the following verbs.

1. hacer las maletas
2. tener paciencia
3. no doblar a la derecha
4. escribir tu lección
5. no vender tu bicicleta
6. no ir al centro
7. buscar tus libros
8. seguir derecho
9. beber leche
10. no hablar por teléfono

Situaciones

Direcciones

a) **A pie al banco**

—Perdón, señora, ¿dónde está el banco?

—¿El banco? Está cerca de aquí, señor. Camine Ud. por la Calle Bolívar hasta la Avenida de la Paz. Doble a la derecha y camine tres cuadras y allí está la Plaza de la Revolución. Cruce la plaza y allí en la Calle Colón está el banco.

—Muchísimas gracias, señora.

—De nada, señor.

b) **En coche en Valencia**

—¿Hay un sitio para estacionar el coche en el centro?

—Sí, sí. Es muy fácil. Escucha. Toma la Calle San Vicente Mártir y dobla a la derecha en la Calle Xátiva. Sigue derecho dos cuadras y dobla a la izquierda en la Avenida Marqués de Sotelo. Pasa por delante de la Plaza del País Valenciano y sigue derecho tres cuadras más. Allí a la derecha hay un sitio para estacionar el coche. ¿De acuerdo?

—De acuerdo.

c) **En coche al Alcázar de Segovia**

—Perdón, señor, ¿dónde está la Calle Velarde? Queremos ir al Alcázar.

—Bien, sigan derecho por esta calle —la Calle Agustín. Pasen por delante de la Iglesia de San Esteban y después de una cuadra doblen a la izquierda. Allí está la Calle Velarde. Sigan la Calle Velarde derecho por más o menos diez cuadras. Allí van a ver Uds. el Alcázar.

—Muchas gracias, señor.

—De nada.

d) **A pie a la farmacia**

—¡Hola, Marirrosa! ¿Qué haces por aquí?

—Leira, yo estoy buscando una farmacia. ¿Hay una cerca de aquí?

—Sí, claro que sí. Hay una farmacia en la Calle Miramonte.

—¿La Calle Miramonte? ¿Dónde está? No conozco muy bien este barrio.

—Es muy fácil. Sigue esta calle —Calle Juárez— una cuadra hasta la esquina y dobla a la derecha.

—¿No está a la izquierda?

—No, no. A la izquierda está la Calle Cholula. Tú quieres la Calle Rivera. Sigue derecho y a la derecha vas a ver una plaza grande. Es la Plaza de Armas. Cruza la plaza y allí está la Calle Miramonte. ¿Comprendes?

—Sí, sí. Comprendo. Muchísimas gracias. Hasta luego.

—Hasta luego, Marirrosa.

¡Aquí te toca a ti!

H. Match the conversations on page 35 with the following drawings.

1.

2.

3.

4.

I. *Por las calles de Madrid* Using the map of Madrid on page 37, give directions for each of the following situations. Pay attention to where you are, where the other person wishes to go, and whether this person is someone with whom you would use **tú** or **Ud.**

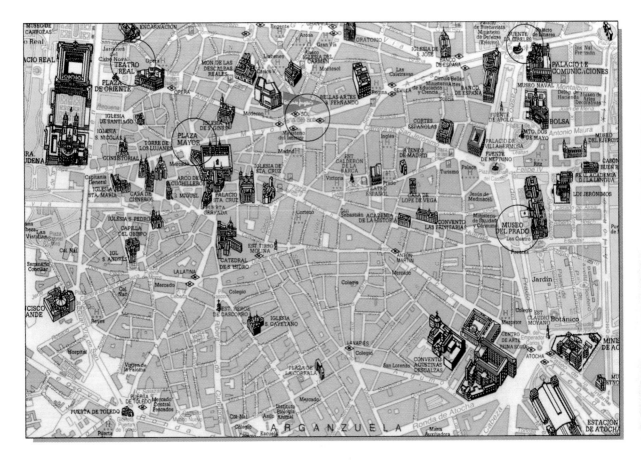

You are at the	You are speaking to	He or she wishes to go to
1. Fuente de la Cibeles	an older man	Puerta del Sol
2. Puerta del Sol	a person your age	Museo del Prado
3. Plaza Mayor	a person your age	Teatro Real
4. Teatro Real	an older woman	Museo del Prado

Actividad

J. En tu ciudad You and your partner want to get together after school to study for an exam. First, discuss your schedules to see when you can meet. Then, give each other directions to where you live and decide which home will be more convenient for meeting.

Cooperative Learning

Learning Strategies:

Scheduling, giving directions, reaching agreement

Tarjetas de vocabulario

Para hablar del tiempo que tarda en llegar

Tarda… minutos para ir a pie (en coche, etc.).
         horas
         días

Para indicar cómo vamos

Yo tomo el autobús.   Yo voy a pie.   en coche.
        el metro.   en bicicleta.   en metro.
        el tren.   en autobús.   en tren.

Para dar direcciones

Doble (Dobla) a la derecha.
             a la izquierda.
Siga (Sigue) derecho hasta…
Tome (Toma) la calle (la avenida)…
Cruce (Cruza) la calle (la avenida, la plaza).

Para indicar qué día es

¿Qué día es hoy?
Hoy es lunes.
　　　　martes.　　　　　　viernes.
　　　　miércoles.　　　　sábado.
　　　　jueves.　　　　　　domingo.

Para indicar la hora

¿Qué hora es?
Es la una.
　　　una y cuarto.
　　　una y media.
Son las dos menos cuarto.
¿A qué hora vienes?
Vengo a las diez y veinte de la mañana (10:20 a.m.).
　　　　　　　　　　　de la noche (10:20 p.m.).

¿QUÉ HACEMOS?

Mercado Libertad, Guadalajara, México

Objectives:

>>> **R**eview words and expressions needed to shop and to order food and beverages.

>>> **R**eview the verbs **hacer** and **ir.**

>>> **P**ractice making comparisons.

>>> **P**ractice placing actions in the past, present, and future.

>>> **P**ractice shopping and ordering.

Strategies:

>>> **L**isting

>>> **M**aking plans

>>> **R**eaching agreement

>>> **C**ategorizing

>>> **E**valuating

PRIMERA ETAPA

Vamos de compras

En Madrid, como en cualquier ciudad grande, hay muchos sitios para ir de compras. Hay tiendas pequeñas que se especializan en un sólo producto: zapaterías, joyerías, librerías, etc. También hay grandes almacenes donde hay de todo. Mi favorito es un almacén grande que se llama El Corte Inglés. Es una tienda donde puedes comprar cualquier cosa. Por ejemplo, en un piso venden comida, en otro venden ropa y aún en otro venden libros. También hay una joyería donde me gusta ir a ver los diamantes y las perlas. En otra sección de la tienda venden discos compactos y cintas. Allí es donde vamos mis amigas y yo cuando queremos comprar el disco compacto más reciente de Gloria Estefan o de Phil Collins porque tienen una selección buena.

María

En Guadalajara hay muchas tiendas y supermercados modernos, pero para ir de compras a veces vamos al Mercado Libertad. Éste es el mercado más grande del Hemisferio Occidental y allí puedes comprar cualquier producto imaginable. En una sección puedes comprar fruta fresca como sandías, melones, mangos, naranjas, limones y manzanas o vegetales como zanahorias, pepinos, chiles, aguacates, cebollas y tomates. En otra parte venden todo tipo de carne —res, puerco y pollo— y varios tipos de queso. En otra sección compramos tortillas de maíz o pan dulce. Después de hacer las compras, puedes pasar a otra parte del mercado donde hay muchos restaurantes pequeños. Allí puedes comer muchos de los platos típicos de esta región de México como el pozole, la birria, el cabrito asado o pollo en mole.

Esteban

Comprensión

A. ¿Cierto o falso?
Based on the comments on page 41, indicate whether the following statements are true, false, or if there is not enough information to answer.

1. **El Corte Inglés** is a large open-air market.
2. María likes to shop at the specialty shops scattered throughout Madrid.
3. She and her friends buy CDs and tapes at a store near **El Corte Inglés.**
4. You can buy clothes at **El Corte Inglés,** but not jewelry.
5. Guadalajara has several open-air markets.
6. **El Mercado Libertad** is a huge department store.
7. You can get a good meal at **El Mercado Libertad.**
8. Along with fruits and vegetables, you can also buy meat at **El Mercado Libertad.**

Learning Strategies:

Asking for information, providing personal information, supporting decisions

Critical Thinking Strategy:

Comparing and contrasting

B. ¿Tienes algo que hacer?
Answer the following questions, then ask them of a classmate. Compare your answers with those of your partner to decide if you would be compatible shopping companions. Be able to give reasons for your decision.

1. ¿Hay un centro comercial cerca de tu casa? ¿Vas allí de vez en cuando? ¿Qué centro comercial prefieres?
2. ¿Prefieres comprar algo o solamente mirar?
3. ¿En general, qué compras en el centro comercial? ¿Qué tiendas prefieres?
4. ¿Vas tú con un(a) amigo(a) a hacer las compras de vez en cuando?
5. ¿Normalmente, quién hace las compras en tu casa? ¿Te gusta ir con él (ella)?
6. ¿Cuándo hace él (ella) las compras? ¿Todos los días? ¿Dos o tres veces por semana? ¿Una vez por semana?
7. ¿Adónde va él (ella) a comprar las frutas y vegetales? ¿a comprar carne? ¿Qué mercado prefieres tú?

El Rastro, Madrid

REPASO

The verb *hacer* (present tense)

	hacer		
yo	**hago**	nosotros(as)	**hacemos**
tú	**haces**	vosotros(as)	**hacéis**
él		ellos	
ella }	**hace**	ellas }	**hacen**
Ud.		Uds.	

1. When the verb **hacer** is used in a question, the answer often requires a verb other than **hacer**, usually a form of a verb that expresses what you do.

—¿Qué **haces** tú los sábados por la mañana?
—Yo **juego** al fútbol con mis amigos.
—¿Qué **van a hacer** ellos el sábado por la noche?
—Ellos **van a ver** una película.

2. Expressions with **hacer.**

hacer las compras	*(to do the shopping)*	**hacer la cama**	*(to make the bed)*
hacer un mandado	*(to run an errand)*	**hacer un viaje**	*(to take a trip)*
hacer las maletas	*(to pack)*		

C. Replace the words in italics with those in parentheses and make the necessary changes.

1. ¿Qué hace *Juan* los viernes por la noche? (ella / tú / Ud. / Uds. / vosotros)

2. *Yo* no hago nada los domingos por la tarde. (tú / Uds. / ellos / ella / nosotros / vosotras)

D. La familia Lamas   Tell your parents about a Hispanic family's weekly routine. Based on the drawings on page 44, answer your parents' questions.

Modelo: ¿Qué hace Miguel los lunes por la mañana?
Él va al colegio.

Learning Strategy:

Reporting based on visual information

43

1. ¿Qué hace Marirrosa los martes por la tarde?
2. ¿Qué hacen la Sra. y el Sr. Lamas los lunes por la mañana?
3. ¿Qué hace Miguel los viernes por la noche?
4. ¿Qué hacen la Sra. y el Sr. Lamas los sábados por la noche?
5. ¿Qué hace Miguel los domingos por la tarde?
6. ¿Qué hace Marirrosa los viernes por la tarde?

Learning Strategies:

Asking for information, providing personal information, supporting opinions

Critical Thinking Strategy:

Comparing and contrasting

E. ¿Y tú? Answer the following questions, then ask them of a classmate. Compare your answers with those of your partner to find out how many activities you and your families have in common. Summarize your findings with a statement like the following:

Tenemos mucho en común, por ejemplo... o:
Mi compañero(a) y yo no tenemos mucho en común porque él (ella)... y yo...

1. ¿Qué haces los viernes por la noche?
2. ¿Qué hacen tus padres?
3. ¿Qué hacen Uds. los sábados por la tarde?
4. Y tu hermano(a), ¿qué hace?
5. ¿Qué van a hacer Uds. esta noche?
6. ¿Qué van a hacer Uds. mañana?

7. ¿Qué van a hacer Uds. el viernes por la noche?
8. ¿Qué van a hacer Uds. el sábado por la tarde?

F. ¿Qué haces en tu tiempo libre?   What do the people in the following drawings do in their free time? What do you do in your free time?

1.   2.   3.   4.

5.   6.   7.

8.   9.   10.

G. ¿Qué deportes te gustan?   Review the **Tarjetas de vocabulario** for sports on page 51 and indicate what sports you like and don't like. Ask a classmate what sports he or she likes and dislikes.

REPASO

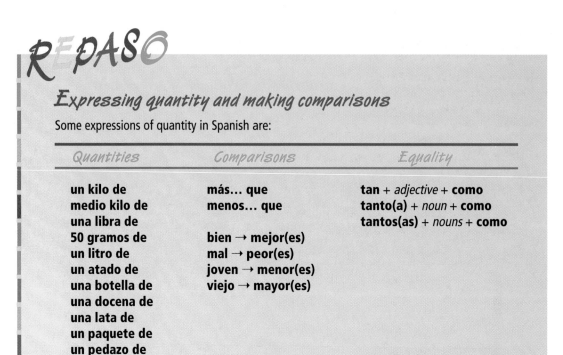

Expressing quantity and making comparisons

Some expressions of quantity in Spanish are:

Quantities	Comparisons	Equality
un kilo de	más... que	tan + *adjective* + como
medio kilo de	menos... que	tanto(a) + *noun* + como
una libra de		tantos(as) + *nouns* + como
50 gramos de	bien → mejor(es)	
un litro de	mal → peor(es)	
un atado de	joven → menor(es)	
una botella de	viejo → mayor(es)	
una docena de		
una lata de		
un paquete de		
un pedazo de		

H. ¿Qué necesita? Based on the drawings, indicate how much of each item the following people need to buy.

1. Luisa   **2.** Roberto   **3.** mi mamá

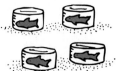

4. Alicia   **5.** Marisol

¿Recuerdan?

The demonstrative adjective is used to point out specific things. Its forms in Spanish are:

close to speaker	close to listener	far from both
este	ese	aquel
esta	esa	aquella
estos	esos	aquellos
estas	esas	aquellas

1. Las frutas y los vegetales   You are in an open-air market. As you choose some fruit or vegetables that you like, your friend always points out others that are better. Follow the model.

—*Quiero estas manzanas.*
—*Pero esas manzanas son mejores.*   o:
—*Aquellas manzanas son mejores.*

1. fresas
2. maíz
3. limones
4. peras
5. lechuga
6. cebollas
7. naranjas
8. zanahorias

Situaciones

Las compras

a) —Buenos días, señor.
   —Buenos días. Mi hijo va a comenzar la escuela mañana y necesita varias cosas. ¿Dónde están los lápices y bolígrafos?
   —Están por aquí. ¿Cuántos quiere?
   —Quiero seis lápices y dos bolígrafos.
   —¿Necesita algo más?
   —Sí, necesito papel, también.
   —El papel está allí.
   —Bien, voy a llevar tres cuadernos.
   —¿Algo más?
   —Sí, busco una mochila buena.
   —Las mochilas están por aquí.
   —Muy bien, quiero esa mochila azul.

—¿Es todo?

—Sí, es todo. ¿Cuánto es?

—Dos mil seiscientas setenta y ocho pesetas.

—Aquí tiene, señor.

—Muchísimas gracias. Hasta luego.

b) —¿En qué puedo servirle, señora?

—Busco un regalo para mi hijo. ¿Me puede sugerir algo?

—¿Qué deportes le gustan?

—¡Le gustan todos los deportes!

—Aquí están las raquetas de tenis.

—No, ya tiene una raqueta.

—Allí están las pelotas de fútbol.

—No, también tiene una pelota de fútbol y de básquetbol
y de fútbol americano.

—¿Por qué no compra unos zapatos de tenis? ¡Éstos aquí están
muy de moda!

—¡Estupenda idea! ¿Tiene ésos de allí, de color rojo, azul y blanco de
tamaño 42?

—Voy a ver. Creo que sí.... Sí, aquí están. ¿Va a pagar en efectivo o con
tarjeta de crédito?

—En efectivo. ¿Cuánto es?

—Dos mil quinientas pesetas.

—Aquí tiene.

—Muchísimas gracias.

—¡Gracias a Ud. por la magnífica sugerencia!

c) —Señores, señoras. Compren vegetales… fruta… tomates, guisantes,
naranjas, manzanas…. ¿Señora, qué va a llevar?

—Quiero un kilo de tomates, por favor.

—¿Estos tomates?

—No, quiero esos tomates grandes de allí.

—Muy bien. ¿Qué más?

—Tres kilos de bananas. Es todo.

—Bien, vamos a ver… un kilo de tomates a treinta pesetas el kilo y tres kilos
de plátanos a quince pesetas el kilo… setenta y cinco pesetas por favor.

—¿Tiene cambio de quinientas pesetas?

—Sí, claro. Aquí tiene el cambio.

—Señores, señoras. Compren vegetales… fruta…

d) —¿Vas a comprar alguna cosa?

—Creo que sí. Si tengo suficiente dinero, voy a comprar un disco compacto.

—¿Qué vas a comprar?

—Quisiera comprar el nuevo disco compacto de Jon Secada.

—Ah, sí, dicen que es excelente.

—Te gusta la música de Miami Sound Machine, ¿verdad?

—Sí, me gusta muchísimo. ¿Sabes que tienen un disco compacto nuevo?

—Sí, pero no tengo suficiente dinero para comprar el disco compacto.
—Puedes comprar la cinta.
—Tienes razón. Voy a preguntar si tienen la nueva cinta de Miami Sound
   Machine aquí.

¡Aquí te toca a ti!

J. ¿Dónde están?   Indicate where each of the conversations on pages 47–49 took place. Possible locations: **la panadería, la papelería, la tienda de deportes, la tienda de música, el mercado, la carnicería, la tienda de ropa, el supermercado.**

Critical Thinking Strategy:

Drawing inferences

Actividades

K. Al mercado   You and a classmate will play the roles of shopper and grocery store clerk.

Cooperative Learning

Learning Strategies:

Listing, making plans

One of you must prepare a large salad for a family dinner. That student should make a list of items (four or five, at least) needed for the salad. Your list should include how much of each item you will need and about how much you want to spend for each one.

The person playing the grocery store clerk should prepare two lists. On the first, write the names of six to eight items, including fruits and vegetables that you have in stock, indicating the price of each per bottle, kilo, etc. On the second list, write the names of five or six items that you do *not* have in your store.

Work on your lists separately. Before beginning your conversation look at the following five points which should be included in your conversation. Review the **Situationes** on pages 47–49 for ideas.

1. Greet each other at the market.
2. Discuss which produce items are needed and available.
3. Discuss the price of the items selected by the customer.
4. Conclude the purchase/sale.
5. Say good-bye.

L. De compras   Choose three stores and write down three items you need to buy at each. Work with a partner to role play the conversation you have at each store. Remember that there are several ways to indicate what you would like to buy: **Yo quisiera..., Yo necesito..., ¿Tiene Ud.... ?,** and **Yo voy a llevar....** Try to vary the expressions you use.

Tarjetas de vocabulario

Lugares adonde vamos

la biblioteca
un restaurante
la piscina
el cine
la fiesta
la playa
el museo
el parque

el parque zoológico
el gimnasio
el concierto
la casa de un(a) amigo(a)
el centro
el médico

Para hablar de lo que hacemos en el centro

Yo voy al centro para ir al cine.
                              ir de compras.
                              hacer un mandado.
                              ver a mis amigos.

Para indicar la cantidad

un kilo de	50 gramos de	una botella de	una lata de
medio kilo de	un litro de	una docena de	un paquete de
una libra de	un atado de	un pedazo de	

En el mercado yo compré bananas.   melones.   guisantes.   papas.
   el supermercado   fresas.   naranjas.   cebollas.   tomates.
                          limones.   peras.   lechuga.   zanahorias.
                          manzanas.   uvas.   maíz.

En la papelería yo compré una hoja de papel para escribir a máquina.
                                        papel de avión.
                un sobre.
                una tarjeta de cumpleaños.
                            del Día de las Madres.
                            del Día de los Padres.

Para comprar alguna cosa

Yo quisiera…
¿Tiene Ud.…?
Aquí tiene…
¿Tiene Ud. cambio *(change)*
  de 500 pesetas?
Es todo.
¿Cuánto cuesta?
Un(a)… por favor.

Deportes

En mi tiempo libre me gusta jugar…
  al béisbol.
  al baloncesto.
  al fútbol americano.
  al fútbol.
  al tenis.
  al golf.
  al vólibol.

También me gusta…
  levantar pesas.
  patinar.
  patinar en ruedas.
  jugar al hockey.
  jugar al hockey sobre hierba.
  montar en bicicleta.
  hacer ejercicio aeróbico.

Deportes de verano

Durante el verano me gusta practicar…
  el esquí acuático.
  el windsurf.
  la vela.
  el alpinismo.
  el ciclismo.
  el surfing.

También me gusta…
  tomar el sol.
  nadar / la natación.
  bucear / el buceo.
  ir de pesca / la pesca.
  ir de camping.
  caminar en la playa.

  hablar por teléfono.
  escuchar música.
  alquilar vídeos.
  montar en bicicleta.
  escribir cartas.
  ir al cine.

En mi tiempo libre me gusta…
  desayunar en un restaurante.
  escuchar el estéreo.
  pasar tiempo con mi familia.
  mirar la televisión.
  cenar con un(a) amigo(a).
  caminar al centro.
  comprar un disco compacto.
  visitar a un(a) amigo(a).
  hacer ejercicio.
  hacer un mandado.

SEGUNDA ETAPA

Vamos a comer algo

Cuando mi padre tiene hambre, le gusta comer en un buen restaurante. En Madrid hay muchísimos restaurantes, y el domingo pasado mi padre y un amigo fueron a cenar en un restaurante que se llama La Casa Gallega. Allí se especializan en platos típicos de Galicia. A mi papá le gusta la comida gallega y dice que es la más sabrosa de toda la comida española. Mi hermano y yo preferimos los restaurantes pequeños donde podemos comer bocadillos. Nos gustan los bocadillos de todo tipo. A veces comemos bocadillos de chorizo o bocadillos de jamón con queso y muchas veces comemos mi favorito: un bocadillo de calamares fritos.

El sábado por la tarde, como no hay escuela, normalmente voy con mis amigos al centro. Allí conversamos con otros amigos y, de costumbre, vamos a comer en nuestro restaurante favorito: El Farolito. El Farolito es una taquería donde puedes comer tacos de todo tipo: de carne o de pollo. También nos gustan las quesadillas. Tienen la mejor ensalada de guacamole de toda Guadalajara y también tienen varias salsas —unas picantes y otras que no son tan picantes. Para tomar hay limonada y varios tipos de licuados —de mango, melón y fresas. Después de comer allí, generalmente vamos al cine o damos un paseo por el parque.

Esteban

Comprensión

A. *Mis gustos* Scan the paragraphs on page 52 to find all the different foods that María and Esteban like. As you find them, add them to one of three lists. In the first, list all the foods mentioned that *you* have eaten. In the second, list foods that you have never eaten but that you would like to try. In the third, list foods that you don't think you would like.

When you have completed your lists, compare your categories with those of your partner. Make another set of the three lists, this time listing only the items that you have in common for each category.

B. *Prefiero comer con...* Based on their food preferences, decide whether you would rather go out to dinner with María or with Esteban. Be ready to explain your choice.

REPASO

The preterite of -ar, -er, and -ir verbs

hablar, comer, escribir

yo	hablé comí escribí		nosotros(as)	hablamos comimos escribimos
tú	hablaste comiste escribiste		vosotros(as)	hablasteis comisteis escribisteis
él ella Ud.	habló comió escribió		ellos ellas Uds.	hablaron comieron escribieron

C. Replace the words in italics with those in parentheses and make the necessary changes.

1. Yo *canté una canción* anoche. (mirar la tele / comprar unos libros / escuchar mi estéreo / tomar el autobús / caminar al centro / hablar por teléfono / bailar en una discoteca)
2. Ella *asistió a clase* ayer. (vender su bicicleta / escribir una carta / correr dos millas / aprender el vocabulario / salir de casa temprano / perder su libro / volver a casa tarde / compartir su bocadillo con un amigo[a])

¿Recuerdan?

The preterite of *ir*

yo	**fui**	nosotros(as)	**fuimos**
tú	**fuiste**	vosotros(as)	**fuisteis**
él		ellos	
ella	**fue**	ellas	**fueron**
Ud.		Uds.	

D. *El sábado de Marisol*   Based on the verbs and drawings provided below and on page 55, tell what Marisol did last Saturday. Follow the model.

Modelo: hablar por teléfono
El sábado pasado Marisol habló por teléfono con Tomás.

1. salir de   2. caminar a un restaurante   3. comer con Tomás

4. ir al centro comercial   **5.** ir a la tienda de música   **6.** comprar un disco compacto

7. volver a casa de Marisol   **8.** escuchar discos compactos   **9.** mirar la televisión

E. *Mi sábado* Now imagine that you spent your Saturday much as Marisol did. Use the drawings in Activity D, but substitute names and places from your own life when appropriate. (If you would not normally do something that Marisol did, use **no** + the verb to indicate what you did not do.) Follow the model.

Learning Strategy:

Reporting based on personal knowledge

> *Modelo:* *El sábado pasado, hablé por teléfono con mi amiga Janet.*

F. *Ayer: un día loquísimo* (crazy) Imagine that yesterday nothing went as usual for you. Make a list of eight to ten things that usually happen in your daily routine. Include events such as (1) when you have breakfast, (2) what you eat for breakfast, (3) when you leave for school and what mode of transportation you use, (4) when your parents leave for work, (5) when you arrive at school, (6) what you do when you get there, (7) when you go to lunch, (8) what and how much you eat for lunch (e.g., **dos bocadillos y una ensalada**), (9) what time you leave school, (10) where you go, (11) with whom you go, (12) when and where you have dinner, (13) what you and your family do after dinner, and (14) how long you study.

Learning Strategies:

Listing, reporting based on personal knowledge, asking questions based on context

When you have completed your list, discuss with your partner what normally happens and how things didn't happen as usual yesterday. Follow the model.

> *Modelo:* **Estudiante 1:** *De costumbre, tomo el almuerzo en la cafetería, pero ayer no comí en la cafetería.*
> **Estudiante 2:** *¿No? ¿Dónde comiste?*
> **Estudiante 1:** *Comí en el restaurante con mi padre.*

 R PASO

Talking about past, present, and future events

1. Use the preterite to express a past action.

Ayer **nosotros fuimos** al centro.	Yesterday *we went* downtown.
Salió de la casa hace una hora.	*He left* the house an hour ago.

2. Use the present tense of the verb to indicate a habitual action or a present condition.

De costumbre yo ceno a las 6:00.	*I usually eat dinner* at 6:00.
Yo tengo 17 años.	*I am* seventeen.
Hoy es miércoles.	*Today is* Wednesday.

3. Use the present progressive (**estar** + **-ndo** *participle*) to emphasize that an action is going on at the moment of speaking.

Ahora ellos **están mirando** la tele.	Right now *they are watching* TV.
En este momento él **está leyendo** una revista.	At this moment he *is reading* a magazine.

4. Use the immediate future (**ir** + **a** + *infinitive*) to express a future action.

Esta noche **vamos a ver** una película.	Tonight *we are going to see* a movie.
Nosotros **vamos a trabajar** el lunes próximo.	We *are going to work* next Monday.

¿Recuerdan?

To express how long ago something happened or how long ago you did something, you would use:

hace + *length of time* + **que** + *subject* + *verb in the preterite*
Hace dos semanas **que** comí en un restaurante.

You may also use:

subject + *verb in the preterite* + **hace** + *length of time*
Yo comí en un restaurante **hace** dos semanas.

Some expressions for expressing length of time are:

un minuto, dos minutos, tres minutos, etc.
una hora, dos horas, tres horas, etc.
un día, dos días, tres días, etc.
una semana, dos semanas, tres semanas, etc.
un mes, dos meses, tres meses, etc.
un año, dos años, tres años, etc.

G. *La última vez que...*   Indicate the last time you did each of the following activities. Use expressions such as **el martes pasado, el año pasado, la semana pasada,** or **hace** + *length of time*. Follow the model.

Modelo: ¿Cuándo fue la última vez que comiste pizza?
Comí pizza el viernes pasado.   o:
Comí pizza hace dos semanas.

¿Cuándo fue la última vez que...

1. comiste en un restaurante?
2. fuiste al cine?
3. hiciste tu tarea?
4. visitaste a un(a) amigo(a)?
5. estudiaste para un examen?
6. fuiste a un partido de fútbol?
7. hiciste tu cama?
8. tomaste el autobús?
9. leíste un libro?
10. escribiste una carta?

H. *¿Cuándo vas a...?*   Now indicate the next time you are going to do the following things. Use expressions such as: **mañana, mañana por la tarde, la semana próxima, el mes próximo, el año próximo.**

Modelo: ¿Cuándo vas a comer pizza?
Voy a comer pizza el viernes próximo.   o:
No voy a comer pizza.

¿Cuándo...

1. vas a hablar por teléfono con un(a) amigo(a)?
2. vas a viajar a Europa?
3. vas a hacer la tarea?
4. vas a nadar en la piscina?
5. vas a leer una revista?
6. vas a tomar un autobús?
7. vas a visitar a un(a) amigo(a)?
8. vas a comprar un disco compacto o una cinta?
9. vas a jugar al tenis?
10. vas a mirar la televisión?
11. vas a escribir una carta?
12. vas a ir de compras?

1. *El mes de Juan Robles* This month has been, is, and will continue to be a very busy time for Juan Robles. Based on the drawings and the calendar that follows, answer the questions about his current, past, and future activities. Today is the 24th of the month.

L	M	M	J	V	S	D
1	2	3	4	5	6	7
8	9	10	11	12	13	14
15	16	17	18	19	20	21
22	23	24	25	26	27	28
29	30	31				

1. ¿Qué día es hoy?
2. ¿Qué van a hacer los padres de Juan esta noche?
3. ¿Cuándo fue el Sr. Robles a Madrid?
4. ¿Qué va a hacer Juan mañana por la tarde?
5. ¿Cuándo celebraron el cumpleaños de Juan?
6. ¿Cuándo fue Juan al museo?
7. ¿Qué hizo Juan el 11?
8. ¿Qué va a hacer el 29?
9. ¿Qué hizo el 13?
10. ¿Qué hace Juan los domingos por la mañana?

Situaciones

Vamos a comer algo...

a) **Ángela y Mauricio**
—Por favor, camarero.
—Sí, señorita, ¿qué desea?
—Quisiera un sándwich de jamón.
—¿Y para tomar?
—Quisiera una limonada.
—Y Ud., señor, ¿qué va a pedir?
—Yo quisiera una hamburguesa con queso y un licuado de mango.
—¿Alguna cosita más?
—No, es todo. Gracias.

b) **Mario y Ernesto**
—Ay, Mario. ¡Qué hambre tengo!
—Yo también. Vamos a la Taquería Mixteca. Está muy cerca de aquí.
—De acuerdo.

(Media hora después)
—Por favor, señorita. Tráigame dos tacos al carbón, una salsa picante y un té helado. ¿Tú, qué quieres, Mario?
—Tres quesadillas y un agua mineral sin gas, por favor.
—¿Es todo?
—Sí, señorita, es todo.

c) **Antonio y Margarita**
—Antonio, ¿tienes hambre?
—Sí, por supuesto. Tengo mucha hambre.
—¿Quieres comer alguna cosa?
—¡Claro que sí! ¿Por qué no vamos a la pizzería nueva que está en la esquina de la Calle Ocho y la Avenida Bolívar?
—Vamos, pues.

(Media hora después)
—Buenas tardes, ¿qué van a pedir?
—Por favor, quisiéramos una pizza grande con mucho queso, aceitunas y cebollas.

d) **Carolina y Filomena**
—Mira. Hay muchísima gente.
—Como siempre.
—¿Tienes suficiente dinero?
—Sí. Tengo 500 pesetas.

—Yo también.
—¿Qué quisieras comer?
—¿Por qué no comemos unas tapas?
—Buena idea. Yo quisiera unas aceitunas y patatas bravas.
—Está bien. ¿Vamos a pedir unos calamares también?
—Sí, ¡cómo no!
—¿Qué vas a tomar?
—Agua mineral con limón. ¿Y tú?
—Agua mineral también, pero sin limón.

¡Aquí te toca a ti!

J. ¿Dónde comen? Based on the four conversations on pages 59–60, indicate where each group of people is eating or planning to eat.

K. En el restaurante You and two friends go to a restaurant for lunch. Discuss what each of you would like to eat and drink. Then call the waiter and place your order.

Actividad

L. ¿Qué vamos a comer?
You and some friends are spending the afternoon together. Your friend's dad offers to pick up some carry-out lunches for you. Agree on what kind of food you all want (e.g., **tapas, tacos, pizza, sándwiches**), then make your individual decisions about what you want to eat and drink. One member of the group needs to write down what each of you wants.

BUFFET DE TACOS N$12.00

TACOS AL PASTOR N$1.50

DESAYUNO COMPLETO N$8.00

MENU ECONOMICO N$10.00

Tarjetas de vocabulario

Para indicar adonde vamos a comer

Yo quiero ir a un restaurante.
Vamos a una taquería.
Quisiéramos ir a comer pizza.
¿Por qué no vamos a comer unas tapas?

Para aceptar

De acuerdo.
¿Por qué no?
¡Vamos!

Para indicar qué queremos beber o comer

En el restaurante, yo pido…
  café (con leche).
  chocolate.
  un licuado de fresas.
        de banana.
        de mango.
  una limonada.
  un agua mineral con (sin) gas (con limón).
  té (con limón).
  té helado.

En el restaurante, yo como…
  un sándwich de jamón con queso.
  un bocadillo.
  una pizza.
  una hamburguesa (con queso).

En una taquería yo como…
  tacos de carne.
      de pollo.
  unas quesadillas.
  una ensalada de guacamole.
  una enchilada.
  frijoles.
  salsa picante.
      no muy picante.

En un bar de tapas yo como…
  unas aceitunas.
  unos calamares.
  patatas bravas.
  chorizo y pan.
  queso.
  tortilla de patatas.

Para pedir algo para comer o beber

Perdón señor (señorita),   Nosotros quisiéramos…
Yo quisiera…   Por favor, tráigame…
Mi amigo(a) quisiera…

Períodos de tiempo

un minuto, dos minutos, tres minutos, etc.
una hora, dos horas, tres horas, etc.
un día, dos días, tres días, etc.
una semana, dos semanas, tres semanas, etc.
un mes, dos meses, tres meses, etc.
un año, dos años, tres años, etc.

Para indicar la última vez que hiciste alguna cosa

hace tres días
hace tres meses
hace tres años

Para hablar de una actividad habitual

de costumbre
normalmente
por lo general

siempre
todos los días

Para hablar del pasado, presente y futuro

ayer	hoy	mañana
ayer por la mañana	esta mañana	mañana por la mañana
ayer por la tarde	esta tarde	mañana por la tarde
anoche	esta noche	mañana por la noche
el lunes pasado		el lunes próximo
la semana pasada	esta semana	la semana próxima
el mes pasado	este mes	el mes próximo
el año pasado	este año	el año próximo

¿Qué ves?

>> ¿Dónde está la gente en las fotografías?

>> ¿Qué hacen las personas aquí?

>> ¿Qué estación del año es y qué tiempo hace?

>> ¿Qué hay en las montañas?

>> ¿Qué piensas de este deporte? ¿Tú lo practicas?

OBJECTIVES

IN THIS UNIT YOU WILL LEARN:

- **T**o talk about the weather;
- **T**o understand weather reports;
- **T**o describe objects;
- **T**o describe people.

Capítulo uno: ¿Qué tiempo hace?

Primera etapa: **¡Hace frío hoy!**
Segunda etapa: **¡Hoy va a nevar mucho!**
Tercera etapa: **¿Qué tiempo va a hacer mañana?**

Capítulo dos: ¿Cómo es?

Primera etapa: **Descríbeme…**
Segunda etapa: **¿Qué piensas?**

Capítulo tres: ¿Cómo es tu amiga?

Primera etapa: **Nuestros vecinos y nuestros amigos**
Segunda etapa: **El carácter**

Descripciones

UNIDAD UNO

¿QUÉ TIEMPO HACE?

Un día nublado en Miami.

Objective:

>>> **D**escribing the weather and understanding weather reports and meteorological maps

Strategies:

>>> **R**eporting based on visual information

>>> **A**sking for information

>>> **M**aking associations

PRIMERA ETAPA

Preparación

›› **W**hat kinds of questions do you normally ask when talking about the weather?

›› **W**hat are some of the weather expressions used frequently in English to describe weather conditions?

›› **D**o you know where the equator is? What is the weather like there?

›› **W**here is the country of Ecuador located?

Learning Strategy:

Previewing

¡Hace frío hoy!

Hace sol.
Hace calor.
Está despejado.

Hace mal tiempo.
Truena. Hay tormenta.

Llueve.
Llovizna.

Hace buen tiempo.
No hace mucho frío.
No hace mucho calor.

Nieva.
Hace frío.

Está nublado.
Hay nubes.

Hace viento.
Hace fresco.

Hay niebla.
Hay neblina.

Hay hielo.
Está resbaloso.

¡Aquí te toca a ti!

A. ¿Qué tiempo hace?   Describe el tiempo en cada dibujo.

Modelo: Hace sol.
Hace mucho calor.
Está despejado.

1.   2.   3.   4.   5.   6.

B. ¿Hace buen tiempo hoy?   You're traveling around the United States with your friend's family. Each time you call home, your parents want to know what the weather is like. Answer their questions negatively. Then give the indicated weather condition. Follow the model.

Modelo: ¿Hace buen tiempo hoy? (mal)
No, no hace buen tiempo hoy. Hace mal tiempo.

1. ¿Hace calor hoy? (frío)
2. ¿Llueve hoy? (nieva)
3. ¿Está nublado? (sol)
4. ¿Hay tormenta? (buen tiempo)
5. ¿Hace fresco? (mucho frío)

6. ¿Hace calor? (viento)
7. ¿Hace sol? (nubes)
8. ¿Hace frío? (bastante calor)
9. ¿Está despejado? (nublado)

ESTRUCTURA

Los meses del año

enero	abril	julio	octubre
febrero	mayo	agosto	noviembre
marzo	junio	septiembre	diciembre

All the months of the year are masculine and are used without articles. They are not capitalized. To express the idea of *in* a month, use **en** or **en el mes de.**

En enero, nieva mucho.   *In January*, it snows a lot.
Hace calor **en el mes de agosto**.   It's hot *in the month of August.*

Aquí practicamos

C. *¿Qué tiempo hace donde vives tú?* Para cada mes, describe el tiempo.

 Modelo: septiembre
En septiembre, hace fresco y hace viento.

1. enero
2. julio
3. marzo
4. noviembre
5. mayo
6. agosto
7. diciembre
8. junio

COMENTARIOS CULTURALES

El clima

There is more variety in the weather patterns within very short distances in Latin America than in any other region of the world. Most Latin American countries north of the equator, such as Mexico, Costa Rica, and Venezuela, have a warm rainy season of about six months during the summer (April–October) and a dry, colder season the rest of the year during the winter months. In July, for example, the temperatures reach over 80° F or 27° C in most of the Latin American countries in the Northern Hemisphere, while 60° F or 16° C is the average during January.

South of the equator, however, the seasons follow the reverse pattern. Temperatures in January, for instance, climb to over 80° F or 27° C in the Southern Hemisphere, while July brings snow to the southernmost countries like Argentina and Chile.

69

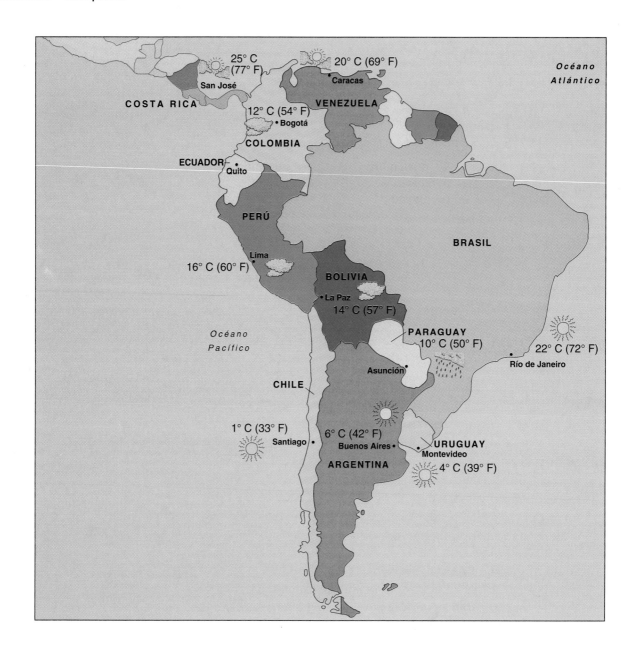

//-//-//-//-//-//-//-//-//

D. *Yo nací* (I was born) *en el mes de...*   Diles a tus compañeros de
clase en qué mes naciste *(you were born)* y qué tiempo generalmente hace
en ese mes. Sigue el modelo.

Modelo: *Yo nací en el mes de julio. Siempre hace mucho calor.*

Palabras útiles

La fecha

¿Cuál es la fecha de hoy?	
¿Qué fecha es hoy?	*What is today's date?*
¿A cuántos estamos?	
Hoy es el 5 de octubre.	*Today is October 5.*
¿Cuál es la fecha de tu cumpleaños?	*What is the date of your birthday?*
Yo nací **el primero de febrero de mil novecientos setenta y cinco.**	*I was born on the first of February 1975.*
Mi hermana nació **el once de junio de mil novecientos setenta y seis.**	*My sister was born on June 11, 1976.*

To express the date in Spanish, use the definite article **el,** a cardinal number **(treinta, diez, cinco)**, and the name of the month. The one exception is the first of the month, expressed by **el primero.** The day, the month, and the year of any date are connected by **de.**

Aquí practicamos

E. ¿En qué año? Lee las fechas que siguen. Sigue el modelo.

 July 4, 1776 — la independencia de los Estados Unidos
el cuatro de julio de mil setecientos setenta y seis — el día de la independencia de los Estados Unidos

1. October 12, 1492 — el descubrimiento de América
2. November 20, 1910 — la revolución mexicana
3. April 23, 1616 — las muertes *(deaths)* de Cervantes y Shakespeare
4. July 14, 1789 — la revolución francesa
5. September 16, 1821 — la independencia de México
6. November 22, 1963 — el asesinato del Presidente Kennedy
7. July 21, 1969 — el primer hombre en la luna *(moon)*
8. November 9, 1989 — la caída *(fall)* del muro *(wall)* de Berlín
9. ? — tu cumpleaños

Palabras útiles

Las estaciones del año

la primavera

el verano

el otoño

el invierno

All the nouns for the seasons are masculine except **la primavera.** To express the idea of *in* a particular season, use **en** and the appropriate definite article.

En el otoño jugamos al fútbol.	*In the fall* we play soccer.
En el invierno hace frío.	*In the winter* it is cold.
Llueve mucho **en la primavera**.	It rains a lot *in the spring*.
Todos van a la playa **en el verano.**	Everybody goes to the beach *in the summer.*

Aquí practicamos

F. *Donde tú vives*   Describe el tiempo durante las estaciones del año en la región donde vives.

Modelo: ¿Qué tiempo hace en el invierno donde vives?
En el invierno nieva y hace mucho frío.

1. ¿Qué tiempo hace en el invierno donde vives?
2. ¿En el otoño?
3. ¿En el verano?
4. ¿En la primavera?

G. *¿Cuándo practicas... ?*   Indica la estación en que normalmente juegas a los siguientes deportes. Entonces, explica por qué el tiempo de esta estación es bueno para el deporte. Sigue el modelo.

Modelo: jugar al fútbol
Juego al fútbol en el otoño porque hace buen tiempo.   o:
... porque no hace demasiado calor en el otoño.   o:
... porque no llueve mucho en el otoño.

1. jugar al tenis
2. jugar al básquetbol
3. jugar al béisbol
4. nadar
5. jugar al golf
6. jugar al jai alai
7. practicar el alpinismo
8. patinar
9. ir de pesca
10. hacer proyectos de artesanía

H. *¡Preguntas, preguntas, tantas preguntas!*   Trabajas con unos niños hispanos en los Estados Unidos. Te hacen muchas preguntas. Contesta sus preguntas.

1. ¿Cuántas estaciones hay en un año?
2. ¿Cuáles son los meses del verano aquí?
3. ¿En qué estación es posible esquiar?
4. ¿En qué estación vamos a la playa?
5. ¿En qué estaciones jugamos al fútbol? ¿al básquetbol?
6. ¿En qué estación celebramos el día de Acción de Gracias?
7. ¿Cuál es la fecha de hoy?
8. ¿Cuál es la fecha del primer día de las vacaciones del verano?

Aquí escuchamos:
"¿El mar o las montañas?"

Antes de escuchar

It's the month of July and the Valenzuela family, from Chile, has eight days of vacation. But there is a problem. The mother and father want to go skiing and the children prefer to go to the beach. Look at the following questions and identify a few things you expect to hear them talk about.

Después de escuchar

1. ¿Cuál es la estación del año donde vive la familia? ¿Qué tiempo hace?
2. ¿Adónde quieren ir los padres para las vacaciones? ¿Por qué?
3. ¿Adónde prefieren ir los hijos?
4. ¿Adónde va a pasar las vacaciones la familia, por fin?

¡Aquí te toca a ti!

1. ¿Qué tiempo hace en...?

Usa la información que sigue para imitar la conversación del modelo.

Modelo: agosto / Portillo, Chile

Estudiante 1: *Yo quiero ir a Portillo en agosto.*   o:
Yo no quiero ir a Portillo en agosto.

Estudiante 2: *¿Por qué (no)? ¿Qué tiempo hace en Portillo en agosto?*

Estudiante 1: *Hace frío. Nieva y hace viento.*

1. agosto / Acapulco

2. febrero / Buenos Aires

3. octubre / Aspen

4. noviembre / Miami

EJERCICIO ORAL

J. Un(a) estudiante extranjero(a)

Un(a) estudiante extranjero(a) del sur de Perú acaba de llegar y te hace preguntas sobre el tiempo y las estaciones donde tú vives. Él (Ella) quiere saber cuáles son los meses del invierno, verano, etc. y qué deportes y actividades tú haces en estos meses. Usando lo que sabes *(Using what you know)* del clima de Perú, trabaja con un(a) compañero(a) para comparar los dos climas. Hagan una tabla como la siguiente para tomar notas. Ahora imaginen que uno(a) de Uds. es el (la) estudiante extranjero(a) y conversen.

Las estaciones	Los meses		El tiempo		Los deportes y las actividades	
	En Perú	Aquí	En Perú	Aquí	En Perú	Aquí
primavera						
verano						
otoño						
invierno						

EJERCICIO ESCRITO

K. Las estaciones y mis actividades.

Write a paragraph of four or five sentences about the season of the year that you prefer. Describe its weather in detail as well as what you normally like to do during this particular season and why.

SEGUNDA ETAPA

Preparación

>> **C**an you give some examples of when the weather makes the headlines in the newspaper or on television?

>> **D**oes the weather change much throughout the year where you live? Why or why not?

>> **W**hen you read or hear a weather report, what information do you expect to get?

Learning Strategy:

Previewing

Critical Thinking Strategy:

Making associations

¡Hoy va a nevar mucho!

¡Hoy va a nevar mucho!: Today it's going to snow a lot!

¡35°! ¡Calor increíble en la capital!

¡Los esquiadores están contentos!

Tormenta tropical localizada en el golfo

¡Seis semanas sin sol!

Accidente de dos barcos en el Lago de Chapala

El aeropuerto está cerrado

¡Aquí te toca a ti!

A. ¿Qué tiempo hace?   Indica la descripción que corresponde a lo que dice el periódico *(what the newspaper says)*.

1. Hace mucho viento.
2. Hay niebla.
3. Nieva.
4. Está muy nublado.
5. Llueve mucho.
6. Hace calor.

B. Hoy va a hacer muy buen tiempo. Mira el pronóstico del tiempo *(weather forecast)* y contesta las preguntas. Sigue el modelo.

Modelo: ¿Qué tiempo va a hacer el sábado en Nueva York?
Va a hacer calor. Va a estar un poco nublado.

t = thundershower
pc = partly cloudy
s = sunny
c = cloudy

U.S. TRAVELERS' FORECAST

	FRI	SAT		FRI	SAT
Atlanta	94/74s	92/70t	Minneapolis	79/58s	85/62pc
Atlantic City	86/66t	76/60pc	New Orleans	93/72pc	93/72pc
Boston	81/64t	66/58pc	New York	84/65t	77/57pc
Buffalo	72/53c	70/54s	Orlando	94/74t	95/74pc
Chicago	75/55pc	79/59s	Philadelphia	88/66t	78/60pc
Cincinnati	89/65t	82/59pc	Phoenix	103/80pc	108/78s
Dallas	100/78s	100/78pc	Pittsburgh	80/60t	76/54pc
Denver	90/58pc	90/57s	Portland, OR	80/57pc	75/55s
Detroit	78/55c	77/57s	San Francisco	75/56s	75/58pc
Houston	96/76s	94/76pc	Seattle	72/56pc	70/55pc
Los Angeles	90/70pc	90/70pc	St. Louis	90/67t	87/67pc
Miami	92/76pc	90/75pc	Washington	93/70t	79/65pc

¿Qué tiempo va a hacer el sábado . . .

1. en Boston?
2. en Houston?
3. en San Francisco?
4. en Orlando?
5. en Detroit?
6. en Phoenix?
7. en Buffalo?
8. en Pittsburgh?
9. en Dallas?
10. en Denver?
11. en New Orleans?
12. en Chicago?

Learning Strategy:

Reading for cultural information

COMENTARIOS CULTURALES

La siesta

The custom of taking an afternoon rest is often necessary in tropical countries where temperatures are hottest during the middle of the day. Seeking refuge indoors is practically a must, and the reference to the sixth hour of the day (**la sexta hora**, or high noon) as **la siesta** has become commonplace in Spanish-speaking cultures. In some countries, small businesses close for a few hours during the hottest part of the afternoon, extending store hours into the early evening. **Echar** or **dormir una siesta** means *to take a nap.*

Repaso

C. ¿Cuál es la fecha?   Working with your partner, make a list in Spanish of the 12 months of the year. For any ten months, name and give the date of a holiday or special event which takes place in that month. Some possibilities that you may want to include are **la Navidad** (Christmas), **la independencia de los Estados Unidos, el Año Nuevo, el Día de los Enamorados, tu cumpleaños, el Día de Acción de Gracias** (Thanksgiving). You might refer to Activity E on page 71 for other ideas.

Learning Strategy:

Listing

Critical Thinking Strategy:

Making associations

Stem-changing verbs in the present tense

—Yo siempre **juego** al fútbol
  por la tarde. ¿Y tú?

—Yo también. **¿Juegas** mañana?

—¿Mañana? Sí. Y Juan **piensa**
  jugar también.

—Bueno, **podemos** jugar juntos.

I always *play* soccer in the
afternoon. What about you?

I do, too. *Are you playing* tomorrow?

Tomorrow? Yes. And Juan *is
thinking about* playing also.

Good, *we can* play together.

As you learned in Level 1 of *¡Ya verás!,* some verbs change their stems in the present and preterite tenses. Stem-changing verbs are verbs that have a change in the vowels of the stem (everything before the **-ar, -er,** or **-ir** ending of the infinitive). All the endings, however, remain regular. There are three types of stem-changing verbs in the present: the stem vowels change to **ie, ue,** or **i.**

pensar (ie)		*dormir (ue)*		*pedir (i)*	
pienso	pensamos	**due**rmo	dormimos	**pi**do	pedimos
piensas	pensáis	**due**rmes	dormís	**pi**des	pedís
piensa	**pie**nsan	**due**rme	**due**rmen	**pi**de	**pi**den

Other verbs of this type that you have seen include:

(ie)   comenzar, despertar(se), empezar, querer

(ue)   acostar(se), jugar, poder

(i)   servir

Stem-changing verbs are indicated in the glossary by the notation **(ie), (ue),** or **(i)** after the infinitive form.

Aquí practicamos

D. Combina un elemento de cada columna para formar una oración lógica *(logical sentence)*. Sigue el modelo.

Modelo: Marisol   pensar   ir a la playa.
Marisol piensa ir a la playa.

A	B	C
mis hermanos	volver	ocho horas cada noche
Carlos	comenzar	hablar con los amigos
el (la) profesor(a)	pensar	café con leche
Alonso y Carmen	querer	al tenis
tú	pedir	a estudiar ahora
el camarero	jugar	a la casa después
vosotros	dormir	a los clientes
yo	servir	ir al cine

E. *Encuentra alguien que...* (Find somebody who . . .) Ask questions of your classmates to find someone who fits each of the following descriptions. When you find someone, write a sentence in your notebook using that person's name.

Modelo: *Amy quiere viajar los sábados.*

1. querer viajar los sábados
2. dormir ocho horas cada noche
3. dormir mucho los sábados
4. jugar al básquetbol
5. pedir ayuda con la tarea
6. poder tocar la guitarra
7. pensar ir al cine mañana
8. acostarse después de las 11 de la noche
9. despertarse después de las ocho de la mañana los sábados
10. comenzar a jugar al tenis

F. *¿Qué haces después de las clases?*   Your new neighbor
arrives home from school at the same time that you do. He (She) also
happens to be in your Spanish class. (1) Greet each other. (2) Introduce
yourselves. (3) Tell each other at least three activities that you typically do
after school. (4) Find one activity in common that the two of you would
like to do together this afternoon. Follow the model.

Modelo:

— *Buenos días. ¿Cómo estás?*
— *Muy bien. ¿Y tú?*
— *Bien, gracias. Tú estás en mi clase de español. Me llamo
  Juanita.*
— *Encantada, Juanita. Me llamo Sofía. Oye, ¿qué piensas
  hacer después de las clases?*
— *No sé. Generalmente vuelvo a la casa a las 3:30 y empiezo a
  hacer la tarea. A veces juego al béisbol; a veces miro la tele-
  visión.*
— *No quiero hacer la tarea ahora. No juego al béisbol, pero
  juego al tenis. Pienso ir al café para tomar un refresco y
  después ir al centro. ¿Quieres ir conmigo?*
— *Sí, Vamos. Tengo ganas de tomar un refresco.*

Aquí escuchamos:
"¡Hace mucho frío!"

Antes de escuchar

The Valenzuela family is on vacation in Portillo, but the weather
is bad and the children are unhappy. Look at the following
questions to get an idea of what you will hear in their
conversation.

Después de escuchar

1. ¿Por qué no están contentos
   los hijos?
2. ¿Qué tiempo hace en
   Acapulco, probablemente?
3. ¿Qué hizo la familia ayer?
4. ¿Hay música en el hotel?
5. ¿Qué cosa positiva dice el
   padre?

¡Aquí te toca a ti!

G. *Las vacaciones* Tell your classmates about a vacation you took with your family or friends. Explain (1) where you went and (2) in which month. Then (3) describe the weather and (4) tell three activities that you did. Follow the model.

Dónde:	*Fuimos de vacaciones a Disney World.*
Mes:	*Fuimos en el mes de junio.*
Tiempo:	*Hizo calor. Hizo sol. Hizo muy buen tiempo.*
Actividades:	*Jugamos al tenis, bailamos por la noche y conocimos al Ratón Miguelito.*

¡Adelante!

EJERCICIO ORAL

H. *Mis vacaciones* Find out from one of your classmates about his or her last vacation. Ask (1) where he or she went, (2) with whom, (3) when, (4) what the weather was like, and (5) at least three activities that he or she did, including at least one activity done when the weather was bad. Prepare to report back to the class.

EJERCICIO ESCRITO

I. *Una postal* Write a postcard to a friend, describing what you did during a vacation that you just had with your family. (You may refer to a real vacation or use your imagination.) Tell (1) where you went, (2) when, (3) with whom, (4) one interesting site that you visited, and (5) two other activities that you did, including one done when the weather was bad.

TERCERA ETAPA

Preparación

›› **W**hat do the weather symbols on the map mean?

›› **W**hat temperature system is used in the United States?

›› **W**hat temperature system is more commonly used in the rest of the world?

›› **I**n what areas of the United States does it tend to be particularly hot? particularly cold?

›› **W**hat do you know about weather patterns in the countries of Latin America?

/./././././././././

Learning Strategy:

Previewing

¿Qué tiempo va a hacer mañana?

¡Aquí te toca a ti!

A. La temperatura está en...   Tell your new Spanish-speaking friend what the temperature usually is in your hometown during different months of the year, so that he or she may better understand climate in the U.S. Look at the **Comentarios culturales** below and use Celsius for the temperatures.

Modelo: *En octubre la temperatura en Boston está en cinco grados centígrados.*

B. ¿Qué tiempo va a hacer?   Look at the temperatures given for the various cities on page 83. According to the temperature, say whether it will be warm **(calor)**, cool **(fresco)**, cold **(frío)**, or very cold **(mucho frío)** on May 26, and give a second indicator of the weather in that city according to the icons on the map. Then choose one activity your friends in each location can plan to do outside **(afuera)** on that day.

Modelo: Lima
Va a hacer fresco y va a estar nublado. Mis amigos de Lima pueden jugar al fútbol, pero no deben nadar.

1. Asunción
2. Caracas
3. Santiago
4. San José
5. Buenos Aires
6. La Habana
7. Bogotá
8. La Paz
9. Montevideo

COMENTARIOS CULTURALES

La temperatura

Temperatures in Spain and Latin American countries are given on the Celsius (centigrade) scale. Here is a comparison of Celsius temperatures and their Fahrenheit equivalents.

C:	30°	25°	20°	15°	10°	5°	0°	-5°
F:	86°	77°	68°	59°	50°	41°	32°	23°

To convert from Celsius to Fahrenheit, follow these steps:
   a. Divide by 5   b. Multiply by 9   c. Add 32

For example, if the temperature is 34° Celsius, you would calculate as follows:
   a. 35 divided by 5 = 7   b. 7 x 9= 63   c. 63 +32 = 95° Fahrenheit

C. ¿Qué tiempo va a hacer mañana?   Indícale a un(a)
compañero(a) el tiempo que crees que va a hacer aquí mañana. Pueden referirse a las posibilidades de la lista o añadir *(add)* otras. Sigue el modelo.

Critical Thinking Strategy:

Predicting

llover / hacer sol / estar nublado / estar despejado / hacer frío / hacer fresco / hacer calor

 Modelo: ¿Va a hacer buen tiempo mañana?
No, va a llover.

1. ¿Va a nevar mañana?
2. ¿Va a hacer frío mañana?
3. ¿Va a hacer buen tiempo mañana?

4. ¿Va a estar despejado mañana?
5. ¿Va a llover mañana?

D. Ayer y mañana   Usa las pistas *(cues)* para hablar del tiempo de
ayer y de mañana. Trabaja con un(a) compañero(a) y sigan el modelo.

 Modelo: buen tiempo / también
—*¿Qué tiempo hizo ayer?*
—*Hizo buen tiempo.*
—*¿Qué tiempo va a hacer mañana?*
—*Va a hacer buen tiempo también.*

1. mal / también
2. calor / bastante frío
3. llover / también
4. viento / mucho calor

5. nublado / sol
6. muy buen tiempo / nevar
7. tormenta / buen tiempo
8. fresco / bastante calor

E. ¿Qué hacen?   Describe lo que hacen las personas en los dibujos. Usa los verbos *jugar* y *volver*, y otros verbos que sabes.

Modelo: *Juegan al fútbol.*

1.

2.

3.

4.

ESTRUCTURA

The verb *saber*

—**¿Sabes** quién es ese actor de cine?   *Do you know* who that movie actor is?
—Claro que **sé** quien es. ¡Es Rubén   Sure, *I know* who he is. It's Rubén Blades!
Blades! ¡Y además **sabe** cantar!   And he also *knows* how to sing!

Here is the way to form the present tense of the verb **saber:**

		saber		
yo	**sé**		nosotros(as)	sab**emos**
tú	sab**es**		vosotros(as)	sab**éis**
él			ellos	
ella	} sab**e**		ellas	} sab**en**
Ud.			Uds.	

Saber is used to talk about knowledge of facts or something that has been learned thoroughly, as well as to say that you know how to do something. In this last instance **saber** is used before an infinitive form of another verb.

Rita **sabe bailar** bien. Rita *knows how to dance* well.
Tú **sabes hablar** tres idiomas, ¿verdad? You *know how to speak* three languages, right?

Aquí practicamos

F. Take turns talking with a classmate about what you know and do not know how to do. Refer to the possibilities on the list or add others. Follow the model.

> **Modelo:** —*Yo sé nadar pero no sé esquiar. Y tú, ¿qué sabes hacer?*
> —*Yo sé jugar al tenis pero no sé nadar.*

nadar
esquiar
jugar al tenis
el nombre del
  presidente de México
jugar al fútbol

quién es el (la) mejor
  estudiante de la clase
el número de teléfono
  de la escuela
dónde está el estado
  de Iowa
preparar tacos

manejar un automóvil
hablar español
tocar la guitarra
bailar el mambo
cuántos estudiantes
  hay en la clase hoy
de dónde es el (la) profesor(a)

G. Usa las pistas para hacerles cuatro preguntas a otros estudiantes. Usa el verbo *saber* y los sujetos *tú, Uds., él/ella* y *ellos/ellas.* Sigue el modelo.

> **Modelo:** ¿Sabes tú hablar español?
> ¿Saben Uds. hablar español?

1. hablar francés
2. los meses del año
3. cuándo va a hacer calor

4. si llueve mucho en marzo
5. quiénes son mis amigos
6. jugar al béisbol

H. *Mi amigo(a) nuevo(a)* You are writing your Spanish-speaking pen pal about a classmate you would like to get to know better. Refer to the list of possible topics in Activity F if you need ideas for what your new friend knows and does not know how to do. Tell which things you know about your friend, such as age, telephone number, birthday, etc. Point out special talents (**Él/Ella sabe tocar el piano, patinar...**). Mention to your pen pal which facts you still do not know about this classmate. Use the verb **saber** as many times as you can along with other verbs you know.

Aquí escuchamos:
"¿Va a llover mañana?"

Antes de escuchar

Tomorrow is Saturday. Patricia and her friends talk about their plans for the weekend. Their plans depend on what the weather will be like. Look at the following questions and identify a few things you expect to hear them talk about.

START

Después de escuchar

1. ¿Qué tiempo va a hacer mañana por la mañana? ¿por la tarde?
2. ¿Cómo saben esto las amigas?
3. ¿Adónde quiere ir Margo?
4. ¿Qué van a hacer las amigas por la mañana?
5. ¿Adónde van por la tarde?

¡Aquí te toca a ti!

I. *Planes para el fin de semana* You and two of your friends are making plans for the weekend. Each time one of you makes a suggestion, another uses the weather as a reason for not doing the proposed activity. Then the third person comes up with a suggestion of another activity more appropriate for the weather forecasted. Take turns being the first to suggest an activity. Follow the models.

Modelos: ir a la playa

Estudiante 1: *Vamos a la playa.*
Estudiante 2: *No, va a hacer frío mañana.*
Estudiante 3: *Entonces, vamos al cine.*

mirar la televisión

Estudiante 1: *Vamos a mirar la televisión.*
Estudiante 2: *No, va a hacer buen tiempo mañana.*
Estudiante 3: *Entonces, damos un paseo al parque.*

1. ir a las montañas
2. dar un paseo
3. ir al centro
4. nadar en la piscina
5. jugar al básquetbol
6. ir al cine
7. correr
8. estudiar en casa

EJERCICIO ORAL

J. Una entrevista Working with a partner, imagine that an exchange student from Latin America has just arrived on your campus. The school newspaper has asked you to interview him or her since you know Spanish. Use the following items as guidelines for organizing your interview and take notes on the information you receive. Switch roles and partners after the first interview.

Ask…

1. when he or she arrived in the United States
2. if he or she likes the United States
3. where he or she lives in Latin America
4. what the weather is like in his or her hometown
5. if he or she lives near the beach
6. when he or she was born
7. what his or her parents do
8. if he or she has any brothers or sisters
9. if he or she knows how to ski

Learning Strategies:

Organizing, interviewing, asking for or giving personal information, taking notes

EJERCICIO ESCRITO

K. Los resultados de una entrevista Ahora usa la información obtenida en la entrevista en la Actividad J para escribir el artículo para el periódico de tu escuela.

Learning Strategies:

Compiling and organizing information in an article, paraphrasing, reporting

Vocabulario

Para charlar

Para hablar del tiempo

¿Qué tiempo hace?
Está despejado.
Está nublado.
Está resbaloso.
Hace buen tiempo.
Hace calor.
Hace fresco.
Hace frío.
Hace mal tiempo.
Hace sol.
Hace viento.
Hay hielo.

Hay neblina.
Hay niebla.
Hay nubes.
Hay tormenta.
Llovizna.
Llueve.
Nieva.
Truena.
La temperatura
  está en… grados
  (bajo cero).

Para preguntar y dar la fecha

¿A cuántos estamos?
¿Cuál es la fecha de hoy
  (de tu cumpleaños, etc.)?
¿Qué fecha es hoy?
Hoy es el 5 de abril.
En (el mes de) enero
  (febrero, marzo, etc.)…
Él (Ella) nació…

Temas y contextos

Los meses del año

enero   julio
febrero   agosto
marzo   septiembre
abril   octubre
mayo   noviembre
junio   diciembre

Las estaciones del año

la primavera
el verano
el otoño
el invierno

Vocabulario general

Sustantivos

el mar
la montaña
la neblina
la niebla
la nieve
la temperatura
la tormenta

Verbos

jugar
saber
volver

Otras palabras y expresiones

demasiado
depender de
echar (dormir) una siesta

Lectura CULTURAL

EL TIEMPO ES RELATIVO

Antes de leer

Learning Strategies:

Scanning for cognates, previewing, reading for details

1. What does the word **tiempo** mean in Spanish? Does it have more than one meaning? What do you think it will mean in this reading?
2. In a normal conversation between speakers of English, if the topic of weather comes up, at what point in the conversation does this usually happen?
3. What kinds of words or expressions do you usually find in articles dealing with the weather? Make a list of some of these in Spanish.
4. Do you have any of the following on your list? What do they mean?

Learning Strategy:

Reading for details

condiciones atmosféricas	**hace calor**	**está lloviendo**
hace buen/mal tiempo	**hace frío**	**boletín meteorológico**

Guía para la lectura

A. Scan the passage on page 92 and find the expressions listed at the end of **Antes de leer**.

B. As you come upon the answers in each paragraph, indicate whether the following statements are true or false.

1. El tema del tiempo es de igual importancia en todas las culturas.
2. Cada cultura determina los usos y los significados de una palabra.
3. La palabra tiempo tiene varios significados en español.
4. Cuando hace buen tiempo en los países de habla española no se habla del clima.
5. Es una costumbre entre hispanohablantes iniciar una conversación con comentarios sobre el clima.
6. Hay muchas expresiones para preguntar sobre la salud de una persona.

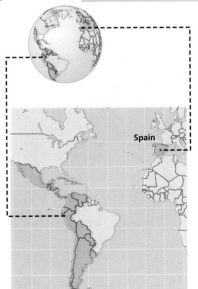

Spain

El tiempo es relativo

José Juan Arrom

Para muchas personas que viven la mayor parte de su vida en Nueva Inglaterra, uno de los primeros temas de una conversación es el tiempo. Esta palabra tiene usos muy variados que dependen de su contexto cultural. Es decir, los significados y la importancia que tiene el tiempo en los países de habla española no siempre corresponden a los que tiene en los países de habla inglesa.

Es evidente que la palabra *tiempo,* tal como se acaba de usar, equivale a *condiciones atmosféricas.* También, como en inglés, es la idea que usamos para hablar de la distancia o la duración de algo que pasa, calculándolo por segundos, minutos, horas, días, meses, años y hasta siglos. Pero aquí vamos a limitar la discusión del tiempo, por ahora, a lo que también se llama *el clima.*

En este sentido de la palabra, en España y en América Latina de vez en cuando se dice que hace buen tiempo o que hace mal tiempo. Pero con más frecuencia, si el tiempo es bueno, se acepta como una realidad y no se dice más. Y si es malo, la gente puede decir que "hace un calor horroroso", que "está lloviendo a cántaros" o que "hace un frío de los mil diablos".

Aun así, hablar del tiempo es una manera poco usada para comenzar una conversación en español. Generalmente, el boletín meteorológico le interesa mucho menos a la persona de habla española que la salud de la persona con quien habla y la de su familia. Por eso el idioma español es tan rico en frases como: "¿Qué tal? ¿Cómo te va? ¿Cómo estás? ¿Qué cuentas? ¿Qué me dices? ¿Qué pasó? ¿Qué anda? ¿Qué hubo? ¿Cómo andan por tu casa? ¿Qué me dices de la familia?," etc. Y la persona que recibe la pregunta sabe que no es de mal gusto contestar con detalles. Al contrario, es importante dar esos detalles.

a cántaros: pitchersfull / *de mal gusto:* in bad taste

¿CÓMO ES?

El Palacio de Bellas Artes,
México, D.F.

Objective:

>>> **D**escribing objects and people

Strategies:

>>> **E**xpressing opinions
>>> **D**escribing
>>> **E**valuating

PRIMERA ETAPA

Preparación

❯❯ **W**hen you describe an object, what details do you take into account?

❯❯ **W**hich is easier to describe—an object, a place, or a person? Why?

❯❯ **W**hat is your favorite color? Your least favorite?

Learning Strategy:

Previewing

Describeme...

Este coche es pequeño.
Este coche es bonito.
Este coche es moderno.
Este coche es bueno.

old

Ese coche es grande.
Ese coche es feo.
Ese coche es **viejo**.
Ese coche es malo.

Este libro es interesante.
Este libro es **fácil**.
Este libro es **ligero**.

Ese libro es aburrido.
Ese libro es **difícil**.
Ese libro es **pesado**.

easy / difficult
light / heavy

What color is it?

¿De qué color es... ?

blanco   morado   anaranjado   negro   azul   rojo

gris   verde   rosado   pardo, café   amarillo   violeta

¡Aquí te toca a ti!

A. ¿Cómo es?   ¿Qué adjetivo describe mejor *(best describes)* cada dibujo?

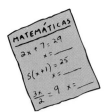

1. ¿Es fácil o difícil el examen?   **2.** ¿Es grande o pequeño el auto?

3. ¿Es vieja o moderna la iglesia?   **4.** ¿Es aburrido o interesante el libro?   **5.** ¿Es bonita o fea la playa?

6. ¿Es buena o mala la película?   **7.** ¿Es ligera o pesada la maleta?   **8.** ¿Es bonito o feo el pueblo?

B. ¿De qué color es?   Escoge *(Choose)* el color que mejor describe el objeto.

1. ¿Es azul o verde el cielo *(sky)*?
2. ¿Son rojas o violetas las manzanas?
3. ¿Es negro o amarillo el sol?
4. ¿Es blanca o azul la nieve?
5. ¿Son grises o amarillos los plátanos?
6. ¿Son verdes o negros los guisantes?
7. ¿Son blancas o anaranjadas las papas?
8. ¿Son amarillas o grises las nubes?

C. Reservaciones computarizadas   Read the following advertisement for a computerized reservation system. As you read it, make a list of the adjectives that you find, along with the nouns they modify. You should be able to find at least ten adjectives. Remember that adjectives give you information about the nouns they modify.

When you have completed your list, work with a partner to verify that you have as many adjectives as possible. Then, together, decide which two qualities of this service you consider most important.

Cooperative Learning

Learning Strategies:

Listing, negotiating

Critical Thinking Strategies:

Comparing and contrasting, evaluating

SU NUEVO SISTEMA DE RESERVACIONES COMPUTARIZADO

Ahora LACSA pone el mundo en sus manos con el nuevo sistema computarizado de reservaciones-SPEEDY. Este nuevo sistema nos permite ayudarle a organizar su viaje hasta el más mínimo detalle y con mayor rapidez.

SPEEDY le brinda acceso al mayor banco de información sobre disponibilidad de espacio en cualquier línea aérea, escoge y organiza los más convenientes vuelos y conexiones para su viaje y le indica las tarifas más económicas.

Con SPEEDY usted puede reservar hasta con 11 meses de anticipación y escoger el asiento que prefiera de antemano. Además, SPEEDY tiene capacidad para informar y reservar en 13,000 hoteles, 125 cadenas hoteleras y 26 compañías de alquiler de automóviles en todo el mundo.

Y como si fuera poco, SPEEDY se encarga de informarle y reservarle espacio en cruceros, excursiones y eventos culturales, así como de darle información sobre su destino desde los lugares de interés turístico hasta ¡qué tipo de ropa llevar! Lo único que SPEEDY no puede hacer por usted es...empacar.

Recuerde, ahora cada vez que viaje con LACSA, usted cuenta con SPEEDY para ayudarle a organizar su viaje hasta el último detalle y con mayor rapidez.

||Lacsa
nos encanta la gente

Pronunciación: *The vowel combination ia*

The combination **ia** in Spanish is pronounced in one single syllable, similar to the *ya* in the English word *yacht*.

Práctica

D. Lee cada palabra en voz alta, pronunciando con cuidado la combinación *ia*.

1. sucia	**4.** gracias	**7.** democracia
2. familia	**5.** gloria	**8.** farmacia
3. estudia	**6.** patria	

Repaso

E. *Comentando sobre* (about) *el tiempo*   Un(a) reportero(a) *(A reporter)* informa sobre el tiempo. Comenta sobre la información. Sigue el modelo.

 La temperatura está en 23 grados centígrados.
Hace buen tiempo.

1. Esta noche la temperatura va a bajar a cinco grados centígrados.
2. El cielo está despejado.
3. Por la tarde va a estar nublado con lluvias y tormentas eléctricas.
4. Mañana la temperatura va a estar en 29 grados centígrados al mediodía.
5. Hace sol, pero va a nevar *(to snow)* por la tarde.
6. Es un día perfecto para salir a jugar al tenis con los amigos.
7. La temperatura está en 15 grados centígrados bajo cero.

F. *¿Qué sabes del tiempo?*   Alternando con un(a) compañero(a) de clase, pregunten y contesten las siguientes preguntas sobre el tiempo.

 ¿Nieva mucho en la ciudad de Miami?
No, no nieva en Miami. Hace mucho calor.

1. ¿Dónde hace más calor en mayo, aquí o en Argentina?
2. ¿En qué meses hace mal tiempo en Seattle?
3. ¿Llueve mucho en Arizona?
4. ¿Qué tiempo hace en Ecuador en diciembre?
5. ¿Cuándo hace mucho viento en Chicago?
6. ¿Cuándo nieva en Chile?
7. Si la temperatura está en 20 grados centígrados, ¿cuánto es en Fahrenheit?
8. ¿Qué tiempo hace en Acapulco, en general?

ESTRUCTURA

Agreement of adjectives

1. As you have already learned, many adjectives end in **-o** if they are masculine and in **-a** if they are feminine. If the masculine form of an adjective ends in **-e**, the feminine form also ends in **-e**. To make these adjectives plural, you simply add **-s**.

El muchacho es **alto.**   La muchacha es **alta.**
El libro es **interesante.**   La pregunta es **interesante.**
Los hombres son **inteligentes.**   Las mujeres son **inteligentes.**

2. An adjective ending in **-sta** has the same ending for both the masculine and feminine forms. To make these adjectives plural, simply add an **-s.**

El abogado es **pesimista.**   Las abogadas son **pesimistas.**

3. If the masculine form of an adjective ends in **-l, -s,** or **-z,** the ending for the feminine form is also **-l, -s,** or **-z.** To make these plural, you add **-es.** Note that in the plural form, **z** changes to **c.**

El examen es **difícil.**   Las preguntas son **difíciles.**
El libro es **gris.**   Las faldas son **grises.**
El niño es **feliz.**   Las niñas son **felices.**

Remember: The exception to this rule is that when an adjective of *nationality* ends in **-s** in the masculine form, the feminine form then ends in **-sa.**

El profesor es **francés.**   La profesora es **francesa.**

Aquí practicamos

G. Da la forma femenina de cada adjetivo del 1 al 7 y la forma plural del femenino de cada adjetivo del 8 al 14. Sigue el modelo.

 Modelo: caro *cara*
negro *negras*

1. aburrido
2. fácil
3. colombiano
4. alegre
5. delicioso
6. feliz
7. normal
8. bonito
9. activista
10. blanco
11. inglés
12. dominante
13. formal
14. malo

H. Ahora da la forma masculina de cada adjetivo del 1 al 10 y la forma plural del masculino para cada adjetivo del 11 al 20. Sigue el modelo.

 Modelo: delgada *delgado*
blanca *blancos*

1. interesante
2. famosa
3. bonita
4. amable
5. optimista
6. gorda
7. anaranjada
8. católica
9. larga
10. real
11. japonés
12. breve
13. café
14. inglesa
15. tranquila
16. musical
17. baja
18. grande
19. realista
20. difícil

I. Mi casa es...   Usa un adjetivo para hacer un comentario sobre cada objeto. Después hazle una pregunta a otro(a) estudiante. Sigue el modelo.

  Modelo: mi casa
—*Mi casa es grande. ¿Y tu casa?*
—*Mi casa es grande también.*   o:
—*Mi casa no es grande. Es pequeña.*

1. mi casa (mi apartamento)
2. mi cuarto
3. mis libros
4. mi amigo(a)
5. mi coche
6. mis discos compactos
7. mi computadora
8. mi ciudad
9. mis padres
10. mi clase de…

Aquí escuchamos:
"¡Es feo este auto!"

Antes de escuchar

Felipe saved some money and finally was able to buy a used car. In this conversation, his friends will give their reaction to the car. Before listening, make a short list of adjectives commonly used to describe cars. Then look at the questions in the next section to anticipate for what information you should listen.

Después de escuchar

1. ¿Le gusta a la muchacha el coche?
2. ¿De qué color es el coche?
3. ¿Qué dice Felipe de su coche?

¡Aquí te toca a ti!

J. Acabo de comprar...   Describe to a classmate something you just bought. Tell him or her what it is, using the adjectives you've learned to describe its color, size, and other characteristics. Suggestions: **una bicicleta, un vídeo, una mochila, un coche, un televisor, una cámara, una computadora, un libro.** Follow the model.

Modelo: *Acabo de comprar una bicicleta. Es francesa. Es azul y gris. Es muy ligera. ¡Es muy rápida también!,* etc.

¡Adelante!

EJERCICIO ORAL

K. ¿Qué es?   (1) Choose someone or something from one of the following categories: **un monumento, una ciudad turística, un lugar en tu ciudad, una película, un programa de televisión popular.** (2) Write out five sentences that describe your choice without explicitly identifying it. These are your clues. Next, working in groups of four, (3) tell your group which category your choice is from (e.g., **Es una ciudad turística.**) and (4) give them one of your clues. (5) They will ask questions and try to guess what person, place, film, or television program you have in mind. (6) Give a new clue after each guess until your group guesses your choice or until you have used all of your clues.

EJERCICIO ESCRITO

L. Un(a) amigo(a) quiere saber   A Spanish-speaking exchange student from Lima, Peru is coming to live in your community for a month, and it's your task to write a brief letter describing your school to him or her. (1) Begin by giving a general description of the school, telling whether it is large or small, modern or old, attractive or not, close to or distant from other places you like to go. (2) Then choose three places on your school's campus that you like. Tell what they are and describe them. Tell what you like about them, using a couple of different adjectives for each one. (3) Finally, tell about some part of your school that you would like to change using a couple of adjectives to tell what is wrong with it and a couple to describe how you would like it to be.

Some areas you may want to consider are **la cafetería, la biblioteca, la piscina, el estadio, la clase de inglés,** and **la clase de matemáticas.**

SEGUNDA ETAPA

Preparación

》》 **W**hat sort of entertainment is available in your town or city?

》》 **W**hen you are planning to go out for entertainment, where do you generally like to go?

》》 **I**f you are going to see a movie or a play, what information do you usually like to have?

》》 **H**ow do you get the information you need before going out?

¿Qué piensas?

NACIO USTED EN ESTE DIA

Es inventivo, nervioso y un poco sensible. Usualmente es talentoso en las líneas creativas. Para lograr sus habilidades tiene que aprender a controlar su temperamento. Tendrá éxito en cualquier carrera que mida sus ideales. Necesita autodisciplina. Tiene buena intuición en la cual debería aprender a confiar. Deje a un lado el escepticismo y la tendencia a ser muy sensitivo.

¿Es un horóscopo muy romántico?
¿Es un horóscopo demasiado pesimista?

Cine BELLAVISTA
HOY 4 y 7:30 p.m. ¢110
GANADORA DE 9 OSCARES
* MEJOR PELICULA
* MEJOR DIRECTOR
* MEJOR GUION ADAPTADO
* MEJOR PARTITURA MUSICAL ORIGI...
* MEJOR DIRECC...
* MEJOR F...
* M...

¡ÚLTIMO DIA! NO DEJE DE VERLA
...DO SEMANA DE EXITO!

Una Historia Verdadera de antiguas tradiciones

EL ÚLTIMO EMPERADOR
DE BERNARDO BERTOLUCCI

¿Es una película interesante?
¿Es una película sensacional?
¿Es una película aburrida?

¿Es un lugar serio y formal?
¿Es un lugar alegre y divertido?

¿Es un libro difícil?
¿Es un libro histórico?
¿Es un libro infantil?
¿Es un libro bonito?

¿Es un programa teatral variado?
¿Es un programa teatral completo?
¿Es un buen programa teatral?
¿Es un programa teatral norteamericano?

¿Es un buen restaurante?
¿Es un restaurante nuevo?
¿Es un restaurante chino?
¿Es un restaurante elegante?
¿Es un restaurante caro?

RESTAURANTE

LUZ DE LUNA

Se complace en invitar al público en general a su

GRAN INAUGURACION

Especialidad en comida china del
oeste a cargo de 4 cheffs internacionales.
Ofrecemos una bebida de cortesía por cada plato de comida.
Oferta válida durante la primera semana

¡Lo esperamos! Dirección: Sabana oeste 125 sur
de canal 7 Teléfono: 20-08-08

Horario:
De 11:00
a.m. a 3:00 p.m. y
de 6:00 p.m. a
11:00 p.m.

¡Aquí te toca a ti!

A. ¿Qué piensas? Usa tres adjetivos para describir cada objeto o para dar tu opinión. Sigue el modelo.

Modelo: *Es una novela buena.*
Es una novela interesante.
Es una novela sensacional.

1. una novela

2. un periódico

3. una obra teatral

4. un programa

5. un cuadro

6. un vídeo

Pronunciación: *The vowel combination* ie

The combination **ie** in Spanish is pronounced in one single syllable, similar to the *ye* in the English word *yes*.

Práctica

B. Lee cada palabra en voz alta, pronunciando con cuidado la combinación *ie*.

1. tiene   3. diente   5. siete   7. también
2. viene   4. cien   6. tiempo   8. cielo

Repaso

C. *Los monumentos* Usa dos adjetivos para describir cada uno de los siguientes monumentos en América Latina. Posibilidades: *pequeño, grande, alto, moderno, viejo, interesante, feo, bonito*, etc. Sigue el modelo.

Modelo: *Es alta y bella.*

arriba, izquierda: Chichén Itzá, México; *arriba, derecha:* El Palacio Presidencial de la Moneda, Santiago de Chile; *abajo, izquierda:* La Torre Latinoamericana, México, D.F.; *abajo, derecha:* La Catedral, México, D.F.

ESTRUCTURA

Position of adjectives

Acabo de comprar una motoneta **nueva.**	I just bought a *new* moped.
Es una motoneta **linda.**	It's a *beautiful* moped.

In Spanish, unlike English, an adjective is almost always placed *after* the noun it describes.

una película **japonesa**   una lección **fácil**   los libros **interesantes**

Adjectives indicating nationality always *follow* the noun.

Los automóviles **japoneses** son buenos.   *Japanese* cars are good.

Aquí practicamos

D. **Mi casa es tu casa.**   Your family is considering making a "home exchange" for a month with a family in Mexico City. With your partner, practice answering the questions that you expect to be asked about your residence. In order to make yourself clearly understood, give a complete response to each question. Follow the model.

Modelo: ¿Es nueva tu casa?
No, no es una casa nueva.

1. ¿Es grande tu casa?
2. ¿Es cómoda *(comfortable)* tu casa?
3. ¿Es bien equipada tu cocina?
4. ¿Son cómodos los cuartos?
5. ¿Es fácil la televisión?
6. ¿Es moderno el baño?

E. **Cadenas** (Chains)   Form a spontaneous "chain" with your classmates. Start with a short sentence. The next person will use that sentence to form a new sentence by substituting a different word. Make any necessary changes as you go along. The process continues as quickly as possible, moving in turn from one association to the next. Follow the model.

Modelo: *La fiesta es estupenda.*
*La **película** es estupenda.*
***Maricarmen** es estupenda.*
*Maricarmen es **simpática.***
*El **profesor** es simpático.*
*El profesor es **chileno.** Etc.*

Position of two adjectives

When two adjectives modify the same noun, they are placed after the noun and connected to each other with **y.**

una escuela **buena y grande**
unos muchachos **inteligentes y responsables**

F. ¿Qué tipo (kind) **de... tienes?** Escoge uno o dos adjetivos de la lista para contestar cada pregunta. Sigue el modelo.

alemán / azul / bonito / blanco / chino / difícil / español / fácil / feo / francés / grande / gris / inteligente / italiano / japonés / joven / largo / moderno / nuevo / pequeño / rojo / simpático / verde / viejo

Modelo: ¿Qué tipo de casa tienes?
Tenemos una casa pequeña y amarilla.

1. ¿Qué tipo de casa tienes?
2. ¿Qué tipo de coche tiene tu familia?
3. ¿Qué tipo de restaurante prefieres?
4. ¿Qué tipos de amigos(as) tienes?
5. ¿Qué tipo de tarea *(homework)* tienes para la clase de español?
6. ¿Qué tipo de viaje haces cuando vas de vacaciones?
7. ¿Qué tipo de bicicleta tienes?
8. ¿Qué tipo de exámenes tienes en la clase de español?

Aquí escuchamos:
"En el Museo de Arte Moderno"

Antes de escuchar

Maricarmen and Ricardo are going to *El Museo de Arte Moderno*. What adjectives would you use in Spanish to describe modern art? Name some painters. Where are they from? Before listening, preview the questions in the next section.

Después de escuchar

1. ¿Cómo es el cuadro que admiran Ricardo y Maricarmen?
2. ¿Qué le gusta más a Ricardo del cuadro?
3. ¿Qué dice Maricarmen del pintor *(painter)*?
4. ¿De dónde es el pintor?

¡Aquí te toca a ti!

G. Intercambio Haz las siguientes preguntas a un(a) compañero(a) de clase. Él (Ella) las contesta.

Learning Strategy:

Asking for and giving information

1. ¿Vive en una casa o un apartamento tu familia? ¿De qué color es? ¿Es grande? ¿Es bonito(a)?
2. ¿Tienes un coche o una bicicleta? ¿De qué color es? ¿Es nuevo(a)? ¿Es americano(a)?
3. ¿De qué color es (son) tu(s)… camisa favorita? ¿pantalones? ¿zapatos?

¡Adelante!

EJERCICIO ORAL

H. Vi una película. Pick a film you've seen recently and describe it to a classmate. Tell whether you like or dislike the film, supporting your opinion by commenting on the content, the actors, the music, the cinematography, the kind of movie it is, and how it held your interest. Some adjectives that you may need in your description: **aburrido, bueno, malo, cómico, divertido, dramático, feo, interesante, sensacional, fantástico, largo, histórico, emocionante, romántico, triste, violento.**

Learning Strategies:

Giving details, describing, supporting an opinion

EJERCICIO ESCRITO

I. Reseña de una película Write a letter to your pen pal in Madrid in which you describe a movie that you have seen recently. Without giving away the plot, tell why you like or dislike the film. Describe the content, the actors, the music, the cinematography, the kind of movie it is, and how it held your interest. Advise your pen pal to see or not to see the film.

Learning Strategies:

Giving details, describing, supporting an opinion

Vocabulario

Para charlar

Para hacer una descripción física

feo(a) / bonito(a)   moderno(a) / viejo(a)
largo(a)   pequeño(a) / grande
ligero(a) / pesado(a)

Para describir el color

amarillo(a)   gris   rojo(a)
anaranjado(a)   morado   rosado(a)
azul   negro(a)   verde
blanco(a)   pardo(a)   violeta
café

Para evaluar cualquier cosa

aburrido(a) / interesante   formidable
alegre / triste   histórico(a)
bueno(a) / malo(a)   infantil
caro(a)   optimista / pesimista
clásico(a)   práctico(a)
completo(a)   regular
delicioso(a)   romántico(a)
divertido(a) / serio(a)   sensacional
económico(a)   teatral
elegante   variado(a)
formal

Vocabulario general

Sustantivos   ### Otras palabras y expresiones

un cuadro   ¿De qué color es… ?
un horóscopo   Descríbeme…
un período   pudo
una reacción

Lectura CULTURAL

EL CINE EN ESPAÑA Y AMÉRICA

Antes de leer

1. Based on the photos and the title, what do you think this article is about?
2. Who are some of the key people involved in the making of a movie?
3. List some words that you associate with movies and movie-making. Did you include some of the following?

película	**director**	**premio**
cinematográficas	**actor**	**filmar**

//-//-//-//-//-//-//-//
Learning Strategies:

Previewing, using cognates for meaning, reading for gist

Guía para la lectura

//-//-//-//-//-//-//-//
Learning Strategies:

Reading for details, reading for main ideas

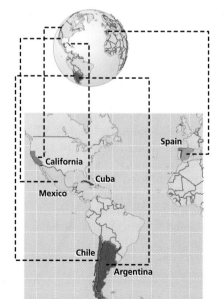

A. Scan the reading and find the words listed at the end of **Antes de leer.** From the context of the reading, what do you think these words mean?

B. Now read the first sentence of each paragraph to get an idea of the overall meaning.
   1. Paragraph l includes information about . . .
   2. Paragraph 2 includes information about . . .
   3. Paragraph 3 includes information about . . .

C. Answer the following questions.
   1. ¿Cuáles son algunos de los países latinoamericanos conocidos por su industria cinematográfica?
   2. ¿Cuáles son dos ejemplos de películas de habla española que ganaron premios internacionales?

El cine en España y América

a producción de películas cinematográficas tiene una larga tradición en España y en algunos países latinoamericanos como Argentina, Cuba, Chile y México. La primera película que se filmó este siglo en España fue en el año 1900. Muchas películas excelentes, como el reciente éxito mexicano *Como agua para chocolate* y *Bella época,* que ganó un Óscar para España en 1994, reciben premios en los festivales cinematográficos más prestigiosos del mundo. Uno de ellos es el famoso festival de cine de San Sebastián en el norte, que tuvo lugar por primera vez en 1952.

Luis Valdéz

Edward James Olmos

Dos de los directores del cine español más conocidos internacionalmente son Luis Buñuel y Pedro Almodóvar. Buñuel vivió muchos años en México donde filmó películas sobre problemas de la sociedad, como en *Los olvidados* y *El ángel exterminador* entre otras. Almodóvar tiene fama por sus películas dramáticas pero que tratan ciertas situaciones con humor, como en *Mujeres al borde de un ataque de nervios* y *¿Qué he hecho para merecer esto?* por ejemplo. Su nuevo proyecto se llama *Kika,* una película de intriga, pero cómica a la vez.

El cine hispano en los Estados Unidos se encuentra en un momento de gran vitalidad. Algunos de los directores más conocidos son Luis Valdéz, Edward James Olmos, Guillermo Varela y Robert Rodríguez.

El éxito de Rodríguez comenzó con su fenomenal película *El mariachi.* Este director mexicano-americano tiene 24 años y vive en Austin, Texas. Desde los 12 años hace películas en que sus nueve hermanos son los actores. Aunque *El mariachi,* una película filmada en español, recibió catorce premios internacionales, sólo costó 7.000 dólares. Robert escribió el guión en tres semanas y filmó la película en 14 días, con la cámara de un amigo.

Los actores de la película "Mujeres al borde de un ataque de nervios"

3

¿CÓMO ES TU AMIGA?

Todos ellos son amigos.

Objective:

>>> **D**escribing people's physical characteristics and personality traits

Strategies:

>>> **L**isting

>>> **O**rganizing information

>>> **C**omparing and contrasting

PRIMERA ETAPA

Preparación

>> **W**hen you describe how a person looks, what kind of information is useful to include?

>> **H**ow would you describe yourself over the telephone to someone who has never seen you before?

Nuestros vecinos y nuestros amigos

neighbor

a bit weak
eyes
hair / short
nose
moustache / beard

Aquí está nuestro **vecino**, el señor Salazar.
Es muy viejo; tiene 82 años.
Es pequeño y **un poco débil**.
Tiene los **ojos** azules.
Tiene el **pelo corto**.
Tiene una **nariz** grande.
Tiene **bigote** y **barba**.

granddaughter

strong
hazel

Aquí está su **nieta**, Susana.
Es joven; tiene dieciséis años.
Es alta y **fuerte**.
Tiene los ojos **castaños**.
Tiene el pelo rubio.
Tiene el pelo largo.
Tiene una nariz pequeña.
Es muy bonita.

¡Aquí te toca a ti!

A. José y la señora Velázquez: retratos (portraits) físicos

Contesta las preguntas según lo que ves en los dibujos.

1. Aquí está José. Tiene dieciséis años. ¿Es viejo? ¿Es grande? ¿Es fuerte? ¿Tiene los ojos negros? ¿Tiene bigote? ¿Tiene la nariz pequeña?

2. Aquí está la señora Velázquez. Tiene sesenta y ocho años. Es vieja, ¿no? ¿Es grande? ¿Es delgada? ¿Tiene el pelo rubio? ¿Tiene la nariz grande?

B. Retrato de un(a) compañero(a)
Choose someone in your class to describe. Make a list of sentences presenting your description one feature at a time. Order your sentences so that each one identifies the person more specifically than the preceding one. For example, if your subject has short, brown hair and there are eight people with brown hair in your class, but only five people have short hair, tell the color before the length. Features that you will want to mention include: height (tall, short), color of eyes, color of hair, and length of hair. Use the descriptions of Sr. Salazar and Susana on page 112 as models.

> **Learning Strategies:**
>
> *Selecting and organizing information, describing, sequencing*

Pronunciación: The vowel combination io

The combination **io** in Spanish is pronounced in one single syllable, similar to the Spanish word **yo**.

Práctica

C. Lee cada palabra en voz alta, pronunciando con cuidado la combinación *io*.

1. rubio
2. Mario
3. adiós
4. acción
5. radio
6. comió
7. bebió
8. microscopio

Repaso

D. ¡Vamos a visitar (Let's visit) el parque de Chapultepec!

You're acting as a guide and showing your friends the Chapultepec castle and park in Mexico City. Use the shorthand notes below to give your descriptions. You may add to the description or change it, as long as you keep to the main idea. Follow the model.

> *Modelo:* parque / inmenso
> *Es un parque inmenso.*   o:
> *Es un parque muy grande.*   o:
> *Estamos aquí en un parque inmenso.*

El parque de Chapultepec

1. parque / interesante
2. turistas / norteamericano
3. lago *(lake)* / bonito / popular
4. estatuas / enorme

El castillo de Chapultepec

5. museo / histórico / mexicano
6. cuadros / viejo
7. terraza / bello / alto
8. patios / elegante / tranquilo

ESTRUCTURA

The verb *conocer*

—¿Quieres **conocer** a ese muchacho guapo?   Do you want *to meet* that good-looking boy?
—¡Cómo no! ¿Tú lo **conoces?**   Of course! *Do you know* him?
—¡Claro que lo **conozco!** Es mi hermano Raúl.   Sure I *know* him! He's my brother Raúl.

Here is the way to form the present tense of the verb **conocer:**

conocer			
yo	cono**zco**	nosotros(as)	cono**cemos**
tú	cono**ces**	vosotros(as)	cono**céis**
él		ellos	
ella }	cono**ce**	ellas }	cono**cen**
Ud.		Uds.	

This verb is used to indicate an acquaintance or familiarity with someone, something, or someplace. It can also be used to talk about the act of meeting someone or visiting a place for the first time.

Aquí practicamos

E. ¿Lo conoces?   Forma una pregunta lógica con el verbo *conocer* y la información en cada columna. Sigue el modelo.

 ¿Ustedes conocen a Raquel?

ustedes	la música española
Carlos	a esos actores de cine
yo	hablar español
Mario y Mercedes	al mejor mesero
mis padres	dónde está el restaurante
el (la) profesor(a)	la hora
la ciudad	quién es ella
vosotros	bailar el tango
el presidente	el número de teléfono
Carlos y tú	a Raquel

F. Preguntas   Hazles preguntas a los otros estudiantes de tu grupo sobre la siguiente información. Usa una variedad de sujetos (tú, Uds., él/ella y ellos/ellas). Sigue el modelo.

 México
¿Conoces tú México? / ¿Conocen Uds. México?

1. Buenos Aires
2. la comida mexicana
3. a Gloria Estefan
4. el castillo de Chapultepec
5. las mejores tiendas de esta ciudad

G. ¿Saber o conocer?   Cuando otro(a) estudiante te hace una pregunta sobre la información en la lista, contesta correctamente con *saber* o *conocer*. Sigue los modelos.

Modelos: la dirección de un hotel cerca de aquí
—*¿Sabes la dirección de un hotel cerca de aquí?*
—*Sí, sé la dirección del hotel.*

Maricarmen
—*¿Conoces a Maricarmen?*
— *No, no conozco a Maricarmen.*

1. el nombre del (de la) profesor(a)
2. los mejores libros de la biblioteca
3. cuántos habitantes tiene México
4. a las hermanas de tus amigos
5. usar la computadora
6. los meses del año
7. qué vamos a estudiar mañana
8. bailar el chachachá

||-||-||-||-||-||-||-||-||

Cooperative Learning

Learning Strategies:

Describing, listing

Critical Thinking Strategy:

Comparing and contrasting

H. Retratos físicos   Prepare descriptions of three of the people in the photographs. Begin your description with a general statement such as **Es una mujer / un hombre / una chica / un chico.** Continue by guessing their ages (**Pienso que él / ella tiene...**) and giving other details about their appearance, including the length and color of their hair, the color of their eyes, their size, and other features you notice. (Consult the descriptions at the beginning of this **etapa.**)

Next, working with a partner, choose one of the five people in the photographs to compare with the other four. List as many different points of comparison and contrast as you can. When you have done your comparing and contrasting, decide which of the other four people has the most in common with your subject.

Sr. Mendoza

Sra. Álvarez

Miguel

Ana y Eduardo

I. *Mi familia* Choose two or three members of your family to describe to your partner. Tell who they are, how old they are (if appropriate), and how they look. Finally, mention some of their interests. For example, what they do for work, their pastimes, likes, and dislikes.

As you listen to your partner's descriptions, ask questions to find out what the members in your two families have in common. As you discuss them, make two lists, one for similarities and one for differences.

Mi hermano tiene diecinueve años. Es delgado y muy alto. Tiene el pelo negro y los ojos verdes. Tiene bigote pero no tiene barba. Es bastante guapo. Él trabaja en un restaurante y es estudiante en la universidad. Mi hermano tiene una nueva motocicleta y le gusta mucho el cine.

Nota gramatical

The personal a

¿Ves **a** Catalina?	Do you see Catalina?
¿Admiras **al** presidente?	Do you admire the president?
¿Ves **a** la mujer alta?	Do you see the tall woman?
¿Llevo **a** mi perro?	Shall I take my dog?
¿Ves el edificio grande?	Do you see the big building?
¿Admiras la inteligencia de Carlos?	Do you admire Carlos's intelligence?

The object of a verb is a person, a thing, or an idea that receives the action of that verb. When the direct object is a specific *human being* or *an animal that is personalized,* it is preceded by **a**. When the definite article in the masculine singular form follows the personal **a**, the contraction **al** is used.

Aquí practicamos

J. Completa las oraciones, usando el modelo. Incluye la *a* personal cuando es necesario.

Miro... (la televisión / los estudiantes).
Miro la televisión. Miro a los estudiantes.

1. Buscamos... (el parque / los turistas / Roberto / el restaurante nuevo / mi perro).

2. Voy a visitar… (el estadio / la señora Mendoza / mis amigos / Buenos Aires).
3. El presidente no comprende… (la gente / los jóvenes / la situación / la lengua japonesa).
4. ¿Necesitas… (el profesor / tu hermano / los libros / el dinero)?
5. Josefina piensa visitar… (el museo / México / su familia / los tíos).

K. *De vacaciones en Hollywood* Imagine that you have won a trip to Hollywood. Your prize allows you to visit your favorite Hollywood personalities and locations from movies or television shows (for example, **la escuela en 90210.**) Using at least four verbs from the list below, tell what you plan to do during your vacation. Mention both people and places in your plans.

ver	**entender**
visitar	**conocer**
mirar	**buscar**
escuchar	**admirar**

Aquí escuchamos:
"¡Es muy guapo mi hermano!"

Antes de escuchar

Cecilia is going to visit Manuel, her older brother, next weekend. She describes Manuel to her friend Claudia. Look at the following questions to get an idea of what she will say.

Después de escuchar

1. ¿Dónde está el hermano de Cecilia?
2. ¿Para qué profesión estudia Manuel?
3. ¿De qué color tiene Manuel el pelo?
4. ¿Cómo reacciona Claudia?
5. ¿Cuál es el problema que menciona Cecilia?

¡Aquí te toca a ti!

L. *Mi cantante* (singer) *preferido(a)* You are discussing your favorite singers with a classmate. Pick the one you like best and give a description of him or her. Tell the singer's name and nationality, and describe as many physical features as you can. Finally, give your general opinion of the singer and his or her music. (Refer to pages 94, 101–102, and 112 for ideas.)

Learning Strategies:

Describing, expressing opinions

Critical Thinking Strategy:

Evaluating

EJERCICIO ORAL

M. *¿Quién es?* Choose a famous person to describe to your classmates. They will try to guess who it is. Begin your description by telling what the person does (**es cantante, es actor/actriz, es profesor[a]**). Continue your description of physical features, nationality, and where the person lives. Prepare your description as a list of clues. (Write at least six sentences.)

Cooperative Learning

Learning Strategies:

Selecting information, describing, guessing

EJERCICIO ESCRITO

N. *¿Cómo soy yo?* Write a physical description of yourself on a piece of paper in six sentences. Then exchange descriptions with one of your classmates and read them to each other to see if either of you can add one more detail about the other person.

Learning Strategies:

Selecting information, providing personal information, reading for details, making suggestions

SEGUNDA ETAPA

Preparación

>> **W**hat are some of the personality traits that are taken into account when you talk about what someone is like?

>> **H**ow would you describe your personality to someone who does not know you?

Learning Strategy:
Previewing

El carácter: Personality

Aquí está mi amigo Eduardo. Él va a estudiar.

☐ Es pesimista.
☐ Es tímido.
☐ Es idealista.
☐ Es honesto.
☐ Es paciente siempre.
☐ Es intelectual.
☐ Es serio.

☐ Es **perezoso.**
☐ Es generoso.
☐ Es independiente.
☐ Es discreto.
☐ Es triste.
☐ Es **casado.**

Aquí está mi amiga Cecilia. Ella **da una vuelta** con su perro.

☐ Es optimista.
☐ Es valiente.
☐ Es realista.
☐ No es deshonesta.
☐ Es impaciente.
☐ Es atlética.
☐ Es simpática.

☐ Es **cómica.**
☐ Es activa y enérgica.
☐ Es generosa también.
☐ Es independiente también.
☐ Es indiscreta a veces.
☐ Es alegre.
☐ Es **soltera,** pero tiene **novio.**

perezoso: lazy / *casado:* married / *da una vuelta:* takes a walk / *cómica:* funny / *soltera:* single / *novio:* boyfriend

¡Aquí te toca a ti!

A. *José y la Sra. Velázquez: retratos psicológicos*

Contesta las preguntas sobre la personalidad de José y de la Sra. Velázquez.

1. A José le gustan mucho los coches rápidos y las actividades peligrosas *(dangerous)*. ¿Es valiente o tímido?
2. La Sra. Velázquez da dinero a los amigos que no son ricos. ¿Es generosa o tacaña *(stingy)*?
3. A José no le gusta trabajar. Prefiere mirar la televisión. ¿Es trabajador o perezoso?
4. La Sra. Velázquez encontró 25.000 pesos. Llamó por teléfono a la policía. ¿Es honesta o deshonesta?
5. A José no le gustan los libros, pero le encanta el fútbol y le gusta esquiar. ¿Es atlético o intelectual?
6. La Sra. Velázquez siempre escucha la radio. Le gustan la música clásica y las discusiones políticas. ¿Es seria o cómica?
7. A José le gusta la vida y tiene muchos amigos. ¿Es triste o alegre?
8. La Sra. Velázquez trabaja mucho. Va al teatro, al museo y al cine. ¿Es activa o perezosa?

B. *Mi mejor amigo(a)*

Tell one of your classmates about your best friend. Give a physical description first. Then describe his or her personality traits. Your classmate will respond by asking you two or more questions about your best friend.

Pronunciación: The vowel combination ua

The combination **ua** in Spanish is pronounced in one single syllable, similar to the *wa* in the English word *water*.

Práctica

C. Lee cada palabra en voz alta, pronunciando con cuidado la combinación *ua*.

1. agua
2. cuadro
3. cuanto
4. suave
5. cuatro
6. guante
7. cuaderno
8. cuarenta

Repaso

D. **Yo soy...**   If you had to meet someone at the airport who had never seen you before, how would you describe yourself over the telephone so that the other person would be sure to recognize you? Give as many details as possible.

ESTRUCTURA

Ser para + pronouns

Esta carta **es para ella.**
Este dinero **es para ustedes.**

Estos cuadros **son para mí.**
Estas camisas **son para ti.**

Pronouns used as objects of prepositions, following such phrases as **ser para**, have the same forms as subject pronouns, except for **mí** and **ti.**

The following object pronouns are used after a preposition such as **para.**

mí	*me, myself*	**nosotros(as)**	*us, ourselves*
ti	*you (fam.), yourself*	**vosotros(as)**	*you (fam.), yourselves*
usted	*you, yourself*	**ustedes**	*you, yourselves*
él	*him*	**ellos**	*them (masc.)*
ella	*her*	**ellas**	*them (fem.)*

Aquí practicamos

E. **¿Para quién es?**   A classmate will ask you if an object on the list on page 123 is for somebody. Answer by saying that it is not for the person in question but for somebody else. Follow the model.

Modelo: la cámara
—*¿La cámara es para ella?*
—*¡Claro que no! Es para él.*

1. el disco compacto
2. la raqueta
3. las fotografías
4. el coche

5. el dinero
6. las cartas
7. la comida
8. el refresco

9. los esquíes
10. la tarjeta
11. la computadora
12. la fiesta

F. *¡Qué generoso(a) eres!* As you point to people in the room, tell each person that you have something for him or her. Think of an object and indicate who it is for. Follow the model.

 Modelo: *Tengo un libro para ti.*
Tengo unas cintas para Uds.

Nota gramatical

Shortened adjectives: *buen, mal, gran*

Ramón es un **buen** muchacho.	Ramón is a good boy. (no emphasis on how good)
Ramón es un muchacho **bueno.**	Ramón is a *good* boy. (emphasis on how good)
Éste es un **mal** día para esquiar.	This is a bad day for skiing. (no emphasis on how bad)
Éste es un día **malo** para esquiar.	This is a *bad* day for skiing. (emphasis on how bad)
Plácido Domingo es un **gran** hombre.	Plácido Domingo is a *great* man.
Plácido Domingo es un hombre **grande.**	Plácido Domingo is a *big* man.

When the adjectives **bueno, malo,** and **grande** are used before a masculine singular noun, they are shortened to **buen, mal,** and **gran.** The meaning of **grande** is radically different when it precedes the noun, for then it means *great* instead of *large.*

Aquí practicamos

G. Usa los adjetivos sugeridos para modificar los sustantivos de la página 124 en dos maneras, cambiando las formas cuando es necesario.

 Modelo: Es un museo. (grande)
Es un gran museo.
Es un museo grande.

1. Es un libro. (bueno)
2. Son unos niños. (malo)
3. Es un hombre. (grande)
4. Son unos amigos. (bueno)
5. Son unas ideas. (bueno)

6. Es una situación. (malo)
7. Es un perro. (grande)
8. Son unos libros. (grande)
9. Es una característica. (bueno)
10. Son unos futbolistas. (malo)

H. *Descripciones* Escoge al menos cinco adjetivos de la lista para primero describirte a ti mismo(a) y después a las personas indicadas. Usa una gran variedad de adjetivos.

1. tú
2. tu amigo(a)
3. tu hermano(a)

4. tu madre o tu padre
5. tu profesor(a)

activo / alegre / antipático / bonito / bueno / cómico / cruel / delgado / discreto / dinámico / egoísta / enérgico / frívolo / fuerte / guapo / generoso / grande / honesto / idealista / imaginativo / impaciente / independiente / indiscreto / ingenuo / inteligente / joven / malo / optimista / paciente / pequeño / perezoso / pesimista / realista / serio / simpático / sincero / tímido / trabajador / triste / valiente / viejo

Aquí escuchamos:
"¡Mi hermana es independiente!"

Antes de escuchar

Roberto is going to visit his sister Silvia next weekend. He describes what his sister is like to his friend Raúl. Look at the questions to get an idea of what Roberto will tell him.

Después de escuchar

1. ¿Cuál es la profesión de la hermana de Roberto?
2. ¿Dónde vive ella?
3. ¿Cuántos años tiene la mujer?
4. ¿Le gustan los deportes?

5. ¿Cómo la describe su hermano?
6. ¿Qué quiere Raúl cuando oye cómo es la hermana de su amigo?

¡Aquí te toca a ti!

I. *Mi pariente* (relative) *preferido(a)*   Describe your favorite family member to one of your classmates. Discuss both physical appearance and personality. Your classmate will ask you follow-up questions. Use **Aquí escuchamos** as a model.

Learning Strategies:

Listing, organizing information

EJERCICIO ORAL

J. *Mi retrato*   You want your friend to tell his or her cousin about you as a possible date. Use at least five of the adjectives listed in Activity H to describe yourself as you want your friend to tell his or her cousin. Give at least one example to explain or support your choice of each characteristic. For example, if you are **atlético(a),** tell what sports you participate in.

Learning Strategies:

Listing, elaborating, supporting an opinion

EJERCICIO ESCRITO

K. *Una descripción*   Write a brief description of a famous person who is visiting in your town or city. Describe the person's physical characteristics and personality, as well as what he or she does.

Learning Strategies:

Describing, organizing ideas in a paragraph

Jon Secada

Vocabulario

Para charlar

Para dar una descripción física de una persona

Tiene...

      los ojos azules / verdes / castaños / negros.
      el pelo corto / largo.
      la nariz grande / pequeña.
      bigote / barba.

Es...

      débil / fuerte.

Para describir la personalidad

Él (Ella) es...

activo(a) / perezoso(a).	idealista / realista.
ambicioso(a).	impaciente / paciente.
atlético(a).	independiente.
cómico(a).	intelectual.
deshonesto(a) / honesto(a).	perfecto(a).
discreto(a) / indiscreto(a).	tímido(a) / valiente.
generoso(a).	

Vocabulario general

Sustantivos

un(a) nieto(a)
un(a) vecino(a)

Verbos

conocer

Adjetivos

casado(a)
soltero(a)

Otras palabras y expresiones

dar una vuelta

Lectura
CULTURAL

DIME QUÉ REGALO QUIERES Y TE DIGO QUIÉN ERES

Antes de leer

1. Look at the pictures on page 128 and the title and think about what this reading is going to be about. What do you think the word **regalo** means?
2. Look the passage over quickly. How is it organized?
3. What do you think the following words from the headings mean? Look at the picture that goes with each section to determine the meaning of the words that you may not know.

| ajedrez | ropa | colección de |
| chandal | bicicleta | discos compactos |

Guía para la lectura

A. Read the introduction. What do you think **prueba de personalidad** means? What do you think this phrase has to do with the rest of the reading?

B. On a separate piece of paper copy the headings. Read the passage, looking for descriptive words and phrases. Next to each heading make a list of the adjectives associated with the kind of person who wants each gift.

C. Work with a partner and decide which description best fits your personalities.

Learning Strategies:

Previewing, scanning for cognates, listing

Cooperative Learning

Learning Strategy:

Supporting an opinion

Critical Thinking Strategy:

Comparing and contrasting

Dime qué regalo quieres y te digo quién eres

No importa a quién vas a pedir los siguientes regalos, a los Reyes Magos, a San Nicolás, a tus padres o a tus abuelos. Lo importante es que tienes que decidir qué quieres. Aquí te presentamos una prueba de personalidad para decirte cómo eres según tu selección. Pero ya sabes que solamente es un juego. ¡No te lo tomes muy en serio!

Un perro

Eres una persona cariñosa y responsable. Te gusta ayudar a otras personas pero a veces exiges mucho de tus amigos o familiares. Tienes que ser menos posesivo(a).

Una colección de discos compactos de tu cantante favorito(a)

Eres extrovertido(a) y dinámico(a). Te gusta divertirte y el futuro no te interesa demasiado. Debes pensar más en tus estudios.

Una colección de libros de historia

Eres una persona original. Piensas mucho en el pasado y no das tu opinión fácilmente. Tienes que tener más confianza en ti mismo(a).

Una cámara fotográfica

Eres introvertido(a) y creativo(a). También tienes mucha imaginación, pero tienes que ser un poco más realista.

Ropa

Te gusta ser el centro de atención. Generalmente tienes muy buen humor y te gusta estar con mucha gente. Eres muy popular, pero también un poquito frívolo(a). Debes pensar un poco más en las otras personas.

Un juego de ajedrez

Eres una persona muy lógica. Piensas mucho antes de y eso te quita naturalidad. Debes ser un poco menos rígido(a). Disfrutarás más de la vida.

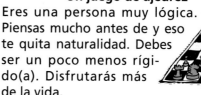

Una bicicleta

Te gusta la naturaleza. Eres romántico(a) y apasionado(a). Tienes que ser menos impulsivo(a) y pensar antes de actuar; así vas a tener más amigos(as).

Un chandal

Eres independiente. Te gusta la aventura y todo lo nuevo. El riesgo es tu elemento. Siempre estás buscando nuevas metas. Un poco de calma en tu vida te va a hacer bien.

Aqui leemos

Estrategia para la lectura

Some kinds of writing are intended to create a particular mood in the reader. Writers use adjectives and other descriptive words to produce moods. (You can use adjective endings to help keep track of the nouns being referred to in such writing.) Some writing, such as poetry, is best read aloud because the author chooses particular words for their sounds and puts them together in ways that emphasize their rhythms. Reading aloud is a good technique to practice because it helps you improve pronunciation while learning how to be more expressive in Spanish.

Reading Strategies:

Use adjective endings to help you interpret meanings.
Pay attention to the mood of the reading.
Read aloud for pleasure and practice.

Antes de leer

This reading is a poem by a well-known Mexican poet, Amado Nervo (1870–1919). His work has two important themes: love and religion. Both are reflected in this poem in which the reader is invited to think about what a divine being might be like. Before reading the poem carefully, look at it to see how it is organized. Then answer these questions before going on to the **Actividades.**

>> **W**hat are some adjectives you might use to describe your idea of a supreme being?

>> **Y**ou can see that the poem is organized as a series of questions about the nature of God. What questions can you ask that might be answered by the adjectives you have thought of?

Read the poem through once to get the general idea and mood. Don't worry about every word. Notice especially how the organization of the poem changes from questions to statements in the last three lines. Then read the poem again, more carefully, making sure the meanings you guess fit the mood and content. Pay attention to the relationship between the title and the rest of the poem, and to the last three lines.

Voluntad: Will

ley: law

fuera: beyond

Tiempo ha que: For a while
  now / *ya no:* no longer

> ### ¿Cómo es?
>
> ¿Es Dios personal?
> ¿Es impersonal?
> ¿Tiene forma?
> ¿No tiene forma?
> ¿Es esencia?
> ¿Es sustancia?
> ¿Es uno?
> ¿Es múltiple?
> ¿Es la conciencia del Universo?
> ¿Es Voluntad sin conciencia y sin fin?
> ¿Es todo lo que existe?
> ¿Es distinto de todo lo que existe?
> ¿Es como el alma de la naturaleza?
> ¿Es una ley?
> ¿Es simplemente la armonía de las fuerzas?
> ¿Está en nosotros mismos?
> ¿Es nosotros mismos?
> ¿Está fuera de nosotros?
> Alma mía, hace tiempo que tú ya no te preguntas estas cosas.
> Tiempo ha que estas cosas ya no te interesan.
> Lo único que tú sabes es que Lo amas…

Actividades

A. Answer these questions by reflecting on the poem. Refer to it whenever you need to.

1. Which of the following statements is the best explanation of the relationship between the question section and the last three lines?
   a. The last three lines are the answers to the questions.
   b. The last three lines suggest that, in spite of all the questions, one thing is known with certainty.
   c. The last three lines are not related to the questions at all.
2. Which statement best describes the relationship between the title and the poem?
   a. The poem gives the answer to the title question.
   b. The last three lines give the answer to the title question.
   c. The title is a general question and the questions in the poem are specific ones included in it.

B. Read the poem again carefully. Next read it aloud, listening to how the words and lines go together. Then answer these questions about how Nervo uses words to create the mood and message of the poem.

1. Quickly list all the adjectives you find in the poem. What do they describe?
2. What rhyming words does the poet use?
3. Nervo uses many pairs of words with opposite meanings. An example is **personal** and **impersonal**. What other pairs like this do you see? What do you think the poet accomplishes with this technique?

C. Read the poem out loud, concentrating on the meaning. Then answer these questions about what the poem means.

1. What is the main question being asked in the poem?
2. What are some specific characteristics of a supreme being that Nervo wonders about? Why do you think Nervo does not actually give any specific answers to his questions?
3. What might be the reason why the poem is divided into so many short lines? Can you relate this pattern of lines to the message of the poem?
4. Who is the speaker in the poem? To whom are the last three lines addressed? What does the poet finally conclude about all his questions?

D. Writing that conveys a mood is intended to get a response from its readers. Read the poem again, thinking about your reaction to its message. The following questions will help you formulate your own response.

1. Do you think many people ask the questions that Nervo has asked? Have you ever wondered about these questions yourself?
2. Do you think there is a more specific answer than the one Nervo gives? Do you agree with his answer?
3. How do you feel when the poet switches from questions to statements? Can you feel the shift from doubt to certainty that he intends you to feel?
4. Do you enjoy the rhythm created by the pairs of oppositions in the questions? What feeling do you get when the pairs are interrupted by the longer statements in the last three lines? Do you think that's what the poet wanted you to feel?
5. Does the poem have more meaning after you work with it for a while? Do you like it better after reading it several times?

Ya llegamos

Actividades orales

A. *Una oportunidad* Imagine that you are a weather forecaster and you have an opportunity to audition for a position on the Spanish-speaking television station in your area. Prepare a weather report for your region, including a mock-up of a weather map to use as a prop and to refer to during your audition.

Announce (1) the weather conditions for yesterday and last night, (2) what the weather is like today, and (3) what you forecast for tonight and tomorrow. Then (4) give your prediction for the upcoming weekend, suggesting appropriate weekend activities according to the weather conditions in your forecast.

B. *Un álbum de la familia* While on a trip you meet two friends and show them pictures of your family.

Materials: Bring photographs of your family members to class. You might include pets and one or two of your best friends. If you are limited in the photographs you have available, you might borrow some, cut them from magazines, or draw them (stick-figure style is OK!), to represent your family and friends.

Scenario: You and two of your traveling companions are talking about people you know—friends and family. Show pictures and tell about the people in your photographs, elaborating on four of them. For the four people that you describe, tell (1) how they are related to you and (2) what they are like (naming at least two of their most outstanding physical traits and two personality traits). Tell also (3) where they live, and (4) two things or activities that they like and/or don't like **[(no) le gusta(n)]**. Finally, (5) mention for each person at least one of their possessions that is of interest to you (giving a description of that possession that includes at least two features).

Remember to speak conversationally, picking up the threads of discourse from each other, for example, "Oh, your grandfather likes fast cars? My Uncle Jim loves fast boats and waterskiing."

Actividades escritas

C. *El aviso meteorológico*   Write a brief weather report for your region. Indicate the weather and temperatures for today, tonight, and tomorrow.

D. *Una entrevista*   Pretend that you work on your school newspaper and that you're writing up an interview with a rock star who is performing in your town. Choose a rock star and imagine his or her answers to your questions about his or her personality, pastimes, favorite music and books, what sports he or she plays or watches, where he or she prefers to live, etc. Then write your article for the paper in interview format.

Learning Strategies:

Describing, organizing information, using appropriate journalistic style

Critical Thinking Strategy:

Making associations

Conexión

La letra y la personalidad

>> Do you think that your handwriting reflects your personality? If so, how?

> Does your teacher's handwriting reflect his or her personality? If so, how?

AL EMPEZAR

The way we do things often says something about who we are. Graphologists make a study of our handwriting, claiming that the way we write tells something about our personalities.

ACTIVIDAD A

Listed below are adjectives used in the following reading. Working with a partner, select adjectives from the list which most closely describe your personality. Now select adjectives which most closely describe your partner's personality. Write the adjectives you choose in your notebook. How are you and your partner alike? How do you differ? Follow the model.

Modelo: *Soy independiente. Mi compañero(a) es sociable.*

extrovertido	introvertido	perfeccionista	motivado
amigable	**suspicaz**	económico	extrovertido
sociable	independiente	organizado	entusiasta
compasivo	meticuloso	agresivo	optimista
cauteloso	modesto	confidente	

suspicious (of others) — suspicaz
compassionate — compasivo
cautious — cauteloso

LA LETRA Y LA PERSONALIDAD

Cada persona tiene su **letra** particular. Por eso es fácil reconocer la letra de un buen amigo o un **pariente.** Pero hay gente que dice que la letra de una persona también expresa su identidad. Los grafólogos estudian los **rasgos** distintivos de la letra, incluyendo el **tamaño** de las letras individuales, y el grado y uniformidad de inclinación, ornamentación y curvatura. La grafología se basa en la teoría de que nuestra forma de escribir refleja las características elementales que forman la personalidad. Se mantiene, por ejemplo, que la persona que hace la letra grande tiene ambiciones. El siguiente esquema nos resume otras afirmaciones comunes de la grafología.

handwriting — letra
relative — pariente

characteristics — rasgos
size — tamaño

Estilo de letra	Características asociadas
Inclinación hacia la derecha	extrovertido, amigable, sociable, compasivo
Inclinación hacia la izquierda	cauteloso, introvertido, suspicaz, independiente
Letra pequeña	meticuloso, modesto, perfeccionista, organizado
Letra grande	agresivo, extrovertido, entusiasta, optimista

ACTIVIDAD B

Based on the information provided in the reading, make suggestions about the people who provided a handwriting sample below. Follow the model.

Modelo: *Damián Flores es muy extrovertido porque su letra es muy grande y está inclinada hacia la derecha.*

María Cubas   Mark T. Smith   Pedro Escobar

Javier Pinares   Damián Flores   Susana del Mar

ACTIVIDAD C

Paso 1: Find your name as you have written it on an old quiz or homework assignment. Answer the following questions.

1. ¿Es grande o pequeña tu letra?
2. ¿Está inclinada hacia la derecha o hacia la izquierda?
3. Según los grafólogos, ¿cuáles son los adjetivos que mejor describen tu personalidad?

Paso 2: Find the lists of adjectives that you and your partner chose to describe your personality before reading the passage. Do they match the ones predicted by the analysis of your handwriting in the previous **paso**?

Modelo: *Sí. Soy _____. Pero no soy _____.*

¿Qué ves?

>> ¿Qué son estos edificios?

>> ¿Cómo se llama el hotel?

>> ¿Cuál es el edificio más elegante?

>> ¿Cuál es el edificio más moderno?

OBJECTIVES

IN THIS UNIT YOU WILL LEARN:

■ **T**o rent and pay for a hotel room;

■ **T**o understand classified ads and brochures for lodging;

■ **T**o describe a house or apartment;

■ **T**o tell time using the 24-hour clock.

Vamos a instalarnos

UNIDAD dos

4

BUSCAMOS UN HOTEL

—¿Qué te parece este hotel?
—Me parece muy típico. Me gusta mucho.

Objectives:

》》 **R**enting and paying for a hotel room

》》 **U**nderstanding classified ads and lodging brochures

Strategies:

》》 **R**eading for details

》》 **F**inding averages

》》 **C**ategorizing

PRIMERA ETAPA

Preparación

>> **D**o you like to travel?

>> **W**hen you travel, where do you stay?

>> **W**hen you plan a trip like a summer vacation, what types of information will you need to organize your trip?

>> **W**here will you get information on hotels?

>> **I**s there some publication that would have that kind of information?

>> **I**f you travel through Spain, the *Guía Michelín* might come in handy.

/./././././././././././

Learning Strategy:

Previewing

La Guía Michelín

La Guía Michelín: The Michelin Guide

La instalación

Las habitaciones de los hoteles que recomendamos poseen, en general, cuarto de baño completo. No obstante puede suceder que en las categorías 🏨, 🏠 y 🏡 algunas habitaciones carezcan de él.

30 hab **30 qto**	Número de habitaciones
🛗	Ascensor
	Aire acondicionado
📺	Televisión en la habitación
☎	Teléfono en la habitación directo con el exterior
♿	Habitaciones de fácil acceso para minusválidos
	Comidas servidas en el jardín o en la terraza
	Fitness club (gimnasio, sauna...)
	Piscina : al aire libre – cubierta
	Playa equipada – Jardín
🎾	Tenis – Golf y número de hoyos
25/150	Salas de conferencias : capacidad de las salas
🚗	Garaje en el hotel (generalmente de pago)
Ⓟ	Aparcamiento reservado a la clientela
🐕	Prohibidos los perros (en todo o en parte del establecimiento)
Fax	Transmisión de documentos por telefax
mayo-octubre	Período de apertura comunicado por el hotelero
temp.	Apertura probable en temporada sin precisar fechas. Sin mención, el establecimiento está abierto todo el año
✉ 28 012 ✉ 1 200	Código postal

139

classifies	El gobierno español **clasifica** los hoteles en cinco categorías:
luxury / bathrooms / (bed)rooms	Hoteles de gran **lujo** —con **salas de baño** en todas las **habitaciones**
	Hoteles **** (cuatro estrellas) —hoteles de primera clase; la mayoría de las habitaciones con sala de baño
comfort elevator	Hoteles *** (tres estrellas) —gran **confort;** muchas habitaciones con sala de baño; **ascensor,** teléfono
	Hoteles ** (dos estrellas) —buena calidad, muy confortables; 30 por ciento de las habitaciones con sala de baño
at least sink / booth	Hoteles * (una estrella) —buena calidad, bastante confortables; **al menos** diez habitaciones con **lavabo; cabina** de teléfono
The following / what the *Michelin Guide* says	Si Ud. viaja a España, es muy útil usar la *Guía Michelín* roja (guía de hoteles y restaurantes). Esta guía usa un sistema un poco diferente de la clasificación oficial española. **Lo siguiente** es **lo que dice la *Guía Michelín*** del Hotel Inglaterra en Sevilla.

They do not permit You don't have to go through the reception desk. credit cards	El Hotel Inglaterra es un hotel de gran confort. Tiene restaurante y está en la Plaza Nueva. El número de teléfono es 422 49 70. Tiene ascensor y hay un televisor en cada habitación. **No permiten** perros en el restaurante. Hay un teléfono en cada habitación con línea directa al exterior. **No hay que pasar por la recepción.** En este hotel hay 109 habitaciones. Una habitación cuesta entre 15.600 y 19.500 pesetas. El desayuno cuesta 1.000 pesetas y no está incluido en el precio de la habitación. Aceptan cinco **tarjetas de crédito:** American Express, Diners Club, Eurocard, Visa y Japan Card Bank.

¡Aquí te toca a ti!

A. *¿Qué significan los símbolos?*   In order to familiarize yourself with the symbols that the ***Guía Michelín*** uses to describe hotels, tell what each symbol on page 141 means. Then find an example of the symbol used in the ***Guía Michelín*** on pages 139 and 140. Follow the model.

Modelo:

Es un hotel con salas de conferencias.

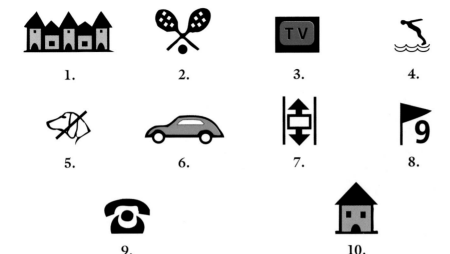

1. 2. 3. 4.

5. 6. 7. 8.

9. 10.

COMENTARIOS CULTURALES

Los hostales

A convenient and economical place for students to stay when traveling in Spain is a youth hostel (**hostal**). **Hostales** are designed to accommodate young people up to the age of 26, primarily students. They offer modest rooms at unbeatable prices, and meals are often served for a nominal fee as well. There are both advantages and disadvantages to staying in **hostales**—there is usually an early curfew after which the doors are locked, and shared rooms are common practice. However, in addition to the economic advantages, you have the opportunity to meet young travelers from all over the world. The chance to make new friends and experience adventures you'll remember for a lifetime are the greatest advantages of the **hostal**.

B. *Los hoteles de Sevilla* Some friends of your parents are planning to visit Sevilla, a city in southern Spain. Because they don't speak Spanish, they ask your help in finding a hotel. Read the excerpt on page 142 from the *Guía Michelín*. Then answer their questions.

/I-/I-/I-/I-/I-/I-/I-/I-/I//

Learning Strategy:

Reading for details

▲▲▲▲ **Alfonso XIII**, San Fernando 2, ✉ 41004, ✆ 422 28 50, Telex 72725, Fax 421 60 33,
« Majestuoso edificio de estilo andaluz » – ... – ▮ 🖭 ☎ 🚗 Ⓟ ⚠ 25/500. AE
Ⓓ Ɛ VISA JCB ℁ rest
Comida 4700 – ☕ 2300 - **129 hab** 29000/39000, 19 suites.   c

▲▲▲▲ **Príncipe de Asturias Radisson H. Sevilla** ⚓, Isla de La Cartuja, ✉ 41092, ✆ 446 22 22,
Fax 446 04 28, ... – ▮ 🖭 ☎ 🚗 – ▲ 25/900. AE Ⓓ Ɛ VISA ℁
Comida 3500 - **288 hab** ☕ 16800/21000, 7 suites.   n

▲▲▲▲ **Tryp Colón**, Canalejas 1, ✉ 41001, ✆ 422 29 00, Telex 72726, Fax 422 09 38, ℔ – ▮ 🖭
🖭 ☎ 🚗 – ▲ 25/240. AE Ⓓ Ɛ VISA JCB ℁
Comida (ver rest. *El Burladero*) 4100 – ☕ 1500 - **211 hab** 15500/19400, 7 suites – PA 7760. s

▲▲▲▲ **Occidental Porta Coeli**, av. Eduardo Dato 49, ✉ 41018, ✆ 453 35 00, Telex 72913,
Fax 453 23 42, ▣ – ▮ 🖭 ☎ 🚗 – ▲ 25/600. AE Ⓓ Ɛ VISA ℁
Comida (ver rest. *Florencia*) – ☕ 1200 - **241 hab** 9500/16000, 3 suites.   a

▲▲▲▲ **Meliá Lebreros**, Luis Morales 2, ✉ 41005, ✆ 457 94 00, Telex 72772, Fax 458 27 26, ...
℔, ... – ▮ 🖭 🖭 ☎ 🚗 – ▲ 25/500. AE Ⓓ Ɛ VISA ℁
Comida (ver rest. *La Dehesa*) – ☕ 1500 - **431 hab** 12250/16575, 6 suites.   v

▲▲▲▲ **Meliá Sevilla**, Doctor Pedro de Castro 1, ✉ 41004, ✆ 442 15 11, Telex 73094,
Fax 442 16 08, ... – ▮ 🖭 🖭 ☎ 🚗 – ▲ 25/1000. AE Ⓓ Ɛ VISA ℁
cerrado julio y agosto – **Comida** 3500 – ▲ 1500 - **361 hab** 14500/18100, 5 suites –
PA 7225.   n

...la Borbolla
... 25. AE Ⓓ Ɛ VISA ...
☕ 1000 – 🖭 **77 hab** 10500/16000, 5 suites.   f

▲▲ **G. H. Lar**, pl. Carmen Benítez 3, ✉ 41003, ✆ 441 03 61, Telex 72816, Fax 441 04 ...
... – ▲ 25/300. AE Ɛ VISA – ▮ 🖭 🖭
Comida 2600 – ☕ 1000 - **129 hab** 12500/18000, 8 suites – PA 4900.   a

▲▲ **Husa Sevilla** ⚓, Pagés del Corro 90, ✉ 41010, ✆ 434 24 12, Fax 434 27 07 – ▮ 🖭 🖭
☎ 🚗 – ▲ 25/220. AE Ɛ VISA JCB ℁
Comida 3250 – ☕ 1100 - **114 hab** 15500/21000, 14 suites – PA 6400.   c

▲▲ **NH Plaza de Armas**, av. Marqués de Paradas, ✉ 41001, ✆ 490 19 92, Fax 490 12 32, ...
– ▮ 🖭 🖭 ☎ 🚗 – ▲ 25/250. AE Ⓓ Ɛ VISA ℁
Comida 2200 – ☕ 1200 - **260 hab** 11200/14000, 2 suites.   a

▲▲ **Sevilla Congresos**, av. Montes Sierra, ✉ 41020, ✆ 425 90 00, Telex 73224, Fax 425 95 00,
– ▮ 🖭 🖭 ☎ 🚗 Ⓟ – ▲ 25/270. AE Ⓓ Ɛ VISA ℁ rest
Comida 2750 – ☕ 1600 - **202 hab** 10500/15000, 16 suites – PA 5680.   a

▲▲ **Emperador Trajano**, José Laguillo 8, ✉ 41003, ✆ 441 11 11, Fax 453 57 02 – ▮ 🖭
☎ 🚗 – ▲ 25/150. AE Ⓓ Ɛ VISA JCB ℁
Comida 2000 – ☕ 1000 - **77 hab** 13640.   Instalado parcialmente   u

▲▲ **San Gil** sin rest, Parras 28, ✉ 41002, ✆ 490 68 11, Fax 490 69 39,
en un edificio típico sevillano de principios de siglo, patio ajardinado – ... 🖭 ☎ AE
Ⓓ Ɛ VISA JCB ℁
☕ 800 - **4 hab** 11200/12800, 5 suites, 30 apartamentos.   c

▲▲ **Álvarez Quintero** sin rest, con cafetería, Álvarez Quintero 9, ✉ 41004, ✆ 422 12 98,
Fax 456 41 41 – ▮ 🖭 🖭 ☎ 🚗 – AE Ⓓ Ɛ VISA ℁
☕ 700 - **40 hab** 9500/13000.   v

▲▲ **Bécquer** sin rest, con cafetería, Reyes Católicos 4, ✉ 41001, ✆ 422 89 00, Telex 72884,
Fax 421 44 00 – ▮ 🖭 🖭 ☎ 🚗 – ▲ 25/45. AE Ⓓ Ɛ VISA ℁
☕ 800 - **120 hab** 10000/15000.   e

▲▲ **Giralda**, Sierra Nevada 3, ✉ 41003, ✆ 441 66 61, Telex 72417, Fax 441 93 52 – ▮ 🖭
🖭 ☎ – ▲ 25/250. AE Ⓓ Ɛ VISA JCB 12650
Comida 2000 – ☕ 950 - **98 hab** 12650.   r

▲▲ **Derby** sin rest, pl. del Duque 13, ✉ 41002, ✆ 456 10 88, Telex 72709, Fax 421 33 91 – ▮
🖭 ☎ AE Ɛ VISA ℁
☕ 550 - **75 hab** 7000/9500.

1. Which is the largest hotel in Sevilla?
2. Which is the most expensive? What justifies the high prices?
3. Which hotels have swimming pools?
4. Which hotels don't have restaurants?
5. Which hotel is the least expensive?
6. Which hotels have meeting rooms?
7. How much does breakfast cost at the Hotel Giralda?
8. How many suites does the Alfonso XIII have?
9. Which hotels allow dogs?
10. Where will it be cheapest to eat breakfast?

ESTRUCTURA

Ordinal numbers

el primero, la primera	**el quinto, la quinta**	**el noveno, la novena**
el segundo, la segunda	**el sexto, la sexta**	**el décimo, la décima**
el tercero, la tercera	**el séptimo, la séptima**	
el cuarto, la cuarta	**el octavo, la octava**	

Ordinal numbers (such as *first, second, third*) are used to order and to rank items in a series. Notice the following special cases:

1. For *the first* use **el primero** or **la primera,** and for *the last* use **la última** or **el último.**
2. Note that ordinal numbers agree in gender with and precede the nouns they modify.
3. The shortened forms **primer** and **tercer** are used before masculine singular nouns: **el primer estudiante, el tercer piso.**
4. Beyond **décimo,** cardinal numbers are generally used. They follow the noun: **el siglo veinte, la Calle Setenta y Ocho.**
5. For dates, Spanish uses the ordinal numbers only for the first day of the month: **el primero de mayo, el primero de junio,** but **el dos de marzo, el tres de abril,** etc.
6. The abbreviated forms of the ordinal numbers are formed as follows:

primero	**1º**	primera	**1ª**	primer	**1er**
segundo	**2º**	segunda	**2ª**		
tercero	**3º**	tercera	**3ª**	tercer	**3er**
cuarto	**4º**	cuarta	**4ª**		
quinto	**5º**	quinta	**5ª**		
etc.					

Aquí practicamos

C. Lee los siguientes en voz alta *(out loud)*.

1. el 1º de abril
2. el 4º libro
3. la 1ª vez
4. la 3ª estudiante
5. el 8º lugar
6. el 1er lugar
7. el 2º año
8. la 5ª avenida
9. el 7º día
10. la 2ª clase
11. la 9ª semana
12. el 3er año

D. Contesta las siguientes preguntas.

1. ¿Cuál es el primer mes del año? ¿el tercer mes del año? ¿el octavo? ¿el último?

2. ¿Cuál es el primer día de la semana en el calendario hispano? ¿el cuarto? ¿el último?

3. ¿A qué hora es tu primera clase? ¿tu segunda clase? ¿tu tercera clase? ¿tu última clase?

Aquí escuchamos:
"¿Tiene Ud. una reservación?"

Antes de escuchar

Linda and her friend Kelly are traveling through Spain on their own and have been using the *Guía Michelín* to organize their trip. They arrive at a hotel in Sevilla and go directly to the registration desk. Look at the following questions and identify a few things you expect to hear during their exchange at the hotel desk. What questions would you ask a clerk when checking into a hotel?

Después de escuchar

1. **¿Tenían Linda y Kelly una habitación reservada?**
2. **¿Para cuántas personas?**
3. **¿Cuánto costó la habitación?**
4. **¿Tiene baño la habitación?**
5. **¿El precio incluye el desayuno?**

¡Aquí te toca a ti!

E. *¿Quisiera Ud. una habitación?*   Use the information given below and on page 145 to tell the desk clerk what kind of a room you want. Follow the model.

Modelo: dos personas / 5.500–7.000 pesetas (5.700 pesetas / sin baño)
—*Buenos días, señor. ¿Tiene Ud. una habitación para dos personas, entre 5.500 y 7.000 pesetas?*
—*Sí, tengo una habitación sin baño por 5.700 pesetas.*
—*Está bien.*   o:
—*Nosotros quisiéramos una habitación con baño.*

1. dos personas / 7.000–7.500 pesetas (7.300 / sin baño)

2. tres personas / 9.000–9.500 pesetas (9.400 / con baño)
3. una persona / 4.500–5.000 pesetas (4.900 / con baño)
4. una persona / 4.200–5.500 pesetas (4.250 / sin baño)

EJERCICIO ORAL

F. Sí, yo tengo una reservación. You arrive at a hotel where you have made a reservation. Go to the front desk and talk to the employee (played by your partner). **Estudiante A** begins.

Estudiante A	Estudiante B
1. Greet the employee.	1. Greet the hotel guest.
2. Find out whether the hotel has a room for two people.	2. Find out whether the guest prefers a room with or without a private bath.
3. Say that you prefer a private bathroom and find out how much such a room costs.	3. Tell how much a room costs with bath (5,000 pesetas) and without bath (4,740 pesetas).
4. Ask whether breakfast is included.	4. Say that breakfast costs an additional 300 pesetas.
5. Thank the employee for the information. Tell which room you want and whether you want breakfast. **(Prefiero...)**	5. Give the guest the room key and welcome him or her to the hotel. **(Muy bien. Bienvenido al Hotel...)**

EJERCICIO ESCRITO

G. El Hotel Montecarlo Imagine that you are Linda or Kelly (**Aquí escuchamos**). Write a postcard to a friend describing the hotel where you're staying. Comment on (1) the location of the hotel, (2) how the hotel is classified by the **Guía Michelín,** (3) how many rooms the hotel has, (4) what floor your room is on, (5) one of the amenities in your room (such as television or telephone), and (6) how many days you are going to stay at the hotel. (7) Remember to date and sign your postcard.

145

SEGUNDA ETAPA

Preparación

As you begin this **etapa,** review the symbols used by the *Guía Michelín* on pages 139–140 for the various features of a hotel.

>> **W**hat information would you expect to see included in a hotel brochure?

>> **W**hich features do hotels usually highlight to attract customers?

>> **W**hat are some of the features you might expect to find in a highly rated hotel?

/-/-/-/-/-/-/-/-/-/-/-/-/-//

Learning Strategy:

Previewing

En una habitación

Hotel INGLES, situado en el corazón de Madrid, tan próximo a su tradición e historia monumental, como a sus núcleos comerciales y de diversión. En la capital de España, en el lugar preciso, siempre vecino a los puntos de interés.

Equipado con 58 habitaciones (Suites, Dobles, Individuales), disponiendo cada una de ellas de: Baño completo, Calefacción, Teléfono, así como de los servicios particulares del Hotel: Cafetería-Pub, Salón de TV (color), Hilo musical, Caja de Seguridad individual, Parking privado, Gimnasio.

UN PUNTO
IDEAL
EN EL CENTRO
DE LA CIUDAD

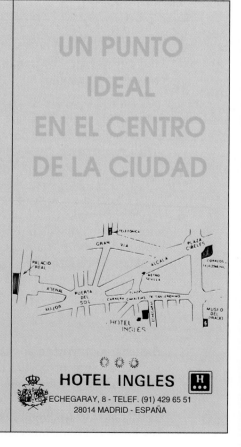

HOTEL INGLES

ECHEGARAY, 8 - TELEF. (91) 429 65 51
28014 MADRID - ESPAÑA

¡Aquí te toca a ti!

A. El gran hotel...
Basándote en el folleto (*brochure*) de la página 146, contesta las siguientes preguntas.

1. In what part of Madrid is the hotel located?
2. Near what tourist sights is the hotel located?
3. How many stars does the hotel have? What does that mean?
4. How many rooms does the hotel have?
5. What amenities does a typical room have?
6. Does each room have a television?

la lámpara

la mesita de noche   el lavabo

el espejo   el bidé

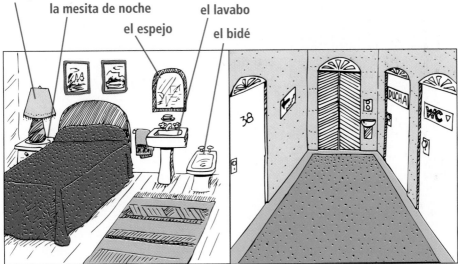

la habitación   el pasillo

B. La habitación del hotel
Basándote en el dibujo de la habitación y el pasillo, contesta las siguientes preguntas. Usa las pistas entre paréntesis cuando aparecen (*when they appear*).

1. ¿Cuántas camas hay en la habitación?
2. ¿Dónde está la mesita de noche? (cerca de)
3. ¿Dónde está el lavabo? (al lado de)
4. ¿Dónde está el bidé? (al lado de)
5. ¿Dónde está el ascensor? (al fondo de)
6. ¿Dónde está el WC? (en frente de)
7. ¿Dónde está la ducha (*shower*)? (al lado de)
8. ¿De qué color es la lámpara?

147

//·/·//·//·/·//·/·//·//·//

COMENTARIOS
CULTURALES

▪ *Los números de los pisos*

In Spanish, the word **piso** is used for floors above the ground level.
The term for *ground floor* is **la planta baja** (literally, the level of
the pavement). This is abbreviated **PB** or sometimes **B** in elevators.
Consequently, each **piso** is numbered one floor lower than its des-
ignation would be in English:

American hotel	**Spanish hotel**
4th floor	3er piso
3rd floor	2° piso
2nd floor	1er piso
1st floor	Planta baja (PB/B)

To indicate that a room is *on* a certain floor, use **en: en el segundo piso.**

Repaso

C. ¿Cuál es el primer hotel de la lista?   You and a friend are
reviewing the list of hotels that follows. He or she asks you about a specific hotel, referring to it by its place on the list using ordinal numbers.
You respond to the question. Follow the model.

Modelo: —*¿Cuál es el primer hotel de la lista?*
—*El primer hotel es el NH Ciudad de Sevilla.*

NH Ciudad de Sevilla, av. Manuel Siurot 25, ✉ 41013, ✆ 423 05 05, Fax 423 85 39, ⌕
– ⬧ ▤ TV ☎ ⚙ 🚗 – ⚎ 25/300. AE ⓓ E VISA ⚓
Comida 3500 – ⚏ 1400 – **90 hab** 25400/31800, 3 suites.
                                                                                           r

Pasarela sin rest, av. de la Borbolla 11, ✉ 41004, ✆ 441 55 11, Telex 72486, Fax 442 07 27,
⬧ ⬧ ▤ TV ☎ ⚎ 25. AE ⓓ E VISA
⚏ 1000 – **77 hab** 10500/16000, 5 suites.
                                                                                           n

G. H. Lar, pl. Carmen Benítez 3, ✉ 41003, ✆ 441 03 61, Telex 72816, Fax 441 04 52 – ⬧
▤ TV ☎ ⚙ 🚗 – ⚎ 25/300. AE ⓓ E VISA
Comida 2600 – ⚏ 1000 – **129 hab** 12500/18000, 8 suites – PA 4900.
                                                                                           f

Husa Sevilla ⚓, Pagés del Corro 90, ✉ 41010, ✆ 434 24 12, Fax 434 27 07 – ⬧ ▤ TV ☎
🚗 – ⚎ 25/220. AE ⓓ E VISA JCB ⚓
Comida 3250 – ⚏ 1100 – **114 hab** 15500/21000, 14 suites – PA 6400.
                                                                                           a

NH Plaza de Armas, av. Marqués de Paradas, ✉ 41001, ✆ 490 19 92, Fax 490 12 32, ⌕
– ⬧ ▤ TV ☎ ⚙ ♿ – ⚎ 25/250. AE ⓓ VISA
Comida 2200 – ⚏ 1200 – **260 hab** 11200/14000, 2 suites.
                                                                                           c

Sevilla Congresos, av. Montes Sierra, ✉ 41020, ✆ 425 90 00, Telex 73224, Fax 425 95 00,
⌕ ⛭, ▥, – ⬧ ⬧ ▤ TV ☎ ♿ 🚗 ℗ – ⚎ 25/270. AE ⓓ E VISA ⚓ rest
Comida 2750 – ⚏ 1600 – **202 hab** 10500/15000.
                                                                                           a

Emperador Trajano, José Laguillo 8, ✉ 41003, ✆ 441 11 11, Fax 453 57 02 – ⬧ ▤ TV
☎ 🚗 ⚎ 25/150. AE ⓓ E VISA JCB
Comida 2000 – ⚏ 1000 – **77 hab** 13640.
                                                                                           a

San Gil sin rest, Parras 28, ✉ 41002, ✆ 490 68 11, Fax 490 69 39,   Instalado parcialmente
en un edificio típico sevillano de principios de siglo, patio ajardinado , ⌕ – ▤ TV ☎ AE
ⓓ E VISA JCB ⚓
⚏ 800 – **4 hab** 11200/12800, 5 suites, 30 apartamentos.
                                                                                           u

Álvarez Quintero sin rest, con cafetería, Álvarez Quintero 9, ✉ 41004, ✆ 422 12 98,
Fax 456 41 41 – ⬧ ▤ TV ☎ ⚙ 🚗 AE ⓓ E VISA ⚓
⚏ 700 – **40 hab** 9500/13000.
                                                                                           c

Bécquer sin rest, con cafetería, Reyes Católicos 4, ✉ 41001, ✆ 422 89 00, Telex 72884,
Fax 421 44 00 – ⬧ ▤ TV ☎ ⚙ 🚗 – ⚎ 25/45. AE ⓓ E VISA ⚓
⚏ 800 – **120 hab** 10000/15000.
                                                                                           v

Giralda, Sierra Nevada 3, ✉ 41003, ✆ 441 66 61, Telex 72417, Fax 441 93 52 – ⬧ ▤ TV
☎ – ⚎ 25/250. AE ⓓ E VISA JCB
Comida 2000 – ⚏ 950 – **98 hab** 12650.
                                                                                           e

Derby sin rest, pl. del Duque 13, ✉ 41002, ✆ 456 10 88, Telex 72709, Fax 421 33 91 – ⬧
▤ TV ☎ AE ⓓ E VISA ⚓
⚏ 550 – **75 hab** 7000/9500.
                                                                                           r

ESTRUCTURA

The preterite of the verb dormir

—¿**Dormiste** mucho anoche?   *Did you sleep* a lot last night?
—Sí, **dormí** ocho horas.   Yes, *I slept* eight hours.

	dormir		
yo	**dormí**	nosotros(as)	**dormimos**
tú	**dormiste**	vosotros(as)	**dormisteis**
él		ellos	
ella	} **durmió**	ellas	} **durmieron**
Ud.		Uds.	

The verb **dormir** in the preterite is irregular only in the third person singular and plural. Notice that in these forms, only the **o** of the stem changes to a **u.**

A common expression with **dormir** is **dormir la siesta** *(to take a nap):*

—¿**Dormiste la siesta** ayer?   *Did you take a nap* yesterday?
—Sí, **dormí una siesta** de dos horas.   Yes, *I took* a two-hour *nap.*

Aquí practicamos

D. ¿Cuántas horas durmieron tus amigos? Di hasta qué
hora durmieron tú y tus amigos el sábado pasado.

A	B	C	D
yo	dormir	hasta las	8:00
tú			8:30
Elena			9:00
nosotros			9:30
?			10:00
			10:30
			11:00
			11:30
			12:00

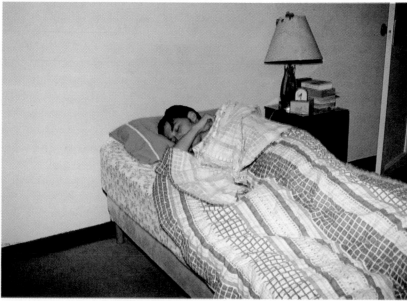

Ayer Eduardo
durmió una siesta
de tres horas.

E. Working in pairs, ask each other the following questions, noting both your answers and those of your partner. Determine which of you generally gets more sleep.

Cooperative Learning

Learning Strategy:

Asking for and giving personal information

Critical Thinking Strategy:

Comparing

1. ¿Hasta qué hora dormiste ayer?
2. ¿Hasta qué hora dormiste el sábado pasado?
3. ¿Dormiste en una cama matrimonial *(double bed)* o en una cama sencilla *(twin bed)*?
4. ¿Cómo dormiste anoche? ¿Bien? ¿Mal?
5. ¿Cuántas horas dormiste anoche?
6. ¿Cuántas horas dormiste el sábado pasado?
7. ¿Dormiste la siesta ayer?
8. ¿Dormiste la siesta el fin de semana pasado?

F. ¿Duermen mucho Uds.? Tú quieres saber más acerca de *(about)* cuántas horas duermen varios compañeros de clase. Hazle una pregunta a un(a) compañero(a) acerca de cuánto duerme él o ella y tres preguntas más sobre otros compañeros de clase.

Learning Strategy:

Asking questions

Modelo: —*¿Cuántas horas duermes en general?*
—*Duermo nueve horas cada noche.*
—*¿Cuántas horas duerme Susana?*
…

Aquí escuchamos:
"¡Es una habitación bonita!"

Antes de escuchar

Linda and her friend Kelly get the key from the hotel clerk and go up to check out their room. Look at the questions below and identify a few things you expect to hear during their conversation in the room.

Learning Strategy:

Previewing

Después de escuchar

1. ¿Qué habitación tienen y dónde está?
2. ¿Dónde está el ascensor?
3. ¿Qué hay en la habitación?
4. ¿Dónde están el baño y la ducha?
5. ¿Qué piden para usar la ducha?

Learning Strategy:

Listening for details

¡Aquí te toca a ti!

G. *Perdón, señor*   Estás en un hotel y necesitas información. Usa las palabras entre paréntesis para hacer preguntas en la recepción. Sigue el modelo.

 the location of the elevator (**dónde está**)
Perdón, señor, ¿dónde está el ascensor?

1. what your room number is (**cuál es**)
2. the location of the toilet (**dónde está**)
3. the location of the shower (**dónde está**)
4. the location of the restaurant (**dónde está**)
5. whether breakfast is included in the price of the room (**está incluido**)
6. if he has the key for the shower (**tiene Ud.**)

EJERCICIO ORAL

H. *En la recepción*   You are at the reception desk of a hotel.

1. Greet the hotel clerk.
2. Say that you would like a room with a bath.
3. The room is for one person for four nights.
4. You would like a room on the fifth floor, if there is an elevator.
5. Find out the price of the room.
6. Ask if breakfast is included.
7. Ask if there is a **metro** station nearby.
8. Thank the hotel clerk.

EJERCICIO ESCRITO

I. *Mi habitación*   Write a postcard to a friend in the U.S. describing your hotel room in Barcelona, Spain. Tell (1) the name of the hotel, (2) what floor your room is on, (3) whether there is an elevator, (4) whether there is a private bathroom, (5) how the room is furnished, (6) whether breakfast is included in the price, (7) whether you like the hotel and the room and why. (8) Remember to date and sign your card.

TERCERA ETAPA

Preparación

>> **W**hat types of information would you expect to find on a bill from a hotel?

>> **B**efore you proceed to **Activity A**, take a look at the bill below.

>> **W**hat information is included?

Learning Strategy:
Previewing

Learning Strategies:
Previewing, reading for details

La cuenta

I.S.S.A.
C. P. A-40000390
C: JUAN BRAVO, 30
Teléfono 43 4011 ...
40001-SEGOVIA

Nº 11583

Habitación n.º **402**

1

Hotel Residencia
Las Sirenas

Sr. D. ...*Miss Janet Dracksdorf*...

Se suplica el pago de la factura a su presentación.
On est prié de payer la facture dès sa présentation - Please pay the weekly bill on presentation

A - SERVICIOS ORDINARIOS   IMP. VDA. DE MAURO LOZANO SEGOVIA

Mes de **Octubre** de 19**96**	Día **23** Pesetas	Día **24** Pesetas	Día — Pesetas	TOTALES Pesetas
Habitación	**3950**			
Total del día, pesetas	**3950**			
Suma anterior		**3950**		
Total serv. ordinarios				

B - OTROS SERVICIOS

Lavado y planche				
Teléfono.	TELEFÓNO.			
Total del día, pesetas				
Total otros servicios				

2490003

TOTAL FACTURA	**3950**
IVA 8%	**231**
Total a abonar por el cliente	**4181**

¡Aquí te toca a ti!

A. La cuenta Answer the questions based on the bill.

1. What is the name of the hotel?
2. In what city is the hotel located?
3. What are the dates of the hotel stay?
4. How many rooms is the bill for?
5. How many nights is the bill for? How much did the room cost per night?

En este hotel, se puede pagar la cuenta con **cheques de viajero** *(traveler's checks)* o **en efectivo** *(cash)*. No aceptan **tarjetas de crédito** *(credit cards)*.

Repaso

B. ¿Cuántas horas dormiste tú? You have heard that high-school students have strange sleeping habits—some sleep a lot and some sleep very little. You want to conduct an informal survey on this. When your teacher gives the signal, circulate around the room and ask how much sleep several of your classmates got on various nights during the past week. Try to find out if there are differences between weekday and weekend nights.

C. En la recepción Go to the hotel desk and ask for a room. The student playing the role of the desk clerk will use the suggested information to answer your questions. Follow the model.

 Modelo: una persona / con / 3.500 pesetas / 350 pesetas / 1er / 19
—*¿Tiene Ud. una habitación para una persona con baño?*
—*Sí, tenemos una habitación por 3.500 pesetas la noche.*
—*¿Está el desayuno incluido en el precio?*
—*No… Tiene que pagar 350 pesetas más.*
—*Bien. Quiero la habitación.*
—*De acuerdo. Está en el primer piso. Es la habitación 19.*

1. dos personas / sin / 3.900 pesetas / 250 pesetas / 2º / 24
2. una persona / con / 4.600 pesetas / 360 pesetas / 5º / 51
3. dos personas / con / 5.950 pesetas / incluido / 4º / 43
4. dos personas / sin / 6.250 pesetas / incluido / 3er / 16

ESTRUCTURA

The verbs salir and llegar

Mi hermano **sale con** María.	My brother *goes out* **with** María.
Salgo para Madrid mañana.	I *leave for* Madrid tomorrow.
Yo **salgo de** la escuela a las 4:00.	I *leave* school at 4:00.
¿A qué hora **llegas a** casa?	What time *do you get* home?
Yo **llego a** casa a las 4:30.	I *get* home at 4:30.
Mi papá **llega de** Nueva York el viernes próximo.	My father *arrives from* New York next Friday.

yo	**salgo**	**llego**	nosotros(as)	**salimos**	**llegamos**
tú	**sales**	**llegas**	vosotros(as)	**salís**	**llegáis**
él			ellos		
ella	**sale**	**llega**	ellas	**salen**	**llegan**
Ud.			Uds.		

In the present tense, only the **yo** form of **salir** is irregular. The verb **llegar** is completely regular in the present tense.

Mi hermano **salió con** María el viernes pasado.	My brother *went out* **with** María last Friday.
Yo **salí de** la escuela a las 4:00 ayer.	I *left* school at 4:00 yesterday.
¿A qué hora **llegaste a** casa?	What time *did you get* home?
Yo **llegué a** casa a las 4:30.	I *got* home at 4:30.
¿Cuándo **llegó de** Valencia tu amiga?	When did your friend *arrive from* Valencia?

yo	**salí**	**llegué**	nosotros(as)	**salimos**	**llegamos**
tú	**saliste**	**llegaste**	vosotros(as)	**salisteis**	**llegasteis**
él			ellos		
ella	**salió**	**llegó**	ellas	**salieron**	**llegaron**
Ud.			Uds.		

The **yo** form of **llegar** has a spelling change in the preterite. The verb **salir** is completely regular in the preterite.

Salir para means *to leave for* a place.
Salir de means *to leave from* a place.
Salir con means *to go out with* someone.
Llegar a means *to arrive at* a place.
Llegar de means *to arrive from* a place.

Aquí practicamos

D. *¿Cuándo llegaste?* Di a qué hora tú y varios compañeros de clase salieron de la escuela y a qué hora llegaron a casa el miércoles pasado.

A	B	C
yo	salir de casa	a las 3:30
tú	llegar a casa	a las ?
?		
nosotros		
? y ?		

E. ¿A qué hora?   Use the cues suggested to find out at what time your partner does certain routine activities (present time) or at what time he or she did a particular activity (past time). Your partner will answer by making up an appropriate time of day. Follow the model and be careful that the time used is appropriate for the activity being discussed.

Modelo: Ud. / salir para Chicago mañana
—*¿A qué hora sale Ud. para Chicago mañana?*
—*Salgo para Chicago a las 9:00.*

1. tú / salir de casa por la mañana en general
2. ellos / salir del trabajo anoche
3. Uds. / salir para Miami este verano
4. tus padres / salir para el cine el sábado pasado
5. tú / salir del restaurante ayer
6. ellos / salir de Nueva York mañana
7. ella / salir de su clase de español todos los días
8. Uds. / salir de la biblioteca el martes pasado

Aquí escuchamos:
"Arregle la cuenta, por favor."

Antes de escuchar

Linda and her friend Kelly are getting ready to check out of the hotel in Sevilla. Look at the following questions and identify a few things you expect to hear during Linda's conversation with the hotel clerk.

Después de escuchar

1. ¿Qué pide Linda?
2. ¿Qué toman para el desayuno?
3. ¿Cuántas noches estuvieron en el hotel?
4. ¿Cuántos desayunos tomaron?
5. ¿Cuánto y cómo pagaron?

¡Aquí te toca a ti!

F. Por favor, señor(a).   Your tour group is checking out of the hotel. You need to settle your account. Greet the hotel clerk and find out…

1. if he or she has prepared the bill.
2. how much the bill is.
3. if they accept credit cards.
4. if the train station is far from the hotel.
5. if there is a restaurant at the train station.

Thank the desk clerk and say good-bye.

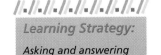

Learning Strategy:

Asking and answering questions

EJERCICIO ORAL

G. Intercambio   You and your partner are sharing details about family vacations. Interview each other giving information about either a real or imaginary trip that you have taken or would like to take with your family. Include information about some of the following:

adónde / cuándo / dormir en hotel o en casa de amigos o parientes *(relatives)* **/ salir por la noche / museos / parque de atracciones / restaurantes / pagar en efectivo o con una tarjeta de crédito o con cheques de viajero / viajar en coche o en tren o en avión / escribir cartas o tarjetas postales**

Cooperative Learning

Learning Strategies:

Interviewing, narrating in the past

Critical Thinking Strategies:

Comparing and contrasting, categorizing

EJERCICIO ESCRITO

H. Una comparación de hoteles   Choose any two of the hotels listed on page 149 and write a short comparison of the two. How are they similar? How are they different?

Critical Thinking Strategy:

Comparing and contrasting

157

Vocabulario

Para charlar

Para hablar de una habitación en un hotel

Yo quisiera…
Nosotros quisiéramos…
Necesitamos…
Buscamos…
Tenemos una reservación.

una habitación para dos personas.
por tres noches.
con baño.
sin baño.
en el primer piso.
con televisor.
con teléfono.

Para pagar la cuenta

¿Puede Ud. arreglar la cuenta?
¿Tiene Ud. la cuenta para la habitación 38?
Yo voy a pagar en efectivo.
　　　　　　con cheques de viajero.
　　　　　　con una tarjeta de crédito.

Temas y contextos

En el hotel

una alfombra
un ascensor
un baño (una sala de baño)
un bidé
una cabina de teléfono
un corredor
una cuenta
el desayuno (incluido en el precio
　o no incluido en el precio)
una ducha

un espejo
una lámpara
un lavabo
una mesita de noche
el (primer, segundo, tercer,
　cuarto, quinto) piso
la planta baja
la recepción
el WC

Los números ordinales

el (la) primero(a) / el primer
el (la) segundo(a)
el (la) tercero(a) / el tercer
el (la) cuarto(a)
el (la) quinto(a)
el (la) sexto(a)
el (la) séptimo(a)
el (la) octavo(a)
el (la) noveno(a)
el (la) décimo(a)

Vocabulario general

Sustantivos	Adjetivos	Verbos	Otras expresiones
la calidad	confortable	clasificar	al menos
la categoría	incluido(a)	dormir (ue, u) (la siesta)	¡Claro que no!
el confort	simple	llegar de (a)	hay que pasar por…
el lujo	útil	salir con	lo que dice la
el sistema de clasificación		de	*Guía Michelín*
		para	lo siguiente
			no permiten

Lectura CULTURAL

LOS PARADORES

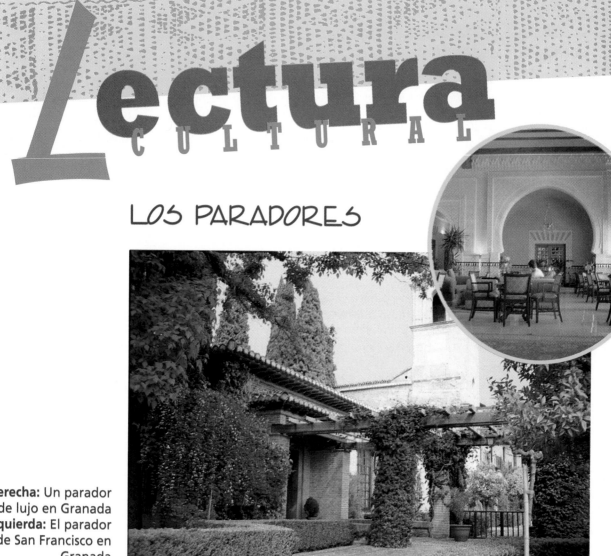

Derecha: Un parador
de lujo en Granada
Izquierda: El parador
de San Francisco en
Granada

Antes de leer

1. When people travel in the U. S., what are some of the places where they can
   stay overnight? Can you think of at least three types of places?
2. Look at the pictures that accompany this reading. What do you think the
   places featured are?
3. Look at the map that accompanies this reading. Where do you think these
   places are?
4. What do you think a **parador** is?

Guía para la lectura

A. Now read the first paragraph and answer the following:

1. Un parador es un tipo de _____.
   a. hotel
   b. restaurante
   c. viaje
2. ¿Qué hicieron el Marqués de la Vega-Inclán y el rey Alfonso XIII en 1926?
3. ¿Cuántos paradores hay en España?

B. Now read the second paragraph and answer the following question:
¿Dónde deciden en España establecer un parador?

Los paradores

La palabra *parador* aparece en muchos textos literarios españoles. Tradicionalmente en otros tiempos, el parador servía como un lugar donde los viajeros podían pasar la noche. Tomando esta tradición, en 1926 el Comisario Regio de Turismo, el Marqués de la Vega-Inclán, junto con el rey Alfonso XIII empezaron el proyecto de establecer una red de paradores en toda España. El primer parador se construyó en la Sierra de Gredos. Después se construyeron otros como el Parador de Manzanares y el Parador de Oropesa. Hoy día la red de paradores consiste en ochenta y seis establecimientos.

La filosofía básica es establecer un parador en una parte de España donde no hay muchos hoteles privados. Pero también hay un segundo punto importante en la concepción del Marqués de la Vega-Inclán. Y es que siempre que sea posible, se establezcan los paradores en antiguos monumentos como palacios, castillos o conventos.

Un viaje a los paradores no es sólo un viaje por las tierras de España. Es también un viaje por la historia. Usted puede dormir en la misma habitación en que durmió el Emperador Carlos V en el castillo de Jarandillo de la Vera. También puede comer en las salas que eran parte de la Universidad Complutense, fundada por el Cardenal Cisneros en Alcalá de Henares en 1498.

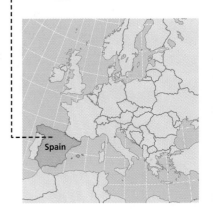

Spain

5

UN AÑO EN CASA DE LOS ÁLVAREZ

Vista de la ciudad de Granada desde la Alhambra, maravilla de la arquitectura árabe.

Objectives:

>>> **D**escribing furniture and items in a room

>>> **T**elling time using the 24-hour clock

Strategies:

>>> **C**alculating

>>> **N**arrating in the past

>>> **A**nalyzing

PRIMERA ETAPA

Preparación

In this chapter you will be focusing on an American student who is studying abroad.

>> **D**o you know of anyone who has studied in a foreign country? in which country?

>> **W**ould you like to study in a foreign country?

>> **I**n which one? What are your reasons for that choice?

>> **W**hat are other reasons that someone might have for wanting to study in another country?

Learning Strategies:

Previewing, supporting choices

Critical Thinking Strategy:

Hypothesizing

Un programa de intercambio

Un programa de intercambio: An exchange program

PROGRAMA DE INTERCAMBIO

Escuela _Santa Fe Capital High School_

Apellido _McGill_

Nombre _Patrick_

Edad _16_

Dirección: Calle _1606 Jay St._

Ciudad _Santa Fe_

Estado _Nuevo Mexico 87502_

País _Estados Unidos_

Teléfono _(505) 555-4321_

Nombres de sus padres _Susan, Charles_

¿Ha vivido en el extranjero?   Sí __✓__   No____   ¿Ha visitado el extranjero?   Sí __✓__   No____

País: _Canadá_   Duración de la visita: _2 semanas_

Chile   _1 mes_

Edad: Age

Estado: State

¿Ha vivido en el extranjero?: Have you lived outside the country? / *Ha visitado:* Have you visited

163

Pensión: student lodging

En Granada, prefiere vivir _____ ✓ _____ con una familia

_____ en una pensión con otros estudiantes norteamericanos.

Escriba un párrafo en que explique por qué quiere estudiar en una escuela española.

Hace cinco años que estudio español y quiero ser profesor de español algún día. También estudio francés y alemán. Me gustan mucho las lenguas extranjeras y me encanta el español. Mi madre es chilena y mi hermana, Mía, visitó España el año pasado. Quisiera conocer a unos españoles de mi edad y quiero perfeccionar mi español. Un año en Granada va a darme la oportunidad para estudiar la cultura española. Creo que es importante conocer otras culturas y estoy seguro de que voy a beneficiar de este viaje.

PARA SU INFORMACIÓN:

Los cuartos en las pensiones y con las familias contienen una cama, un sillón, un escritorio, unos estantes para libros y una cómoda con tres o cuatro cajones. Los estudiantes tienen la responsabilidad de traer toallas y jabón para lavar la ropa sucia.

sillón: armchair / *cajones:* drawers / *toallas:* towels / *jabón:* soap / *lavar la ropa sucia:* to wash dirty clothes

¡Aquí te toca a ti!

A. *Un retrato* (portrait) *de Patrick* Contesta las siguientes preguntas según *(according to)* la información que nos da Patrick en el formulario.

1. ¿Dónde vive Patrick?
2. ¿Cuál es la nacionalidad de su madre?
3. ¿Cuántos años tiene Patrick?
4. ¿Qué países extranjeros ha visitado Patrick?
5. ¿Cuánto tiempo pasó en cada país?
6. ¿Por qué va a Granada?
7. ¿Prefiere él vivir en una pensión o con una familia?

COMENTARIOS
CULTURALES

■ *Vivir con una familia en el extranjero* ■

Many exchange programs offer students the possibility of living with a family during their stay in the country where they will be studying. Becoming a member of the family allows students to truly live the culture and isolates them from other American students with whom they would probably speak English. Generally, the families with whom students are placed speak little English, allowing students interaction with native speakers and plenty of practice speaking Spanish!

Patrick McGill

Pronunciación: The vowel combination *ue*

The combination **ue** in Spanish is pronounced in one single syllable, similar to the *we* in the English word *wet.*

Práctica

B. Lee cada palabra en voz alta, pronunciando con cuidado la combinación *ue*.

1. bueno	**3.** luego	**5.** después	**7.** fuerte
2. abuelo	**4.** cuerpo	**6.** puerta	**8.** nuez

Repaso

C. Responde a las siguientes preguntas con la expresión que significa lo opuesto *(the opposite)* de la expresión en cursiva. Sigue el modelo.

Modelo: *¿Llega* él *al* banco?
*No, él **sale del** banco.*

1. *¿Llega* ella *de* Roma?

2. *¿Sale* él *de* la biblioteca?

3. *¿Llega* él *a* la escuela?

4. *¿Llegan* ellos *a* Madrid?

5. *¿Sale* ella *del* mercado?

6. *¿Llega* él *de* Oaxaca?

ESTRUCTURA

Some time expressions

No me gusta llegar **tarde,** y no me gusta llegar **temprano.** Me gusta llegar **a tiempo.**	I don't like to arrive *late,* and I don't like to arrive *early.* I like to arrive *on time.*
La clase comienza **en** cinco minutos.	The class begins *in* five minutes.
Yo salí de la escuela **hace** media hora.	I left school half an hour *ago.*
El profesor habló **por** una hora.	The professor spoke *for* an hour.

Here are some expressions associated with time.

1. **Temprano, a tiempo, tarde:** To express the ideas of *early* and *late* in relation to a specific moment in time (for example, an appointment or the departure time of a plane), use **temprano** and **tarde.** The expression **a tiempo** means *on time.*

   El concierto comenzó a las 8:00. Paula llegó a las 7:30; ella llegó **temprano.** Olivia llegó a las 8:30; ella llegó **tarde.** Santiago llegó a las 8:00; él llegó **a tiempo.**

2. **En:** To indicate when a future action will take place, use the preposition **en** as the equivalent of *in.*

   Son las 7:55. El concierto va a comenzar **en** cinco minutos.

3. **Hace, por:** As you have learned, **hace** is used with the preterite to indicate *how long ago* a past action occurred, and **por** is used to indicate *for how long* an action continued, continues, or will continue.

   Ahora son las 8:20. El concierto comenzó **hace** veinte minutos.
   El concierto terminó a las 10:00. La orquesta tocó **por** dos horas.

Aquí practicamos

D. La clase de matemáticas comienza a las 9:00.

Contesta las pregunts basándote en la información que tienes. (Recuerda que la clase comienza a las nueve.)

1. Ahora son las 8:50. Joaquín está durmiendo. Él vive lejos de la escuela. ¿Va a llegar a tiempo a su clase de matemáticas?
2. Ahora son las 7:30. Gabriela se está desayunando. Ella va a salir de casa en veinte minutos. Ella vive muy cerca de la escuela. ¿Va a llegar a tiempo para su clase de matemáticas?

Learning Strategy:
Calculating

Critical Thinking Strategy:
Analyzing time relationships

3. Ahora son las 8:30. ¿En cuántos minutos va a comenzar la clase de matemáticas?

4. Ahora son las 9:15. ¿Cuánto hace que comenzó la clase de matemáticas?

Learning Strategy:

Calculating

Critical Thinking Strategy:

Analyzing time relationships

E. ***En la Sierra Nevada***   La temporada de esquí *(The ski season)* empieza *(begins)* en la Sierra Nevada el primero de diciembre. Basándote en esto, contesta las siguientes preguntas.

1. Hoy es el 1º de noviembre. ¿Cuándo va a comenzar la temporada de esquí?

2. Podemos esquiar hasta el 1º de abril. ¿Por cuántos meses podemos esquiar en la Sierra Nevada?

3. Hoy es el 1º de febrero. ¿Cuánto hace que comenzó la temporada del esquí?

4. Nos gusta esquiar el primer día de la temporada. Hoy es el 10 de noviembre. Tenemos dos semanas de clase antes de nuestras vacaciones. Necesitamos tres días para llegar a la Sierra Nevada. ¿Vamos a llegar tarde para el primer día de la temporada?

Palabras útiles

Parts of an hour

un cuarto de hora	*a quarter of an hour*
media hora	*half an hour*
tres cuartos de hora	*three quarters of an hour*
diez minutos	*ten minutes*
cuarenta minutos	*forty minutes*

Learning Strategy:

Calculating

Critical Thinking Strategy:

Analyzing time relationships

F. ***Ahora son las 2:30.***   Ahora son las 2:30. Contesta las siguientes preguntas.

1. Juan va a llegar en un cuarto de hora. ¿A qué hora va a llegar?

2. Eva salió de casa hace media hora. ¿A qué hora salió ella de casa?

3. Donaldo salió de su trabajo hace un cuarto de hora. Él trabajó por una hora. ¿A qué hora comenzó a trabajar?

4. Sara va a estar en el museo una hora y tres cuartos. Ella va a llegar al museo en media hora. ¿A qué hora va a salir del museo?

Aquí escuchamos:
"¡Aquí está tu habitación!"

Antes de escuchar

Patrick has just arrived at the home of the Álvarez family. Sra. Álvarez will show him his room. Look at the questions below and identify a few things you expect to hear during Patrick's conversation with Sra. Álvarez.

Learning Strategy:

Previewing, predicting

Después de escuchar

1. ¿Qué le muestra *(show)* la familia a Patrick?
2. ¿Qué hay en la habitación?
3. ¿Dónde está el baño y qué hay allí?
4. ¿Dónde puede dejar su ropa sucia?
5. ¿Cuándo lava la ropa la Sra. Álvarez?

Learning Strategy:

Listening for details

¡Aquí te toca a ti!

Learning Strategy:

Describing based on visual cues

G. *¿Qué hay en la habitación de Patrick?* Describe Patrick's room according to what you see in the drawing.

EJERCICIO ORAL

H. *Aquí está tu habitación.* Imagine that a Spanish-speaking friend is spending a semester at your home and you have volunteered to share your room with your guest. Tell him or her (1) where your room is located in the house and (2) where the bathroom is located in relation to the room. Describe (3) what is in the room and (4) where each item is located. A classmate will play the role of your friend and ask you follow-up questions to each one of your statements. Follow the model.

Modelo:
—*Mi habitación está en el segundo piso a la izquierda de la escalera y enfrente del cuarto de mis padres. El baño está al final del corredor.*
—*¿Cuántas habitaciones hay arriba?*

EJERCICIO ESCRITO

I. *La hoja de inscripción* (Registration form) Following is a registration form for the summer program at the University of Salamanca. On a separate piece of paper, write information you'd need to fill out the form.

C U R S O S INTERNACIONALES	Reservado a Secretaría		FOTOGRAFÍAS 2
	9 3		
		Preinscripción: Alojamiento:	

Apellido

Nombre

Fecha de Nacimiento   Día   Mes   Año 1 9   Sexo: Fem.   Masc.

Pasaporte (Número)   Nacionalidad

Dirección

Teléfono (Número)   Fax (Número)

ALOJAMIENTO

VERANO: Señale con los números 1, 2, 3 y 4 su orden de preferencias, cubriendo todas las opciones.
RESTO DEL AÑO: Señale con los números 1 y 2 su orden de preferencia dentro del alojamiento en familia.

RESIDENCIA (Sólo en verano)		FAMILIA (Todo el año)	
Habitación doble (54.000 ptas. el mes)	Habitación individual (62.000 ptas. el mes)	Habitación doble (1.800 ptas. diarias)	Habitación individual (2.000 ptas. diarias)

SEGUNDA ETAPA

Preparación

At the beginning of this **etapa,** Patrick writes a thank-you note to the Álvarez family.

>> **H**ave you ever written a thank-you note?

>> **W**hat sorts of information do you expect to find in a thank-you note Patrick would write after spending a year in the Álvarez home?

//-//-//-//-//-//-//-//

Learning Strategy:

Previewing

Una carta de agradecimiento

*Una carta de agradeci-
    miento:* A thank-you
    letter

Santa Fe, 10 de julio de 1996

Queridos Sr. y Sra. Álvarez,

    Hace quince días que salí de Granada y los extraño. Mi estancia en su casa fue inolvidable y les agradezco con todo el corazón su hospitalidad. Yo aprendí mucho en España y voy a continuar mis estudios de español en mi escuela y después en la universidad. Voy a hablarles a mis amigos de mi escuela de Granada y de mi familia española.

    Mil gracias y espero que Uds. puedan visitar la ciudad de Santa Fe algún día. Mis padres quisieran conocerlos.

                    Un abrazo,
                    Patrick

Queridos: Dear

los extraño: I miss you /
    estancia: stay
inolvidable: unforgettable /
    les agradezco: I thank you /
    corazón: heart

hablarles a mis amigos: talk
    to my friends

espero que Uds. puedan: I
    hope that you can
conocerlos: to meet you

abrazo: hug

171

¡Aquí te toca a ti!

A. *Comprensión*   Contesta las siguientes preguntas según la información en la carta de Patrick en la página 171.

1. How long ago did Patrick leave Granada?
2. What is he going to do when he returns to school?
3. Is he going to continue studying Spanish? Where?
4. What does he hope the Álvarez family will do?

B. *Hace... que*   Patrick is telling his friends at school about his stay in Spain and how long ago he did certain things. Follow the model and be sure to use the preterite of the verbs.

> **Modelo:**   dos semanas / salir
> *Hace dos semanas que salí de España.*

1. quince días / salir de Granada
2. un mes / nadar en el Mar Mediterráneo
3. dos meses / visitar el Museo del Prado en Madrid
4. seis meses / ir a Barcelona
5. un año / conocer a la familia Álvarez
6. dos días / volver a la escuela aquí

Now imagine you are telling a friend about what Patrick did.

> **Modelo:**   dos semanas / salir
> *Hace dos semanas que salió de España.*

Los parques del Generalife en la Alhambra

172

Pronunciación: *The vowel combination uo*

The combination **uo** in Spanish is pronounced in one single syllable, similar to the English word *woe*.

Práctica

C. Lee cada palabra en voz alta, pronunciando con cuidado la combinación *uo*.

1.	continuo	**3.**	antiguo	**5.**	mutuo	**7.**	arduo
2.	monstruo	**4.**	continuó	**6.**	cuota	**8.**	actuó

Repaso

D. *El día de Juan José*   Describe el día de Juan Jose según los dibujos.

Modelo: ¿Hasta qué hora durmió Juan José?
Él durmió hasta las 8:00.

Learning Strategies:

Reporting based on visual cues, narrating in the present, past, and future

1. ¿En cuántos minutos comienzan sus clases?

2. ¿Va a llegar a tiempo para su primera clase?

3. ¿A qué hora sale de la escuela?

4. ¿Llegó tarde para el autobús?   **5.** ¿En cuántos minutos llega a casa?   **6.** ¿Qué hace hasta las 4:30?

7. ¿Va a llegar a tiempo para la cena?   **8.** ¿En cuánto tiempo hace su tarea *(homework)*?

//·//·//·//·//·//·//·//·//

Learning Strategy:

Reading for cultural information

ESTRUCTURA

The 24-hour clock

El partido comienza a las **19:00.**	The game begins at *7:00 p.m.*
Nosotros llegamos a las **20:45.**	We arrived at *8:45 p.m.*

You have already learned the conversational method of telling time in Spanish. But in airports and railroad stations, on radio and TV, and at concerts and movies, official time based on the 24-hour clock is used in the Spanish-speaking world. Note that military time in English is also expressed in official time. The basic differences between the two are as follows.

Conversational time	Official time
• Is based on the usual 12-hour clock	• Is based on the 24-hour clock (0 = midnight, 12 = noon)
• Divides the hour into two 30-minute segments (after and before the hour)	• Treats the hour as a 60-minute whole (that is: only moves forward, never uses **menos**)
• Uses the expressions **y cuarto, y media, menos cuarto, medianoche, mediodía**	• Uses only cardinal numbers such as **y quince, y treinta, y cuarenta y cinco, veinte y cuatro horas, doce horas**

The easiest way to switch from official time to conversational time is to *subtract* twelve from the hour of official time, *unless* the hour is already less than twelve.

Conversational time		*Official time*	
9:45 a.m.	las diez menos cuarto	9:45	nueve horas y cuarenta y cinco
12:30 p.m.	las doce y media	12:30	doce horas y treinta
2:50 p.m.	las tres menos diez	14:50	catorce horas y cincuenta
11:15 p.m.	las once y cuarto	23:15	veintitrés horas y quince

Aquí practicamos

E. Cambia de hora oficial a hora conversacional.

Modelo: 15:00
las tres de la tarde

1. 13:00 **3.** 22:00 **5.** 3:15 **7.** 20:45
2. 9:00 **4.** 12:00 **6.** 15:30 **8.** 18:06

F. *Horarios de avión* En clase conociste (**conocer** = *to meet*) a Pepe, un estudiante de Tenerife. Estás considerando la posibilidad de pasar una semana en su casa durante las vacaciones de Pascua *(Easter)*. Cada semana, Iberia y British Caledonia Airways (BCA) tienen cuatro vuelos *(flights)* de Madrid a Santa Cruz de Tenerife. Mira los horarios en la página 176 e indica si las afirmaciones a continuación son verdaderas o falsas *(true or false)*.

Learning Strategy:

Reading a timetable

Madrid-Tenerife — Salidas del Aeropuerto Barajas

	Vuelo	Salida	Llegada
martes	Iberia 831	08:15	11:30
jueves	BCA 29	20:30	23:45
sábado	BCA 37	10:45	14:00
domingo	Iberia 867	21:15	00:30

Tenerife-Madrid — Llegadas al Aeropuerto de Barajas

	Vuelo	Salida	Llegada
lunes	Iberia 868	13:30	16:45
miércoles	Iberia 832	6:15	9:30
viernes	BCA 30	12:40	15:55
domingo	BCA 38	17:15	20:30

1. Los lunes el avión de Iberia llega a Madrid a las cinco menos cinco.
2. Los martes el vuelo de Iberia sale de Madrid a las ocho y media.
3. Los lunes el avión de Iberia 868 sale a la una y media y llega a las cinco menos cuarto de la tarde.
4. Los sábados el vuelo de BCA 37 llega a Tenerife a las dos de la tarde.
5. Los domingos el avión sale de Madrid a las nueve y cuarto de la mañana y llega a Tenerife a las 12 y veinticinco del mediodía.
6. La duración del vuelo es de tres horas y cuarto.

G. Una pequeña prueba   Para practicar cómo se usa el tiempo oficial, Pepe te hace las siguientes preguntas.

1. El avión de Madrid a Barcelona tarda una hora en llegar (*flight = 1 hour*). ¿Quieres estar en Barcelona a las 9:00 de la noche. ¿Vas a tomar el avión de las 20:00 o el de las 21:00?
2. Quieres ir al cine pero tienes que volver a casa antes de las 6:00 de la tarde. La película es de dos horas y empieza a las 13:00, 16:00, 19:00 y 22:00. ¿A qué hora vas a poder ir al cine?
3. Vas a la estación de trenes para recoger (*to pick up*) a tus padres. El tren llega de Barcelona a las 17:30. Llegas a la estación a las 4:30 de la tarde. ¿Llegaste a tiempo?
4. Invitaste a un(a) amigo(a) a un concierto. El concierto empieza a las 21:00. Se tarda media hora en ir de tu apartamento al concierto. ¿A qué hora tiene que llegar tu amigo(a) a tu apartamento?

Aquí escuchamos:
"La salida"

Antes de escuchar

Patrick is getting ready to leave and will say good-bye to a friend. Later he will say good-bye to the Álvarez family at the train station. Look at the following questions and identify a few things you expect to hear during Patrick's conversations.

START

Después de escuchar

1. ¿Qué hace Patrick el día que sale?
2. ¿A qué hora sale su tren?
3. ¿Qué avión toma?

4. ¿Qué quiere hacer Miguel?
5. ¿Cuándo piensa volver Patrick a España?

¡Aquí te toca a ti!

H. *Mil gracias*   You have just spent a month with a Spanish family and are about to return to the United States. As your classmate plays a member of the family, enact the following conversation.

1. Thank him or her for everything.
2. Ask if he or she is going to visit the United States next summer.
3. Say that you would like to return to Spain very soon.
4. Tell him or her that you learned a lot and that you are going to tell your friends in the United States about Spain.

¡Adelante!

EJERCICIO ORAL

I. *Un viaje a las Islas Canarias*   You are helping a friend plan a trip to the Canary Islands. He or she is starting from Valencia. Use official time to discuss the plans.

1. Ask if he or she wants to travel in the morning or afternoon.
2. Explain that the morning flight leaves Tuesday at 10:15 a.m. and arrives in Tenerife at 12:35 p.m. The afternoon flight leaves Saturday at 12:55 p.m. and arrives in Tenerife at 2:25 p.m.
3. Tell him or her that the cost of the ticket is 20,000 pesetas.
4. Find out in how many days your friend is going to leave for Tenerife.
5. Find out which flight your friend is going to take.
6. Find out how much time your friend will spend in Tenerife.
7. Explain that you would like to go to Tenerife too, but that you don't have enough money. You are going to spend the vacation at home.

EJERCICIO ESCRITO

J. *Una carta de agradecimiento*   Write a short thank-you note to an imaginary family with whom you spent the last year in Spain. Remember to (1) give the name of your town and today's date in the heading, (2) greet your host family by name, (3) tell how long you have been gone from their home, (4) comment on how much you learned while living with their family, (5) tell how your experiences in Spain will be important to you, (6) express your appreciation, and (7) include a friendly closing. (Use the letter on page 171 as a model.)

Vocabulario

Para charlar

Para hablar del horario

llegar a tiempo
llegar tarde
llegar temprano
en (veinte minutos, etc.)
por (una hora, etc.)
hace (un año, dos días, etc.)
un cuarto de hora
media hora
tres cuartos de hora
diez (etc.) minutos

Para decir que extrañamos a alguien

Te extraño
Los extraño

Para dar las gracias

Les agradezco.
Les agradezco con
  todo el corazón su
  hospitalidad.
Mil gracias por…
Muchas gracias
  por...

Temas y contextos

Los muebles de una habitación

una cama
un clóset
una cómoda con dos cajones
                 cuatro cajones

un escritorio
un estante
una lámpara
una silla
un sillón

Vocabulario general

Sustantivos

la edad
un estado
un país
un programa de intercambio
una salida

Verbos

beneficiarse
extrañar
lavar
perfeccionar

Otras palabras y expresiones

un abrazo
durante
espero que Uds. puedan visitar
el jabón
prestar atención
querido(a)
queridos(as)
la ropa sucia
una toalla

Lectura
CULTURAL

LA ALHAMBRA

Antes de leer

1. Look at the photos that accompany this reading. What kind of place do you think this is?
2. Where do you think it is located?
3. Have you ever heard about the Alhambra? It has been described in detail by Washington Irving in his famous book *Tales from the Alhambra*.
4. Note the arches in the photos. Are they different from other arches you have seen? In this reading, you will learn about their design.

El patio de los Leones en la Alhambra

Guía para la lectura

A. Read the first paragraph to determine the following:

1. Who built the Alhambra with its beautiful arches?
2. When did this group of people invade Spain?
3. What part of Spain was influenced most by this group?

B. Now finish reading the passage and answer the following questions.

1. What does the phrase **"Calat Alhambra"** mean?
2. What illusion does the water and marble create?
3. How did they get the water to flow out of the lions' mouths?

La Alhambra

Spain

ANDALUCIA
Granada

n el año 711 los moros (también conocidos como árabes) invadieron la Península Ibérica y se establecieron en la parte del sur hasta 1492. Su influencia arquitectónica es evidente en toda esta región de España que también se conoce como Andalucía. Esta influencia se ve muy claramente en las tres ciudades principales de Andalucía: Sevilla, Córdoba y Granada. Pero de todos los monumentos que construyeron los moros en España, ninguno es tan espectacular como La Alhambra.

La "Calat Alhambra" o castillo rojo es una de las fortalezas más notables que ha construido el ser humano. Está situada en una colina desde donde se contemplan bonitas vistas de la ciudad. La mayor parte fue construida en el siglo XIV y es un conjunto de patios, salones y jardines extraordinarios. La mezcla del mármol con el agua de las fuentes causa una confusión entre lo líquido y lo sólido para el visitante. El famoso Patio de los Leones es una maravilla de la arquitectura medieval. El agua que sale de la boca de los doce leones es traída por una serie de canales y acequias desde las alturas de la Sierra Nevada. El agua sale sin la ayuda de una bomba—sale con la simple fuerza de gravedad que trae el agua desde las alturas de la sierra.

Los arcos árabes de la Alhambra

6

BUSCO UN APARTAMENTO

Muchos ciudadanos españoles viven en edificios grandes y modernos como éste.

Objectives:

>>> **U**nderstanding classified ads and lodging brochures

>>> **D**escribing a house or apartment

Strategies:

>>> **U**sing cognates for meaning

>>> **N**egotiating

>>> **I**magining

PRIMERA ETAPA

Preparación

〉〉 **H**ave you ever looked at an apartment ad?

〉〉 **W**hat kind of information would you expect to find in such an ad?

〉〉 **B**elow are some ads for apartments in Madrid. How many ads are there?

〉〉 **W**hat do you think the boldface words in each ad mean? (Hint: Think back to the Madrid **metro**. Remember the names of the **metro** stops?)

Anuncios del periódico

Anuncios del periódico: Newspaper ads

Goya. Vacío. Dos dormitorios. 60 m^2. Cocina amueblada. Comedor. Baño. Teléfono. Terraza. 5º piso. Ascensor. Tel. 2 43 94 54

Prado. Completamente amueblado. 225 m^2. Aire acondicionado. Piscina. Tres dormitorios. Garaje. Dos baños. Dos terrazas. 4º piso. Ascensor. Llamar después de las 20h. Tel. 4 20 28 87

Lavapiés. Un dormitorio. Baño. Teléfono. Cocina amueblada. Piscina. Jardín. Tenis. Llamar después de las 16h. Tel. 5 31 67 06

Ventas. Vacío. 185 m^2. Cuatro dormitorios. Dos baños. Dos terrazas. Cocina grande. Estacionamiento. Comedor. 7º piso. Dos ascensores. Tel. 5 73 34 30

Plaza de España. Completamente amueblado. Sala de estar grande. Dos dormitorios. 125 m^2. Cocina grande. Baño. 3er piso. Llamar mañanas. Tel. 2 45 85 42

Centro. Tres dormitorios. Cocina amueblada. Garaje. Piscina. Jardín. Algunos muebles—mesa, sofá— para vender. Tel. 4 52 58 24 noche.

Vacío: Vacant
Cocina amueblada: Furnished kitchen / *Sala de estar:* Livingroom / *Comedor:* Dining room / *Terraza:* Terrace / *Jardín:* Garden

Estacionamiento: Parking *muebles:* furniture

¡Aquí te toca a ti!

Learning Strategy:

Using cognates for meaning

A. Lee los anuncios en la página 183 con cuidado *(carefully)*. ¿Qué piensas que significan *(mean)* las siguientes palabras?

1. aire acondicionado
2. completamente
3. dormitorio
4. tenis
5. garaje
6. llamar

Learning Strategy:

Describing, paraphrasing

B. *¡No comprendo!* You are looking over the apartment ads in today's newspaper. Call one of your Spanish friends and describe one of the apartments to him or her. Base your description on one of the ads on page 183.

Modelo: El apartamento está cerca de la estación de metro Goya. Está vacío y tiene dos dormitorios. Tiene unos 60 metros cuadrados (square meters) y la cocina está amueblada. También tiene un comedor, baño, teléfono y terraza. Está en el quinto piso y hay un ascensor en el edificio.

> **Goya.** Vacío. Dos dormitorios. 60 m². Cocina amueblada. Comedor. Baño. Teléfono. Terraza. 5°piso. Ascensor. Tel. 2 43 94 54

Pronunciación: The vowel combination ui

The combination **ui** in Spanish is pronounced in one single syllable, similar to the English word *we*. Note that in the word **muy,** the same sound is spelled **uy.**

Práctica

C. Lee cada palabra en voz alta, pronunciando con cuidado la combinación *ui*.

1. fui
2. Luis
3. Ruiz
4. ruido
5. muy
6. fuimos
7. buitre
8. cuidado

Repaso

D. ¿A qué hora presentan los programas? Imagine that you and your friends are on a class trip in a Spanish-speaking country. Your roommate wants to watch TV but is having trouble figuring out the television schedule because the times are based on the 24-hour clock. As you and your partner look over a program listing taken from a Spanish newspaper, take turns expressing interest in certain programs and answering your partner's questions (page 186) using conversational time.

Learning Strategies:

Calculating time conversions, reading for details

Modelo:
—Me gustaría ver "Blossom" en el canal uno. ¿A qué hora lo (it) presentan?
—Lo presentan a las siete de la tarde.

P R O G R A M A C I O N

07.30 Estamos de vacaciones.
11.30 Vacaciones de cine.
 "El hombre más fuerte del mundo"
13.00 McGyver.
14.00 Informativo territorial.
14.30 No te rías que es peor.
15.00 Telediario.
15.30 Alejandra.
16.30 Marielena.
17.30 Telefilme.
18.30 Vídeos de primera.
18.55 Noticias.
19.00 Blossom.
19.30 Justicia ciega.
20.30 Los problemas crecen.
21.00 Telediario-2.
21.27 El tiempo.
21.30 Pret a porter.
22.00 Cine español.
 "El tesoro"
24.00 Noches de gala.
01.15 Telediario 3.
01.45 Sobre mi cadáver.
02.35 Testimonio.
02.40 Dime luna.
03.30 Diga 33.
04.00 Despedida y cierre.

07.30 Euronews.
09.00 Epoca de cambios.

10.00 **La película de la mañana** .
 "Una mujer peligrosa"
11.35 Clip clip ¡hurra!
13.00 Pinnic.
15.00 Cifras y letras.
15.30 Grandes documentales.
17.00 Sueños de Olimpia.
17.30 **La película de la tarde.**
 "Entre la luz y las tinieblas"
19.10 Ruta Quetzal 94.
19.40 Planeta sur.
20.10 Habitación para dos.
20.35 El superagente 86.
21.00 Lingo.
21.30 Informa-2.
22.00 Fútbol.
 Bielorusia-España
24.00 Dudas razonables.
01.00 Los veranos de La 2.

TELEMADRID

07.15 Telenoticias (R).
07.35 La línea Onedin.
08.25 A saber.
08.55 Hermanas.
09.20 Gente casada.
09.45 Tele Empleo (R).
10.00 Avance informativo.
10.15 **Star Treck: la nueva generación.**
11.10 Primeros besos.
11.35 Dirty dancing.

12.00 La banda.
13.30 Los picapiedra.
14.00 Telenoticias.
15.00 Roseanne.
15.30 Cine de tarde.
17.15 Ole tus vídeos.
18.00 A través del tiempo.
18.45 Tele Empleo.
19.00 Madrid directo.
20.30 Telenoticias.
20.55 El tiempo.
21.00 Colegio mayor.
21.30 Cine: una de acción.
23.30 Un momento, por favor.
01.00 Telenoticias.
01.05 Tele Empleo .
01.20 Cine: sala de madrugada.
03.00 Información cultural de la CAM.

07.00 Programación.
07.30 Noticias.
08.00 Tras 3 Tris, vacaciones.
11.00 Punky Brewster.
11.30 Somos diez.
12.00 Colmillo blanco.
12.30 Aventuras en Africa.
13.00 Star Treck.
14.00 Un mundo diferente.
14.30 El príncipe de Bel Air.
15.00 Noticias.
15.30 Telecine.
17.30 Catwalk.
18.30 Salvados por la campana.
19.00 Paradise Beach.

19.30 **Los vigilantes de la playa.**
20.30 A toda página.
21.00 Noticias.
21.30 Cine.
23.30 Telecine.
24.00 Cine.
01.30 Noticias.
02.00 Línea América.
02.30 Cine de madrugada.
04.00 Televenta.
05.30 Cine de madrugada.

07.15 Entre hoy y mañana (R).
07.45 Los periódicos.
08.00 La tele es tuya, colega.
10.55 Webster.
11.20 Grandullón.
11.45 Apartamento para tres.
12.15 Hotel.
13.15 La ruleta de la fortuna.
14.00 Veredicto.
14.30 Las noticias.
15.00 Veredicto (II)
15.30 Sensación de vivir.
16.30 Melrose Place.
17.30 Remington Steele.
18.30 Déjate querer.
19.30 Su media naranja.
20.30 Las noticias.
21.00 Telecupón.
21.10 Karaoke.
21.45 Cine.
23.45 Misterio para tres..

00.45 Las pesadillas de Freddy.		14.30 Kate y Allie.	21.57 Primer plano.
01.45 Entre hoy y mañana.		15.00 Cine (Cod).	22.00 Estreno Canal Plus. (Cod).
02.15 Cine.		*"La novia del candidato"*.	*"Homicidio"*.
04.15 Novedades increíbles.	08.05 **ABC World News.**	16.28 Cine (Cod).	23.40 Cine. (Cod).
04.45 Los días y las noches de	08.30 Dibujos.	*"Juegos prohibidos de una*	*"La ciudad de la alegría"*.
Molly Dodd.	08.55 Videominuto.	*dama"*.	01.50 Piezas. (Cod).
05.15 Novedades increíbles.	09.52 Noticias.	18.07 Especial "Los jóvenes	02.17 Música noche. (Cod).
05.45 Cine.	10.00 Cine. (Cod).	flamencos"(Cod).	03.10 Sesión especial (Cod).
	"El beso del sueño"	19.35 Dibujos. (Cod).	*"Vivir por nada"*
	12.01 Cine. (Cod).	20.05 Los 40 principales.	04.37 Golf. (Cod)
	"El invitado".	20.30 Sigue soñando.	05.37 Cine (Cod).
	13.35 Los 40 principales.	21.00 Primos lejanos.	*"Más allá de la inocencia"*
	14.00 Noticias.	21.30 Noticias.	
	14.05 Mi viejo rockero.	21.53 Información deportiva.	

1. ¿A qué hora presentan "Star Trek: la nueva generación"?
2. ¿A qué hora presentan "Grandes documentales"?
3. ¿A qué hora presentan la película "El tesoro"?
4. ¿A qué hora presentan "Vídeos de primera"?
5. ¿A qué hora presentan "Hermanas"?
6. ¿A qué hora presentan el partido de fútbol entre Bielorusia y España?

ESTRUCTURA

The verb *decir*

—**¿Dicen Uds.** la verdad? Are *you telling* the truth?
—Claro! Siempre **decimos** la verdad. Of course! We always *tell* the truth.
—¿Qué **dijo Juan?** What *did Juan say*?
—**Dijo que** no. *He said* no.
—**Él dijo que** va a nevar. *He said that* it is going to snow.
—**María dijo que** Juan no estudió. *María said that* John didn't study.

The verb **decir** *(to say, to tell)* is irregular in both the present and the preterite tenses.

Present			
yo	**digo**	nosotros(as)	**decimos**
tú	**dices**	vosotros(as)	**decís**
él		ellos	
ella	**dice**	ellas	**dicen**
Ud.		Uds.	

	Preterite		
yo	**dije**	nosotros(as)	**dijimos**
tú	**dijiste**	vosotros(as)	**dijisteis**
él		ellos	
ella	**dijo**	ellas	**dijeron**
Ud.		Uds.	

Note that **decir que** can be used to report something.

Aquí practicamos

E. ¿Qué dicen ellos?
You're sitting inside a café with a large group of friends. Because of the street noise outside, you can't hear what some of your friends are saying; so you have to keep asking what's going on. Use the cues to ask your questions.

> **Modelo:** ellos
> *¿Qué dijeron ellos?*

1. ella
2. tú
3. Uds.
4. él
5. ellas
6. ellos

F. Ellos dicen que...
Now that you've asked, the person sitting next to you at the table repeats everything that is said.

> **Modelo:** ellos / no hace buen tiempo hoy
> *Dijeron que no hace buen tiempo hoy.*

1. ella / va a nevar
2. yo / hay niebla por las calles
3. nosotros / hace mucho frío
4. él / no hay escuela mañana
5. ellas / van a jugar en la nieve
6. ellos / van a esquiar

Palabras útiles

Expressions with decir

Para decir la verdad, no me gusta el francés.	*To tell the truth*, I don't like French.
¿Qué quiere decir esto?	*What does* this *mean*?
¿Cómo se dice "documentary" en español?	*How do you say* "documentary" *in Spanish*?

The verb **decir** is used in a variety of everyday expressions:

para decir la verdad	*to tell the truth*
decir que sí (no)	*to say yes (no)*
querer decir	*to mean*
¿Cómo se dice... ?	*How do you say . . . ?*
¿Qué dijiste?	*What did you say?*

G. Decide which of the **decir** expressions best fits the following situations.

1. You want to know how to say "apartment building" in Spanish.
2. You didn't hear what your brother said to you.
3. You explain that, to tell the truth, you are not sure.
4. You want to find out what someone means by what he or she said.
5. You explain that you mean that your teacher is very difficult.
6. You want to tell someone that the teacher said no.

Aquí escuchamos:
"Buscamos un apartamento"

Antes de escuchar

Patrick is looking at some apartment ads in the newspaper. Look at the following questions and identify a few things you expect to hear during Patrick's conversation with his friend. Is the rent (el alquiler) for apartments expensive in your town?

START

Después de escuchar

1. ¿Qué leen los dos amigos?
2. ¿Qué encuentra Patrick?
3. ¿Dónde está?
4. ¿Cómo es?
5. ¿Qué deciden buscar al final?

Learning Strategy:

Listening for details

¡Aquí te toca a ti!

H. Buscamos un apartamento. You and your friend are now college students and have just arrived in Madrid on a study abroad program from your university. Part of the experience is that you must find your own lodging. Look at the apartment ads from the classified section of the newspaper and carry out the following tasks: (1) Brainstorm together on the features that are most important to have in an apartment and rank your top three preferences; (2) Take turns describing the apartments in the ads to one another; (3) decide which apartments do not suit you both and give your reasons; (4) decide together which apartment you are going to rent (**alquilar**) and why.

Cooperative Learning

Learning Strategies:

Paraphrasing, supporting opinions, negotiating

Critical Thinking Strategies:

Comparing and contrasting, prioritizing

Cuatro Caminos. Amueblado. Cuatro dormitorios. Dos baños. Comedor. Dos terrazas. Piscina. 95.000 ptas. Tel. 4 12 54 40

Argüelles. Tres dormitorios. Cocina grande. Comedor. Todo amueblado excepto salón. 50.000 ptas. Tel. 6 10 90 87

Lavapiés. Amueblado. Comedor. Un dormitorio. Teléfono. Terraza. Piscina. Tenis. 70.000 ptas. Tel. 8 14 23 85

Delicias. Un dormitorio grande. Cocina amueblada. Aire acondicionado. Jardín. 45.000 ptas. Tel. 7 21 40 89 noche.

Legazpi. Vacío. Dos dormitorios. Comedor. Baño. Cocina. 30.000 ptas. Tel. 4 50 17 76

Goya. Amueblado. Dos dormitorios. Comedor. Cocina. Baño. Terraza. 60.000 ptas. Tel. 3 15 41 55

¡Adelante!

EJERCICIO ORAL

I. Mi casa / Mi apartamento

Describe your dream house or apartment to one of your classmates. Where is the house or apartment located? How do you get from there to school? How many rooms does it have? Name the rooms. How big are the rooms? On what floor are the rooms located? Is there a garden? Do you have a garage? Is there an elevator? Your classmate will ask you questions to get more information.

EJERCICIO ESCRITO

J. Mi apartamento ideal

Write an ad for your ideal apartment. Base it on those that appear on pages 183 and 189.

SEGUNDA ETAPA

Preparación

>> **I**f you were to rent an unfurnished apartment, with what sorts of items would you need to furnish it? Make a list of them.

>> **W**hat are the basic necessities?

>> **W**hat are some of the luxury items?

>> **L**ook at the drawings for some basic apartment furnishings.

Learning Strategies:

Previewing, listing

Critical Thinking Strategies:

Categorizing, evaluating

Mi apartamento

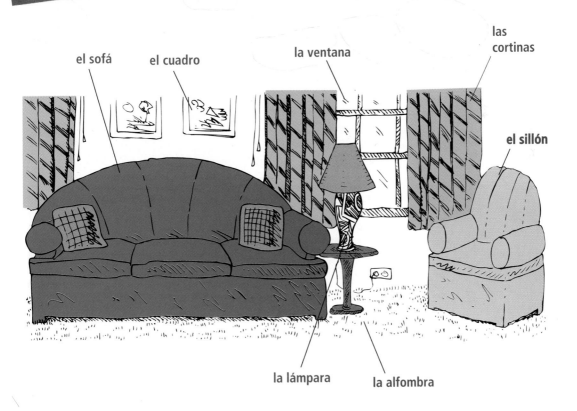

el sofá   el cuadro   la ventana   las cortinas

el sillón

la lámpara   la alfombra

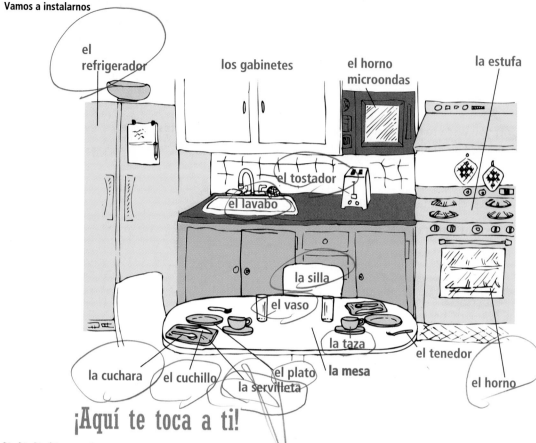

el
refrigerador   los gabinetes   el horno
microondas   la estufa

el tostador
el lavabo
la silla
el vaso
la taza
el tenedor
la cuchara   el cuchillo   el plato   **la mesa**   el horno
la servilleta

¡Aquí te toca a ti!

A. *Un apartamento nuevo* You and your family are about to move into a new apartment. Using words you already know and the new vocabulary in the drawings, imagine how you'll furnish each room. Use the verb **poner** *(to put)* in the infinitive form, according to the model.

Modelo: el dormitorio
En el dormitorio voy a poner una cama, un televisor, etc.

1. la cocina
2. el dormitorio
3. la oficina
4. la sala de estar

B. *Donde yo vivo* Describe los muebles en cada cuarto (in each room) de la casa o apartamento donde vives.

Pronunciación: *The vowel combination ai*

The combination **ai** in Spanish is pronounced in one single syllable, similar to the English word *eye.* Note that it can also be spelled **ay,** as in the Spanish words **hay** and **ay.**

Práctica

C. Lee cada palabra en voz alta, pronunciando con cuidado la combinación *ai*.

1. aire	**3.** paisaje	**5.** hay	**7.** caimán
2. baile	**4.** habláis	**6.** ¡ay!	**8.** compráis

Repaso

D. *¿Qué dijiste?* You are talking about what you and some of your classmates did last night. One of your classmates, who didn't hear, will ask you what you said. You will respond using the verb **decir.** Follow the model.

Modelo: ella / estudiar
—*Ella estudió para un examen.*
—*¿Qué dijiste?*
—*Dije que ella estudió para un examen.*

1. ella / hablar por teléfono   **5.** nosotros / ir al partido
2. yo / ir al cine   **6.** ellas / mirar la televisión
3. ella / estudiar para un examen   **7.** ellos / comer pizza
4. él / salir con una amiga   **8.** él / alquilar un vídeo

E. *Su casa está...* Describe the homes of the people listed below to a group of your classmates. In addition to saying where each home is located, be precise about what it is like (rooms, furnishings, etc.). Use sentences like: **Su casa está...** and **Su casa tiene....**

1. a teacher   **3.** a professional athlete
2. a famous actress   **4.** a famous rock star

Learning Strategies:

Listing, describing

Critical Thinking Strategies:

Imagining, comparing and contrasting, making associations

ESTRUCTURA

The verb *poner*

Voy a poner el sofá en la sala de estar.	*I'll put* the couch in the living room.
Ella puso el televisor en el dormitorio.	*She put* the television in the bedroom.
Yo puse el estante en mi oficina.	*I put* the bookcase in my office.
Yo pongo la mesa.	*I set (I'm setting)* the table.

The verb **poner** has several meanings. It may mean *to put* or *to place* something somewhere. It can also be used in the idiomatic expression **poner la mesa** *(to set the table)*.

Present

yo	**pongo**	nosotros(as)	**ponemos**
tú	**pones**	vosotros(as)	**ponéis**
él		ellos	
ella }	**pone**	ellas }	**ponen**
Ud.		Uds.	

Notice that, like **decir**, only the **yo** form of **poner** is irregular in the present, but all preterite forms are irregular.

Preterite

yo	**puse**	nosotros(as)	**pusimos**
tú	**pusiste**	vosotros(as)	**pusisteis**
él		ellos	
ella }	**puso**	ellas }	**pusieron**
Ud.		Uds.	

Learning Strategy:

Reading for cultural information

COMENTARIOS
CULTURALES

El piso

In large cities like Madrid, because of the way space is used, it is rare to find suburbs as we know them in this country. What happens is that large apartment-like buildings are constructed that contain units with several rooms each. A unit, called **un piso,** can consist of a kitchen, living room, dining room, bathrooms, and bedrooms. People in Madrid buy **pisos** (similar to our condominiums) the same way we would buy houses in the suburbs.

Aquí practicamos

F. ¿Dónde pones los libros? Di donde tú y tus compañeros de clase ponen sus libros cuando llegan a casa. Usa las pistas *(cues).*

A	B	C
yo	poner en	la mesa
tú		el estante
?		el escritorio
nosotros		
? y ?		

G. ¿Dónde pusiste... ? All the new furniture for your apartment arrived while your sister or brother was spending the weekend with a friend. You decided where to put the new items and rearranged the apartment while your sibling was away. Now telephone him or her. When asked, tell where you put each item.

 Modelo: la cómoda
—¿Dónde pusiste la cómoda?
—Puse la cómoda en el dormitorio.

/-/-/-/-/-/-/-/-/-/-/-/

Learning Strategy:

Asking and answering questions

Critical Thinking Strategy:

Making associations

Aquí escuchamos:
"Vamos a arreglar el apartamento."

Antes de escuchar

Patrick and his friend are looking at their new apartment and deciding where they are going to put their furniture. Look at the following questions and identify a few things you expect to hear during Patrick's conversation with his friend.

START

/-/-/-/-/-/-/-/-/-/-/-/

Learning Strategy:

Previewing

Después de escuchar

1. ¿Qué hacen?
2. ¿Qué ponen en la cocina?
3. ¿Quién sabe cocinar?
4. ¿Cómo arreglan *(arrange)* la sala de estar?

5. ¿Qué deciden hacer al terminar?

¡Adelante!

EJERCICIO ORAL

//-/-//-/-//-/-//-/-//-/
Cooperative Learning

Learning Strategies:

Negotiating, describing

Critical Thinking Strategies:

Creating a floor plan, making associations, comparing and contrasting

H. ¡Vamos a arreglar el apartamento!   Using the furniture names you have learned, work with several classmates to create a floor plan for an apartment and decide how you're going to arrange your furniture. When your group has finished, compare your arrangement with that of another group. Use the present tense of **poner** when you make your plans. (**Pongo las dos camas en el segundo dormitorio.**) Then use the *preterite* to explain to the other group what you did. (**Pusimos las dos camas en el segundo dormitorio.**)

EJERCICIO ESCRITO

I. Mi apartamento ideal   Write a description of your dream apartment. Tell what furniture is in at least four of the rooms. Place a minimum of twelve pieces of furniture.

Vocabulario

Temas y contextos

Los anuncios en el periódico para una casa o un apartamento

aire acondicionado
(completamente) amueblado(a)
la cocina
el comedor
el dormitorio
el estacionamiento

el garaje (para dos coches)
el jardín
la sala de estar
la terraza
vacío(a)

La cocina y los muebles

las cortinas
el cuadro
la cuchara
el cuchillo
la estufa
el horno (de microondas)
el plato

el refrigerador
la servilleta
el sofá
la taza
el tenedor
el tostador
el vaso

Vocabulario general

Sustantivos

el alquiler
el periódico
el plan
la ventana

Verbos

arreglar
cocinar
decir
poner

Adjetivos

increíble

Otras palabras y expresiones

¿Cómo se dice… ?
decir que sí (no)
m² (metros cuadrados)
para decir la verdad
¿Qué dijiste?
querer decir

Lectura CULTURAL

MACHU PICCHU

Los jardines en terrazas de Machu Picchu

Antes de leer

1. Look at the photos that accompany this reading. What do you think this place is?
2. Where do you think this place is? Who do you think lived there?
3. Are you familiar with the major indigenous civilizations that existed in the Americas long before the arrival of the Spaniards? Which ones do you know about?
4. Look at the title. Have you ever heard of this place?

Guía para la lectura

A. Read the first paragraph and answer the following questions.

1. ¿En qué país está Machu Picchu?
2. ¿Quién construyó esta ciudad?
3. ¿Por qué era tan importante Cuzco?
4. ¿En qué montañas está Machu Picchu?

B. Now finish the passage and answer the following questions.

1. ¿Por qué fue difícil encontrar esta ciudad?
2. ¿Quién era Hiram Bingham y por qué es importante?

Machu Picchu

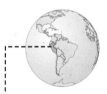

En un lugar de privilegiada belleza y difícil accesibilidad de los Andes peruanos, se levantan las ruinas de Machu Picchu. En tiempos antiguos, la ciudad fue ciudad-fortaleza de los incas. Hoy es uno de los principales atractivos turísticos del Perú. Los restos arqueológicos están situados en una de las zonas más elevadas de los Andes, muy cerca de Cuzco, la antigua capital del imperio inca. Machu Picchu fue construida en un altiplano situado a unos 2.400 metros de altitud.

En cierto momento fue abandonada por sus antiguos pobladores y quedó cubierta por la vegetación durante siglos. Aunque los habitantes de la región creían en la mítica existencia de esta ciudad nadie la podía encontrar. Es que las ruinas estaban muy aisladas y eran accesibles a través de un camino muy difícil y montañoso. En el año 1911 una expedición encabezada por el profesor Hiram Bingham, de la Universidad de Yale, por fin encontró esta ciudad maravillosa.

Aqui leemos

Reading Strategies:

Read first for main ideas, then for details.
Use titles, subtitles, and words that stand out as clues to the topic or main idea.
Pay attention to the contexts of words you are guessing.

Estrategia para la lectura

As you know, most of the time, you do not need to understand every word in a reading. It is more important to figure out the main idea, then go on to the details, since you look for details only when you need them. Main ideas are usually given in the titles or subtitles and in the first (and sometimes the last) sentence or paragraph. You should concentrate on these parts of a reading first. When you need to guess the meaning of a word, remember that surrounding context is extremely important, especially for false cognates. Be sure the guess you make fits the context.

Antes de leer

Here are some ads for vacation chalets in Spain. Before reading them, answer these questions.

>> **W**hat kind of information is typically included in house ads?

>> **W**hat information is usually highlighted?

>> **W**hat are some words you know are used in real estate ads?

Read the ads carefully, noticing what they have in common. Then go on to the **Actividades.**

Actividades

A. Based on the way the ads here and on page 201 highlight different words, what do you think the person who placed the ads most wants to stress? Choose two of the following features.

1. amount of space in the chalet
2. name of development or neighborhood where chalet is located
3. price of chalet
4. description of individual rooms
5. lot size

B. These words are cognates. Try to figure out their meanings from context as well as by thinking of the English words they resemble.

1. chimenea
2. parcelas
3. estudio
4. fase

These words are not cognates. Use context and background knowledge to guess what they mean.

5. sala de juegos
6. aseo
7. bodega
8. entrada

These words are false cognates. You will have to depend completely on context and your background knowledge to help you guess them. Here's a hint: Like **entrada**, these words have to do with the way people pay for houses.

9. facilidades
10. resto

C. Use the vocabulary you learned in this unit to help you answer the following questions.

1. How many bedrooms will you have at **Los Juncos**?
2. Which chalets are on more than one floor?
3. Which ad advertises a separate dining room?
4. Do all the chalets have a double garage?

D. Using these ads as models, design an ad for a house in your region of the country.

Ya llegamos

Actividades orales

A. Una habitación de hotel You and your family are checking into a hotel. With a partner who will play the clerk, enact the following situation.

1. Greet the desk clerk.
2. Tell him or her you have reservations for two rooms for five nights.
3. You want two rooms with bathrooms.
4. Say you want the first floor. You don't like elevators.
5. Ask how much the rooms cost.
6. Ask if they take traveler's checks.
7. Thank the desk clerk and say good-bye.

B. Adiós... Hasta luego. You've just spent some time at the home of some Spanish friends and are about to return home. Thank your friends for everything they did for you, ask them to visit you in the United States, tell them you plan to return to Spain next summer, and say good-bye. Work with a partner.

Cooperative Learning

Learning Strategies:

Describing, negotiating

Critical Thinking Strategy:

Prioritizing

C. Yo busco un apartamento. You have gone to an apartment rental office in Spain to rent an apartment for you and your friend during your semester-long stay. With a partner who will play the role of the rental agent, negotiate the following.

Rental Agent	**Client**
1. Greet the new client.	1. Return the greeting.
2. Ask how you can help him or her.	2. Say you want an apartment with two bedrooms.
3. Ask how many rooms are wanted.	3. Say you want a living room and a small dining room.
4. Ask what is wanted in the kitchen.	4. Say you need a kitchen equipped with a refrigerator and stove, etc.
5. Ask what floor is preferred and if an elevator is needed.	5. Say you want to live several stories off the street level so it will be quieter. You want to have an elevator.
6. Ask what special amenities are desired.	6. Say you prefer an apartment with a swimming pool.
7. What part of town is preferred?	7. You prefer to live downtown.

The rental agent should decide on one element on the client's list that cannot be provided, and the client should decide on two elements he or she cannot give up. An agreement then should be negotiated with an acceptable price.

Actividades escritas

D. Muchas gracias Write a thank-you note to someone you visited recently.

E. Un hotel en España Write a postcard describing the hotel you are staying in on your vacation in Spain. Use the *Michelin Guide* descriptions on pages 142 and 149 for inspiration.

F. Una carta You've just moved into an apartment. Write a letter to your Spanish family describing the apartment and your furniture.

Conexión

Los inmigrantes en los Estados Unidos

AL EMPEZAR

ancestors
native Northamericans
Because of
roots

Casi todos los norteamericanos tienen **antepasados** que salieron de otros países para vivir en los Estados Unidos. Hace quinientos años, sólo los **indígenas norteamericanos** vivieron en este continente. **A causa de** la inmigración, somos un país de personas con diversas **raíces** étnicas y culturales.

ACTIVIDAD A

Abajo hay una lista de las regiones principales del mundo. ¿Cuáles regiones representan el origen de tus antepasados?

- África
- Asia
- Australia y las islas del Pacífico
- Europa
- Norteamérica (los indígenas)
- Latinoamérica

La tabla en la página 205 tiene los principales grupos étnicos que salieron para los Estados Unidos. ¿Cuántos de estos nombres reconoces? ¿Tienes antepasados que llegaron con uno de estos grupos?

ACTIVIDAD B

Primero, mira el esquema en la página 205. Después, contesta las preguntas.

1. ¿Cuáles grupos de inmigrantes llegaron a los Estados Unidos antes de 1820?
2. ¿Cuáles grupos de inmigrantes llegaron recientemente?
3. ¿Quiénes llegaron primero, los africanos o los alemanes? ¿los cubanos o los polacos? ¿los irlandeses o los ingleses?
4. ¿Durante cuantos años llegó el grupo principal de judíos?
5. ¿Cuántos italianos llegaron entre 1880 y 1930?
6. ¿Hace cuánto tiempo que llegó el primer grupo de mexicanos?
7. ¿Con cuáles grupos llegaron tus antepasados?

con la sociología

GRUPOS DE INMIGRANTES PRINCIPALES EN LOS ESTADOS UNIDOS

¿Quiénes llegaron?	¿Cuándo?	¿Cuántos?	¿Quiénes llegaron?	¿Cuándo?	¿Cuántos?
africanos	1700-1810	400.000	ingleses, franceses y escoceses	1700-1810	500.000
alemanes	1840-1890	4 millones			
austriacos, húngaros, checos y eslovacos	1880-1930	4 millones	irlandeses	1840-1860	1,5 millones
			italianos	1880-1930	4,5 millones
chinos, coreanos y filipinos	1960-1990	1 millón	judíos de Europa oriental	1880-1930	2,5 millones
cubanos	1960-1990	700.000	mexicanos	1910-1990	3 millones
daneses, noruegos y suecos	1870-1910	1,5 millones	polacos	1880-1930	1 millón
dominicanos, haitianos y jamaiquinos	1970-1990	900.000	vietnamitas	1970-1990	500.000

Source: World Book Encylcopedia, Vol. "I", p. 82, 1994.

ACTIVIDAD C

Work with a partner to put the following immigrant groups in order according to when they arrived in the United States. You will need to refer to the immigration table to complete this activity. One person should cover the table and ask questions, while the other should look at the table and provide the necessary information.

Modelo: **Estudiante 1**: *¿Quiénes llegaron hace doscientos años?*
Estudiante 2: *Los ingleses llegaron hace doscientos años.*

africanos	chinos	cubanos	mexicanos	polacos
judíos	irlandeses	alemanes	ingleses	

LLEGARON...

... hace 200 años	... hace 150 años	... hace 100 años	... hace 30 años

¿Qué ves?

>> ¿Dónde está y qué hace la gente que se ve en cada foto?

>> ¿Crees que hacen lo mismo todos los días? ¿Por qué?

>> ¿Cuáles de las fotos muestran la vida diaria? ¿Cómo sabes?

OBJECTIVES

IN THIS UNIT YOU WILL LEARN:
- **T**o talk about your daily routine;
- **T**o organize weekend activities;
- **T**o discuss vacation plans.

Capítulo siete: ¿Qué haces de costumbre?

Primera etapa: Una mañana en la casa de Cristina Gallegos
Segunda etapa: Una tarde con Enrique Castillo
Tercera etapa: Una noche en la casa de Marilú Méndez

Capítulo ocho: ¿Qué haces este fin de semana?

Primera etapa: La revista *Cromos*
Segunda etapa: Te invito a una fiesta

Capítulo nueve: ¿Cuándo son las vacaciones?

Primera etapa: Las vacaciones con la familia
Segunda etapa: Una visita a un parque nacional

Nuestro día

207

¿QUÉ HACES DE COSTUMBRE?

La calle de la Ronda es una calle típica de una sección de Quito, la capital de Ecuador.

Objectives:

>>> **T**alking about daily routines

>>> **O**rganizing weekend activities

>>> **D**iscussing vacation plans

Strategies:

>>> **R**eporting based on personal information

>>> **T**aking notes in a chart

>>> **C**omparing and contrasting

PRIMERA ETAPA

Preparación

›› **W**hat do you usually do on weekdays? on weekends?

›› **W**hen and with whom do you talk about your daily activities?

›› **H**ow is a typical day different from an extraordinary one?

Una mañana en la casa de Cristina Gallegos

Me levanto a las 7:20 y me desayuno. Siempre me sirvo un chocolate bien caliente y luego me preparo para ir a la escuela. Esto tarda tres cuartos de hora, más o menos. Salgo para la escuela a las 8:10. Voy a pie porque el autobús no va directamente a la escuela. Llego en un poco menos de 20 minutos. Generalmente mis clases comienzan a las 8:30. Casi siempre llego a tiempo.

Por lo general, los fines de semana comienzan para mí el viernes después de la escuela, cuando voy al centro con mis amigos. Allí charlamos, cenamos y vamos al cine o a una fiesta. Los sábados y domingos no me levanto muy temprano por la mañana —me quedo en cama hasta las 10. Después me desayuno con mis padres.

Me levanto: I get up / *me desayuno:* I eat breakfast / *me sirvo:* I prepare / *caliente:* warm / *me preparo:* I get ready / *Casi:* Almost / *charlamos:* we chat / *me quedo:* I stay

209

¡Aquí te toca a ti!

A. ¿Verdadero o falso?
Basándote en la descripción de Cristina en la página 209, indica si los siguientes comentarios son verdaderos (V) o falsos (F). Si es falso, di *(say)* por qué.

1. Cristina se levanta muy temprano todas las mañanas.
2. Se queda en cama tarde los sábados y los domingos.
3. Se desayuna, después se prepara para ir a la escuela.
4. Se prepara para ir a la escuela en menos de una hora.
5. Vive cerca de la escuela.
6. Toma el autobús para llegar allí.
7. Su primera clase es a las 8:30.
8. Los fines de semana de Cristina son parecidos a *(are similar to)* los fines de semana norteamericanos.

COMENTARIOS CULTURALES

Actitudes hacia el tiempo

The word **mañana** means both *morning* and *tomorrow,* but is also commonly used in Spanish-speaking cultures to mean at some indefinite future time, rather than specifically the next morning or the next day, as might be assumed. It is also important to understand that references to **la mañana, la tarde,** and **la noche** are often much broader in meaning than they are in English. There is a different attitude on the part of Spanish speakers regarding the amount of time in which they allow themselves and other people to do things.

When used specifically, **la mañana** is viewed as any time before noon. After that, **la tarde** can go on into what is considered "evening" to a person from an English-speaking culture.

La noche begins after 8:00 or 9:00 p.m. or thereabouts. There is not a big concern with dividing the day into precise, inflexible units of time.

This is good to know because it also means that people in Spanish-speaking cultures often function according to a general time range when it comes to social occasions. It is perfectly acceptable, and even expected, for example, for someone to agree to meet at 7:00 and then arrive 30–45 minutes after that. This is not viewed as rude behavior, but rather as dealing in a kind of "comfort zone" in which everyone is assumed to live. When it comes to business or medical appointments, however, sticking to a precise hour is understood to be the agreement.

The present tense of reflexive verbs

Me levanto temprano.	*I get up* early.
Mi amiga Isabel **se levanta** temprano también.	My friend Isabel *gets up* early, too.
Nos llamamos por teléfono todas las mañanas.	*We call each other* on the telephone every morning.

Reflexive verbs can be used to express two different meanings:

1. an action that reflects back on the subject

Yo me lavo.	*I wash (myself).*
Ella se levanta.	*She gets up.* (Literally, *she gets herself up.*)

2. an action in which two or more subjects interact

Nosotras nos reunimos por la tarde.	*We get together* in the afternoon.
Ellas se miran.	*They look at each other.*

In either case, the subject (noun or pronoun) is accompanied by a corresponding reflexive pronoun (**me, te, se, nos, os, se**).

---

bañarse (to bathe)

yo	**me baño**	nosotros(as)	**nos bañamos**
tú	**te bañas**	vosotros(as)	**os bañáis**
él		ellos	
ella	**se baña**	ellas	**se bañan**
Ud.		Uds.	

To express that the subject does something to himself/herself/themselves, the reflexive pronoun must agree with the subject of the verb with which it is used. When the verb is conjugated, the pronoun usually precedes it; with an infinitive, the pronoun is normally attached to it.

Yo **me levanto** temprano todos los días.
Yo quiero **levantarme** temprano mañana.

Here is a list of some frequently used reflexive verbs. (The pronoun **se** attached to an infinitive means that the verb is reflexive.)

acostarse (ue)	*to go to bed*
afeitarse	*to shave*
cepillarse (el pelo, los dientes)	*to brush (one's hair, teeth)*
darse prisa	*to hurry up*
desayunarse	*to eat breakfast*
despertarse (ie)	*to wake up*
divertirse (ie, i)	*to have a good time*
dormirse (ue, u)	*to fall asleep*
ducharse	*to take a shower*
lavarse (las manos, el pelo, los dientes)	*to wash (one's hands, hair; to brush one's teeth)*
maquillarse	*to put on makeup*
peinarse	*to comb one's hair*
ponerse	*to put on*
quedarse	*to stay, to remain*
sentarse (ie)	*to sit down*
vestirse (i, i)	*to get dressed*

Aquí practicamos

B. Usa la información entre paréntesis para crear oraciones nuevas.

1. *Yo* me despierto a las nueve. (Juana / nosotros / tú / tus amigos / vosotros)
2. *Él* se viste antes de desayunarse. (María y Carlos / yo / Uds. / ella / tú)
3. *Ellas* se llaman mucho por teléfono. (Uds. / mis hermanas / nosotros / ellos)
4. *Ud.* se ducha después de levantarse. (yo / Uds. / Marta / ellos / tú / vosotras)
5. *Tú* te acuestas muy temprano. (nosotros / él / mis padres / Carlos y tú / ella)

C. Pedro o Ana María y yo   Compare your activities with those, on page 213, of Pedro (if you are male) or those of Ana María (if you are female).

Los muchachos

 Pedro se despierta a las siete.
Yo me despierto a las siete menos cuarto.

1. Pedro se queda en cama por media hora y se levanta a las siete y media.
2. Pedro no se baña por la mañana de costumbre.
3. Pedro se lava los dientes una vez al día.
4. Pedro se afeita de vez en cuando.

Las muchachas

 Ana María se despierta a las siete.
Yo me despierto a las seis y media.

1. Ana María se queda en cama por un cuarto de hora.
2. Ana María se levanta a las siete y cuarto.
3. Ana María se baña todas las mañanas.
4. Ana María se cepilla el pelo y se maquilla.

D. *Una familia*   Tu compañero(a) describe la rutina diaria de su familia. Tú le haces algunas preguntas usando la información entre paréntesis.

Modelos: Mi madre se baña todas las mañanas. (cepillarse el pelo)
¿Se cepilla el pelo también?

Mi padre siempre se queda en cama. (a qué hora / levantarse)
¿A qué hora se levanta?

1. Mi hermano se despierta a las seis. (a qué hora / levantarse)
2. Yo no me quedo en cama por la mañana. (por qué / levantarse inmediatamente)
3. Mi hermana se cepilla el pelo todas las mañanas. (maquillarse)
4. Yo me baño todas las mañanas. (lavarse el pelo)
5. Mi padre se baña, se viste y sale de la casa. (cuándo / afeitarse)
6. Yo me levanto, me baño y me desayuno. (cuándo / vestirse)

E. *¿Y tú?*   You and two of your friends are discussing the morning routines of your families. First, name the members of your family. Then use the suggested verbs to tell something about the members of your family and to ask your partners about theirs. Follow the model.

Modelo: despertarse muy temprano
Estudiante A: *Mi padre se despierta muy temprano.*
Estudiante B (a Estudiante C):   *¿Tu padre se despierta muy temprano también?*
Estudiante C: *Sí, se despierta muy temprano también.* o:
No, de costumbre se despierta a las nueve.

1. despertarse
2. levantarse antes de… (la hora)
3. quedarse en cama hasta… (la hora)
4. cepillarse / lavarse los dientes… veces por día
5. ducharse todas las mañanas
6. afeitarse todos los días / a veces
7. maquillarse todos los días / a veces
8. vestirse antes / después del desayuno

Learning Strategy:
Reporting based on personal information

Critical Thinking Strategy:
Comparing and contrasting

Learning Strategy:
Asking questions

Learning Strategies:
Reporting based on personal information, asking questions

213

Aquí escuchamos:
"Una mañana en casa de Juan Manuel y Cecilia"

Antes de escuchar

Juan Manuel, 18, and Cecilia, 14, are brother and sister. Both are students at the **Escuela Simón Bolívar.** For each of them every morning is the same. What do you typically do each morning? Look at the following questions in order to help you listen for the details of Juan Manuel's and Cecilia's schedule.

START

Después de escuchar

1. ¿Qué dice Juan Manuel que Cecilia hace por las mañanas?
2. ¿Qué hace Juan Manuel cuando se despierta?
3. ¿A qué hora dice Cecilia que se levanta su hermano?
4. ¿Qué no tiene tiempo de hacer Juan Manuel?
5. ¿Siempre se desayunan los hermanos?

¡Aquí te toca a ti!

F. En casa de Victoria Mornings at Victoria's house are very different from those at Juan Manuel's and Cecilia's. Based on the drawings below and at the top of page 215, describe what Victoria and her brother Miguel do in the morning. Use the following verbs and expressions: **despertarse, levantarse, quedarse en cama, ducharse, lavarse, cepillarse, maquillarse, vestirse, peinarse, desayunarse, irse.**

Miguel

Victoria

G. ¿Y tú?   Now describe your own morning activities. Talk about the same topics as mentioned in the conversation with Juan Manuel and Cecilia, but fit the information to your personal situation.

> *Modelo:*   *De costumbre, yo me despierto a las 6:30…*

¡Adelante!

EJERCICIO ORAL

H. Intercambio   Conversa con un(a) compañero(a) usando las siguientes preguntas.

1. ¿A qué hora se levantan en tu casa?
2. ¿Quién se levanta primero?
3. ¿Quién se ducha?
4. ¿Quién se lava el pelo por la mañana?

EJERCICIO ESCRITO

I. Una mañana típica   Your family has registered to host an exchange student from a Spanish-speaking country. In preparation for the visit, the student has written you asking for an idea of your family's daily routine.

Write a letter to him or her. (1) Give the names of your family members with a brief description of each. (2) Describe the early morning routine of your family, (3) commenting on specific times when certain family members do certain things. In the next paragraph, (4) tell where everyone goes during the day and (5) two facts about each one's day. In the final paragraph, describe the family's evening at home, (6) telling what you do together and (7) what you do individually, including preparation for bed and what time you go to sleep. Don't forget to (8) use appropriate letter format with date, salutation, and closing.

SEGUNDA ETAPA

Preparación

>> **W**hat is a typical afternoon like for you?

>> **W**hat do you do on Fridays after school that you don't do on other days of the week?

Una tarde con Enrique Castillo

Las clases comienzan a las 9:00 y duran 55 minutos. Los lunes, mi primera clase es el latín. Después, tengo una hora de español y una hora de francés. ¡A veces no sé qué lengua estudio!

Al mediodía tengo una hora para comer: de las 12:00 hasta la 1:00. Almuerzo en la cafetería de la escuela y hablo con mis amigos. Después del almuerzo, tengo una hora libre (para hacer la tarea) o salgo de la escuela para dar un paseo con mis compañeros.

Las clases comienzan de nuevo a las 2:00. Por la tarde, tengo ganas de echar una siesta, pero no puedo porque tengo una hora de historia y geografía, luego siguen las clases con una hora de matemáticas, luego una hora de física y química. ¡Es mucho! Después de las clases estoy cansado. Siempre me quedo un buen rato en frente de la escuela para charlar con mis amigos. Luego regreso a casa. Llego en muy poco tiempo porque vivo cerca de la escuela.

Esta tarde sólo es un ejemplo, porque tengo un horario diferente para cada día de la semana. Por ejemplo, los martes, comienzo a las 8:30, almuerzo de las 11:30 a las 12:30 y termino a las cuatro. Y los cursos mismos son diferentes: estudio también inglés y ciencias naturales, y tengo dos horas de deportes por semana.

duran: last / *tarea:* homework / *de nuevo:* again / *siguen (seguir):* continue / *un buen rato:* a good while / *sólo:* only / *ejemplo:* example / *mismos:* themselves

¡Aquí te toca a ti!

A. *Los cursos de Enrique* Here are some of the courses offered in **escuelas secundarias** or **colegios** in Spanish-speaking countries. Indicate which courses are part of the **programa** Enrique just described on page 216 and which are not.

el español
el alemán
el inglés
el francés
el griego *(Greek)*
el latín
las matemáticas

la física
la química
las ciencias naturales
   (la biología, la geología)
la educación física
la historia

la geografía
la economía
la música (instrumento,
   canto, baile)
las artes plásticas
   (pintura, escultura)

B. *Enrique y tú* Compare your school day with the one Enrique describes. For each statement Enrique makes, either say that your situation is similar **(Para mí, es lo mismo...)** or explain how it is different **(Para mí, es diferente...).** Follow the model.

> **Modelo:** Generalmente, mis clases comienzan a las 9:30.
> *Para mí, es diferente. Mis clases comienzan a las 8:45.*

1. Las clases en mi escuela duran 55 minutos.
2. Los lunes por la mañana tengo tres clases.
3. En nuestra escuela tenemos una hora y media para comer.
4. Yo almuerzo en la cafetería de la escuela.
5. Después de almorzar, salgo de la escuela para dar un paseo con mis amigos.
6. Las clases terminan a las tres de la tarde.
7. Después de las clases, me quedo un buen rato en frente de la escuela.
8. Siempre llego a casa en cinco minutos porque vivo muy cerca de la escuela.
9. Tomo cursos de español, inglés, francés, latín, historia, geografía, física, química, biología, geología y matemáticas.

Learning Strategy:

Identifying

Critical Thinking Strategy:

Comparing and contrasting

C. *No es verdad...* Indicate that the statements on page 218 are incorrect. For at least three items, provide more accurate statements based on the drawings. Follow the model.

Learning Strategy:

Reporting based on visual information

 Modelos: Pablo se levanta antes de las siete. *No es verdad. No se levanta antes de las siete. Se levanta a las ocho y media.*

Yo me levanto muy temprano. *No es verdad. Tú no te levantas muy temprano. Te levantas después de las diez.*

1. Jorge se lava los dientes una vez al día.

2. Consuelo y su hermano se dan prisa para ir a la escuela.

3. Yo me afeito todas las mañanas.

4. Juana se viste antes de desayunarse.

5. Después de las clases, nos gusta dar un paseo por el parque.

Repaso

Learning Strategy:

Giving personal information

D. ¿Qué hago y qué no hago?   Para cada actividad en la página 219, indica si es verdad para ti o no. Sigue el modelo.

 **Modelo:**   despertarse muy temprano
Yo me despierto muy temprano.   o:
Yo no me despierto muy temprano.

Actividades: despertarse muy temprano / levantarse inmediatamente / quedarse en cama / ducharse por la mañana / lavarse el pelo todos los días / afeitarse / maquillarse / vestirse rápidamente / desayunarse antes de ir a la escuela / salir para la escuela antes de las siete y media / darse prisa para llegar a tiempo / cepillarse los dientes después de la comida

E.   *¡Dime!* (Tell me!)   Habla con un(a) compañero(a) de clase sobre su rutina diaria. Usa la información entre paréntesis.

Learning Strategy:

Requesting and giving personal information

1. ¿A qué hora… ? (levantarse durante la semana / levantarse el sábado por la mañana / levantarse en el verano)
2. ¿Cuántas veces al día (a la semana)… ? (lavarse los dientes / lavarse el pelo / ducharse)

ESTRUCTURA

Ud. and Uds. command forms of reflexive verbs

Levántese Ud. ahora mismo, por favor.	*Get up* right now, please.
Levántense Uds. antes de las 10:00, hijos.	*Get up (all of you)* before 10:00, children.
Póngase la camisa azul.	*Put on* the blue shirt.
Pónganse los zapatos, niños.	*Put on* your shoes, kids.
No **se duerma** en clase.	Don't *fall asleep* in class.
No **se duerman** aquí.	Don't *(all of you) fall asleep* here.

Reflexive verbs form their command forms the same way that other infinitives do. The only difference is that command forms for reflexive verbs must also include reflexive pronouns.

219

To form the **usted** affirmative formal command of reflexive **-ar** verbs, add **-e** to the stem of the **yo** form of the verb in the present tense. For **-er** and **-ir** verbs, add **-a** to the stem of the **yo** form of the verb. Then attach the reflexive pronoun **se** to this command form.

yo qued**o**	qued-	qued**e**	qu**é**d**ese**
yo pong**o**	pong-	pong**a**	p**ó**ng**ase**
yo duerm**o**	duerm-	duerm**a**	du**é**rm**ase**

The negative formal command is formed the same way, except that the reflexive pronoun **se** is used *before* the command form. Notice that **no** is placed *before* the reflexive pronoun.

yo qued**o**	qued-	qued**e**	**no se** qued**e**
yo pong**o**	pong-	pong**a**	**no se** pong**a**
yo duerm**o**	duerm-	duerm**a**	**no se** duerm**a**

The plural formal affirmative and negative command forms add **-n** to the singular command forms. The reflexive pronoun **se** is positioned the same as it is in each singular form.

yo qued**o**	qued-	qued**e**	qu**é**d**ense**
			no se qued**en**

Note that a written accent appears on the third syllable from the end of all command forms when the reflexive pronoun is attached. This indicates that the original stress remains despite the changes to the word.

quédese   **qué**dense   **pón**gase   **pón**ganse   **duér**mase   **duér**manse

Aquí practicamos

F. ¡Órdenes, órdenes! (Orders, orders!)   Using a reflexive verb, a classmate will ask you if he or she or everyone should do something. You respond by using the same verb in the appropriate **Ud.** or **Uds.** affirmative command forms. Follow the models.

 Modelos: ¿Me quedo aquí?
Sí, quédese aquí.

¿Nos lavamos las manos?
Sí, lávense las manos.

1. ¿Me levanto temprano?
2. ¿Me baño ahora?
3. ¿Nos sentamos aquí?
4. ¿Me lavo los dientes?
5. ¿Nos llamamos por teléfono?
6. ¿Me peino antes de salir?
7. ¿Me maquillo para la fiesta?
8. ¿Me pongo el abrigo?
9. ¿Nos acostamos a las 7:00?
10. ¿Nos divertimos con la música?

G. ¡No, no, no y tres veces que no!
This time, respond to questions asked by your classmate by using the appropriate **Ud.** or **Uds.** *negative* command forms of the reflexive verbs. Follow the models.

> **Modelos:**   ¿Me quedo aquí?
> *¡No, no, no! No se quede aquí.*
>
> ¿Nos levantamos tarde?
> *¡No, no, no! No se levanten tarde.*

1. ¿Me siento en la mesa?
2. ¿Nos ponemos tres suéteres?
3. ¿Me afeito en la cocina?
4. ¿Me cepillo los dientes con jabón *(soap)*?
5. ¿Nos acostamos a la una?
6. ¿Me divierto con el coche nuevo de papá?
7. ¿Me duermo en la clase de español?
8. ¿Nos bañamos a la medianoche?
9. ¿Me afeito en la biblioteca?
10. ¿Me levanto a las 4:00 de la tarde?
11. ¿Me peino en la iglesia?
12. ¿Nos quedamos en tu casa por dos meses sin salir?

H. El (La) director(a)
Pretend you are directing a commercial for personal hygiene products. You must tell the actors exactly what to do or not to do during the filming of scenes typical of a family's routine early in the morning. Give at least six orders, using the **Ud.** and **Uds.** forms of reflexive verbs in affirmative or negative command forms. Suggested verbs to use: **afeitarse, peinarse, sentarse, maquillarse, acostarse, levantarse, cepillarse, lavarse, despertarse, ponerse,** etc. Each actor/actress will act out what the director asks him or her to do.

Learning Strategies:

Organizing, sequencing

Aquí escuchamos:
"La tarde de Juan Manuel y Cecilia"

Antes de escuchar

Juan Manuel and Cecilia talk with their Uncle Pedro about their life in school. Look at the questions on page 222 to help you anticipate what they might tell him about a typical school day.

START

//-/-/-/-/-/-/-/-/-/
Learning Strategy:

Listening for details

Después de escuchar

1. ¿Qué quiere saber el tío Pedro?
2. ¿Van a la escuela juntos Juan Manuel y Cecilia?
3. ¿Qué estudia Juan Manuel?
4. ¿Dónde almuerzan los dos?
5. ¿A qué hora regresa Juan Manuel a casa? ¿y Cecilia?
6. ¿Cómo se llama la escuela?

//-/-/-/-/-/-/-/-/-/
Learning Strategy:

Reading for cultural information

COMENTARIOS
CULTURALES

La cortesía

The use of direct commands is usually avoided in Spanish except in specific instances when the speaker wishes to be quite firm, express a degree of anger or impatience, or is in an "ordering about" or agitated frame of mind. Gentler, more indirect ways of getting people to do things are preferred by most Spanish-speaking people in everyday social situations. For example, **¿Quiere abrir la puerta?** or **¿No me abre la puerta?** are used as kinder alternatives to a direct **Abra la puerta,** even if this affirmative command is used with **por favor.**

In other words, basic courtesy is an important characteristic of the Spanish language as most people around the world speak it. They don't think it is overly polite or "flowery" to use the higher frequency expressions that convey wishes instead of using command forms. In fact, to some Spanish speakers who do not know the English language well, the normal and acceptably frequent use of commands in English often seems brusque and even rude.

¡Aquí te toca a ti!

1. ¿Y tú? With a partner, ask and answer the questions on page 223 about your school routine.

1. ¿A qué hora sales de casa por la mañana?
2. ¿Tu colegio está lejos de tu casa?
3. ¿Cómo vas a la escuela?
4. ¿A qué hora comienzan las clases?
5. ¿Hasta qué hora tienes clases por la mañana?
6. ¿Cuánto tiempo tienes para comer?
7. ¿Dónde almuerzas?
8. ¿A qué hora vuelven a comenzar tus clases por la tarde?
9. ¿A qué hora sales de la escuela?
10. ¿A qué hora regresas de costumbre a casa?

Learning Strategy:

Requesting and giving personal information

EJERCICIO ORAL

J. ¿Tú, no?   Identify five things in Activity D on page 219 that you do *not* do. Then question your classmates until, *for each activity,* you find at least two other people who do not do it either. In order to report back to the class, create a chart of your findings. Follow the model.

Modelo:

NO	Yo	Mi amigo(a)	Mi amigo(a)
1. lavarse el pelo todos los días	X	*Carmen*	*Jaime*
2. maquillarse	X	*Juan*	*Carlos*
3.	X		
4.	X		
5.	X		

Cooperative Learning

Learning Strategies:

Taking notes in a chart, interviewing

EJERICIO ESCRITO

K. Por la tarde...   Write six to eight sentences describing what you normally do in the afternoon. Don't forget to include weekends as well. Make a calendar of the week to illustrate your afternoon activities.

Learning Strategy:

Taking notes on a calendar

TERCERA ETAPA

Preparación

》》 **W**hat do you do in the evening during the week? on weekends?

》》 **W**hat time do you go to bed when you have school the next day?

》》 **W**hat do you like to do on Sunday evenings?

Una noche en la casa de Marilú Méndez

Normalmente mis clases duran hasta las 5:00. Entonces regreso a mi casa. Vivo bastante lejos del colegio. Por eso tomo el autobús. El autobús hace el viaje en 40 minutos, más o menos.

Ya en casa, hago mi tarea para el día siguiente. En mi casa cenamos a eso de las 7:45. Mi madre se encarga de preparar las comidas. Después de la cena, yo quito la mesa y lavo los platos. Después hay más tarea que hacer y tengo que ocuparme de los animales —tengo un gato y un perro. Por lo general, me acuesto a las 10:30. Es un poco aburrido, pero nadie tiene la culpa. ¡Siempre hay tanto que hacer!

Por eso prefiero el fin de semana. Los sábados por la noche voy al centro con mis amigos. Vamos al cine o vamos a bailar. Los domingos por la noche casi siempre miro la televisión porque generalmente hay buenas películas esa noche.

bastante: rather, pretty / *Ya en casa:* Once I'm home / *a eso de:* at about, around / *se encarga de:* she's in charge of / *quito la mesa:* I clear the table / *ocuparme de:* to take care of / *tiene la culpa:* is to blame

¡Aquí te toca a ti!

A. ¿Dónde está Marilú? ¿Qué hace ella?
On the basis of what you have read on page 224, indicate for each day and time where Marilú probably is and what she is doing. Follow the model.

 Modelo: martes a las 15:00
Marilú está en la escuela. Está en clase.

1. martes a las 18:15
2. miércoles a las 20:00
3. jueves a las 21:00
4. viernes a las 23:00
5. sábado a las 21:00
6. domingo a las 21:00

Learning Strategies:

Reading for information, answering questions

B. Una entrevista
Radio Futuro quiere entrevistarte *(interview you)* sobre tu rutina diaria. Contesta las siguientes preguntas.

1. ¿Generalmente, hasta qué hora duran tus clases?
2. ¿Vives cerca del colegio?
3. ¿Cuánto tiempo tarda para regresar a la casa?
4. ¿Qué haces, ya en casa?
5. ¿A qué hora cenan ustedes en tu casa?
6. ¿Quién prepara la comida? ¿Quién quita la mesa? ¿Quién lava los platos?
7. ¿Qué haces los fines de semana?
8. ¿Qué haces los domingos por la noche?

Learning Strategy:

Answering questions based on personal information

Repaso

C. Durante las vacaciones...
During vacations, people want to get away from their daily routines. Use the **Uds.** command form of the verbs suggested to indicate to your friends what they should or should not do when they are on vacation. Follow the model.

 Modelo: *Durante las vacaciones acuéstense tarde y no se levanten temprano.*

Possible verbs: acostarse / despertarse / dormirse / divertirse / levantarse / ducharse / lavarse / vestirse / desayunarse / darse prisa / comer / descansar / estudiar / bailar / dormir

ESTRUCTURA

Tú command form of reflexive verbs

¡Levántate, Marisa! Ya es tarde.	*Get up*, Marisa! It's late.
¡Muévete, por favor!	*Move (yourself)*, please!
¡No **te duermas** otra vez!	Don't *fall asleep* again!
¡No **te acuestes** tan tarde mañana!	Don't *go to bed* so late tomorrow!

The affirmative **tú** command form of most reflexive and nonreflexive verbs, whether they are **-ar, -er,** or **-ir** verbs, is exactly the same as the third person singular of the present indicative tense.

él, ella **habla**	**¡Habla** (tú)!	*Speak!*
él, ella **come**	**¡Come** (tú)!	*Eat!*
él, ella **escribe**	**¡Escribe** (tú)!	*Write!*

When the verb is reflexive, the familiar reflexive pronoun **te** and an accent are added to the command form.

levanta (tú)	**¡Levántate** (tú)!	*Get up!*
duerme (tú)	**¡Duérmete** (tú)!	*Go to sleep!*

The negative **tú** command form of most reflexive and nonreflexive verbs is the same as the **Ud.** command form, except that an **-s** is added to it and **no** goes before the word.

hable Ud. **no** habl**es** (tú)   coma Ud. **no** com**as** (tú)   escriba Ud. **no** escrib**as** (tú)

When the verb is reflexive, the reflexive pronoun **te** is used *before* the verb. Notice that **no** is placed *before* the reflexive pronoun.

no levantes   **no te** levantes (tú)   no duermas   **no te** duermas (tú)

Aquí practicamos

D. Give the affirmative **tú** command form of the following verbs.

> **Modelo:** lavarse
> *¡Lávate!*

1. levantarse
2. ducharse
3. vestirse
4. quedarse
5. acostarse
6. moverse
7. maquillarse
8. dormirse

E. Give the negative **tú** command form of the following verbs.

Modelo: afeitarse
¡No te afeites!

1. peinarse
2. mirarse
3. moverse

4. desayunarse
5. dormirse
6. darse prisa

7. sentarse
8. acostarse

F. **Díle a ella** (Tell her) First tell your friend Ana María to do each of the activities suggested. Then change your mind and go through the list again, telling her *not* to do them. Follow the model.

Modelo: levantarse
¡Ana María, levántate!
¡Ana María, no te levantes!

1. despertarse
2. darse prisa
3. cepillarse los dientes

4. acostarse
5. lavarse el pelo
6. divertirse

7. maquillarse
8. peinarse

G. **Díles a ellos** (Tell them) Tell the small children you are taking care of to do each of the activities suggested. Then go through the list again, telling them *not* to do those things.

Modelo: levantarse
¡Levántense!
¡No se levanten!

1. cepillarse los dientes
2. darse prisa
3. acostarse

4. peinarse
5. dormirse
6. lavarse las manos

7. ducharse
8. despertarse

H. **Diálogos para completar** Complete each mini-conversation with the affirmative or negative command of one of the following: **levantarse, acostarse, darse prisa, lavarse, vestirse, despertarse.**

Modelo: —¡Andrés! ¡Andrés! *¡Despiértate!*
—¿Cómo? ¿Qué pasa?
—Tienes que levantarte para ir a la escuela.

1. —¿Qué hora es, Francisco?
—Son las 9:55, papá.
—¿Cómo? ¿Las 9:55? ¿Por qué estás todavía en la cama? ¡_____!

2. —¡Maricarmen! ¡Maricarmen!
—¿Sí, mamá?
—Vamos a cenar, mi hija. _____ las manos y siéntate.
—Sí, mamá.

Learning Strategies:

Reading for main ideas, selecting appropriate meaning from context

Critical Thinking Strategy:

Making associations

227

3. —¡Carlos! ¡Ya son las 7:30!
   —¿Qué pasa, mamá?
   —¡La película comienza dentro de media hora! ¡_____!

4. —¡Luis! ¡Anita! ¿Qué hacen ustedes?
   —Ehhh, una cosa, mamá.
   —Ya es medianoche. ¡_____, hijos!
   —Un momento más, mamá.

Aquí escuchamos:
"La noche con Juan Manuel y Cecilia"

Antes de escuchar

The parents of Juan Manuel and Cecilia are on a trip. Their aunt and uncle are spending the weekend with them at their house. When Juan Manuel and Cecilia arrive home from school, their Aunt Margarita is waiting for them. What are some of the household tasks you do in the afternoon and evening at your house? Look at the following questions in preparation for listening to their conversation.

START

Learning Strategy:
Listening for details

Después de escuchar

1. ¿Qué trabajo va a hacer Juan Manuel?
2. ¿Quién va a preparar la comida?
3. ¿A qué hora comen Juan Manuel y Cecilia?
4. ¿Quién quita la mesa?
5. Como ya terminó su tarea, ¿qué quiere hacer Juan Manuel para divertirse?
6. ¿A qué hora se acuesta Juan Manuel? ¿y Cecilia?

Learning Strategy:
Requesting and giving personal information

¡Aquí te toca a ti!

1. ¿Y tú? Alternando con otro(a) estudiante, hagan y contesten las preguntas abajo y en la página 229 sobre su rutina en casa.

1. ¿A qué hora regresas del colegio?

2. ¿Cuándo haces tu tarea generalmente?
3. ¿Ayudas *(Do you help)* con los quehaceres *(chores)* de la casa?
4. ¿Quién se encarga de lavar la ropa en tu casa?
5. ¿Quién lava los platos en tu casa?

EJERCICIO ORAL

J. Encuentra a alguien que... (Find someone who . . .) Make a chart like the following one. In the second column (1) fill in the information about how you will ask certain questions of your classmates. (2) Then add the appropriate information about yourself in the third column. (3) When your teacher gives the signal, circulate around the classroom asking questions of your classmates to find out information about their routine and home life. (4) When you find a student with an answer that matches one of your own, enter the person's name in the appropriate cell in the last column. *Note:* you cannot use the same person's name more than once.

<table>
<tr><th colspan="4">¿Qué tenemos en común?</th></tr>
<tr><th></th><th>La pregunta que voy a hacer en español</th><th>Mi información</th><th>Nombre de amigo(a) con quien tengo algo en común</th></tr>
<tr><td>time you get home from school</td><td></td><td></td><td></td></tr>
<tr><td>time you do your homework</td><td></td><td></td><td></td></tr>
<tr><td>time your family has dinner</td><td></td><td></td><td></td></tr>
<tr><td>which household chores you do</td><td></td><td></td><td></td></tr>
</table>

EJERCICIO ESCRITO

K. Un día típico Write a description of a typical day for you. First tell what you usually do on a weekday. Then describe what you do on weekends as well.

229

Vocabulario

Para charlar

Para hablar de las actividades de todos los días

acostarse (ue)
afeitarse
bañarse
cepillarse el pelo,
  los dientes
darse prisa
desayunarse
despertarse (ie)

divertirse (ie, i)
dormirse (ue, u)
ducharse
lavarse (las manos,
  el pelo, los dientes)
levantarse
maquillarse
peinarse

ponerse
prepararse
quedarse en cama
sentarse (ie)
servirse (i, i)
tardarse
vestirse (i, i)

Temas y contextos

Los quehaceres de la casa

encargarse de
lavar los platos

lavar la ropa
ocuparse de

poner la mesa
quitar la mesa

Vocabulario general

Sustantivos

la culpa
un ejemplo
el latín
una tarea

Verbos

comenzar (ie)
charlar
durar
encargarse de

irse
llamarse
mirarse
moverse (ue)

regresar
reunirse

Adjetivos

caliente
conveniente
mismo(a)

Adverbios

bastante
casi
directamente
sólo
ya

Preposiciones

en frente de

Otras palabras y expresiones

a eso de
un buen rato
de nuevo
¡Dense prisa!
los espera
ya en casa

Lectura CULTURAL

ESPAÑA JOVEN

Antes de leer

1. Look at the photo and the title to help you decide what this reading is about.
2. What do you think young teenagers do in Spain in their spare time?
3. What sorts of things do you think they like?
4. How do you think they like to dress in general?
5. Do you think their interests are fairly similar to or very different from yours?

//-//-//-//-//-//-//-//-//

Guía para la lectura

A. Look at the five headings to determine what the content of each section will be. What are they?

B. What sorts of information does the introduction suggest will be covered in the reading?

C. Find out what Spanish young people do in their free time on weekdays and weekends.

D. According to the next paragraph, what do they spend their money on?

E. Read the fourth paragraph and tell what kinds of clothes they wear. What do you think a **pendiente en la oreja** means?

F. Read the last paragraph and point out a problem that they worry about.

España joven

Hoy hay más de tres millones de españoles entre los doce y los dieciséis años de edad. ¿Cómo son estos jóvenes? ¿Qué hacen normalmente? ¿Qué les interesa? ¿Qué les preocupa? La siguiente información viene de entrevistas que se hicieron con varios grupos de estos jóvenes que representan el futuro de España.

Vida diaria

Durante la semana los adolescentes españoles casi no salen. Generalmente dividen su tiempo entre la casa y el colegio. Cuando están en casa, además de estudiar, pasan mucho tiempo hablando por teléfono y escuchando música. Pero los fines de semana nadie se queda en casa. Normalmente todos salen con sus amigos, sobre todo a bailar. A veces van a comer en grupo en un restaurante o café.

Sus gustos

Los jóvenes gastan su dinero en lo que más les apasiona: la música, la ropa de marca y los vídeojuegos que, junto con el "walkman", son sus juguetes favoritos. Van bastante al cine y ven todo tipo de películas.

La ropa

A los chicos les gusta llevar vaqueros y un pendiente en la oreja. Las chicas también llevan vaqueros durante la semana, pero para ir a la discoteca prefieren las faldas cortas o los vestidos largos.

Cómo ven el futuro

A muchos adolescentes les preocupa la crisis económica en su país. Saben que hay mucha gente sin trabajo en España y temen que la situación vaya a afectar su futuro. Muchos opinan que los ecologistas son las únicas personas que se preocupan por salvar el planeta.

Spain

8

¿QUÉ HACES ESTE FIN DE SEMANA?

Buenos Aires es una ciudad importante en la costa atlántica de Argentina. Es la capital, con más de diez millones de habitantes.

Objectives:

>>> **I**ssuing invitations for leisure-time activities

>>> **O**rganizing and coordinating plans for various activities

Strategies:

>>> **R**eading for cultural information

>>> **N**egotiating

>>> **D**etermining preferences

PRIMERA ETAPA

Preparación

》》 **W**hat plans do you have for the weekend?

》》 **D**o you read a particular magazine or a newspaper entertainment section to decide what you are going to do on weekends?

》》 **W**hat kind of information does the newspaper give you about possible activities for the weekend?

Learning Strategies:

Previewing, brainstorming

La revista Cromos

Cromos es una revista popular en Bogotá, Colombia, que se vende cada semana en los quioscos de periódicos. Contiene artículos sobre varios temas, entrevistas con personas interesantes y también información sobre el teatro, el cine y la televisión, entre otras cosas.

TEATRO

El *Teatro Esquina Latina* comienza a partir del 11 de junio, todos los domingos y lunes festivos del resto del año, la programación para niños. Teatros, títeres y marionetas con los grupos más representativos de la región llevan a los niños realizaciones artísticas de alta calidad.

El *Teatro Santa Fe* presenta "Yerma" con Waldo Urrego y Natalia Giraldo en los papeles de los protagonistas. Después de mucho éxito esta temporada, la inmortal obra de Federico García Lorca se despide en dos semanas de los bogotanos para visitar otras ciudades del país. *"Yerma"*, a cargo del grupo Teatral Actores de Colombia y bajo la dirección de Jaime Arturo Gómez. Calle 57 No. 17-13, Tel. 255 05 92.

En el *Auditorio Crisanto Luque,* durante los próximos días, se estará presentando la obra *"Outside Okey"* del grupo Teatro Quimera, dirigida por Carlos Alberto Sánchez. La obra tiene como tema central las relaciones entre el fútbol, la música, el teatro y la filosofía. Se presentará en escena hasta el 17 de junio. Calle 20 No. 9-45.

TELEVISIÓN

viernes 9

Quinceañera (15:00, cadena uno). Beatriz, a causa de un accidente, pierde a su hijo. Por eso entran en discusiones amigos y parientes.

The Monsters (16:30, cadena uno). Lily descubre que la cuenta bancaria de Herman no tiene dinero y decide trabajar en un salón de té para ayudar a la familia.

La naturaleza de las cosas (18:30, cadena tres). El oso polar, estudios científicos sobre su vida y campañas para salvar este animal de la extinción.

TELEVISIÓN

sábado 10

El túnel (20:00, cadena uno). Película basada en la novela del escritor argentino Ernesto Sábato. Un pintor se obsesiona con una tímida mujer casada.

La bella y la bestia (20:30, cadena dos). Muere su padre y Catherine se va "abajo" a vivir con Vincent para siempre.

Cómo casarse con un millonario (22:00, cadena tres). Película. Tres chi-cas deciden, cada una, "pescar" un millonario. Actúan las cómicas y guapas Marilyn Monroe, Lauren Bacall y Betty Grable.

domingo 11

El espíritu de Asia (18:30, cadena tres). Mundo de sombras: El Ganges, sagrada fuente de la primera religión del mundo, el hinduísmo.

Matar o morir (19:30, cadena uno). Vicente Fernández en una película de pasiones y emoción.

Crónica de una muerte anunciada (21:45, cadena dos). Película basada en la novela de Gabriel García Márquez, narra la triste historia de un pequeño pueblo colombiano y su reacción al crimen de Santiago Nassar.

¡Aquí te toca a ti!

A. ¡Dínos! (Tell us!)   Contesta las preguntas sobre *Cromos* en inglés.

1. How many movies are being shown on television over the weekend? On which network(s) *(cadena)* are they presented? What time(s) are they on?
2. Which documentary programs are listed? What are they about? Which one seems to be the most serious?
3. What other programs are mentioned in these listings? What kind are they?
4. Which theater listing mentions what the play is about? Which theater seems to have booked the most successful show? How do you know this?
5. If you had to pick just one of these productions to see, which one would you choose? Why?

Pronunciación: The vowel combination *ei*

The combination **ei** in Spanish is pronounced in one single syllable, similar to the *a* in the English word *date*. Note that in some words, such as **rey** and **mamey,** this sound is spelled **ey**.

Práctica

B. Lee las siguientes palabras en voz alta, pronunciando con cuidado la combinación *ei*.

1. peine
2. veinte
3. reina
4. aceite
5. ley
6. buey
7. afeitar
8. vendéis

235

//-//-//-//-//-//-//-//-//
**Critical Thinking
Strategy:**

*Seeing cause-and-
effect relationships*

Repaso

C. *Los consejos* (Advice)   In each of the following situations, advise the person or people involved to do or not to do each of the actions mentioned. First, give advice to a friend who has a difficult exam tomorrow.

 Modelos: acostarse temprano
¡Acuéstate temprano!

estudiar hasta las tres de la mañana
¡No estudies hasta las tres de la mañana!

1. estudiar hasta las diez de la noche
2. acostarse tarde
3. levantarse temprano
4. desayunarse

Now talk to a friend who is planning to go to a semiformal dance.

5. ducharse primero
6. lavarse el pelo
7. peinarse
8. vestirse elegantemente
9. comer antes de ir al baile

Finally, talk to the *three* children for whom you are babysitting.

10. mirar la televisión
11. cepillarse los dientes
12. acostarse temprano
13. levantarse durante la noche

ESTRUCTURA

Direct object pronouns

—¿El policía mira **mi coche?**   Is the police officer looking at *my car?*
—Sí, el policía **lo** mira.   Yes, he's looking at *it.*

—¿María quiere **la cámara japonesa?**   Does María want the *Japanese camera?*
—Sí, **la** quiere.   Yes, she wants *it.*

—¿Ven **a los muchachos?**   Do they see *the children?*
—No, no **los** ven.   No, they don't see *them.*

—¿Prefiere José **novelas de aventura?**   Does José prefer *adventure novels?*
—Sí, **las** prefiere.   Yes, he prefers *them.*

A direct object is the person or thing that is directly affected by a verb; it tells whom or what is acted upon. In the Spanish sentences you just read, **mi coche, la cámara japonesa, los muchachos,** and **novelas de aventura** are all direct objects.

Whenever possible, speakers take shortcuts by using pronouns. Direct objects can be replaced by direct object pronouns. The pronouns agree with the direct object they stand for in both number (singular and plural) and gender (masculine and feminine).

masculine singular: lo
El niño no ve **mi cuaderno.**   The child doesn't see *my notebook.*
El niño no **lo** ve.   The child doesn't see *it.*

feminine singular: la
Escuchamos **música clásica.**   We listen to *classical music.*
La escuchamos.   We listen to *it.*

masculine plural: los
Despierto **a mis hermanos.**   I wake *my brothers.*
Los despierto.   I wake *them.*

feminine plural: las
No compramos **las entradas.**   We don't buy *the tickets.*
No **las** compramos.   We don't buy *them.*

Aquí practicamos

D. *En pocas palabras*   Shorten each sentence on page 238 by replacing the direct object noun or noun phrase with the corresponding direct object pronoun. Follow the model.

    Ruth llama a Francisco por teléfono.
Ruth lo llama por teléfono.

1. Hago la tarea ahora.
2. Los estudiantes no leen el libro.
3. No como carne.
4. Compramos los cuadernos en la librería.
5. Invitan a las muchachas.
6. Dan una película después de la clase.

E. ¿Sí o no? You and a classmate take turns asking each other the following questions. Answer them briefly and use a direct object pronoun for the noun or phrase provided. Follow the model.

Modelo: ¿Hablas alemán?
Sí, lo hablo.   o: *No, no lo hablo.*

1. ¿Miras la televisión por la noche?
2. ¿Tomas el autobús a la escuela?
3. ¿Tus profesores dan mucha tarea?
4. ¿Practicas deportes mucho?
5. ¿Quién prepara la comida en tu casa?
6. ¿Lees el periódico cuando te desayunas?

Nota gramatical

Position of direct object pronouns

¿El edificio? **Lo** conozco.	The building? I'm familiar with *it.*
¿El número? Es importante saber**lo.**	The number? It's important to know *it.*
¿Las cartas? Puedes poner**las** allí.	The letters? You can put *them* there.
¿Los libros? **Los** quiero comprar ahora.	The books? I want to buy *them* now.

The direct object pronoun is placed immediately *in front of* the conjugated verb.

Leo **la revista.**   I read *the magazine.*
La leo.   I read *it.*

When used with an infinitive, the direct object pronoun is *attached* to it.

Es posible vender **el coche.**   It's possible to sell *the car.*
Es posible vender**lo.**   It's possible to sell *it.*

When a conjugated verb and an infinitive are used together, the direct object pronoun can be placed *either* in front of the conjugated verb or it may be attached to the end of the infinitive. Attaching the pronoun to the infinitive is probably the more common practice.

Prefiero comprar **la cámara.**   I prefer to buy *the camera.*
La prefiero comprar. }   I prefer to buy *it.*
Prefiero comprar**la.**

F. *¡Ya lo hice!* When your mother tells you to do something, you indicate that you have already done it. Follow the model.

> *Modelo:*   ¡Lava los platos!
> *¡Ya los lavé!*

1. ¡Compra el pan!
2. ¡Prepara el desayuno!
3. ¡Come tus vegetales!
4. ¡Quita la mesa!
5. ¡Lava el coche!
6. ¡Termina tu tarea!
7. ¡Escucha mi nuevo disco compacto!
8. ¡Busca mis llaves!

G. *No quiero hacerlo... no voy a hacerlo...* You are in a particularly bad mood one evening. Whenever you are asked if you are going to do what you normally do, you indicate that you don't want to do it and, moreover, you are not going to do it. Follow the model.

> *Modelo:*   preparar la cena
> —*¿Vas a preparar la cena esta noche?*
> —*No, no quiero prepararla esta noche.*
> —*Pero, vas a prepararla de todas maneras* (anyway), *¿no?*
> —*No quiero prepararla y no voy a prepararla.*

1. lavar la ropa
2. ayudar a tu hermano
3. quitar la mesa
4. leer el libro
5. terminar tu tarea
6. mirar la televisión
7. escribir tu composición
8. lavar los platos

Aquí escuchamos:
"¡Vamos a ver la nueva película!"

Learning Strategy:

Previewing

Antes de escuchar

Juan Manuel and Cecilia work hard during the week, so they like to have a good time on weekends. Juan Manuel likes to go to the movies. Look at the following questions before you listen to the conversation he has with his friends Mario and Enrique.

START

Learning Strategy:

Listening for details

Después de escuchar

1. ¿Cuántas personas hablan aquí?
2. ¿Cuál es el problema que tienen?
3. ¿Qué ideas tienen para divertirse?
4. ¿Qué dice Mario de las películas de horror?
5. ¿A qué hora deciden reunirse los amigos?
6. ¿Dónde van a reunirse?

Learning Strategy:

Reading for cultural information

COMENTARIOS CULTURALES

El cine

Going to the movies is a very popular activity for people of all ages and backgrounds in Spanish-speaking countries. Movie theaters abound in the cities and towns and show a variety of films, particularly those that are produced in the U.S. These movies are generally dubbed in Spanish. Newspapers always carry several pages of movie advertisements. In some countries, like Mexico, box-office prices are kept within a certain range by the government so that practically anyone can afford to buy a ticket. Many times the ticket lines wind around the block!

¡Aquí te toca a ti!

H. ¿Qué van a ver?   Using the listings from *Cromos* on pages 234–235, recommend shows for your friends. (1) First, they will tell you what kind of programs, films, or plays they like. (2) Respond with a suggestion. Your friends will then ask you questions about (3) what time a program is on television, (4) where a play is being presented, and (5) which country the show represents. Suggested types of shows: **película (de aventuras, de ciencia-ficción, de terror, policíaca** *[police story]*), **comedia, drama psicológico, obra teatral, programa documental, telenovela,** etc.

Modelo: películas cómicas
—*A mí me gustan las películas cómicas.*
—*Debes ver "Cómo casarse con un millonario".*
—*¿A qué hora la dan* (are they showing it)?
—*A las 10:00 de la noche en el canal tres.*
—*¿Es una película mexicana?*
—*No, es una película norteamericana.*

¡Adelante!

EJERCICIO ORAL

I. ¿Qué hacemos esta noche?   Using the listings from *Cromos* on pages 234–235, make arrangements with another student to watch a program on television or go to a play. Imagine that you are talking on the telephone. Be sure to discuss the kind of program, movie, or play you would like to see, make a selection, and arrange where and when you will meet.

EJERCICIO ESCRITO

J. Más programas de televisión   Write descriptions of two different television programs (real or imagined) in Spanish to be included with the other entries in *Cromos*. Include time, channel, and a few sentences that give an idea of the content of each of the programs.

SEGUNDA ETAPA

Preparación

>> **W**hat kind of information does a written invitation contain?

>> **W**hat are some social events that require an invitation?

Te invito a una fiesta

dentro de: within

aprovechar: to take advantage of / *darles:* to give them / *despedida:* send-off / *desearles:* to wish them

¿Te parece bien?: Does that sound O.K.? / *Cuento contigo:* I'm counting on you. / *Contéstame cuanto antes:* Answer me as soon as possible. / *no les digas nada:* don't say anything to them / *será una sorpresa:* will be a surprise / *No te preocupes:* Don't worry / *traer:* to bring

Querida amiga,

Eduardo y Carmelita salen para los Estados Unidos dentro de quince días. Queremos aprovechar la ocasión para darles una despedida y desearles un buen viaje. Estoy organizando una pequeña fiesta en casa… el viernes, 4 de septiembre, a las 20:30.

¿Te parece bien? Cuento contigo. Contéstame cuanto antes. Y sobre todo… ¡no les digas nada a nuestros invitados de honor! La fiesta será una sorpresa para ellos.

No te preocupes —no debes traer nada. Sólo queremos pasar un rato agradable con los amigos en casa.

Afectuosamente,
Mercedes

Estimada señorita:

  En la ocasión de la quinceañera de nuestra hija Marisol, la familia está organizando una fiesta en nuestra casa, Calle Sur N.º 112, el sábado 17 de julio a las 21:00.

  Nos daría mucho gusto tenerle a usted y a su hermano Carlos entre nosotros esa noche para la celebración.

  Tenga la bondad de responder tan pronto como le sea posible.

  Sin más por ahora, reciba los mejores deseos de,

  Teresa Camacho Del Valle

quinceañera: fifteenth birthday

Nos daría mucho gusto: It would give us great pleasure

Tenga la bondad de responder: Please be kind enough to answer / *como sea posible:* as possible

---

El señor y la señora Rafael Bolaños de la Garza

invitan cordialmente a Rosario Vega Arroyo a disfrutar de

la celebración del segundo aniversario de su boda que

ofrecerán en su residencia el sábado 17 de febrero

a las 20:00   R.S.V.P.

Calle Jardín 87   Tel. 28 03 94

disfrutar de: to enjoy

boda: wedding

ofrecerán: they will offer

¡Aquí te toca a ti!

A. *Las tres invitaciones* Contesta en inglés las preguntas sobre las tres invitaciones en las páginas 242 y 243.

1. Which invitation is the most formal? the least formal? What words and expressions in Spanish support your answer?
2. What is the occasion for each invitation?
3. Except when writing to close friends, Spanish-speakers tend to use formalized expressions in making invitations. Find in Sra. Camacho Del Valle's note the Spanish equivalent of the following expressions:
   a. Dear
   b. for Marisol's fifteenth birthday
   c. R.S.V.P.
   d. Very truly yours
4. In what situations might Americans send similar invitations?

COMENTARIOS CULTURALES

La quinceañera

In most Spanish-speaking countries, it is still a popular tradition to have an extra special birthday party when a girl reaches the age of fifteen. The celebration is called **la quinceañera** and includes all extended family members and many friends. It is the equivalent of the "sweet sixteen" party that marks the beginning of a new phase in the life of a teenager.

Generally, the party includes dinner, music, dancing, and, of course, gifts. It may be a lavish affair held at a family club or a smaller party that takes place in the home. In either case, it is a dress-up occasion that people enjoy attending and celebrating.

Pronunciación: *The vowel combination oi*

The combination **oi** in Spanish is pronounced in one single syllable, similar to the *oi* in the English word *oink*. Note that in the words **voy, doy, hoy, estoy,** and **soy,** among others, the sound is spelled **oy.**

Práctica

B. Lee las siguientes palabras en voz alta, pronunciando con cuidado la combinación *oi.*

1. oigo
2. boina
3. heróico
4. voy
5. doy
6. hoy
7. estoy
8. soy

Repaso

C. *En casa de Raúl y en casa de Graciela*   Raúl, his parents, and his sister lead a very traditional life. Guess who probably does the following household chores in Raúl's family: **su papá, su mamá, su hermano, su hermana,** or **Raúl.** Use a direct object pronoun in your answer.

 Modelo: ¿Quién lava la ropa?
Su mamá (Su hermana) la lava de costumbre.

1. ¿Quién prepara las comidas?
2. ¿Quién quita la mesa?
3. ¿Quién lava los platos?
4. ¿Quién hace los mandados?
5. ¿Quién lava el coche?

Graciela, on the other hand, lives in a nontraditional family. Household chores are not assigned by gender. Guess who did the following chores last week at her house: **su padre, su madre, su hermano,** or **Graciela.** Use a direct object pronoun in your answer. Follow the model.

Modelo: ¿Quién lavó la ropa?
Su padre (Su hermano) la lavó.

6. ¿Quién preparó las comidas?
7. ¿Quién quitó la mesa?
8. ¿Quién lavó los platos?
9. ¿Quién hizo los mandados?
10. ¿Quién lavó el coche?

D. *En tu casa*   Ask a classmate who in his or her house usually takes care of the household chores on page 246. Then ask if that person *is going to do* that chore at the indicated time. Use a direct object pronoun when possible. Follow the models.

Modelo: lavar los platos / esta noche
—*¿Quién lava los platos de costumbre en tu casa?*
—*Mi hermana los lava.*
—*¿Ella va a lavarlos esta noche?*
—*Sí, ella va a lavarlos esta noche.*   o:
—*No, mi padre va a lavarlos esta noche.*

Learning Strategy:

Expressing present and past time

Critical Thinking Strategy:

Making associations

Learning Strategy:

Expressing present and future time

Critical Thinking Strategy:

Making associations

1. preparar la cena / esta noche
2. quitar la mesa / esta noche
3. lavar la ropa / esta semana
4. hacer los mandados / esta semana
5. lavar el coche / este fin de semana

ESTRUCTURA

The immediate future of reflexive verbs

—Mi hermana y yo **nos vamos a levantar** a las seis de la mañana.
My sister and I *are going to get up* at six in the morning.

—**¿Te vas a lavar** el pelo?
Are you going to wash your hair?

—Sí, **voy a lavarme** el pelo.
Yes, *I'm going to wash* my hair.

—Nuestros padres **van a reunirse** en el centro.
Our parents *are going to get together (meet)* in town.

The immediate future of reflexive verbs is formed in the same way as the immediate future of any other verb—that is, with **ir** plus **a** and an infinitive. The reflexive pronoun that accompanies the reflexive verb agrees with the subject of **ir**. This pronoun can be placed immediately before the conjugated form of **ir** or attached to the infinitive.

Aquí practicamos

E. Hoy y mañana   Di lo que tienes que hacer hoy y lo que vas a hacer mañana. Usa una de las sugerencias de cada columna de una manera lógica. Sigue el modelo.

 Modelo: yo   darse prisa   divertirse
Yo tengo que darme prisa hoy pero mañana voy a divertirme.

A	B	C
yo	dormirse	llamarse por teléfono
ustedes	quedarse	reunirse en el centro
mis amigos(as) y yo	ducharse	levantarse
el (la) profesor(a)	prepararse	lavarse el pelo

F. El sábado próximo   Next Saturday is a special day. Consequently, you are not planning to follow your usual weekend routine. Use the first cue to describe what you normally do on Saturday. Then use the cue in parentheses to tell how next Saturday is going to be different.

quedarse en casa (pasearse con los amigos por el campo)
Normalmente me quedo en casa los sábados. Pero el sábado próximo, me voy a pasear con mis amigos por el centro.

1. despertarse tarde (despertarse temprano)
2. quedarse en cama (levantarse inmediatamente)
3. bañarse (ducharse)
4. no lavarse el pelo (lavarse el pelo)
5. vestirse después del desayuno (vestirse antes del desayuno)
6. cepillarse los dientes después del desayuno (no cepillarse los dientes)

G. *El lunes próximo*   On the other hand, next Monday promises to be a perfectly ordinary day. Imagine that you and the other members of your family are going to do what you normally do every Monday. Describe your activities. Follow the model.

Modelo: *El lunes próximo, mi papá y mi mamá van a levantarse como a las 7:00. Mi hermana y yo vamos a quedarnos en cama hasta las 7:30,* etc.

Aquí escuchamos:
"Una fiesta en la casa de Cecilia"

Antes de escuchar

Cecilia wants to give a party. Saturday night is a perfect time because her brother will not be there; he'll be in town. What are some of the things she'll need to think about when organizing the party? Look at the following questions in preparation for the conversation she has with her parents about her plans.

START

Después de escuchar

1. ¿Quién va a organizar la fiesta?
2. ¿Cuántas personas van a ir a la fiesta?
3. ¿Dónde va a ser la fiesta?
4. ¿A qué hora comienza? ¿Cuándo va a terminar?
5. ¿Qué dice Cecilia que van a hacer durante todo este tiempo?

Cooperative Learning

Learning Strategies:

Listing, organizing, negotiating

Critical Thinking Strategy:

Analyzing

¡Aquí te toca a ti!

H. ¿Qué vas a hacer tú?
You and your friends have decided to organize a party. In groups of four, decide how each one of you will participate in the preparations. Using the following list as a starting point, determine all the necessary activities to assure the success of the party. Agree on a list of responsibilities for each member of your group.

> **Modelo:** *Yo voy a preparar una ensalada. ¿Y tú?*

Actividades: comprar la fruta / comprar jugo de fruta / comprar la comida / preparar una ensalada / traer las cintas / traer el estéreo y la grabadora / tocar la guitarra / invitar a los amigos / arreglar la comida / hacer un pastel / lavar los platos

¡Adelante!

Learning Strategy:

Negotiating

EJERCICIO ORAL

I. ¡Organicen una fiesta!
You and a friend decide to organize a party. Decide when and where you will have it. Then talk about the preparations. Share the responsibilities as follows:

You: invite the guests (talk about how many and who to invite) and arrange the location

Your friend: take care of the food (three things to eat and two kinds of beverages) and provide activities

Learning Strategies:

Organizing, writing an invitation

Critical Thinking Strategies:

Imagining, creating

EJERCICIO ESCRITO

J. Una invitación escrita
Write an informal invitation to the members of your Spanish club to a surprise birthday party for an exchange student from Bolivia. Give the important details about time, place, food to be served, and the fact that it is a surprise for the guest of honor. Also indicate some of the activities that are planned, such as a movie, dancing, or other entertainment.

Vocabulario

Para charlar

Para hacer invitaciones

Nos daría mucho gusto…
Tenga la bondad de responder
  tan pronto como sea posible.
Cuento contigo…
Contéstame cuanto antes.

Será una sorpresa; no les digas nada.
¿Por qué no?
Nos vemos a / en…
¿Te parece bien?

Vocabulario general

Sustantivos

una boda
una quinceañera
una respuesta

Verbos

aprovechar
seguir (i, i)
traer

Otras palabras y expresiones

darles la despedida
dentro de
desearles
disfrutar de
Espero que no sea…
Exacto.
No se preocupen.
tal vez

Lectura
CULTURAL

LOS CANALES DE TELEVISIÓN EN ESPAÑA

Antes de leer

1. Look at the reading's photo and the title. What do you think it is about?
2. What does the word **canales** in the title mean?
3. Look at the layout of the reading. Of what does it remind you?
4. What sorts of words do you expect to find in a reading about television?

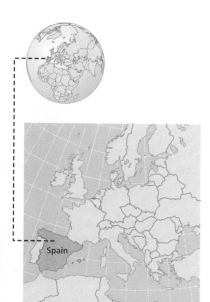

Spain

Guía para la lectura

Learning Strategies:

Scanning, taking notes in a chart, reading for details

A. Now scan the reading and find the following words. According to the context, what do you think they mean?

canales	programa	noticias	caja
cadenas	tele	programación	el mando
transmitiendo	documentales	alboroto	

B. How many "speakers" are there in the passage and what are their names?

C. Make a chart with the following headings. Read the **mini-drama** and fill in the information about each speaker.

Los chicos   Los canales que prefieren   Tipo de programación

Los canales de televisión en España

n el siguiente mini-drama unos jóvenes andaluces hablan sobre los programas de las cadenas nacionales y los de Canal Sur, la cadena regional.

Son las ocho de la noche y está lloviendo, así que Juan, Pedro, Borja y Javier se reúnen en casa de Borja para ver la "tele".

Juan: Vamos a ver qué hay en la "tele". ¡Ah! en Tele 5 ponen ese concurso tan cómico, con esas chicas guapas…

Pedro: No puedo creer que te gusta la Tele 5. ¡Es una cadena tan superficial! A mí me parece que la 2 es la única cadena con un poco de inteligencia.

Javier: No exageres, Pedro. La 2 sólo tiene documentales, noticias y deportes. Puede ser un poco aburrida… Antena 3 es una cadena seria e interesante.

Borja: ¡Que no!, ¡que no! que Canal Plus es la que tiene mejores películas. Tienes que pagar, pero te ofrecen una programación de calidad…

Juan: ¡Dame el mando, que me pierdo mi programa favorito en Tele 5!

Pedro: ¡Sobre mi cadáver! ¡La 2 sí que está bien!

Javier: ¡Antena 3 o me voy!

Borja: Pero Canal Plus está transmitiendo este programa tan interesante…

Todos terminan peleándose por el mando y arman gran alboroto en la casa.

Madre de Borja: ¡Chicos! ¿Por qué no dejáis ya de ver la caja tonta? Acaban de llamar unas amigas para ir al cine…

Borja: Bueno… la verdad es que es un poco tonto el discutir por los canales de la "tele".

Los demás: Pues sí, tienes razón. ¿Y si nos vamos al cine?

Juan: Sí, vamos al Astoria, que tiene "pelis" muy de moda.

Pedro: ¡Ni lo pienses! ¡Yo sólo voy a ver películas de calidad…!

Los demás: ¡Oh no! ¡Otra vez!

¿CUÁNDO SON LAS VACACIONES?

Situada en la costa del Caribe, Cartagena Colombia tiene el clima ideal para navegar a vela.

Objectives:

>>> **T**alking about vacation routines as opposed to normal daily routines

>>> **A**dvising people where to go and not to go for vacation

>>> **D**escribing vacation activities

Strategies:

>>> **L**istening for details

>>> **S**upporting an opinion

>>> **E**valuating

PRIMERA ETAPA

Preparación

>> **W**hat do you do when you are on vacation from school?

>> **W**hat did you do last summer?

>> **W**hat are some of the activities you enjoy most during the summer?

/·/·/·/·/·/·/·/·/·/·/
Learning Strategies:

*Brainstorming,
previewing*

Las vacaciones con la familia

Me llamo Natalia Romero y vivo en Bogotá. Todos los veranos voy de vacaciones con mi familia a Cartagena, una ciudad que está en la costa. En mi familia a todos nos gusta mucho nadar. Además, mi hermano Andrés practica **la navegación a vela.** Tiene un pequeño **velero** y **una tabla vela.** Mi hermana Victoria **se dedica** al **esquí acuático.** Cuando no estoy en la playa, mi deporte **preferido** es **la equitación.** Mi madre y yo **montamos a caballo** en un **centro ecuestre.** Además, nos gusta salir a correr. Por la tarde, cuando ya no hace mucho sol, jugamos al vólibol con Andrés y Victoria. ¿Cómo? No hablé de mi padre. ¡Ah, pues él no es muy atlético! ¡Prefiere leer, descansar y tomar el sol!

sailing / sailboat / sailboard
devotes herself / waterskiing
favorite / horseback riding /
  ride horses /
  equestrian center

253

¡Aquí te toca a ti!

A. La familia de Natalia
Based on Natalia's description of her family vacations on page 253, play the role of each family member and explain what that person does during the summer.

1. su hermano Andrés
2. su madre
3. su hermana Victoria
4. su padre
5. Natalia

Pronunciación: The vowel combination *au*

The combination **au** in Spanish is pronounced in one single syllable, similar to the *ou* of the English word *ouch*.

Práctica

B.
Lee las siguientes palabras en voz alta, pronunciando con cuidado la combinación *au*.

1. aula
2. causa
3. autor
4. auto
5. aunque
6. gaucho
7. pausa
8. jaula

Repaso

//-//-//-//-//-//-//-//
Critical Thinking Strategy:

Seeing cause-and-effect relationships

C. Consecuencias lógicas
Usa verbos reflexivos para decir lo que probablemente van a hacer, o no van a hacer, las siguientes personas en las situaciones que siguen. Sigue el modelo.

 Modelo: Enrique sale con Beatriz. Ella está cansada; está triste.
No van a divertirse.   o:
Van a aburrirse.

1. Son las 6:00 de la mañana. Cecilia se despierta. No tiene clases antes de las 9:00.
2. Son las 8:45 de la mañana. Juan Manuel se despierta. Tiene una clase a las 9:15.
3. Hace buen tiempo. Tenemos dos horas libres *(free)*. Hay un parque muy bonito cerca de la casa.
4. Tienes el pelo sucio *(dirty)*. Vas a salir con tus amigos esta noche.
5. Cecilia tiene mandados que hacer en el centro. Isabel también. Van a ver una película en el Cine Palacio.
6. Cecilia comió muchos dulces y helado. No le gusta ir al dentista.

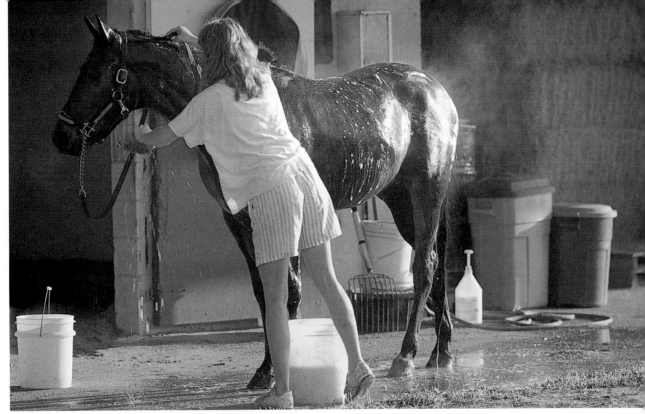

Ella lava el caballo porque el caballo no puede lavarse.

ESTRUCTURA

Reflexive versus nonreflexive verbs

Many Spanish verbs have both a reflexive and a nonreflexive form. In some cases, the meanings of the verbs change when they are used with reflexive pronouns:

Siempre **duermo** ocho horas.	I always *sleep* eight hours.
Casi siempre **me duermo** cuando estudio en la biblioteca.	I almost always *fall asleep* when I study in the library.

Me pongo los zapatos.	I *put on my* shoes.
Pongo los zapatos afuera.	I *put* the shoes outside.

In other cases, the meaning of the verbs is the same, but the meaning of the sentence changes. The nonreflexive verb expresses an action that goes from the subject to the object. The reflexive verb expresses a reciprocal action (the idea of *each other*):

Llamo a Claudia por teléfono a menudo.	I *call* Claudia on the telephone often.
Claudia y yo **nos llamamos** por teléfono a menudo.	Claudia and I *call each other* on the telephone often.

In most cases, however, the nonreflexive verb indicates an action that the subject does to someone or something else, and the reflexive verb expresses an action that the subject does to itself.

Yo **lavo** el coche.	I *wash* the car.
Yo **me lavo.**	I *wash myself.*
Yo **me lavo** las manos.	I *wash my* hands.

Aquí practicamos

D. *En inglés*   Give the equivalent in English of the following sentences.

1. Maricarmen se viste.
2. Maricarmen viste a los niños.
3. Mi hermano escucha la radio.
4. Mis padres no se escuchan.

5. No te levantas temprano.
6. No levantas a tu hermano temprano.

E. *Se lava la cara* (face).   Use the verbs provided to describe the activities of the people portrayed in the drawings. For each pair of drawings, decide which activity requires the reflexive form of the verb and which activity can be expressed with the nonreflexive form.

Modelo: lavar
Miguel se lava la cara.
La Sra. Pérez lava el coche.

Miguel

Sra. Pérez

Sr. Jiménez

Sr. Jiménez / Jaime

1. despertar

Sra. Galindo

Juan José

2. mirar

Sra. Fernández

ella / los jóvenes

3. hablar

Aquí escuchamos:

"¡Siempre vamos a la costa!"

Antes de escuchar

Cecilia talks with her friend Isabel about her summer vacation. Based on your own experience, anticipate what she might say. Look at the following questions before you listen to what Cecilia tells her friend.

START

Después de escuchar

1. ¿Adónde va la familia de Isabel todos los veranos?
2. ¿Dónde vive la familia durante las vacaciones?
3. ¿Se aburre Isabel?
4. ¿Qué hace la familia durante el día por lo general?
5. Por la noche, ¿cómo se divierten todos?

Learning Strategy:

Listening for details

¡Aquí te toca a ti!

F. *Las vacaciones de verano*   Describe un día típico, para Isabel y para sus hermanos según los dibujos. Sigue el modelo.

Modelo: *Por la mañana Isabel se levanta a las ocho y media.*

/./././././././././././
Cooperative
Learning

Learning Strategies:

*Active listening,
describing, reporting
based on personal
knowledge*

*Critical Thinking
Strategy:*

Sequencing

EJERCICIO ORAL

G. Mis vacaciones Tell a classmate about your family's usual summer vacation or about your ideal summer vacation. (1) Say where you go and what activities you do. (2) Describe a typical day, giving the time of day you get up and go to bed as well as at least five activities during the day. (3) Then listen to your partner's description. (4) Decide on the one most interesting activity that each of you does during your typical vacation day.

EJERCICIO ESCRITO

/./././././././././././
Cooperative
Learning

Learning Strategies:

*Organizing informa-
tion, listing, describing,
commenting on prefer-
ences, reading for main
ideas, negotiating, sup-
porting an opinion*

*Critical Thinking
Strategies:*

*Comparing and con-
trasting, evaluating*

H. ¿Adónde fuiste y qué hiciste? Write a letter to a Spanish-speaking friend about where you went and what you did during a recent vacation. (1) Describe the location and the weather. (2) Describe the hotel or other place(s) that you stayed. (3) Name at least five activities in which you participated. (4) Tell which one you liked the best and why. (5) Describe the most interesting meal that you ate. (6) Tell whether you want to return to the same place again. Then, in groups of four, read one another's letters. Decide which one of the location spots the four of you will choose for a vacation together next summer. Give three reasons for your choice.

SEGUNDA ETAPA

Preparación

>> **D**o you know the name of a national park?

>> **H**ave you ever been to a national park? When? What did you do there?

>> **W**hat kind of information is usually contained in a brochure about a national park?

Learning Strategy:

Previewing

Una visita a un parque nacional

SERVICIOS

- Información a cargo de guías y guardaparques
- Servicios sanitarios
- Agua potable
- Estacionamiento
- Refugio para almorzar
- Área de almuerzo
- Centro de visitantes
- Sendero
- Mirador
- Área de juego
- Área de acampar

Parque Nacional Volcán Poás

PARQUE NACIONAL: VOLCAN POÁS

El servicio de Parques Nacionales de Costa Rica administra veintidós áreas silvestres entre parques nacionales y otras reservas afines. Estas áreas cubren 425.329 hectáreas, lo que equivale a un ocho por ciento del territorio nacional.

El principal objetivo del Servicio de Parques Nacionales es preservar áreas naturales para beneficio y disfrute de las generaciones futuras.

El Parque Nacional Volcán Poás, área de gran interés geológico, es importante también porque en él nacen varios ríos que alimentan a otros que dan origen a las cuencas hidrográficas: río Grande de Tárcoles y río Sarapiquí.

BIENVENIDO al Parque Nacional Volcán Poás, una muestra de la actividad geológica y de la belleza del paisaje de Costa Rica.

Esperamos que su visita sea agradable y provechosa.

HORARIO

De 8:00 A.M. a 4:00 P.M.

Agradecemos su colaboración en el mantenimiento del aseo.

DATOS DE INTERÉS

Punto más alto: 2.708 metros

Altura del mirador del cráter: 2.560 metros

Altura del mirador de la Laguna Botos: 2.675 metros

Profundidad del cráter: 320 metros

Diámetro de la Laguna Botos: 400 metros

Superficie de la Laguna Botos: 12 hectáreas

Extensión del parque: 53.173 hectáreas

¡Aquí te toca a ti!

A. *Un parque nacional de volcanes*   Some friends of your parents are going to visit the national parks of Costa Rica, famous for their volcanos, rare birds, and plant life. They bring you a brochure for the **Parque Nacional Volcán Poás** (on page 260) and ask for your help in reading it. You don't know many of the words, but you are able to read enough to get the general idea. Answer the friends' questions about the national park.

Learning Strategies:

Scanning for cognates, reading for main ideas, reading for details

1. How big is the national park system?
2. Is there a place to camp?
3. Is there parking?
4. Are there toilet facilities?
5. Is there a restaurant there?
6. What are some of the other facilities?
7. How high up (**altura**) is the volcano viewpoint?
8. How deep (**profundidad**) is the crater?
9. What time does the park close?
10. What is the main objective of this national park service?

Pronunciación: The vowel combination *eu*

To pronounce the combination **eu**, start with your lips spread, positioned to smile, as you pronounce the Spanish vowel **e**. Bring them slowly to a rounded position as though you were going to whistle. All this should be done in one smooth motion—in one single syllable.

Práctica

B. Lee las palabras en voz alta, pronunciando con cuidado la combinación *eu*.

1. Europa
2. deuda
3. neutro
4. neurosis
5. seudo
6. seudónimo
7. ceuta
8. neurótico

Repaso

C. *Un día en la playa*   En el verano vas a la playa con tu hermana los sábados. Usa la información en la página 262 para decir que hacen Uds. típicamente. Sigue el modelo.

Modelo: yo / levantarse a las 7:30
Yo me levanto a las 7:30.

1. mi hermana / levantarse a las 8:00
2. ella / ducharse
3. yo / bañarse
4. nosotros(as) / desayunarse juntos(as)
5. nosotros(as) / vestirse
6. ella / navegar en la tabla vela
7. yo / jugar al vólibol
8. nosotros(as) / reunirse a las 6:00 de la tarde
9. nosotros(as) / comer mariscos
10. nosotros(as) / regresar como a las 9:00
11. yo / acostarse en seguida *(right away)*
12. ella / acostarse a eso de la medianoche

ESTRUCTURA

The use of pronouns with commands

¡Cálma**te**!	Calm *yourself!* (Take it easy!)
¡Levánten**se**!	Get *(yourselves)* up!
¡No **te** preocupes!	Don't worry *(yourself)*!
¡No **se** despierten!	Don't wake *each other* up!

You have already learned that the reflexive pronouns for **Ud., Uds.,** and **tú (se, se, te,** respectively) are attached to the end of the affirmative command and are placed *before* the verb form in the negative command.

The direct object pronouns **lo, la, los, las** follow the same pattern with command forms.

¡Lléva**lo**!	Take *it!*
¡Láven**la**!	Wash *it!*
¡Tráe**los**!	Bring *them!*

¡No **la** mires!	Don't look at *her!*
¡No **los** compren!	Don't buy *them!*

Aquí practicamos

D. Use the cues on page 263 to form affirmative commands.

 tú / levantarse
¡Levántate!

1. tú / llevarla
2. tú / mirarlo
3. Uds. / llamarse
4. Ud. / comprarlos
5. tú / despertarse

6. Uds. / levantarse
7. tú / acostarse
8. Ud. / comerlos
9. tú / traerla
10. Uds. / lavarse

E. Now use the cues in Activity D to form negative commands.

 tú / levantarse
¡No te levantes!

F. ¡Buena idea!... ¡No, no, no! Cecilia and Isabel are talking about the plans for their party. Two of their friends respond to their comments—the first positively and the second negatively. Follow the model.

 Voy a comprar el nuevo disco compacto de Rubén Blades.
—*¡Buena idea! ¡Cómpralo!*
—*¡No, no, no! ¡No lo compres!*

1. Voy a invitar a Ricardo Núñez.
2. Voy a preparar la ensalada esta tarde.
3. Voy a acostarme a descansar.

4. Voy a llevar a mis primos.
5. Voy a traer el nuevo disco compacto de Los Lobos.

 Vamos a invitar a Mario y a su hermano.
—*¡Buena idea! ¡Invítenlos!*
—*¡No, no, no! ¡No los inviten!*

6. Vamos a invitar a Ana María y a su amiga.
7. Vamos a servir la carne primero.
8. Vamos a lavar los platos mañana por la mañana.
9. Vamos a preparar la comida esta tarde.
10. Vamos a darnos prisa.

Aquí escuchamos:
"¡Vamos a acampar!"

Antes de escuchar

Cecilia and Juan Manuel talk about their upcoming vacation with their parents. Look at the questions on page 264 in preparation for their conversation.

START

Después de escuchar

1. ¿Qué idea tiene el padre para las vacaciones este año?
2. ¿Qué piensan los hijos de la idea de su padre?
3. ¿Qué quiere hacer Juan Manuel?
4. ¿Qué cosas tiene el coche-caravana *(camper)*?
5. ¿Qué dice el padre al final de la conversación?

¡Aquí te toca a ti!

G. *El camping tradicional... el camping moderno...*

"Traditional" campers often make fun of "modern" campers. Compare the activities of traditional and modern campers, using the suggested expressions. Divide these expressions into two lists: one of activities unique to traditional campers and the other of activities unique to modern campers. Would you identify yourself as traditional or modern? Why?

Actividades: acampar / ir al bosque *(woods)* / dormir bajo las estrellas *(under the stars)* / dormir en el coche-caravana / dormir en una tienda de campaña *(tent)* / hacer una fogata *(bonfire)* con leña *(firewood)* / guardar *(to keep, to store)* las bebidas en el refrigerador/en el agua fría / preparar las comidas en una estufa / ducharse / bañarse en el río

H. *Las vacaciones de primavera*

Discuss with two classmates where to go for spring vacation. (1) Choose possible destinations from the list in Column A. (2) Select appropriate activities for each site, one from Column B and one from Column C. (3) Add any other activities that you would like to do in each of these locations. (4) Finally, agree on a destination for spring vacation this year. Follow the model.

A	B	C
ir a las montañas	tomar el sol	patinar
acampar	esquiar	ver a la Casa Blanca
ir a la costa	alquilar un coche-caravana	descansar
ir a España	visitar el Senado	esquiar en agua
ir a Washington	alquilar un coche	visitar las provincias
	nadar	dormir en una tienda de campaña

Modelo: Estudiante A: *¿Cómo vamos a pasar las vacaciones este año?*
Estudiante B: *Yo quiero ir a la costa.*
Estudiante C: *Es una buena idea. Podemos nadar.*
Estudiante A: *Y podemos descansar.*

¡Adelante!

EJERCICIO ORAL

I. *Las vacaciones de la familia* Discuss with another student your family's vacation plans for the summer. Talk about (1) where you are going, (2) when you are going to leave (**salir**), and (3) what you are going to do. (4) Discuss at least four activities, including one that you can do when the weather is bad. (5) If some people in your family would like to do something different, talk about their wishes, too. Each of you will take notes on the plans of each other's family in order to make a report to the class. Be sure to ask questions of your partner about anything that you do not clearly understand.

Learning Strategies:

Requesting and giving personal information, taking notes, expressing future time

EJERCICIO ESCRITO

J. *Mis planes para las vacaciones* Write a letter to your pen pal about your plans for an upcoming vacation. Describe (1) when and (2) where you will go, (3) with whom, (4) for how long, and (5) what you will do during the vacacion. (6) Describe at least four activities that you hope to participate in, including at least one plan for a rainy day. (7) Don't forget to date and sign your letter. (Remember to use **ir a** + *infinitive* and verbs like **pensar** and **querer** in your letter.)

Learning Strategies:

Expressing future time, listing, organizing ideas, writing a letter

Critical Thinking Strategy:

Making associations

265

Vocabulario

Para charlar

¿Por qué no… acampamos en una área de acampar?
alquilamos un coche-caravana?
dormimos en una tienda de campaña?
pasamos las vacaciones en… ?
tomamos el sol?
vamos a la costa / a las montañas?
visitamos un centro ecuestre para hacer equitación?

Temas y contextos

Las actividades deportivas

esquiar en agua montar a caballo
practicar la navegación a vela / tabla vela
el esquí acuático
la equitación

Vocabulario general

Sustantivos	*Otras palabras y expresiones*
un pueblo	en seguida
	¡Magnífico!

Verbos	*Adjetivos*
costar (ue)	anterior
dedicarse	

Lectura CULTURAL

LLEGARON LAS VACACIONES

Antes de leer

1. Look at the photos and title to learn what the reading is about.
2. What do you usually like to do during vacation months away from school?
3. What might you expect young people in a Spanish-speaking country to talk about when referring to activities during vacation?

Learning Strategy:

Previewing

Abajo: A Eva le gusta acampar durante las vacaciones.
Derecha: Vicente disfruta del clima gallego.

Guía para la lectura

A. When does summer vacation start in Spain?

B. Now read each description and record the information using a chart with the following headings:

| Name | Age | Destination | Activities |

C. Based on the information you recorded in your chart, answer the following questions.

   1. ¿Qué piensa hacer la chica que va al campamento de verano?
   2. ¿Quiénes van a ser más activos en cuanto a deportes durante sus vacaciones?
   3. ¿Cuáles de las tres vacaciones te gustan más? ¿Por qué?

Llegaron las vacaciones

 finales de junio los colegios de toda España cierran sus puertas. Chicos y chicas comienzan a hacer sus maletas para irse a la playa, a las montañas o a un campamento juvenil.

Tres jóvenes españoles hablan de lo que van a hacer durante sus vacaciones de verano.

Eva Lamas (15 años): Este verano voy a ir a un campamento de verano. Allí vamos a estar al aire libre todo el día, incluso vamos a dormir en tiendas de campaña. Vamos a hacer excursiones, queremos practicar montañismo, vamos a encender hogueras por las noches y vamos a cantar canciones alrededor del fuego. Espero divertirme igual este año.

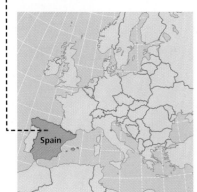

Spain

Vicente Pazuelos (16 años): Yo soy de Madrid y en verano hace muchísimo calor, así que todos los veranos mis padres alquilan una casita en un pueblo de Galicia, en el norte de España, donde no hace tanto calor. Allí hay mucha gente joven de todas partes de España. Durante el día vamos a la playa, nadamos, navegamos en tabla vela y por las tardes vamos de paseo en motocicleta. Me lo paso fenomenal.

Sara Ramírez (18 años): Voy a ir a un campo de trabajo en Valencia, en el este de España, a recoger naranjas durante el mes de agosto. Es un trabajo voluntario, así que no voy a ganar dinero, pero como pienso vivir con la familia dueña de la finca, tampoco lo necesito. Estoy segura de que va a ser una experiencia inolvidable.

Aquí leemos

Estrategia para la lectura

The reading techniques you have learned so far work in longer passages, even about topics that are somewhat unfamiliar. Usually, the main idea is found at the beginning and may be summarized again at the end. Even if there are some words you don't know, you will be able to recognize many others. By using cognates, word families, context, and your background knowledge, you will be able to guess even more. This information is often enough to give you the general idea. A good approach is to treat a reading as a puzzle to be solved, but in order to do so, you must focus on what you do understand rather than on what you do not. Read for details only when you need to.

Reading Strategies:

Look for main ideas in the first and last sentences or paragraphs of a reading.

Pay more attention to what you understand than to what you don't.

Look for details only when you need to.

Antes de leer

People of all ages are fascinated by mountain climbing, a very popular sport in much of Latin America. The degree of difficulty can range from a casual hike up a gradual slope to a demanding and daring assault on unbelievably high peaks. The article on pages 270–271, reproduced in part from the Peruvian newsmagazine *Caretas,* reports on four young Peruvian men who recently climbed to the top of the spectacular snow-capped Alpamayo peak in the Andes. Before reading it, think about the following questions.

>> **W**hat do you already know about hiking and mountain climbing?

>> **W**hat kinds of people do you think are likely to be mountain climbers?

>> **W**hat, if anything, do you already know about the Andes in Peru? Try to find Alpamayo on a map.

>> **T**hink about vocabulary you might need to read about a mountain-climbing adventure: words related to mountains (peak, summit, etc.); words related to climbing (e.g., base camp); words for snow or weather; words for equipment and supplies.

Read over the article quickly. Don't worry about words you don't understand. Just try to see how it is organized, figure out what kinds of information it contains, and identify the main idea.

Una expedición de alpinistas peruanos logró conquistar la cima del Alpamayo, nevado de 5.947 metros de altura en la Cordillera Blanca de los Andes, una de las montañas más bellas del mundo. Lo notable es que son los primeros en subir por la ruta llamada "francesa" que, según explican, es la más larga y la más difícil. "Nadie creía que lo podíamos hacer", dice, riendo, Renzo Uccelli, uno de los miembros de la exitosa expedición Alpamayo Suroeste 87.

A pesar del escepticismo general, Uccelli, fundador y presidente de la Asociación de Andinismo de la Universidad de Lima, junto con Antonio Rodríguez Verdugo, 24 años, Hugo Mugling, 32 y Ronald Bottger, 23, dice que siguieron un plan de entrenamiento no muy profesional, pero con el que tuvieron éxito. Durante meses, todos los días, corrieron un par de horas e hicieron muchos ejercicios abdominales. Al mismo tiempo, preparaban el temperamento para estar mentalmente listos para la dura aventura.

Y así, la noche del 16 de julio, los cuatro compañeros viajaron en ómnibus a Huarás, con 45 kilos de equipos y comida, "miles de paquetes de tallarines, porque no hay plata para comprar otras cosas". Dos días más tarde, alquilaron unos animales de carga y caminaron hasta que llegaron al campamento base, a 3.900 metros de altura.

Una vez al pie de la montaña, se dieron cuenta de que podían subir por la "ruta francesa", la más larga y peligrosa de la Cordillera Blanca. Durante los dos días siguientes, transportaron el equipo hasta el campamento, avanzando a 4.500 metros de altura.

Al despertarse el 24 de julio, los cuatro alpinistas estaban impacientes por atacar la cumbre porque las condiciones climatológicas eran perfectas. La nieve tenía una consistencia ideal para seguir adelante, pero los esperaban un par de días muy largos.

los tallarines: noodles

Por el lado suroeste del Alpamayo hay una famosa pared de hielo y nieve, prácticamente vertical, de 450 metros de alto y una inclinación de 55 a 65 grados. Es el último gran reto para conquistar la cima del Alpamayo, y los alpinistas que se atreven a afrontarla deben tener una excelente técnica "y los cinco sentidos listos".

Afortunadamente, los miembros de la expedición tienen mucha experiencia, pues han escalado juntos muchos nevados en Europa y América del Sur. ¿Qué se siente cuándo se trepa por una pared? "Te sientes bien", comenta Uccelli. "Hay que tener calma y serenidad. Tienes que hacer todos tus movimientos con mucho cuidado."

Así, durante 19 horas, 16 de las cuales estuvieron en la pared, escalaron por la peligrosa "ruta francesa". A cinco metros de la cima perdieron una mochila llena de equipo y comida que cayó rodando centenares de metros más abajo. "Pero eso ya no era tan importante", dice Uccelli. "Subimos a la cumbre y al llegar arriba uno puede sentir mil cosas... ¡Como estamos tan contentos a veces hasta lloramos!"

Lo más importante de esta conquista del Alpamayo es que estos cuatro hombres han demostrado que el alpinismo peruano está mejorando su nivel técnico, y con esto se abren las puertas hacia el camino de las grandes y difíciles escaladas.

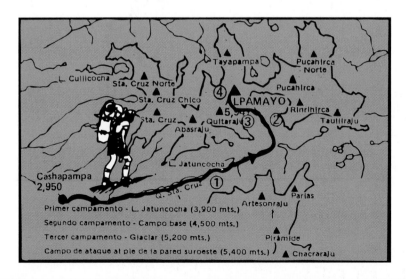

reto: challenge / *escaladas:* climbs

Actividades

A. 1. Read the first and last paragraphs. Based only on the information you find there, write a one-sentence summary of the article.

2. Look for these names mentioned in the article. Use immediate context to identify why they are important. The ones marked * occur more than once.
   a. **Alpamayo***
   b. **Alpamayo Suroeste 87**
   c. **Renzo Uccelli***
   d. **Asociación de Andinismo de la Universidad de Lima**
   e. **ruta francesa***

3. This article is mostly a chronological account of the progress of the expedition. By following the dates and the activities, you get the general idea about the most important content. Here is a list of dates. The ones in parentheses are not mentioned directly in the article but can be deduced from it. Match each date with the activity associated with it during the expedition.

   ___ **16 de julio**   a. move equipment and advance 600 meters
   ___ **(18 de julio)**   b. weather is perfect and climb begins
   ___ **(20 de julio)**   c. arrive at the summit (5947 meters)
   ___ **24 de julio**   d. travel by bus to Huarás
   ___ **(26 de julio)**   e. arrive at base camp (3900 meters)

B. 1. What are some new cognates that you can identify immediately?
2. List the adjectives that are applied to each of the following:
   a. the climbers
   b. Alpamayo peak
   c. the **ruta francesa**
3. How many synonyms can you find for **la cima**? for the four climbers?
4. Find at least three reflexive verb forms. What are the best English equivalents?
5. Uccelli is quoted three times in the article (Paragraphs 1, 7, and 8). Each time his quotes refer to emotions associated with aspects of the expedition. What words (in the quotes or in their contexts) express these emotions?

C. Answer the following questions by referring to the article. Pick out a key word or phrase that provides the answer. (You may not understand a word exactly but can still recognize it as the answer.)

1. What makes the four mountain climbers' accomplishment a "first"?
2. What sort of training program (**entrenamiento**) did they use to prepare for this particular climb?
3. What did the men take with them to the base camp?
4. What was the final obstacle the climbers had to face near the top?
5. Did all four men have a lot of previous climbing experience?
6. What does one climber say is required to climb up a sheer wall?
7. How many hours did they spend scaling the most dangerous part of the mountain?
8. What fell during the very final stage of the climb?
9. How does Uccelli describe the feeling of reaching the very top?
10. According to the article, what is the most important thing about this conquest of Alpamayo overall?

D. 1. Imagine that a book is being written based on the conquest of Alpamayo. Design a book jacket using adjectives, quotes, and other material from this article to highlight the excitement of mountain climbing.
2. With another student, play the roles of Uccelli and a newsmagazine writer. Conduct the interview that would have resulted in this article.
3. Imagine that you are a participant in this expedition, and you are keeping a diary of your adventures. Be sure to include some entries that describe the training, the shopping, the travel, the early stages of the climb, and the arrival at the summit itself. Use everything you have learned so far—descriptions, actions in the past, expression of emotions—to make your writing as vivid as possible.

Ya llegamos

Actividades orales

A. ¿Qué es la telenovela?
In groups of three or four, agree among yourselves on the television soap opera that you want to describe for the class. Have each member of your group select a main character in the soap opera and prepare a description of (1) at least two physical characteristics and (2) two personality traits of that character, as well as (3) a detailed description of that person's daily routine, naming four specific activities typical for that character. Do not give any names or titles that would give away which soap opera or character you are describing.

While each group is giving its presentation, the other members of the class should take notes. Record at least (1) two descriptive facts about each character and (2) two details in each character's daily routine. The small groups should then get together to compare notes, try to name the soap opera, and then ultimately the individual characters. Each group can turn in a written group report for each presentation.

B. Mis vacaciones favoritas
Think back on past vacations you have spent either on a trip or at home, or even in your imagination. Prepare a description of the vacation before coming to class, and bring in some photos that were taken during that time. (If you have none available, cut some appropriate pictures from a magazine or draw some yourself.) In groups of three or four, describe your vacation to your other group members, (1) showing pictures, (2) describing the people you spent time with, including their physical and personality traits, (3) explaining the daily routine you kept during that vacation time, and finally, telling (4) two positive features and (5) one negative feature of the vacation.

After all members of your group have made their presentations, decide together, (1) the person who got the most rest (**la persona que descansó más**), (2) the person who was the busiest (**que estaba la más ocupada**), (3) the one who was the most athletic during that vacation time (**que era la más atlética**), and (4) two other similar features that apply to your group. Be prepared to report these results to the class.

C. En el restaurante
You and some friends meet downtown in a restaurant. Greet each other, order something to drink and/or eat, and then use the *Cromos* listing on pages 234–235 to decide on a television program or a play to see.

Actividades escritas

D. *Las vacaciones* Write about one of your favorite vacations. If possible, bring in photos and describe your activities and those of the other people who were with you.

E. *Un día feriado* (A holiday) You and your friends are making plans for a one-day holiday from school. Write out your schedule of activities, including sports, movies, and the like. Be detailed in your plans—determine times, places to meet, etc.

F. *Una invitación a una fiesta* You and your friends are planning a party. Write an invitation indicating who is giving the party, the time, place, and reason. Look at the invitations on pages 242–243 for ideas if you need them.

Conexión

Los sueños: dreams

>> ¿Do you dream?

>> ¿What images are usually in your dreams?

>> ¿Do you know how to interpret your dreams?

Los sueños

AL EMPEZAR

In the passage below you will read about dreams and what they mean.

LA INTERPRETACIÓN DE LOS SUEÑOS

Todos nosotros soñamos 4 o 5 veces cada noche aunque no siempre recordamos nuestros sueños. Los sueños son importantes para nuestra salud mental y física. Pero, ¿qué significan los sueños?

Nuestras experiencias, **recuerdos**, emociones, **temores** y esperanzas forman la base de nuestros sueños. Pero a veces no los comprendemos fácilmente porque soñamos con símbolos. Se ha escrito mucho sobre la simbología de los sueños. Todos tenemos experiencias y recuerdos diferentes. Por eso, soñamos con diferentes cosas. Sin embargo, hay ciertos símbolos universales. Se presentan algunos en la siguiente tabla.

recuerdos: memories, *temores:* fears

Símbolo	Significado
un barco	representa el viaje de la vida con sus buenos y malos momentos
un coche	representa ambición y deseo de tener un futuro positivo
las nubes	Las nubes claras representan felicidad; las oscuras representan depresión y tristeza.
la luna	representa el amor y las emociones sentimentales
un desierto	simboliza la soledad
un río	representa el actual estado emocional de la persona que sueña
una casa	Cada cuarto de la casa representa un aspecto de nuestra personalidad.
una biblioteca	simboliza nuestra experiencia y conocimiento
un museo	representa nuestros recuerdos, familia y herencia cultural
un restaurante	indica nuestro deseo de estar con amigos
un laberinto	representa una decisión difícil

ACTIVIDAD A

Paso 1: We all have good dreams, bad dreams, and neutral dreams. What type of dreams do the symbols you have read about represent?

Write the symbols down in your notebook. Indicate whether they are positive (**positivo**), negative (**negativo**) or both (**los dos**). Compare your responses with a partner.

Expresiones útiles:

Creo que <u>la luna</u> *es un símbolo positivo.*   I believe
Creo que <u>un río</u> *puede ser un símbolo positivo o negativo.*

Paso 2: With a partner, think of other common symbols which appear in dreams.

lugares: _____

la naturaleza: _____

medios de transporte: _____

otro: _____

¿Creen Uds. que son positivos, negativos o neutrales estos símbolos?

¿Representan felicidad, tristeza, enojo, **paz**, estrés o soledad?   peace

ACTIVIDAD B

How often do you dream about the symbols you read about? Write the symbols in your notebook. Next to them indicate how often you dream about them: **nunca, a veces, frecuentemente.**

When you are done, compare your answers with a partner. Do you dream about the same things or different things?

Expresiones útiles:

¿Con qué frecuencia sueñas con <u>la luna</u>?
Sueño con <u>la luna</u> *frecuentemente.*

277

¿Qué ves?

>> *¿Quiénes son estas personas?*

>> *¿Dónde están?*

>> *¿Qué alimentos ves en la foto a la derecha?*

OBJECTIVES

IN THIS UNIT YOU WILL LEARN:

- **T**o talk about your own and other people's health and physical conditions;
- **T**o refer to habitual actions in the past;
- **T**o use reflexive verbs in the past.

La salud

10

¿CÓMO TE SIENTES?

Después de una carrera de bicicleta se siente cansado pero feliz.

Objectives:

>>> **T**alking about parts of the body and physical complaints

>>> **T**alking about past routines and habitual activities

Strategies:

>>> **I**nterviewing

>>> **R**eporting in the past

>>> **C**omparing and contrasting

PRIMERA ETAPA

Preparación

>> **D**o you know the words for any body parts in Spanish?

>> **W**hen would you need to refer to various body parts?

El cuerpo humano: The human body

El cuerpo humano

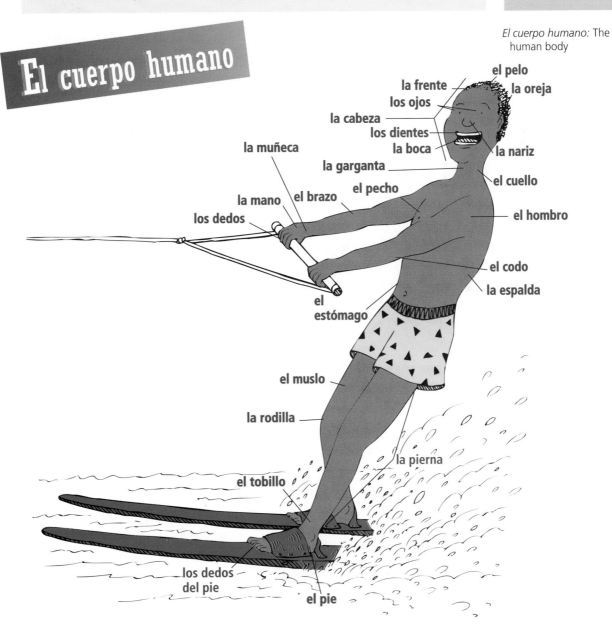

el pelo
la frente
la oreja
los ojos
la cabeza
los dientes
la boca
la nariz
la muñeca
la garganta
el cuello
el pecho
la mano   el brazo
el hombro
los dedos
el codo
la espalda
el estómago
el muslo
la rodilla
la pierna
el tobillo
los dedos del pie
el pie

¡Aquí te toca a ti!

A. *Un amigo extraterrestre* Describe el cuerpo de tu amigo extraterrestre *(your extraterrestrial friend)*. Compara su cuerpo con tu cuerpo, basándote en el dibujo. Sigue el modelo.

Modelo: la cabeza
Yo tengo una cabeza.
Mi amigo tiene una cabeza también.

1. los ojos
2. las orejas
3. los dientes
4. los brazos
5. los dedos
6. las piernas
7. las rodillas
8. los pies

B. *Las partes del cuerpo* Identifica la(s) parte(s) del cuerpo que asocias con *(that you associate with)* las siguientes actividades.

1. playing the piano
2. jogging
3. testing perfume
4. eating

ESTRUCTURA

The imperfect

¿Dónde **vivías** cuando tenías
  10 años?
Yo **vivía** en Indiana.
¿Qué **hacías** durante el verano?
Yo **nadaba y jugaba** al tenis
  todos los días.

Where *did you used to live*
  when you were 10 years old?
I *used to live* in Indiana.
What *did you used to do* during the summer?
I *used to swim and play* tennis
  every day.

You have already learned to express actions in the past by using the preterite. Now you will learn a second past tense, the imperfect, which will allow you to describe what you *used to do*.

To form the imperfect, begin by dropping the **-ar, -er,** or **-ir** of the infinitive and adding the imperfect endings **-aba, -abas, -aba, -ábamos, -abais, -aban** for **-ar** verbs, and **-ía, -ías, -ía, -íamos, -íais, -ían** for **-er** and **-ir** verbs.

The imperfect tense has three equivalents in English:

Ella vivía en España. { *She lived* in Spain.
She used to live in Spain.
She was living in Spain.

	hablar *habl-*	*comer* *com-*	*vivir* *viv-*
yo	habl**aba**	com**ía**	viv**ía**
tú	habl**abas**	com**ías**	viv**ías**
él, ella, Ud.	habl**aba**	com**ía**	viv**ía**
nosotros(as)	habl**ábamos**	com**íamos**	viv**íamos**
vosotros(as)	habl**abais**	com**íais**	viv**íais**
ellos, ellas, Uds.	habl**aban**	com**ían**	viv**ían**

Aquí practicamos

C. ¿Qué hacían Uds.? Di lo que hacían tú y tus amigos(as) *(what you and your friends used to do)* durante el verano cuando tenían diez años.

A	B	C	D
yo	(no)	nadar	todos los días
tú		estudiar	
?		jugar…	
nosotros(as)		beber…	
Uds.		montar en bicicleta	

Nota gramatical

The imperfect of *ver, ser,* and *ir*

The verbs **ver, ser,** and **ir** are conjugated in this way:

	ver	*ser*	*ir*
yo	**veía**	**era**	**iba**
tú	**veías**	**eras**	**ibas**
él, ella, Ud.	**veía**	**era**	**iba**
nosotros(as)	**veíamos**	**éramos**	**íbamos**
vosotros(as)	**veíais**	**erais**	**ibais**
ellos, ellas, Uds.	**veían**	**eran**	**iban**

D. Sustituye las palabras en cursiva con las palabaras entre paréntesis y haz los otros cambios necesarios.

1. *Ellos* iban a la playa cada verano. (yo / ellas / nosotras / tú / Juan y su familia / vosotras)
2. *Nosotros* no veíamos a Juan a menudo. (yo / Uds. / ellas / Mirta y Guillermo / tú / vosotros)
3. ¿Era *él* de España? (tú / ellas / Mario / Ud. / ella / Uds. / vosotras)

E. *El año pasado... cada jueves por la tarde*   Di lo que hacían *(used to do)* cada jueves el año pasado las personas en los siguientes dibujos. Sigue el modelo.

Modelo: *El año pasado, Carmen corría cada jueves por la tarde.*

Carmen

1. Carlos

2. Dina y su novio

3. Jaime

4. Mónica

5. Olga y Lucía

6. Alberto

7. Miguel y Patricio

8. Isabel

F. El año pasado, mi amigo y yo...   Now imagine that every Saturday afternoon, you and a friend did what the people in the drawings in Activity E did. Repeat each item following the model.

> *Modelo:*   *El año pasado, corríamos cada jueves por la tarde.*

Aquí escuchamos:
"¡Pobre Martín!"

Antes de escuchar

Dina and Felipe run into their friend Martín who doesn't feel too well. Look at the following questions and identify a few things you expect to hear during their conversation.

START

Después de escuchar

1. ¿Cómo se ve Martín según Dina?
2. ¿Qué tiene Martín?
3. ¿Cómo se ve Martín según Felipe?
4. ¿Qué dice Dina que debe hacer Martín?
5. ¿Qué va a hacer Martín?

¡Aquí te toca a ti!

G. No te ves muy bien. (You don't look very good.)   Talk to a classmate about his or her state of health. Follow the general pattern of the models while varying the health expressions that you use.

> *Modelos:*   —*¿Qué tal?*
> —*No me siento muy bien.* (I don't feel very well.)
> —*¿Qué te pasa?* (What's wrong?)
> —*Tengo dolor de cabeza (estómago,* etc.*).*
>
> —*¡Hola, amigo! No te ves muy bien.*
> —*¿Verdad? Tengo dolor de cabeza (espalda,* etc.*).*
> —*Pobre. Debes descansar.*
> —*Tienes razón.* (You're right.) *Voy a volver a casa.*

ESTRUCTURA

The imperfect: habitual actions

Todos los veranos **íbamos** a la playa.	Every summer *we used to go* to the beach.
Cada noche **escribíamos** postales.	Every evening *we used to write* postcards.

The imperfect tense is used to describe something that happened over and over again in the past. Certain adverbs and expressions that convey the idea of a routine often accompany the imperfect tense. They reinforce the idea of habitual actions and of things that *used to be done* repeatedly. You already have learned some of the following adverbs and expressions.

a menudo	*often*
a veces	*sometimes*
cada día (viernes, sábado, tarde, mañana, noche, semana, mes, etc.)	*every day (Friday, Saturday, afternoon, morning, night, week, month, etc.)*
con frecuencia / frecuentemente	*frequently*
con regularidad	*regularly*
de vez en cuando	*from time to time*
muchas veces	*many times*
normalmente	*normally*
siempre	*always*
todos los días (lunes, martes, etc.)	*every day (Monday, Tuesday, etc.)*
una vez al día (a la semana, mes, año, etc.)	*once a day (week, month, year, etc.)*

Aquí practicamos

H. *El verano pasado* Last year Silvia's parents went away for a couple of weeks. Use the suggested elements and the imperfect to tell what Silvia and her brother did while their parents were gone.

> **Modelo:** Cada sábado por la noche / yo / salir con mis amigos
> *Cada sábado por la noche salía con mis amigos.*

1. cada día / nosotros / despertarse temprano
2. muchas veces / yo / quedarse en cama una hora o dos
3. de costumbre / mi hermano / levantarse en seguida
4. todos los días / nosotros / ducharse
5. normalmente / nosotros / desayunarse juntos

I. *Cuando tú tenías siete años...* Create a chart like the one on page 287. Decide if each item on the list was true for you when you were seven and mark it to the left of the items. Then interview your partner about his or her situation at the same age. Mark his or her responses in the columns on the right. Follow the model.

: ir a la escuela
—*Cuando tú tenías siete años, ¿ibas a la escuela?*
—*Sí, iba a la escuela.*

Yo			Mi amigo(a)	
Sí	No		Sí	No
X	___	ir a la escuela	X	___
___	___	vivir aquí	___	___
___	___	tener hermanos y hermanas	___	___
___	___	ir a la playa	___	___
___	___	dormir una siesta	___	___
___	___	comer mucho	___	___
___	___	ser travieso(a) *(mischievous)*	___	___
___	___	jugar con los compañeros	___	___
___	___	levantarse temprano	___	___
___	___	beber mucha leche	___	___

 delante!

EJERCICIO ORAL

J. ¿Qué hacías el verano pasado? Think back to what you used to do last summer. (1) Make a list of at least eight activities that you did repeatedly. (2) Using the expressions on page 286, mark down how often each week you participated in each of the activities. (3) Get together with a partner and interview each other about last summer. (4) Compare your partner's activities with yours, noting two similarities and one difference.

EJERCICIO ESCRITO

K. Cuando yo era niño... After spending an afternoon with your ten-year-old niece, you recall your own life at that age. Write a short description in your diary about things that you used to like to do when you were ten or twelve years old. (1) Include at least five activities in which you liked to participate. (2) Tell how often you were involved in these activities. (3) Tell which of these activities was your favorite.

SEGUNDA ETAPA

Preparación

〉〉 **W**hat do you do for exercise?

〉〉 **L**ook at the photograph. What do you think the reading will be about?

〉〉 **W**hat does the title of the reading suggest to you?

El ejercicio ideal

El ejercicio ideal: The ideal exercise

Ventajas: Advantages
peso: weight
tonificarte: to tone up / *lastimarse:* to hurt oneself

las coyunturas: the joints
ponerte en forma: to get in shape / *Aseguran:* Assure

sencilla: simple / *los pulmones:* the lungs

sudando: sweating / *levantar pesas:* to lift weights / *trotar:* to jog

Tírate: Throw yourself

En el agua vas a bajar de peso y vas a tonificarte el cuerpo. No hay manera más eficiente y divertida de ponerte en forma.

¿Buscas una manera **sencilla** y agradable de ponerte en forma? ¿Te gusta la idea de pasar horas **sudando** en un gimnasio? ¿No? Entonces, la solución para ti puede ser la natación. Además de ser un excelente deporte, la nata-

ción puede ser un divertido evento social. En la piscina puedes reunirte con tus amigos... a la vez que trabaja tu sistema cardiovascular.

¿Por qué?
Porque cuando tú nadas, el corazón y **los pulmones** trabajan a su capacidad máxima porque tu cuerpo demanda una gran dosis extra de oxígeno. El movimiento continuo hace de la natación un excelente ejercicio aeróbico.

Ventajas
Una de las grandes ventajas de este deporte es que es difícil **lastimarse** porque cuando tu cuerpo flota en el agua, no hay presión en **las coyunturas**. **Aseguran** los expertos que la persona que nada 15 minutos consecutivos todos los días va a mantenerse en condiciones óptimas sin tener que **levantar pesas** o **trotar**.

¿Quieres ponerte en forma? **Tírate** al agua y nada, nada, nada...

¡Aquí te toca a ti!

A. Contesta las siguientes preguntas sobre la lectura en la página 288.

1. What does the headline say are two benefits of this exercise?
2. In the first paragraph, what is another benefit of this activity, in addition to its being a good sport in general?
3. Why is it a good aerobic exercise?
4. Why is it difficult to injure yourself while doing this activity?
5. How often should you do this activity in order to stay in good shape, according to the experts?

Learning Strategy:

Reading for details

Repaso

B. Tiene dolor de...   Indica dónde tiene dolor cada persona.

Learning Strategy:

Reporting based on visual cues

1. Sara   **2.** mi papá   **3.** mi mamá   **4.** Magda

C. Recuerdos   Marcos and Lucila remember the days when they were students in elementary school. They talk about what they used to do on days they had to go to school. If you are a boy, play the role of Marcos and if you are a girl, play the role of Lucila. Use the imperfect for all verbs.

Learning Strategy:

Expressing past time

> **Modelo:**   Marcos y Lucila / despertarse / 7:00
> **Marcos:**   *Cada día, mi hermana y yo nos despertábamos a las siete.*
> **Lucila:**   *Cada día, mi hermano y yo nos despertábamos a las siete.*

1. Lucila / levantarse / 7:15
2. Marcos / levantarse / 7:30
3. Lucila / ducharse
4. Marcos / afeitarse
5. Marcos / beber leche
6. Lucila / beber jugo de naranja
7. Lucila y Marcos / lavarse los dientes
8. Marcos y Lucila / ir a la escuela / 8:00

ESTRUCTURA

The imperfect: additional uses

Mientras **hablábamos,** ella **leía** una revista.	While *we were talking*, she *was reading* a magazine.
Ella **tenía** los ojos azules.	She *had* blue eyes. (Her eyes *were* blue.)
Yo **creía** que **era** bonita.	I *thought she was* pretty.

In addition to indicating habitual past actions, the imperfect tense is used to talk about several other kinds of situations in the past.

1. To indicate actions that *were going on* at the time about which you are speaking.

Mientras **hablábamos,** ella **leía** una revista.	While *we were talking*, she *was reading* a magazine.

2. To describe the physical attributes of people you are remembering.

Ella **tenía** los ojos azules.	She *had* blue eyes.

3. To express attitudes and beliefs that were held at that time in the past, using verbs such as **creer, pensar,** etc.

Yo **creía** que era bonita.	I *thought* she was pretty.

4. To express how old someone was in the past.

Él **tenía** cincuenta años.	He *was* fifty years old.

5. To describe past states of health.

Yo **no me sentía** bien.	I *didn't feel* well.

6. To set the background or context for a story that takes place in the past.

Eran las nueve de la noche.	*It was* 9:00 at night.
Yo **estaba de visita** en Phoenix.	I *was visiting* Phoenix.
Era invierno, pero **hacía** muchísimo calor allí. **Estábamos** en un pequeño restaurante.	*It was* winter, but *it was* very hot there. *We were* in a tiny restaurant.

Aquí practicamos

D. La fiesta de Cecilia

Daniel llegó tarde a la fiesta de Cecilia. Basándote en el dibujo, usa el imperfecto *(the imperfect tense)* para describir lo que hacían sus amigos cuando llegó a la fiesta.

Cecilia

Mónica Liliana Sr. Castañeda Jorge Verónica

Óscar

Joaquín

Enrique

Jaime

Modelo: Óscar
Óscar escuchaba discos compactos.

1. Jaime, Enrique y Joaquín
2. Mónica y Liliana
3. Jorge y Verónica
4. Cecilia
5. Sr. Castañeda
6. todo el mundo

E. Anoche a las 8:00

You are going to tell a story about something that happened to you. Set the scene by explaining where you were and what you were doing when the story's action began. For the first situation, you are given questions to help you. For the other situations, give similar descriptions on your own.

1. Ayer por la noche a las 8:00 —¿Dónde estabas? ¿Qué hacías? ¿Qué tiempo hacía? ¿Cómo te sentías? ¿Estabas solo(a) *(alone)* o con otras personas? ¿Qué hacían ellas?
2. Esta mañana a las 7:30
3. El sábado pasado a las 10:00 de la noche
4. El viernes pasado por la noche
5. Un momento importante de tu vida

Aquí escuchamos:
"¡Tú siempre estás en forma!"

Antes de escuchar

Magda and Sofía are talking about what they do to stay in shape. Look at the following questions and identify a few things you expect to hear during their conversation.

START

Después de escuchar

1. ¿Qué desea hacer Magda?
2. ¿Qué piensa Madga de Sofía?
3. ¿Por qué está Madga siempre en forma?
4. ¿Cuántas veces por semana hace gimnasia *(work out)* Magda?
5. ¿Cuántas veces por semana va Magda a una discoteca?

¡Aquí te toca a ti!

F. Ellas hacen gimnasia.
Look at the pictures of young women and how they stay in shape. Then answer the questions that follow to match the names of the appropriate activities with the women who do them.

Dina **Virginia** **María Teresa** **Carmen**

1. ¿Quién juega al tenis?
2. ¿Quién nada?

3. ¿Quién levanta pesas?
4. ¿Quién practica yoga?

G. *Intercambio*   Hazle las siguientes preguntas a un(a) compañero(a). Tu compañero(a) va a responderte según su experiencia personal.

1. ¿Eres activo(a)? ¿Te gusta practicar un deporte o mirar los partidos en la tele?
2. ¿Haces ejercicios aeróbicos? ¿Practicas yoga?
3. ¿Nadas de vez en cuando?
4. ¿Te gusta bailar? ¿Ballet o rock?
5. ¿Estás en forma? ¿Tus amigos piensan que tú eres fuerte o débil? ¿Levantas pesas? ¿Quisieras levantar pesas?

¡Adelante!

EJERCICIO ORAL

H. *¿Estás en forma?*   Ask several classmates what they used to do a couple of years ago and what they do now to stay fit. Create a chart like the following one to record their responses and to prepare for class discussion. Start your conversation with: **¿Qué hacías hace dos años para estar en forma? Y ahora, ¿qué haces?** Share with the class some of the common responses as well as the most unusual response.

Hace 2 años	Compañero(a) de clase	Ahora
nadaba	*Cecilia*	*juega al tenis*

EJERCICIO ESCRITO

I. *Soy muy activo(a). ¿Y tú?*   Write a note to your Spanish-speaking pen pal in Argentina telling him or her what you do to stay in shape. (1) Tell at least three things that you do and describe your usual diet. (2) Compare your current activities to what you used to do two or three years ago. (3) Then ask what people your age in Argentina do for exercise. (4) Request photographs of people engaged in popular sports or activities.

TERCERA ETAPA

Preparación

As you start this **etapa,** think about physical ailments. How would you express such things as:

〉〉 a hurt knee?   〉〉 a sprained ankle?

〉〉 a stomachache?   〉〉 other aches and pains?

〉〉 a headache?

Learning Strategy:

Previewing

Niña atropellada

Nívea Lucero, una niña de 7 años, fue atropellada por un automóvil ayer a las 9:30 de la mañana en la Calle Cervantes. La niña caminaba a la escuela y el coche la atropelló cuando cruzaba la calle. En el accidente la niña se quebró un brazo y una pierna y se cortó la frente. Fue transportada al Hospital Santa Cruz en una ambulancia de la Cruz Roja.

Dos lastimados

Un accidente ocurrió ayer a las 2:30 de la tarde en la Avenida Bolívar. Dos jóvenes que andaban en motocicleta chocaron con un automóvil. El motociclista, Alejandro Bernal, 14 años, y su pasajero, Tomás Ferrer, 14 años, se lastimaron en el choque. Fueron transportados al Hospital San Juan en una ambulancia de la Cruz Roja.

¡Aquí te toca a ti!

A. *Estudio de palabras* Based on the context of the two newspaper articles, answer the following in order to figure out the meanings of some of the words you may not know.

1. Find a word that means *to be struck, banged into,* or *knocked down.*
2. Find a word that means *collided.*
3. Find a word that means *driver.*
4. Find a word that means *passenger.*
5. Find a word that means *to be injured.*

B. *Artículos cortos* (Short articles) Los dos artículos de periódicos en la página 294 dan mucha información en pocas líneas. Contestan para cada artículo estas preguntas: ¿quién?, ¿qué?, ¿dónde?, ¿cuándo?

Repaso

C. *El comienzo de un cuento* Aquí tienes el comienzo de un cuento. Cambia los verbos del presente al imperfecto.

Es una noche del mes de diciembre. Hace mucho frío y nieva. Mi hermana y yo estamos en el coche de mi papá. El coche no funciona porque no tiene gasolina. Al lado de la carretera está una mujer vieja. Ella tiene el pelo blanco y una nariz muy larga. Ella camina con un gato negro y canta una canción de Counting Crows. *Mi hermana y yo pensamos que todo eso es muy extraño.*

Now invent the beginning of a second story, based on the drawing to the right. Instead of telling the whole story, establish the scene by using the imperfect to describe the setting, the situation, and the characters.

ESTRUCTURA

The preterite of reflexive verbs

Yo **me acosté** a las nueve anoche.	I *went to bed* at 9:00 last night.
Mi hermana **se levantó** a las 7:30 ayer.	My sister *got up* at 7:30 yesterday.
Nos encontramos en el centro.	*We met each other* downtown.

In **Capítulo 7**, you learned about reflexive verbs in the present tense. As they do in the present tense, these verbs may have two meanings in the preterite:

1. an action that reflects back on the subject

Mi hermana **se levantó** a las 7:30 ayer.	My sister *got up* at 7:30 yesterday.

2. an action in which two or more subjects interact

Nos encontramos en el centro.	*We met each other* downtown.

In both cases, the subject (noun or subject pronoun) is accompanied by its corresponding reflexive pronoun **(me, te, se, nos, os, se).**

Aquí practicamos

D. *Ayer me levanté a las...* Indica algunas actividades que tú y tu hermano(a) hicieron ayer. Sigue el modelo.

 Modelo: yo / levantarse / 7:30
Me levanté a las 7:30 ayer.

1. yo / despertarse / 6:30
2. mi hermano / despertarse / 7:00
3. yo / levantarse / 7:30
4. mi hermana / levantarse / inmediatamente
5. yo / ducharse / 7:45
6. mi hermano / bañarse / 7:15
7. mi hermana / maquillarse
8. yo / afeitarse (maquillarse)
9. mi hermana y yo / cepillarse los dientes
10. mis hermanos y yo / desayunarse juntos

E. *Ayer, anoche y esta mañana* (1) Make a chart like the following one and fill in information about your own activities yesterday, last night, and this morning (following the model information shown). (2) Interview three other members of your class to determine if they did some of those activities. For each one they did, (3) find out some additional detail about it, as suggested in the chart on page 297.

¿Qué hicimos ayer y esta mañana?				
Actividad	Yo	Nombre de amigo(a)	Nombre de amigo(a)	Nombre de amigo(a)
llegar a casa tarde (¿a qué hora?)	*sí; a las cinco*			
hacer deporte (¿por cuánto tiempo?)	*jugué al tenis dos horas*			
salir anoche (¿dónde y hasta qué hora?)	*salí a la casa de Pete hasta las 10*			
acostarse (¿a qué hora?)	*a las once y media*			
cepillarse los dientes (¿cuántas veces?)	*dos veces*			
dormir bien o mal (¿por cuántas horas?)	*bien; por siete horas*			
despertarse (¿a qué hora?)	*a las seis y media*			
levantarse en seguida (¿a qué hora?) o quedarse en la cama (¿hasta qué hora?)	*no, quedé en la cama hasta las siete*			
maquillarse o afeitarse (¿por cuánto tiempo?)	*me maquillé por quince minutos*			
desayunarse con la familia o solo	*con mi hermana*			

Aquí escuchamos:
"¡No me digas! ¿Te rompiste la pierna?"

Antes de escuchar

Carlos and Felipe are talking on the telephone about an accident that Felipe had yesterday. Look at the questions on page 298 and identify a few things you expect to hear during their conversation.

START

Después de escuchar

1. ¿Por qué no fue Felipe a la escuela?
2. ¿Qué parte del cuerpo se lastimó Felipe?
3. ¿Cómo pasó el accidente?
4. ¿Qué hacía Felipe?
5. ¿Se lastimó otra persona también? ¿Dónde se lastimó?

¡Aquí te toca a ti!

F. Un accidente In Spanish, you often use the verbs **lastimarse** *(to hurt oneself)*, **torcerse** *(to twist)*, **romperse** *(to break)*, and **cortarse** *(to cut)* with parts of the body to describe the results of an accident. Use the following expressions and those on page 299 to indicate what happened to you. Follow the model.

Modelo: Yo me lastimé…
Yo me lastimé la mano.

1. Yo me lastimé…

 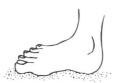

2. Yo me torcí…

  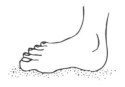

3. Yo me rompí…

4. Yo me corté …

G. *¿Qué pasó?* Identify three people you know who have had an accident that resulted in an injury at one time or another. (You may use yourself as one of those people, if appropriate.) Then share that information with a partner. At the end of your conversation, identify together: (1) any acquaintances who have had the same injury and (2) the person who had the most serious injury.

Cooperative Learning

Learning Strategies:

Selecting and providing information, reporting in the past, negotiating

Critical Thinking Strategy:

Evaluating

EJERCICIO ORAL

H. *Tuve un accidente.* Think of a time when you or a close acquaintance was hurt in an accident. Imagine that the accident just happened. Call up a friend on the telephone to report the news of the accident. Your partner will express appropriate concern, asking about the circumstances of the accident. Discuss (1) when it happened, (2) where, (3) what the injured person was doing before and when the accident occurred, (4) who the person was with, and (5) what the specific injury was.

Learning Strategies:

Asking for and providing information, reporting in the past

EJERCICIO ESCRITO

I. *Un accidente* Imagine that your local newspaper wants to include some articles in Spanish in its weekend edition as a service to the Spanish-speaking population of your city. An editor has asked your Spanish class to submit some articles to be judged for determining who would be offered a position as freelance reporter in Spanish. Using the clippings on page 294 as models, write a short article about an accident (either imaginary or real) that happened recently. Include who, what, where, and when in your article.

Learning Strategies:

Selecting information, organizing details in a sequence, selecting appropriate journalistic tone

299

Vocabulario

Para charlar

Para hablar de tu estado físico

bajar de peso
cortarse
lastimarse
mantenerse en condiciones óptimas
ponerse en forma
romperse
(no) sentirse bien (mal)
sudar
tener dolor de…
tener un accidente
tonificarse
torcerse (ue)

Para hablar del estado físico de otra persona

¿Cómo te sientes?
¿Te sientes bien (mal)?
No te ves muy bien.
¿Estás en forma?
¿Qué te pasa?
¿Qué te pasó?
¿Te lastimaste?
¿Tuviste algún accidente?

Temas y contextos

Las actividades físicas

hacer gimnasia
levantar pesas

El cuerpo

la boca	el diente	el ojo
el brazo	la espalda	la oreja
la cabeza	el estómago	el pecho
la cara	la frente	el pelo
el codo	la garganta	el pie
el corazón	el hombro	la pierna
la coyuntura	la mano	el pulmón
el cuello	la muñeca	la rodilla
el dedo (de la mano)	el muslo	el tobillo
el dedo del pie	la nariz	

Vocabulario general

Sustantivos

la capacidad
una dosis
un evento social
un gimnasio
una manera
un movimiento
el oxígeno
la presión
el sistema cardiovascular
una solución
una ventaja

Verbos

asegurar
demandar
flotar
tirarse

Adjetivos

agradable
consecutivo(a)
continuo(a)
eficiente
experto(a)
grave
máximo(a)
sencillo(a)

Adverbios

normalmente

Otras palabras y expresiones

a menudo
a veces
cada día (viernes, sábado, tarde, mañana, noche, semana, mes, etc.)
con frecuencia
con regularidad
de vez en cuando
muchas veces
tener razón

Lectura CULTURAL

EL CICLISMO EN ESPAÑA

Antes de leer

1. Look at the title of this reading. What do you think **ciclismo** means?
2. What do we do in the U.S. to stay in shape? Do you do anything in particular?
3. Look at the photographs that accompany the reading. Do you know who some of these people are? Where do you think they are from?

Arriba: La bicicleta es mi ejercicio favorito.
Derecha: Miguel Induráin

Un muchacho en bicicleta en el Retiro, Madrid

Guía para la lectura

A. Read the first paragraph and answer the following questions.

1. ¿Qué dice el artículo sobre la popularidad del ciclismo en España?
2. Según el artículo, ¿qué no hay en las ciudades para los ciclistas?

B. Now read the second paragraph and answer the following questions.

1. ¿Quién es Miguel Induráin?
2. ¿Qué se necesita para ser un gran ciclista?
3. ¿Cuál es la carrera que Induráin ganó cuatro veces?
4. ¿Qué información sabemos sobre el corazón de Induráin?

El ciclismo en España

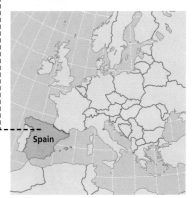

Spain

Aunque las carreteras españolas no son un paraíso para los ciclistas, el número de los aficionados a este deporte crece cada día. Cada día hay más y más jóvenes que van a la escuela en bicicleta, a pesar de que no hay carriles-bici en las ciudades. Mucha de esta popularidad se debe al éxito del gran ciclista español Miguel Induráin.

Induráin es el mejor ciclista del mundo en la actualidad y probablemente uno de los mejores ciclistas en la historia de este deporte. El ganó el prestigioso Tour de France en los años 1991, 1992, 1993 y 1994 y en 1992 y 1993 también ganó el Giro de Italia. Para ser un ciclista como Induráin se necesita estar en forma excelente. Para darles un ejemplo de la forma en que está Induráin vamos a hablar de los latidos del corazón humano. Cuando una persona está en forma, el corazón late más o menos 72 veces por minuto. El corazón de Induráin es tan fuerte que cuando está descansando, el corazón le late 28 veces por minuto.

¡VE A LA FARMACIA!

¡*Ve a la farmacia!*: Go to the pharmacy!

Una farmacia típica en el centro de Madrid

Objectives:

》》 **D**escribing illnesses and complaints

》》 **S**uggesting medical remedies

》》 **G**iving advice about health-related topics

Strategies:

》》 **D**escribing

》》 **L**isting

》》 **M**aking associations

PRIMERA ETAPA

Preparación

Think about the various common illnesses we tend to get in the winter.

》》 **W**hat are some of these illnesses? What are the symptoms?

》》 **W**hat are some of the medicines we take for these illnesses? Are these over-the-counter medicines? Do you need a prescription?

La gripe: un virus anual

La gripe: un virus anual: The flu: an annual virus

Cada invierno los microbios cruzan **las fronteras**. Llegan de todas partes del mundo. Es la temporada del **catarro** y de la gripe. La epidemia de la gripe **alcanza** su **punto** más alto en diciembre, enero y febrero. El Sr. Valdés está enfermo. Tiene la gripe. Noten los síntomas que tiene.

borders
cold
reaches / point

Él tose.

Él estornuda.

Él tiene dolor de garganta.

Él tiene escalofríos.

Él tiene dolor de estómago.

Él tiene fiebre.

Él tiene dolor de cabeza.

¡Aquí te toca a ti!

A. *¿Qué tienen?* Describe los síntomas de las personas en los dibujos. Sigue el modelo.

Modelo: *El Sr. González tiene dolor de estómago.*

Sr. González

1. Sra. López **2.** Simón **3.** Beatriz **4.** Sr. Torres **5.** Srta. Martín **6.** Isabel

Repaso

B. *Mi hermana y yo* Paula Ramírez describes how she and her sister Luisa spent the day yesterday. Use the preterite to recreate her sentences, making sure to distinguish between reflexive and nonreflexive verbs.

Modelo: Luisa y yo / despertarse temprano
Luisa y yo nos despertamos temprano ayer.

1. Luisa / levantarse en seguida
2. yo / quedarse en cama por media hora
3. ella / hacer gimnasia
4. ella / ducharse / lavarse el pelo
5. yo / ducharse / no lavarse el pelo
6. nosotras / desayunarse juntas
7. yo / ir al centro
8. ella / quedarse en casa
9. nosotras / cenar / las 6:30
10. ella / mirar un programa de televisión
11. yo / leer una revista
12. nosotras / lavarse los dientes
13. nosotras / acostarse a las 10:45

C. *¿Se lastimó… ?* A friend is asking you about slight accidents that friends of yours had yesterday. You explain what happened. Work with a partner, use the cues, and follow the model.

> **Modelo:** Juan / cortarse / la frente
> —*¿Se lastimó Juan?*
> —*Sí, se cortó la frente.*

1. Alicia / romperse / brazo
2. Roberto / torcerse / tobillo
3. Carlos / cortarse / mano

4. Bárbara / romperse / pierna
5. Elena / torcerse / muñeca
6. Horacio / cortarse / pie

ESTRUCTURA

The verb *doler*

—¿Cómo estás?
—No muy bien. **Me duele** la garganta.
—**¿Te duele la cabeza?**
—Sí, y **me duelen la espalda y las piernas** también.

How are you?
Not too well. *My* throat *hurts.*

Does your head ache?
Yes, and *my back and legs hurt* also.

The verb **doler** is like the verb **gustar** in that it is used with the pronouns **me, te, le, nos, os,** and **les.** Furthermore, like **gustar,** only the third person singular and plural forms are used, depending on whether what hurts is singular or plural. Notice in the examples that Spanish uses definite articles for body parts where English uses possessives.

Aquí practicamos

D. Sustituye las palabras en cursiva con las palabras entre paréntesis y haz los otros cambios necesarios.

1. Me duele *la garganta.* (la cabeza / los ojos / la mano / la espalda / el tobillo / las piernas)
2. ¿Te duele *el hombro?* (la cabeza / la mano / los pies / la muñeca)
3. Nos duele *el estómago.* (los pies / las piernas / la rodilla / la espalda)
4. A Juan le duelen *los pies.* (la cabeza / el brazo / la rodilla / los ojos)
5. A ellas les duele *el estómago.* (la cabeza / los ojos / los pies / la espalda / las piernas)

Nos duelen los pies.

E. ¿Qué les duele? When your teacher gives the signal, circulate around the room asking several of your classmates if some part of their body hurts. After you finish, tally your responses as a class to find the results of your survey.

Aquí escuchamos:
"Andrés, ¿qué te pasa?"

Antes de escuchar

Emilio runs into Andrés who doesn't look very well. Look at the following questions and identify a few things you expect to hear during their conversation.

START

Después de escuchar

1. ¿Qué le pasa a Andrés?
2. ¿Qué tiene y qué no tiene?
3. ¿Qué hace y qué no hace?

4. ¿Cómo estornuda?
5. ¿Adónde va?

¡Aquí te toca a ti!

F. ¿Qué te pasa? Here are some expressions used to talk about minor physical ailments. Choose the symptoms that would be most likely in each situation.

Síntomas: Me duele(n) la garganta (la cabeza, la espalda, el estómago, los ojos). Toso. Estornudo. No tengo apetito. Estoy mareado(a) *(dizzy)*. No puedo dormir.

1. Tú tienes catarro.
2. Tú comiste mucho.
3. Tú tienes la gripe.
4. Tú tienes una alergia.
5. Tú tienes un examen muy importante y estás muy nervioso(a).

¡Adelante!

EJERCICIO ORAL

G. *No me siento muy bien.*   Think back to the last time you were sick and imagine that you now have the same symptoms. Tell a classmate that you are not feeling well. Answer his or her questions about your symptoms. After having heard the symptoms, he or she will give you some advice: **Tú debes ir a la farmacia (quedarte en casa, ir al médico,** etc.).

EJERCICIO ESCRITO

H. *Mis síntomas*   Write a letter to your grandmother. (1) Tell her that you are not feeling well. (2) Describe at least three symptoms that you are having. (3) Tell her whether or not you have been to see a doctor. (4) Tell her what kinds of medication you are taking. (5) Explain that you cannot visit her this weekend because of the illness. (6) Tell her when you will plan another trip to her house. (7) Remember to date and sign your letter.

Learning Strategies:
Listing, reporting based on personal knowledge, describing
Critical Thinking Strategy:
Analyzing

Learning Strategies:
Listing, describing, providing information, organizing ideas
Critical Thinking Strategy:
Making associations

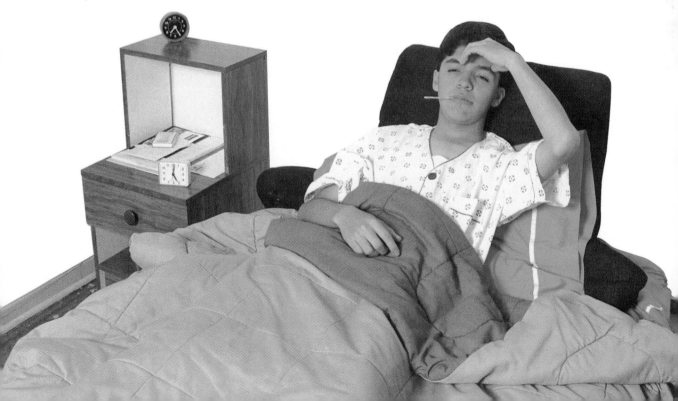

SEGUNDA ETAPA

Preparación

Think about the last time you were sick.

>> **D**id you go to the pharmacy and get an over-the-counter medicine? What was it?

>> **D**id you go to the doctor?

>> **D**id the doctor give you a prescription?

//-//-//-//-//-//-//-//
Learning Strategy:
Previewing

Los remedios

Los remedios:
Treatments

she buys me

cough syrup

gives me
chamomile

Cuando no me siento bien, mi mamá va a la farmacia y **me compra** medicina. Cuando sufro un ataque de alergia y estornudo constantemente, ella me compra un antihistamínico. Cuando toso mucho, ella me compra un **jarabe.** Si tengo la gripe y me duele todo el cuerpo, me acuesto para descansar. Mi mamá **me da** mucha agua o jugo y aspirinas para el dolor. A veces mi mamá prefiere darme los remedios caseros. Ella me da un té de **manzanilla** cuando me duele el estómago.

examines me / takes my
   temperature

prescription

she takes care of me

Cuando estoy muy enferma, tengo que ir a la doctora. Ella **me examina** y **me toma la temperatura.** Si tengo una infección y si tengo fiebre, ella me da una **receta.** Con la receta mi mamá va a la farmacia y me compra un antibiótico. Mi mamá es muy amable y **me cuida** muy bien cuando estoy enferma.

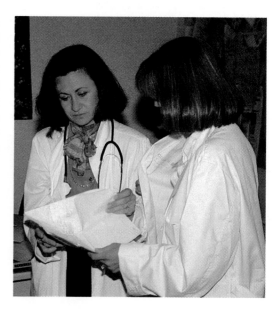

¡Aquí te toca a ti!

A. *Cuando estoy enferma...* Answer the questions based on the information given on the previous page.

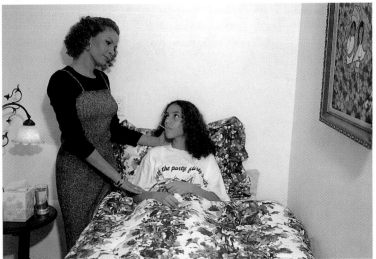

1. What does this person do when she has an allergy attack?
2. What does this person do when she has a cough?
3. What about when she has the flu?
4. When does this person go to the doctor?
5. When does the doctor give this person a prescription?

B. *¿Qué recomiendas?* You are traveling in Uruguay with your family. Whenever someone is not feeling well or needs some medicine, he or she asks you for help. You go to the pharmacy. Based on the information in **Los remedios** on page 310, make the recommendations you think the pharmacist will make to you in each of the following cases.

1. Your sister has a very bad cough.
2. Your father has a backache.
3. Your mother's allergies are acting up and she can't stop sneezing.
4. You have a fever and ache all over.

Repaso

C. *¿Qué le duele?* Describe qué le duele a cada persona en los dibujos en la página 312. Sigue el modelo.

Modelo:

A Jorge le duele la rodilla.

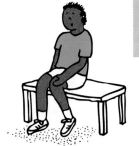

a Jorge

311

1. a Sara

2. al Sr. Lamas

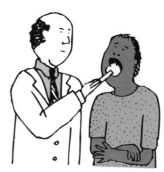

3. a Ricardo

4. a Rita y a Guillermo

ESTRUCTURA

Indirect object pronouns

Él **me** escribió una carta.	He wrote a letter *to me*.
Ella **te** compró un disco compacto.	She bought a CD *for you*.
Tú **nos** vendiste el coche.	You sold the car *to us*.
¿**Le** escribió ella una carta **a Juan?**	Did she write a letter *to Juan*?
No, ella **les** escribió una carta **a sus amigas.**	No, she wrote a letter *to her friends*.

The indirect object pronouns in Spanish are listed below.

me	*to (for) me*	nos	*to (for) us*
te	*to (for) you*	os	*to (for) you*
le	*to (for) him, her, you*	les	*to (for) them, you*

Indirect object pronouns are used to indicate what person or thing receives the direct object.

Aquí practicamos

D. Sustituye las palabras en cursiva con las palabras entre paréntesis y haz los otros cambios necesarios.

1. Ella *me* escribió una carta la semana pasada. (te / nos / le / les / os)
2. Yo le escribí una carta *a Juan*. (a ellos / a Elena / a Margarita y a Marcos / a Ud. / a mi novia / al director / a la profesora)
3. Ellos te enviaron *a ti* una postal de Madrid. (a nosotros / a mis padres / a Ud. / a Ricardo / a Felipe y a Carolina / a mí)

E. *¿Dijo la verdad?*   Your friend is a very naive person and often cannot tell whether people are telling the truth or not. As you watch a mystery story on television, your friend asks you questions about what the main character said to other characters in the program. Follow the model.

Modelo: a María
¿Le dijo la verdad a María?

1. a Juan
2. a la policía
3. a los extranjeros
4. a su novia
5. a su esposa
6. a sus padres
7. a sus hijos
8. al Presidente

Nota gramatical

The verb *dar*

Yo le **doy** el libro a la profesora.	I *give* the book to the teacher.
Ella me **da** la llave.	She *gives* me the key.
—¿Le **diste** la carta a tu novia?	*Did you give* the letter to your girlfriend?
—Sí, le **di** la carta a ella.	Yes, *I gave* the letter to her.
Mi papá nos **dio** dinero para comprar libros.	My father *gave* us money to buy books.

Present

yo	**doy**	nosotros(as)	**damos**
tú	**das**	vosotros(as)	**dais**
él		ellos	
ella	**da**	ellas	**dan**
Ud.		Uds.	

Except for the **yo** form, the verb **dar** is conjugated in the present tense in the same way as other **-ar** verbs.

Preterite

yo	**di**	nosotros(as)	**dimos**
tú	**diste**	vosotros(as)	**disteis**
él		ellos	
ella	**dio**	ellas	**dieron**
Ud.		Uds.	

Although **dar** is an **-ar** verb, it is conjugated in the preterite with the endings that you use for **-er** and **-ir** verbs. The forms **di** and **dio** do *not* take an accent mark.

The verb **dar** is often used with indirect object pronouns that indicate to whom something is being given.

Other verbs commonly used with indirect object pronouns are **hablar, decir, mandar** *(to send),* and **escribir.**

F. *El médico le dio la medicina a...* Indica a quién le dio el médico cada cosa. Sigue el modelo.

Modelo: el jarabe / Mario
Le dio el jarabe a Mario.

1. la medicina / Laura
2. el jarabe / mis hermanos
3. el antihistamínico / Ud.
4. el antibiótico / yo
5. el jarabe / tú
6. la receta / la profesora
7. la aspirina / mi padre
8. las gotas para los ojos / tú
9. la medicina / mis padres
10. las aspirinas / mis primos

G. *¿Qué te da tu mamá cuando...?* Ask several classmates what their mothers give them when they have various illnesses. Suggestions: **la gripe, un catarro, un dolor de cabeza (estómago,** etc.), **una alergia.**

COMENTARIOS
CULTURALES

La farmacia en el mundo hispano

In the Spanish-speaking world, people often consult their local pharmacist when they are not feeling well. If the pharmacist considers the illness to be serious, he or she will advise the customer to see a doctor. In the case of a cold, flu, or minor accident, the pharmacist will recommend over-the-counter medicines and drugs that often require a prescription in the U.S. Many cities and towns in the Spanish-speaking world have at least one pharmacy that remains open all night. Many other pharmacies have signs on their doors indicating that the pharmacy remains open long hours each day.

Here is some useful vocabulary to use in pharmacies throughout the Spanish-speaking world.

Quisiera algo para la garganta.
        los ojos.
        el estómago.

Quisiera algo para la tos.
        la alergia.
        la fiebre del heno.
        el dolor de cabeza.
        la gripe.

Quisiera unas aspirinas.
        un antihistamínico.
        unas pastillas para la garganta.
        unas gotas para los ojos.
        un jarabe para la tos.

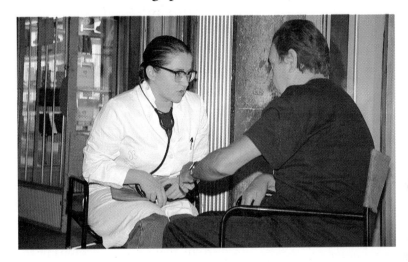

Aquí escuchamos:
"En la farmacia"

Antes de escuchar

Alicia is not feeling well and goes to the pharmacy to get advice from the pharmacist about her symptoms. Look at the following questions and identify a few things you expect to hear during their conversation.

START

Learning Strategies:
Previewing, predicting

Después de escuchar

1. ¿Cómo se siente Alicia?
2. ¿Qué le pasa a ella?
3. ¿Cómo la ve el farmacéutico?
4. ¿Cuánto tiempo hace que está así?
5. ¿Qué le da el farmacéutico?

Learning Strategy:
Listening for details

¡Aquí te toca a ti!

H. Quisiera...
You are traveling in Spain with a group of people who do not speak Spanish. Serve as their interpreter at the pharmacy and make an appropriate request in each situation. Follow the model.

 Modelo: your friend / sore throat
A mi amigo le duele la garganta. Quisiera unas pastillas para la garganta.

1. your friend / headache
2. your sister / stomachache
3. your brother / cough
4. your father / cold symptoms
5. your mother / allergy
6. your friend / flu symptoms

EJERCICIO ORAL

I. En la farmacia
Explain to the pharmacist that you have the symptoms that usually accompany the following medical problems. For each problem, name at least three symptoms. Then the pharmacist (your partner) will recommend at least two possible medicines or ways to treat each problem.

1. catarro
2. la gripe
3. la fiebre del heno

EJERCICIO ESCRITO

J. Cuando me enfermo
A friend of yours from a Spanish-speaking country wants to know more about what we do in this country when we get sick. Write a note to him or her in which you (1) name at least three common ailments and a typical treatment for each. Then (2) describe the symptoms that you had the last time that you were sick enough to miss school. Tell (3) what medicines you took and (4) what you did to get well.

Vocabulario

Para charlar

Para describir los síntomas

Estornudo.
No puedo dormir.
Me duele(n)…
Tengo una alergia.
    catarro.
    dolor de cabeza.
        espalda.
        estómago.

Tengo escalofríos.
    fiebre.
    fiebre del heno.
    la gripe.
    una infección.
    la tos.
    un virus.
Toso.

Para comprar medicina en la farmacia

Quisiera… (remedio)
Quisiera algo para…   }   (parte del cuerpo)
Quisiera alguna cosa para… }

Temas y contextos

Los remedios

un antibiótico	unas gotas para los ojos	una taza de té de manzanilla
un antihistamínico	un jarabe	
una aspirina	unas pastillas	

Vocabulario general

Sustantivos	Verbos	Adjetivos	Adverbios
una epidemia	alcanzar	anual	constantemente
una frontera	cuidar		
un microbio	dar		
un punto	mandar		
	sufrir		

Otras palabras y expresiones

tomar la temperatura

Lectura
CULTURAL

LA MEDICINA EN ALGUNAS PARTES DEL MUNDO HISPANO

//.//.//.//.//.//.//.//.//

Learning Strategies:

Previewing, brainstorming

Critical Thinking Strategy:

Making associations

//.//.//.//.//.//.//.//.//

Learning Strategies:

Reading for cultural information, reading for details

Antes de leer

1. Look at the pictures and the title that accompany this reading. What do you think the people are selling?
2. What connection do you think there is between these items and illness?
3. Are you familiar with any kind of traditional home remedy? If so, what?

Guía para la lectura

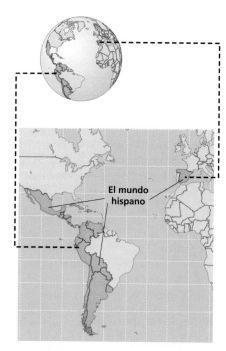

El mundo hispano

A. Read the first paragraph and decide which of the following statements best summarizes the main idea it contains.

1. En general, la gente en países de habla hispana paga por sus visitas al médico.
2. En general, hay programas de medicina muy modernos que el gobierno paga.
3. En general, los remedios en algunas partes del mundo hispano son sólo tradicionales.

B. Read the second paragraph and answer the following questions.

1. ¿Qué solución hay para un(a) enfermo(a) cuando no hay médico?
2. ¿Qué usa esta persona para curar a la gente?
3. ¿Qué tienen en común las medicinas naturales y medicinas producidas por compañías farmacéuticas?

La medicina en algunas partes del mundo hispano

a medicina en algunas partes del mundo hispano es una rara combinación de influencias indígenas, africanas y europeas. Claro que al lado de estas influencias también existen programas de medicina que son tan modernos como los que tenemos en este país, pero a veces, a causa de la historia cultural es muy difícil cambiar las prácticas tradicionales de la gente. Hay países hispanos con programas de medicina muy completos. Si la gente se enferma, va al médico y el gobierno paga la visita. También paga servicios como cirugía, que se hace en un hospital, y visitas del médico a la casa del paciente. En ciertas ocasiones, el gobierno también paga parte de las medicinas.

En las regiones rurales de estos países donde no hay muchos médicos ni grandes hospitales modernos, a veces la gente va a ver al curandero o curandera local. Ésta es una persona que tiene un gran conocimiento de las hierbas y otros ingredientes naturales y sabe cómo usarlas para hacer remedios que curan a la gente. Éstas son medicinas que tienen mucha tradición entre la gente rural. El proceso no parece ser muy científico, pero muchas de las medicinas naturales tienen los mismos ingredientes que las medicinas que recomiendan los médicos en los grandes hospitales modernos.

LA SALUD: MEJOR QUE LA RIQUEZA

*La salud: mejo⬚
la riqueza: H⬚
better than r⬚*

Para la buena salud hay que comer frutas y vegetales y así obtener la fibra, la vitamina C y los minerales necesarios al cuerpo.

Objectives:

>>> **D**escribing dietary and sleeping habits

>>> **A**dvising others what to eat and what not to eat

>>> **A**sking for advice

Strategies:

>>> **R**eading for relevant information

>>> **A**ctive listening

>>> **S**eeing cause-and-effect relationships

PRIMERA ETAPA

Preparación

>> **A**s you begin this **etapa**, think about the interest in healthful food this country has experienced in the past few years. Think about your own eating habits. Do you eat health food? Do you eat junk food? What about red meat? Do you know any vegetarians?

//-//-//-//-//-//-//

Learning Strategy:

Brainstorming

Los cinco grupos alimenticios

Los cinco grupos alimenti-cios: The five food groups

1		**Leches y productos lácteos**	calcio, proteína, **grasa**, vitamina B, vitamina A
2		**Carne, pescado, huevos**	proteína, grasa, **hierro**, vitamina A, vitamina B
3		**Frutas y vegetales**	vitamina C, fibra, minerales
4	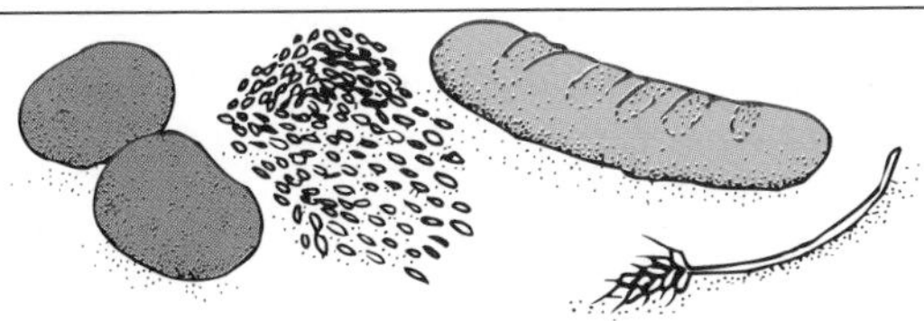	**Pan, cereales, papas, vegetales secos**	**almidón**, proteína, vitamina B
5		**Grasa**	lípidos, vitamina A en la mantequilla y la crema

grasa: oil, fat / *hierro:* iron / *almidón:* starch

Funciones de los cinco grupos alimenticios

Develop / renew / tissues
bones / healthy

Grupos 1 y 2:   **Desarrollan,** mantienen y **renuevan** los **tejidos** del cuerpo. Forman los **huesos** y los dientes; mantienen **sanos** los nervios y los músculos; regulan el tono muscular y el ritmo cardíaco.

Grupo 3:   Facilitan la digestión; mejoran la vista nocturna; ayudan al movimiento muscular.

Grupos 4 y 5:   Le dan energía al cuerpo (calorías).

¡Aquí te toca a ti!

A. *Debes comer los alimentos del grupo...*   Diet has a strong influence on your physical condition. The following people want to supplement their medical treatment with good nutrition. Based on the information at the beginning of the **etapa**, recommend what the following people should eat. Follow the model.

 Paula Lerma tiene problemas cuando maneja *(drives)* el coche de noche; ella no puede ver muy bien.
Debe comer los alimentos del grupo 3, las frutas y los vegetales.

1. Mateo Torres se prepara para una competencia deportiva.
2. Virginia Estrada siempre está cansada.
3. Adela López empieza a echar los dientes *(to teethe).*
4. Pablo Chávez tiene problemas después de comer; le molesta el estómago.
5. Juan José Cisneros se rompió el brazo tres veces.

B. *¿Comes bien?*   Discuss the food that you ate yesterday in terms of the five basic food groups. Your classmate will then tell you whether you ate well or not. Follow the model.

 —*Del primer grupo comí queso para el almuerzo y bebí leche para la cena. Del segundo grupo... etc.*
—*Comiste muy bien.*   o: *Comiste muy mal.*

Repaso

C. *Tú eres el (la) farmacéutico(a).*   Usa el verbo *deber* y un infinitivo para recomendarles a tus clientes *(to recommend to your clients)* lo que deben hacer *(what they should do)* en cada situación en la página 323.

Modelo: Tengo dolor de cabeza.
Debes tomar dos aspirinas.

1. Estornudo sin parar.
2. Tengo la gripe.
3. Tengo una tos terrible.
4. Me duele la garganta.

5. Siempre estoy cansado(a).
6. Tengo fiebre.
7. Me duele el estómago.
8. Me duele todo el cuerpo.

//-//-//-//-//-//-//-//
Critical Thinking Strategies:

Analyzing, making associations, seeing cause-and-effect relationships

D. ¿Qué les dio la doctora?   Indica lo que el médico les dio a tus amigos la última vez que estaban enfermos. Usa pronombres de complemento indirecto *(indirect object pronouns)* con el verbo *dar*. Sigue el modelo.

 Modelo: a ella / un jarabe
La doctora le dio a ella un jarabe.

1. a ellos / dos aspirinas
2. a él / una pastilla para la garganta
3. a nosotros / una receta
4. a ti / un antihistamínico
5. a mí / unas gotas para los ojos
6. a Ud. / un jarabe para la tos

ESTRUCTURA

The verb *pedir*

¿Le **pides** permiso a tu padre cuando quieres salir?

No, yo le **pido** permiso a mi mamá.

¿Le **pediste** permiso al profesor para ir al concierto?

Sí, le **pedí** permiso.

Do you ask your father for permission when you want to go out?

No, I *ask* my mother for permission.

Did you ask the teacher for permission to go to the concert?

Yes, I *asked* him for permission.

Pedir means *to ask for (something)* as opposed to **preguntar,** which means *to ask (questions)*. Here are the conjugations of **pedir.**

Present			
yo	**pido**	nosotros(as)	pedimos
tú	**pides**	vosotros(as)	pedís
él		ellos	
ella	**pide**	ellas	**piden**
Ud.		Uds.	

Notice that the **e** in the stem of **pedir** changes to **i** in all forms of the present except **nosotros** and **vosotros**.

		Preterite	
yo	pedí	nosotros(as)	pedimos
tú	pediste	vosotros(as)	pedisteis
él		ellos	
ella	**pidió**	ellas	**pidieron**
Ud.		Uds.	

Notice that the **e** in the stem of **pedir** changes to **i** in the third person singular and plural preterite forms. Other verbs conjugated like this are

servir   **repetir** *(to repeat)*   **reírse**
medir *(to measure)*   **sonreír** *(to smile)*

Aquí practicamos

E. Sustituye las palabras en cursiva con las palabras entre paréntesis y haz los otros cambios necesarios.

1. *Yo* le pido permiso al profesor. (tú / ella / nosotras / Uds. / Francisco / vosotros)
2. *Yo* le pedí permiso al profesor. (tú / ella / nosotros / Uds. / Francisco / vosotras)
3. ¿Cuánto mide *Francisco*? (tú / tu hermano / Uds. / ella / Ud. / vosotros)
4. *El profesor* repitió la respuesta. (yo / ellos / Ud. / nosotras / Uds. / vosotras)

F. *¿Qué le pidieron al camarero?*   You and several friends are in a busy restaurant and the waiter makes several mistakes when he brings you your food. Follow the model.

Modelo: Marta / ensalada / sopa
Marta le pidió ensalada, pero el camarero le sirvió sopa.

1. Francisco / una hamburguesa / un sándwich de jamón con queso
2. Carolina / sopa / ensalada
3. Carlos / té / café
4. Berta / agua mineral / leche
5. Jorge / una pizza / una hamburguesa con queso
6. Laura / pastel / helado

G. ¿Qué pediste? Create a graph like the following one to record your responses and those of your classmates.

Think about the last time that you ate in a restaurant with a group of your friends when everyone paid his or her own bill. What did you order? Put your name in the appropriate space in the graph. Now ask this question of five of your classmates; put their names in appropriate spaces in the graph to chart their responses.

	Hamburguesa	Pizza	Pollo	Pescado	Tacos	Ensalada
yo						
5						
4						
3						
2						
1						

Now draw another graph. This time think about the last time that you ate out in a restaurant with family or friends when someone else paid the bill. What did you order? Put your name in the appropriate space in the graph. Now ask this question of five of your classmates; put their names in appropriate spaces in the graph to chart their responses.

COMENTARIOS CULTURALES

Metros y kilos

In Spanish-speaking countries, height and weight are expressed in **metros** and **kilos**.

One meter (**metro**) is equivalent to 3.281 feet (a little over 39 inches). Conversely, one foot equals 0.305 meters, and one inch equals 2.5 centimeters. To convert your height to meters and centimeters, multiply your height in inches by 2.5. For example, if you are 5'8" tall, you would be 170 centimeters tall (68" x 2.5). Since there are 100 centimeters in a meter you would say that you are 1 meter 70 centimeters tall, or **"Mido un metro setenta."**

One kilogram (**kilo**) is the equivalent of 2.2 pounds, and one pound equals 454 grams. To convert pounds to kilograms, divide your weight in pounds by 2.2. For example, if you weigh 145 pounds, you would weigh 65.9 kilograms (145 ÷ 2.2) and you would say, **"Peso casi sesenta y seis kilos."**

Aquí escuchamos:
"¿Cuánto mides?"

Learning Strategy:

Previewing

Antes de escuchar

Héctor and Felipe are talking about how tall they are and how much they weigh. Review the **Comentarios culturales**, look at the following questions, and identify a few things you expect to hear during their conversation.

Learning Strategy:

Listening for details

Después de escuchar

1. ¿Cuánto mide Felipe?
2. ¿Cuánto pesa?
3. ¿Cómo guarda la línea?
4. ¿Qué le sirve su mamá?
5. ¿Qué le pide a ella a veces?

¡Aquí te toca a ti!

H. ¿Qué les pides a tus padres?   Your friend asks if you ask your parents for certain foods that are normally not considered good for you. You respond by saying that you do, but that your parents serve you other food instead. Work with a partner and follow the model.

Modelo: dulces / fruta
—¿Les pides dulces a tus padres?
—Sí, les pido dulces, pero me sirven fruta.

1. pasteles / yogur
2. papas fritas / zanahorias y apio (*celery*)
3. dulces / pasas (*raisins*)
4. helado / manzanas o peras
5. galletas / bananas
6. torta / fruta y queso

I. ¿Qué pides en la cafetería?   Tell what kinds of exotic foods you ask for in the school cafeteria and what you actually get served. Use the phrases: **Pido... pero me sirven... .**

EJERCICIO ORAL

J. Una encuesta (survey)   Survey some of your classmates about the eating habits and physical conditions of their family members. Then, without naming names, report to the class your general conclusions about the physical condition of people in your town.

EJERCICIO ESCRITO

K. La semana pasada comí...   Create a food journal for one week. (1) For each day, list everything that you ate. (2) Using the chart of the five food groups on page 321, indicate from which group each item comes. (3) Then place a check mark beside all the foods that are considered healthy for you. (4) Name two changes that you could make in your regular diet that might improve your physical condition and health. (5) Read the food journal of your partner. Add one suggestion for your partner to improve his or her eating habits.

SEGUNDA ETAPA

Preparación

>> **H**ow much sleep do you get in a typical night?

>> **D**oes the amount differ on weekends?

>> **D**o you think getting enough sleep is important for good health?

Los jóvenes duermen mal

A group of doctors carried out a survey **(una encuesta)** and determined that young people between the ages of 15 and 19 don't sleep enough. The following article reports the results of this survey.

Los jóvenes duermen mal

majority / the same

at least in part

nightmares

snore
try to

Aparentemente, los jóvenes se acuestan muy tarde y no duermen lo suficiente. El 75% dice que no duermen más de siete horas cada noche durante la semana. La gran **mayoría** se acuesta a eso de las 22 o 23 horas. La televisión es la causa, **en parte al menos**, por no dormir lo suficiente. Casi el 25% admiten estar muy cansados durante el día y otro 25% duermen la siesta cuando es posible.

Durante el fin de semana, los jóvenes **tratan de** recuperar las horas de dormir que perdieron durante la semana. La mayoría dice que duerme dos horas adicionales los sábados y domingos. Durante las vacaciones también hacen **lo mismo**.

El 25% de estos jóvenes tiene dificultades durmiéndose. Esto es una señal de ansiedad y sin duda una indicación de una vida no muy saludable. Las jóvenes tienen más **pesadillas** que los jóvenes pero los muchachos **roncan** más que las muchachas.

¡Aquí te toca a ti!

A. ¿Verdad o falso?   Basándote en la información en la lectura, indica si las frases en la página 329 son verdaderas o falsas.

1. Los jóvenes típicos duermen ocho horas cada noche durante la semana.
2. Los jóvenes típicos duermen siete horas durante el fin de semana.
3. Los jóvenes típicos se acuestan generalmente a eso de las 10:00 de la noche.
4. El 50% de los jóvenes duermen una siesta durante las vacaciones.
5. Durante las vacaciones los jóvenes de 15 a 19 años duermen poco.
6. El 25% de los jóvenes tiene dificultades durmiéndose.
7. Las muchachas nunca roncan.
8. Los muchachos tienen más pesadillas que las muchachas.

B. ¿Y tú?   Contesta las preguntas sobre tus hábitos de dormir *(sleeping habits)*.

1. Generalmente, ¿a qué hora te acuestas?
2. ¿Miras la tele antes de acostarte?
3. Generalmente, ¿cuántas horas duermes cada noche?
4. ¿Duermes una siesta?
5. Cuando te despiertas, ¿estás cansado(a)?
6. ¿Cuándo te duermes tarde?
7. ¿Te acuestas más tarde durante el fin de semana?
8. ¿Sueñas *(Do you dream)* de vez en cuando?
9. ¿Tienes pesadillas de vez en cuando?
10. ¿Roncas tú?

A Cristina le gusta dormir tarde.

Repaso

C. ¿Cuánto mide... ? ¿Y cuánto pesa?   Tú quieres saber cuánto miden y cuánto pesan varias personas. Trabaja con un(a) compañero(a). Sigue el modelo.

Modelo: José / 1.79 / 68
—¿Cuánto mide José?
—Mide un metro setenta y nueve.
—¿Y cuánto pesa?
—Pesa sesenta y ocho kilos.

1. Marisol / 1.66 / 51
2. Lidia / 1.45 / 48
3. Óscar / 1.96 / 82
4. Verónica / 1.89 / 76

D. Les pedí..., pero me sirvieron... You and your friends asked your parents for certain snack foods. Because your parents thought the foods weren't good for you, they served you something they thought was better. Work with a partner and follow the model.

Modelo: Bárbara / helado / yogur
—*¿Qué les pidió Bárbara a sus padres?*
—*Bárbara les pidió helado, pero le sirvieron yogur.*

1. Lorenzo / pastel / una manzana
2. Rebeca / papas fritas / zanahorias y apio
3. tu hermanito / dulces / pasas
4. ellas / torta / fruta y queso
5. tus amigos / helado / ensalada de fruta
6. ellos / galletas / yogur

ESTRUCTURA

The expressions *desde cuándo, desde (que),*
cuánto tiempo hace, **and** *hace (que)*

—**¿Desde cuándo** estudias español?   *How long (Since when, Since what point in time)* have you been studying Spanish?

—Estudio español **desde que** tenía 15 años.   I have been studying Spanish *since* I was 15.

—Estudio español **desde** el año pasado.   I have been studying Spanish *since* last year.

—**¿Cuánto tiempo hace que** estudias español?   *For how long* have you been studying Spanish?

—**Hace** tres meses **que** estudio español.   I have been studying Spanish *for* three months.

Desde cuándo, cuánto tiempo hace, desde, desde que, and **hace** can be used to ask and answer questions about something that started in the past and is *continuing in the present.*

Question	Answer
¿Desde cuándo + *present tense verb . . . ?*	*Present tense verb +* **desde** + *specific point in time.* *Present tense verb +* **desde que** *+ subject + past tense verb.*
¿Cuánto tiempo hace que + *present tense verb . . . ?*	**Hace** + *length of time* + **que** + *present tense verb.*

Remember that in Unit 5 of *¡Ya verás!, Primer nivel,* you learned to use a similar construction with the preterite tense to express *ago* in Spanish.

Hace cinco años que viví
en Indiana.
I lived in Indiana *five years ago.*

or

Viví en Indiana **hace cinco años.**
I lived in Indiana *five years ago.*

Aquí practicamos

E. *La señora Cortina va al médico.* Your friend Cristina's mother, who has been ill for several days, goes to see the doctor. Before she is examined, the nurse asks her some questions. Use the cues in parentheses to give Sra. Cortina's answers. Follow the model.

Learning Strategy:

Expressing past and present time

> **Modelo:** ¿Desde cuándo vives en Madrid? (1982)
> *Vivo en Madrid desde 1982.*

1. Muy bien, entonces, ¿hace tres años que vive en Madrid? (no / … años)
2. ¿Cuánto tiempo hace que trabaja en el Banco de Bilbao? (diez años)
3. ¿Desde cuándo consulta al Dr. Pérez? (1985)
4. ¿Cuánto tiempo hace que no va al médico? (seis meses)
5. ¿Cuánto tiempo hace que tiene catarro? (tres o cuatro días)
6. ¿Tiene fiebre? ¿Sí? ¿Desde cuándo? (ayer)
7. ¿Qué medicina toma Ud.? ¿Aspirina? ¿Cuánto tiempo hace? (dos días)
8. ¿Durmió bien anoche? ¿No? ¿Cuánto tiempo hace que no duerme bien? (dos días)

Learning Strategy:

Expressing past and
present time

F. ¡Traducciones! (Translations!) Give the Spanish equivalents of the following sentences.

1. I have been feeling poorly for two weeks. I've had a fever since last Monday.
2. Mía has had a cold for a month. She has been coughing for five days.
3. My parents have had sore throats since the beginning (**el principio**) of the week.
4. How long has your stomach been hurting?
5. Since when have you been sleeping badly?
6. I haven't slept well for a month.

Aquí escuchamos:
"¿Dormiste bien?"

Antes de escuchar

Claudia and Rebeca are talking about how much sleep they got last night and why. Look at the following questions and identify a few things you expect to hear during their conversation.

Después de escuchar

1. ¿Cómo ve Rebeca a Claudia?
2. ¿Por qué está cansada Rebeca?
3. ¿Quiénes están de visita en casa de Rebeca?
4. ¿Cuánto tiempo van a estar con Rebeca?
5. ¿Cómo durmió Claudia?

Learning Strategy:

Previewing

Learning Strategy:

Listening for details

¡Aquí te toca a ti!

Learning Strategy:

Requesting and giving
personal information

G. ¿Dormiste bien anoche? Question a classmate about his or her sleeping habits and experiences.

Haga las preguntas para saber…

1. si él (ella) durmió bien anoche.
2. a qué hora se acostó.
3. cuántas horas durmió.
4. cuántas horas duerme generalmente durante la semana.
5. cuántas horas duerme generalmente durante el fin de semana.

¡Adelante!

EJERCICIO ORAL

H. ¿Cuánto dormiste? Work with a partner to compare how much each of you slept during the last week. Create a weekly calendar for each of you to report your sleep for each night. Calculate the average amount of sleep per night that each of you got. For any nights that you slept at least one hour more or less than the average, indicate why on your calendar. Prepare to report to the group for each of you (1) the average amount of sleep per night, (2) the least amount of sleep in any one night, (3) the longest you slept in any one night, (4) and the most interesting reason that you had a "short" night.

EJERCICIO ESCRITO

I. Una encuesta Working with several students, create a survey to find out about the sleeping habits of your classmates and those of their families. Find out information that will either confirm or dispute the following statements. Once you have completed the survey, compile the results, and compare them to the results reported in the article at the beginning of this **etapa.**

1. High school students don't get enough sleep (that is, they go to bed too late and/or get up very early).
2. High school students catch up on lost sleep on weekends and during vacations.
3. Young people fall asleep more easily than older people.
4. Females have nightmares more often than males do.
5. Males snore more often than females do.

Vocabulario

Para charlar

Para hablar del aspecto físico

Mido un metro…   Tengo que subir de peso.
Peso… kilos.   bajar de peso.

Para hablar de un período de tiempo

¿Desde cuándo?   desde (que)
¿Cuánto tiempo hace?   hace (que)

Temas y contextos

Los alimentos y la nutrición

el almidón	el hierro	las papas
el calcio	la leche	los productos lácteos
el cereal	los lípidos	la proteína
la fibra	los minerales	los vegetales
la fruta	el pan	las vitaminas
la grasa		

El sueño

roncar
tener una pesadilla

Vocabulario general

Sustantivos

la ansiedad	una indicación
un artículo	la mayoría
un(a) bebé	un movimiento muscular
unas calorías	un músculo
una causa	un nervio
una dificultad	un resultado
la digestión	el ritmo cardíaco
una duda	la salud
la energía	una señal
una falta	el tono muscular
un hueso	la vista nocturna

Verbos

admitir	regular
desarrollar	renovar
facilitar	repetir (i, i)
formar	sonreír(se) (i, i)
mejorar	tratar de
presentar	
recuperar	

Adverbios

aparentemente
exactamente

Otras palabras y expresiones

en parte al menos
estar de visita
lo mismo
¡Qué envidia!

Adjetivos

adicional
balanceado(a)

Lectura CULTURAL

TRES ALIMENTOS INDÍGENAS

Antes de leer

Learning Strategy:

Previewing

1. Look at the photos and title that accompany the reading. What do you think the reading will be about?
2. Can you identify the foods in the photos? Have you ever seen any of these foods before?
3. Can you name some dishes that contain these ingredients?

Guía para la lectura

Learning Strategy:

Reading for details

A. Read the first paragraph to answer the following question: ¿Qué tienen en común el tomate, el maíz y la papa?

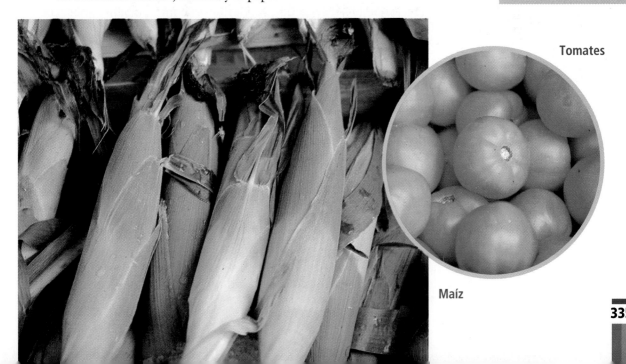

Tomates

Maíz

Papas

B. Now read the second paragraph and answer the following questions.

1. ¿Qué información tenemos sobre el tamaño *(size)* y el color del tomate?
2. ¿Desde cuándo se cultiva esta fruta en las Américas?

C. Read the third paragraph to obtain the following information.

1. ¿De dónde viene la palabra *maíz*?
2. ¿Cuál es una comida importante que se hace con el maíz?

D. Now read the last paragraph and answer the following questions.

1. ¿Por qué no podían cultivar el maíz los incas?
2. ¿Qué inventó la gente de los Andes?

Tres alimentos indígenas

uando los españoles llegaron al Nuevo Mundo, encontraron comidas que eran desconocidas en Europa. Muchas de estas son muy populares en el mundo entero hoy día. Tres de estas comidas son el tomate, el maíz y la papa.

Xitomatl es la palabra para tomate en náhuatl, el idioma de los aztecas. Hoy día en México se usa la palabra *jitomate* en vez de *xitomatl*, pero en otras partes del mundo hispano se usa la palabra *tomate.* Hay muchos tipos de tomates —grandes, pequeños, rojos, amarillos y anaranjados. Se cree que esta fruta se cultiva en México y en partes de la América Central desde hace más de 5.000 años. Los exploradores españoles introdujeron esta fruta en Europa. ¿Pueden imaginar la cocina italiana sin el tomate?

El maíz, conocido como *mahiz* en la lengua de los indios del Caribe, es un producto importantísimo que se originó en las Américas también desde hace más de 5.000 años. En la época pre-colombina se cultivaba desde lo que hoy es Chile hasta el sur de Canadá. El maíz es el ingrediente esencial de muchas comidas de la América Latina, entre ella la tortilla.

En las altas montañas de los Andes no podían cultivar maíz porque hace mucho frío. Allí los indios cultivaban la patata, conocida como *papa* en el quechua, la lengua que hablaban los incas y que hoy todavía se habla en los países andinos. Se cosechaban varios tipos de papa y los indios de los Andes inventaron una manera de conservarlas por medio del frío y el calor, o sea el proceso de conservarlas y deshidratarlas a la misma vez. ¿Se imaginan un mundo sin estas tres comidas?

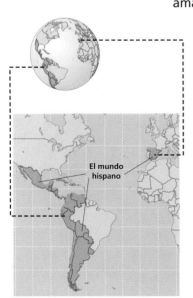

El mundo hispano

Aqui leemos

Estrategia para la lectura

Certain kinds of prose give advice or teach us how to do something. In passages like this, not every word is equally important, but the verb forms that tell what to do are usually especially significant. Sometimes, the order in which information is given is crucial. As always, read first to get an overall idea of content and organization. Then look for the main ideas or topics. Finally, read for specific details either for your own information or because you need them.

Antes de leer

The following article is from **El Regional**, a Puerto Rican newspaper. The article is full of advice for people who want to exercise but have trouble keeping at it. Answer these questions before you read it.

> > **W**hat do you already know about the value of physical exercise for good health?

> > **W**hy do people usually start an exercise program?

> > **W**hat are some reasons people stop exercising?

> > **W**hat are some techniques you use or have heard of that can help make exercise a habit?

Before reading the article, look to see how it is organized. Notice the section titles and the numbered subsections. Look closely at any subsection to see what kinds of verb forms are used. Then go on to the **Actividades.**

Acerca de los dolores musculares

Por Robert P. Sheldon

MANTÉNGASE

Mientras innumerables cantidades de personas comienzan un régimen de ejercicios cada año, otro tanto "tira la toalla" antes de ver algún resultado positivo. Y la cesación de la actividad no está limitada a los principiantes: veteranos, también, frecuentemente abandonan su deporte. La falta de interés y de tiempo y las lesiones son algunas de las razones para renunciar. Los científicos especialistas en comportamiento humano, John Martin, Ph.D. y Patricia Dubbert, Ph.D., de Veteranos y el Centro Médico de la Universidad de Mississippi tienen estos consejos para los deportistas novatos y los no tan novatos, lo mismo que para los profesionales y amigos alentadores:

1) Vaya paso a paso. Comience de una manera fácil, de baja intensidad y gradualmente aumente su ritmo de ejercicios.

2) Control del refuerzo. Siéntase orgulloso de usted mismo. Mantenga una lista que le recuerde sus logros. Cuéntele a sus amigos lo mucho que ha avanzado. Envuélvase en desafíos motivacionales de premios ganados o separe cierta cantidad de dinero por cada milla que corra, nade o corra en bicicleta.

3) Control estimulante. Saque la ropa que va a utilizar en la corrida mañanera la noche anterior, o por la mañana si es que va a correr en la tarde después del trabajo. Evite las amistades que no aprecian el ejercicio. Lleve un historial de su millaje, tenga a la vista carteles y fotografías de personas ejercitándose, programe sus ejercicios semanalmente por adelantado y escriba notas sobre usted mismo.

4) Contratos de comportamiento humano. Escríbase un contrato a usted mismo, y sea realista acerca de sus metas. Guárdelo y cuando haya logrado su meta, celébrelo.

5) Estrategias congénitas. Establezca metas, visualícese logrando éstas, y sea positivo. La gente comienza a ejercitarse por que es bueno para su salud y quiere hacerlo bien. Con un poco de empuje mental y premeditación, usted puede mantenerse en un programa de ejercicios o ayudar a otros a continuar el suyo.

Actividades

 A.
1. Read the first and last sentences. Based only on the information you find there and what you learned from the title, subtitles, illustration, and so on, what seems to be the main idea of the article? In English, write a one-sentence prediction of what you expect the rest of the article to be about.
2. Read the opening paragraph rapidly. According to this paragraph, what are two reasons people give up on their exercise programs? Were these the reasons you had predicted?

3. Read the first few words of each subsection. Based on the subtitle and the first few words, what is the likely content of each subsection?

4. Go to the subsection you previewed in **Antes de leer**. Read it carefully, looking for how each piece of advice relates to the section heading.

B. 1. Return to the opening paragraph and read it more carefully. List all the cognates you see.

2. Go to a numbered paragraph you have not yet read carefully. Read it and list all the command forms you see in it.

3. Based on the content of the reading and the contexts in which the following words and phrases occur, what is the best English equivalent for each one?
   a. régimen
   b. principiantes
   c. lesiones
   d. novatos
   e. refuerzo
   f. logros
   g. evite
   h. semanalmente
   i. metas
   j. empuje mental

C. Answer the following questions in English, based on the reading.

1. Who are John Martin and Patricia Dubbert? Why are they qualified to give advice about exercise?
2. According to number 5, why do people begin exercising?
3. According to number 1, how should you begin an exercise program?
4. According to number 2, how can you reward yourself?
5. What are some suggestions to help maintain a routine when exercising?

D. 1. Imagine you have a friend on an exercise program who is having trouble sticking with it. She has written to ask you for some advice. Using what you learned from this article, write your friend a note in Spanish, giving her some suggestions. Be sure to explain why the things you suggest are important.

2. With a partner, design a flyer that could be posted in your school gym to encourage more people to exercise. Use the information from this article to help you think of important points to emphasize.

3. Prepare a motivational poster for some sport or physical activity that you enjoy. Use the suggestions in number 3 from the article as a starting point. Write slogans and captions in Spanish.

Ya llegamos

Actividades orales

A. *Un amigo te ayuda.* You and your friend are traveling in a Spanish-speaking country. One of you begins to feel ill. The friend notices this and expresses concern. Thus encouraged, the one who is ailing sets about describing his or her symptoms. Since the friend must seek help from the pharmacist, he or she carefully repeats the symptoms to be sure that they are well understood. In addition, he or she inquires about other possible symptoms (for example, **Dices que tienes escalofríos. ¿Tienes fiebre también?**)

Together you should (1) list five symptoms and/or possible causes and (2) think of at least one medication or possible treatment.

B. *Yo no estoy en forma.* Your group of four is comparing notes to determine who is in the worst physical condition. Take turns mentioning facts about your health that could be improved upon and discussing sleeping, eating, and exercise habits. Every time one of the group mentions a reason he or she is not in great shape, try to come up with an even better excuse.

The group should then determine (1) which member needs the most improvement in each of the three areas of sleeping, eating, and exercise (that could be three different students, or one, or two); (2) which of you has the best habits overall; and (3) which one is in the worst overall physical condition. Finally, the group should make recommendations for each of the four members, prescribing what changes each one should make in his or her personal habits in order to improve his or her physical condition.

C. *Voy al médico.* Prepare a skit based on a visit to a doctor's office. One student will play the doctor and the other will play the patient. Be sure to include symptoms, how long the patient has had them, and what medicine the doctor recommends.

Actividades escritas

D. ¿Qué hacías cuando eras niño(a)? You and your friends are comparing what you used to do during summer vacations when you were children. Make a list of at least five activities that reflect how you spent a typical summer day. Then, in pairs, combine your list with a classmate's and write a description of a typical day in the life of a child.

E. ¿Cómo comen los jóvenes? Your family is hosting a foreign exchange student for the year. In order to make your guest more comfortable, you draw up a calendar showing meal times and sleep schedules. Be sure to include weekends, altering meal times and sleep schedules as appropriate.

F. ¿Cómo duermen los jóvenes? Write a letter to a friend in a Spanish-speaking country in which you provide details about your sleeping habits and inquire about theirs.

Conexión

Las enfermedades respiratorias

AL EMPEZAR

Usamos las vías respiratorias para respirar. Cuando inhalamos y exhalamos el oxígeno que nuestros cuerpos necesitan, el aire pasa por las vías respiratorias. A veces los microbios infectan las vías y **nos ponemos** enfermos.

we become

ACTIVIDAD A

¿Cuáles de las siguientes partes del cuerpo forman las vías respiratorias?

la nariz	la boca	los ojos	los brazos
el estómago	la garganta	la tráquea	las rodillas
el cuello	los pulmones	las orejas	
la espalda	el muslo	el corazón	

TRES ENFERMEDADES DE LAS VÍAS RESPIRATORIAS

a bronquitis, la gripe y el resfrío son tres de las enfermedades más comunes de las vías respiratorias. Normalmente los microbios que causan estas enfermedades son víruses. La siguiente tabla tiene una descripción de cada enfermedad.

Enfermedad:	bronquitis	gripe	resfrío
Órganos afectados	los pulmones, la tráquea	todas las vías respiratorias	la nariz, la garganta
Síntomas	una tos fuerte, flema amarilla, fiebre (a veces)	fiebre, escalofríos, dolor de garganta, dolor de cabeza, tos y dolores musculares	estornudos, tos, congestión de la nariz, irritación de los ojos
Tipo de microbio	virus o bacteria	virus	virus
Duración	2-3 días	1-2 semanas	3-4 días

ACTIVIDAD B

Contesta las siguientes preguntas.

1. ¿Cuántos tipos de enfermedades respiratorias hay en la tabla?
2. ¿Cuáles de las enfermedades pueden afectar los pulmones?
3. ¿Cuáles pueden afectar la nariz?
4. ¿Cuáles afectan partes del cuerpo que no están en las vías respiratorias?
5. ¿Cuáles nos dan fiebre? ¿escalofríos? ¿estornudos? ¿tos?
6. ¿Cuál enfermedad dura más tiempo?
7. ¿Hace cuánto tiempo que estuviste enfermo(a) con una de estas enfermedades? ¿Qué tuviste?

ACTIVIDAD C

Think of the last time that you had a respiratory infection and describe the symptoms by answering the following questions.

	Sí	No
¿Tenías fiebre?	_____	_____
¿Tosías?	_____	_____
¿Te dolía la garganta?	_____	_____
¿Tenías escalofríos?	_____	_____
¿Te dolían los ojos?	_____	_____
¿Tenías dolor de cabeza?	_____	_____
¿Estornudabas con frecuencia?	_____	_____
¿Tenías congestionada la nariz?	_____	_____
¿Te dolían los músculos?	_____	_____

¿Otros síntomas? _____

¿Cuánto tiempo duró la enfermedad? ¿Dos o tres días? ¿Cuatro días? ¿Una semana?_____

ACTIVIDAD D

Work with a partner to see if you can correctly diagnose the respiratory infection each of you had. Take turns describing your symptoms using the list in Actividad C. Then complete a medical report like the one below.

Síntomas de mi compañero(a): _____

Mi diagnóstico: _____

¿Qué ves?

>> *¿Te gusta patinar en ruedas?*

>> *¿Cuándo fue la última vez que patinaste en ruedas?*

>> *¿Dónde y con quién lo hiciste?*

OBJECTIVES

IN THIS UNIT YOU WILL LEARN:

- **T**o talk about leisure-time activities;
- **T**o talk about sports;
- **T**o narrate and describe in the past.

Aventura y deporte

13 EL VERANO PASADO

El esquí acuático es un buen ejercicio y una buena manera para divertirse con los amigos.

Objectives:

>>> **U**nderstanding short descriptions of warm-weather sports and pastimes

>>> **T**alking about the recent past

>>> **D**escribing places and events in the past

Strategies:

>>> **R**equesting and providing information

>>> **O**rganizing ideas

>>> **I**magining

PRIMERA ETAPA

Preparación

>> **W**hat is one of your favorite activities?

>> **W**hat did you do last summer?

>> **D**o you like camping? Would you like to windsurf?

Learning Strategies:

Brainstorming, previewing

¿Qué hiciste?

Mi actividad favorita cuando voy a la playa es hacer windsurfing. Es buen ejercicio. En enero fui a Puerto Rico con la familia por una semana y me divertí mucho con los amigos. Una mañana salí temprano para correr en la playa y luego por la tarde hice windsurfing con mi amigo Raimundo. Esa noche fuimos a las discotecas. Pienso volver en el verano si puedo.

Antonio Salazar

Nos gusta mucho acampar. El verano pasado fuimos a Costa Rica donde hay muchos parques nacionales. Llevamos dos tiendas de campaña. Aprendimos mucho sobre los animales y las plantas tropicales. Fuimos a un parque donde vimos el cráter de un volcán y vimos que salía humo del cráter. Me gustó mucho el viaje.

Carmen Rivera

¡Aquí te toca a ti!

A. ¿Quién hizo qué?   Indica las actividades que hizo cada persona
(Carmen o Antonio) basándote en la página 347.

acampó en un parque nacional	vio un volcán
corrió en la playa	fue a Costa Rica
estuvo en Puerto Rico	llevó tiendas de campaña
aprendió mucho sobre la naturaleza	hizo windsurfing
viajó en el verano	viajó en enero
fue a una discoteca	vio humo saliendo de un cráter

ESTRUCTURA

Other verbs in the preterite: *conducir, traer, decir*

Conduje el coche a 55 millas por hora.	I *drove* the car at 55 miles per hour.
¿Quién **trajo** las bebidas?	Who *brought* the drinks?
Tus amigos lo **dijeron.**	Your friends *said* it.

These verbs change their stems in the preterite, but actually have a clear pattern of their own.
Note that they all have **j** in the stem. In addition, the **yo** form does not have an accent on the
last syllable, nor does the **él / ella / Ud.** form ending in **-o.** Also note that the **ellos / ellas /
Uds.** form uses **-eron** (and not **-ieron**) after the **j.**

conducir (to drive)

yo	**conduje**	nosotros(as)	**condujimos**
tú	**condujiste**	vosotros(as)	**condujisteis**
él		ellos	
ella	**condujo**	ellas	**condujeron**
Ud.		Uds.	

traer (to bring)

yo	**traje**	nosotros(as)	**trajimos**
tú	**trajiste**	vosotros(as)	**trajisteis**
él		ellos	
ella	**trajo**	ellas	**trajeron**
Ud.		Uds.	

---

decir (to say)

yo	**dije**	nosotros(as)	**dijimos**
tú	**dijiste**	vosotros(as)	**dijisteis**
él		ellos	
ella	} **dijo**	ellas	} **dijeron**
Ud.		Uds.	

Note that the stem of the verb **decir** has the same vowel change in the preterite, **e** becoming **i,** as in the present tense.

Also, these verbs all have different **yo** forms in the present tense. All the other persons follow the standard present tense endings.

conducir → yo condu**z**co, tú conduces, él / ella / Ud. conduce, nosotros(as) conducimos, vosotros(as) conducís, ellos / ellas / Uds. conducen

decir (i) → yo di**g**o, tú dices, él / ella / Ud. dice, nosotros(as) decimos, vosotros(as) decís, ellos / ellas / Uds. dicen

traer → yo tra**ig**o, tú traes, él / ella / Ud. trae, nosotros(as) traemos, vosotros(as) traéis, ellos / ellas / Uds. traen

Aquí practicamos

B. Forma oraciones completas de una manera lógica, usando elementos de las columnas. Cambia los verbos a la forma apropiada del pretérito.

 Francisco   traer   los discos compactos
Francisco trajo los discos compactos.

A	B	C
Enrique y yo	conducir	los discos compactos
Carlos y José	traer	la verdad
María	decir	el coche de su papá
tú		su tabla vela
Esteban y tú		que vamos a la playa
vosotros		al centro

C. ¿Qué pasó anoche en la fiesta?   Contesta las preguntas
sobre una fiesta. Usa el pretérito e inventa los detalles.

1. ¿Tú condujiste el coche de tus padres a la fiesta de Julián y José?
2. ¿A qué hora dijiste que terminó la fiesta?
3. ¿Qué tipo de cintas trajeron tus amigos?
4. ¿Quién dijo que fue aburrida la fiesta?
5. ¿Quiénes más condujeron anoche?

Aquí escuchamos:
"¿Qué hizo Lorenzo?"

Antes de escuchar

Think about what you usually tell your friends when you talk to them about a vacation you took. Now read the following questions to get a good idea of what to listen for in the conversasation about what Lorenzo did during his vacation.

Después de escuchar

Contesta las preguntas sobre lo que hizo Lorenzo durante sus vacaciones.

1. ¿Adónde fue Lorenzo de vacaciones?
2. ¿Con quién fue de vacaciones?
3. ¿Qué hizo todos los días por la mañana? ¿Y por la tarde qué hizo con su hermano?
4. ¿Cuándo aprendió Lorenzo su nuevo deporte acuático?

5. ¿Qué le dijo Lorenzo a Roberto que le pasó varias veces al principio?
6. ¿Qué sabía hacer ya Lorenzo que le ayudó mucho?
7. ¿Cuál fue la reacción de Roberto a lo que le contó Lorenzo?

¡Aquí te toca a ti!

D. ¿Qué hizo?   Talk with a classmate and (1) find out what three things
he or she did last summer. Then (2) find a second classmate and tell him

or her what the first person you talked to said he or she did last summer. After doing this, (3) ask what three things your second partner did last summer and go on to repeat this process with a third student.

¡Adelante!

E. El verano pasado (1) Talk with a partner about last summer. (2) Create a chart to compare your activities with those of your partner. (3) List at least five activities for each of you. Then (4) find at least two activities that you had in common and two in which only one of you participated. (Use the following list of suggestions to start you thinking.)

Yo		Mi amigo(a)
	ir a la playa	
	hacer windsurfing	
	ir a las discotecas	
	acampar	
	patinar en ruedas	
	ver un volcán	
	hablar por teléfono	
	leer	
	jugar al tenis	
	jugar al vólibol	
	pescar	
	estudiar en la universidad	

F. Una actividad fenomenal Write an entry into your diary in which you tell about a memorable activity. Tell (1) who was involved, (2) your relationship to the principal characters, (3) where the action took place, (4) the goal of the main participants, (5) whether or not they achieved their goal, and (6) how you were affected. (Use several different verbs, paying special attention to the use of the preterite tense.)

//·//·//·//·//·//·//·//·//

Learning Strategy:

Organizing ideas in a paragraph

SEGUNDA ETAPA

Preparación

>> **W**hen was the last time you took a long trip?

>> **W**here did you go and with whom did you go?

>> **W**hat do you remember about that trip?

¡Qué viaje!

Un clavadista en Acapulco, México

dived

unforgettable

*El año pasado fui de vacaciones con la familia a México. Fuimos a Acapulco donde vimos un espectáculo en "La Quebrada" donde unos hombres **se clavaron** al agua desde una altura de 55 metros. Una tarde alquilamos una lancha y mi hermano y yo esquiamos. Una noche fuimos a un excelente restaurante donde comimos mariscos y escuchamos música de mariachi. El último día compramos regalos en las tiendas para los amigos en los Estados Unidos. Fue un viaje **inolvidable**.*

Miguel Martínez

¡Aquí te toca a ti!

A. ¿Qué hizo Miguel?
Indica las actividades que hizo Miguel durante sus vacaciones basándote en la página 352.

Miguel…

escuchó música de mariachi
hizo ciclismo
fue a la Ciudad de México
compró unos discos compactos
comió mariscos
fue a un museo
montó en bicicleta con su hermano
fue a un concierto de rock
se clavó desde una altura *(height)* de 55 m
estuvo en Acapulco
esquió
fue de compras
vio a los clavadistas *(cliff divers)*

Repaso

B. Nuestras vacaciones
Imagina que tu familia fue de vacaciones a México el año pasado. Usa las pistas para hablar sobre tus vacaciones. Sigue el modelo.

Modelo: el año pasado / nosotros / ir de vacaciones a México
El año pasado nosotros fuimos de vacaciones a México.

1. nosotros / divertirse mucho
2. mis padres / decidir / ir a Acapulco
3. mi padre / reservar dos cuartos en el Hotel Presidente
4. el 5 de julio / nosotros / llegar al hotel
5. la familia / pasar dos semanas en Acapulco
6. yo / dar un paseo / todos los días
7. mis hermanos / ir a la playa / mucho
8. una tarde / mi papá / decir "¡Vamos a La Quebrada!"
9. en La Quebrada / nosotros / ver el espectáculo de los clavadistas
10. un experto valiente / clavarse al mar desde una altura de 55 m
11. esa noche / todos nosotros / acostarse muy tarde por la emoción
12. el último día / yo / levantarse temprano / para ir a la playa
13. nosotros / volver a los Estados Unidos / el 29 de julio
14. mi familia y yo / divertirse mucho / durante nuestras vacaciones

ESTRUCTURA

Other verbs in the preterite: *poder, saber, poner*

Traté de hacerlo, pero no **pude**.	I tried to do it, but *I could* not.
Cuando llamó José, **supimos** lo que pasó.	When José called, *we found out* what had happened.
Los niños **pusieron** los paquetes en la cocina.	The children *put* the packages in the kitchen.

These verbs are conjugated in a similar way. Note that the vowel in the stem of each verb changes to **u.** Here are the forms:

poder

pod- → **pud-**

yo	**pude**	nosotros(as)	**pudimos**
tú	**pudiste**	vosotros(as)	**pudisteis**
él		ellos	
ella	**pudo**	ellas	**pudieron**
Ud.		Uds.	

saber

sab- → **sup-**

yo	**supe**	nosotros(as)	**supimos**
tú	**supiste**	vosotros(as)	**supisteis**
él		ellos	
ella	**supo**	ellas	**supieron**
Ud.		Uds.	

poner

pon- → **pus-**

yo	**puse**	nosotros(as)	**pusimos**
tú	**pusiste**	vosotros(as)	**pusisteis**
él		ellos	
ella	**puso**	ellas	**pusieron**
Ud.		Uds.	

Aquí practicamos

C. Contesta las preguntas usando las formas apropiadas de los verbos en el pretérito. Compara tus respuestas con las de un(a) compañero(a). Anota cómo son semejantes o diferentes.

1. ¿Qué deporte pudiste hacer por fin después de practicar mucho?
2. ¿Qué supiste recientemente sobre algún atleta que no sabías antes?
3. ¿Qué deporte no pudiste hacer la primera vez que lo intentaste *(tried)*?
4. ¿Dónde pusieron los estudiantes sus bicicletas cuando llegaron a la escuela?

D. Dime...   Create questions by combining the items in the left column with those in the right column, using the preterite of the verbs in the middle column. A classmate will give answers to your questions.

> *Modelo:*   dónde   poner   las cintas
>   **Estudiante A:**   *¿Dónde pusiste las cintas?*
>   **Estudiante B:**   *Las puse en el coche.*

por qué (no)	poder	la bicicleta
cuándo	conducir	las cintas
quién	saber	salir de la casa
qué	dar	la propina *(tip)* a José
cuánto	poner	los precios del restaurante
dónde	decir	ir a la playa
	traer	el coche de su padre
		la verdad
		las bebidas
		el número de teléfono del hotel
		la silla
		lo que dijo el presidente

Nota gramatical

The verb ponerse

When the verb **poner** is used with a *reflexive pronoun*, it has two very different meanings:

1. to put on (an article of clothing)

Me puse el abrigo.   *I put on* my coat.

2. to get or become (an emotion, a state)

Jorge **se puso** furioso cuando
perdió el partido de tenis.

Jorge *became* furious when he
lost the tennis match.

Mis amigos siempre **se ponen**
nerviosos cuando viajan por avión.

My friends always *get* nervous
when they travel by plane.

 Preguntas   Alternando con otro(a) estudiante, usen las sugerencias para hacer preguntas. Sigan el modelo.

Modelo: cuándo / ponerse nervioso
—*¿Cuándo te pones nervioso(a)?*
—*Me pongo nervioso(a) cuando tengo un examen.*

1. cuándo / ponerse el suéter
2. dónde / poner las bebidas para la fiesta mañana
3. por qué / ponerse nervioso(a) cuando jugar al golf
4. cuándo / ponerse su ropa favorita
5. cuándo / ponerse furioso(a)

Aquí escuchamos:
"Un viaje a Guadalajara"

Antes de escuchar

Review the preterite forms of the verbs you have learned so far in this chapter. Then read the following questions to anticipate what María Elena might say about her trip to Mexico.

Después de escuchar

Ahora contesta las preguntas.

1. ¿Adónde y con quiénes fue de vacaciones María Elena?
2. ¿A quiénes visitó?
3. ¿A qué lugares fueron en la ciudad?
4. ¿Qué más hicieron para divertirse?
5. ¿Adónde condujeron en coche?
6. ¿Qué hicieron en este lugar a dos horas de la ciudad?
7. ¿Qué supieron al volver de su viaje en coche?
8. ¿Cuál fue la reacción ante estas noticias?

¡Aquí te toca a ti!

F. ¿Qué pudiste hacer?   Work with a classmate and ask each other about a memorable trip you each took or can pretend that you took. Ask each other about three things that you were able to do on the trip, using the correct preterite forms of the verb **poder** when asking and answering the questions.

¡Adelante!

EJERCICIO ORAL

G. ¿Qué hiciste la semana pasada?   Use the cues as a starting point to describe at least five things you did last summer in each category. Report facts or make up the information, if you like, using a different verb for each activity you add after the cue. Make sure to relate the activities to the context of that particular cue. Follow the model.

 Modelo: reunirse en la playa / mis amigos y yo
Mis amigos y yo nos reunimos en la playa. Nadamos, tomamos el sol, comimos mariscos, jugamos al vólibol y, por la noche, salimos a bailar.

1. ir al cine / mi familia y yo
2. viajar en coche / con mi papá
3. ir de camping / con unos amigos
4. visitar a mis abuelos / mi familia
5. pasar una semana en la ciudad de México / yo

EJERCICIO ESCRITO

H. Un viaje   Write a letter to your grandmother about an interesting trip that you took, telling (1) where you went, (2) when, (3) how you got there, (4) with whom you went, (5) how long you stayed, and (6) at least four activities in which you participated. (You may base this letter on a real experience or on an imaginary trip.) (7) Don't forget to date and sign your letter.

Learning Strategies:

Expressing past time, listing, reporting based on personal experience

Critical Thinking Strategies:

Making associations, imagining

Learning Strategies:

Expressing past time, organizing details

Critical Thinking Strategy:

Imagining

357

TERCERA ETAPA

Preparación

≫ **W**hat are some of the sports that you play?

≫ **W**hat sports do you play in the summer?

≫ **W**hich sport did you play the most last summer?

≫ **W**hich sport would you like to learn to play?

Learning Strategy:

Previewing

¿A qué jugaste?

—¿A qué jugaste el verano pasado? ¿al tenis?
—No, jugué al béisbol. ¿Y tú?
—Ah, yo jugué mucho al baloncesto.

al golf

al fútbol americano

al béisbol

al vólibol

al tenis

al hockey sobre hierba

al boliche

al dominó

a los naipes

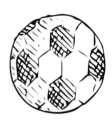

al fútbol

al baloncesto

al ajedrez

a las damas

¡Aquí te toca a ti!

Learning Strategy:

Reporting in the past based on visual cues

A. ¿Qué hizo?   Indica lo que hizo cada una de las personas según los dibujos abajo y en la página 360.

1. Mateo

2. Enrique

3. Susana

4. Alberto

5. Gabriel   **6.** Sara   **7.** Horacio y Elena   **8.** Claudia

Learning Strategies:

Polling, recording information in a chart

B. *¿Qué hiciste tú?*   Your Spanish class has been asked by the school newspaper to participate in a survey to determine which sports and games were played the most last summer by the student body. Your task is to (1) poll five members of the class to find out who played what and (2) record the results of your poll in a chart like the following one. In the last column, (3) total the number of students who played that sport or game. The first column has been done for you.

	Nombre de estudiante: *Lupe*	Nombre: _____	Nombre: _____	Nombre: _____	Nombre: _____	Nombre: _____	Total que lo jugaron:
Deporte: golf	✓						
vólibol							
fútbol	✓						
béisbol	✓						
boliche	✓						
tenis	✓						
baloncesto							
ajedrez							
patinar en ruedas	✓						
esquiar	✓						
naipes							
equitación							
natación	✓						
acampar							

Now, in groups of four or five, (1) compare the results of your surveys. Together, (2) come up with some explanations as to (a) why you think certain activities were the most popular and (b) why the two with the fewest votes were not so popular. Consider geographical location, number of people required for a certain game, season, age of participants, gender of students surveyed, etc. (3) Be prepared to report this analysis to the class. Finally, (4) come up with a possible headline for the newspaper article on the student body's choices of summer activities. Your headline should reflect something about your findings.

Repaso

C. **La carta misteriosa**   Read the following brief passage, changing the underlined present tense verbs into the *preterite* tense. Then work with a group of three or four classmates to decide what happened next, creating your own ending to report back to the entire class.

A las 11:00 de la noche más o menos, Carolina <u>llega</u> a su casa después de un día muy ocupado. Cansada, <u>se sienta</u> por unos momentos. <u>Abre</u> su cartera y <u>saca</u> una carta. La <u>pone</u> sobre la mesita, al lado del sofá, pero luego la <u>mira</u> varias veces y, por fin, <u>decide</u> abrirla. Al principio, no lo <u>puede</u> hacer. <u>Se pone</u> nerviosa pero, por fin, <u>rompe</u> el sobre y <u>mira</u> la carta. Poco después, confundida (confused), <u>pone</u> la carta en el sobre y <u>se levanta</u> muy despacio del sofá. <u>Se da</u> cuenta del silencio total de la casa. Cuando <u>pone</u> el pie en el primer escalón (step) para subir a su cuarto, una voz <u>grita</u> (shouts) desde allí. No <u>puede</u> moverse. <u>Se queda</u> paralizada de terror, sin saber qué hacer.

ESTRUCTURA

Other verbs in the preterite: *leer, caer(se), creer, ver, oír*

Leíste la carta ayer.	*You read* the letter yesterday.
El niño llora porque **se cayó.**	The boy is crying because he *fell down.*
Creímos el cuento de Pablo.	*We believed* Paul's story.
Vi la película el sábado.	*I saw* the movie on Saturday.
Ellos **oyeron** las noticias.	They *heard* the news.

The verbs **leer, caer(se), creer,** and **oír** are conjugated similarly in the preterite. They have in common a **y,** instead of an **i,** in the **él / ella / Ud.** and **ellos / ellas / Uds.** forms.

The other forms follow the normal pattern of **-er / -ir** verbs in the preterite tense.

leer

yo	**leí**		nosotros(as)	**leímos**
tú	**leíste**		vosotros(as)	**leísteis**
él			ellos	
ella	**leyó**		ellas	**leyeron**
Ud.			Uds	

caer(se)

yo	**caí**		nosotros(as)	**caímos**
tú	**caíste**		vosotros(as)	**caísteis**
él			ellos	
ella	**cayó**		ellas	**cayeron**
Ud.			Uds.	

oír

yo	**oí**		nosotros(as)	**oímos**
tú	**oíste**		vosotros(as)	**oísteis**
él			ellos	
ella	**oyó**		ellas	**oyeron**
Ud.			Uds.	

creer

yo	**creí**		nosotros(as)	**creímos**
tú	**creíste**		vosotros(as)	**creísteis**
él			ellos	
ella	**creyó**		ellas	**creyeron**
Ud.			Uds.	

The verb **ver** is conjugated similarly to the verb **dar** in the preterite. Its endings are exactly like those of **-er** and **-ir** verbs.

ver

yo	**vi**	nosotros(as)	**vimos**
tú	**viste**	vosotros(as)	**visteis**
él		ellos	
ella	} **vio**	ellas	} **vieron**
Ud.		Uds.	

Caer(se) and **oír** also have a special **yo** form in the present tense. **Oír** also changes its stem in the present tense.

caerse → me ca**ig**o, te caes, se cae, nos caemos, os caéis, se caen

oír → o**ig**o, oyes, oye, oímos, oís, oyen

Aquí practicamos

D. *Un espectáculo en Acapulco* Sustituye las palabras en cursiva con las palabras entre paréntesis y haz los otros cambios necesarios.

1. *Yo* leí sobre los clavadistas de Acapulco en la guía. (nosotros / ella / tú / mis amigos / vosotras)
2. *Mis padres* no creyeron lo que dije sobre La Quebrada. (Uds. / él / mis hermanos / tú)
3. *Nosotros* vimos, por fin, el espectáculo a la orilla del mar. (yo / ellos / tú / ella / vosotros)
4. *Un clavadista* se cayó de la roca. (Uds. / mi hermano / yo / tú / nosotros)
5. *Yo* oí que no se lastimó. (nosotros / ella / tú / Uds. / vosotros)
6. *Mi papá* les dio una propina *(tip)* a los clavadistas. (ellos / nosotros / yo / tú / Uds. / el Sr. Fuentes)

E. *México* Usa los dibujos en la página 364 para decir lo que *(what)* vieron diferentes estudiantes durante sus vacaciones en México y lo que piensan ver hoy y mañana. Sigue el modelo.

las pirámides

nosotros
Ayer *nosotros vimos las pirámides.*
Hoy *vemos las pirámides.*
Mañana *vamos a ver las pirámides.*

////////////////////
Learning Strategies:
Reporting in the past, present, and immediate future based on visual cues

los volcanes

1. yo

el monumento

2. ella

el clavadista

3. ellos

El Palacio de Bellas Artes

4. nosotros

La Catedral Nacional

5. ustedes

el centro

6. tú

**El Museo Nacional
de Antropología**

7. nosotros

**el zoológico
Bosque de Chapultepec**

8. yo

el mercado

9. ellos

F. El accidente   Cambia los verbos en cursiva al pretérito.

1. Hoy *veo* un accidente en el lago.
2. *Puedo* ver el velero claramente desde el balcón del hotel.
3. El hombre *se cae* del velero y *grita* "¡Auxilio!" *("Help!")*.
4. El velero *da* una vuelta *(turns)* sin el hombre.
5. El hombre *puede* subir al velero cuando *pasa* cerca de él.
6. Al día siguiente *leo* del accidente en el periódico.
7. El hombre *dice* en el artículo que nunca *tiene* miedo durante el accidente.
8. ¡*Me río* cuando *leo* eso!
9. No *creo* al hombre porque lo *oigo* gritar tanto en el agua.

Aquí escuchamos:
"Un espectáculo en Acapulco"

Antes de escuchar

Review the preterite of the verbs you have learned in this chapter. Now read the following questions to focus your listening. You will hear a brief narration about Miguel's trip to Mexico and what happened to a cliff diver while he was in Acapulco.

Learning Strategy:
Previewing

Después de escuchar

Escucha el monólogo otra vez antes de contestar las preguntas.

1. ¿Sobre qué leyó Miguel en la guía?
2. ¿Qué dice Miguel que no creyeron sus amigos?
3. ¿Quiénes vieron el espectáculo?
4. ¿Qué accidente tuvo uno de los hombres?
5. ¿Qué oyó Miguel después del accidente?
6. ¿Qué hizo el papá de Miguel al final?

Learning Strategy:
Listening for details

¡Aquí te toca a ti!

G. ¿Qué jugaste?   Work with a classmate to ask and answer each other's questions about three or four sports that you each played during the past year. Use the verb **jugar** each time you ask or answer a question.

¡**A**delante!

//·//·//·//·//·//·//·//·//

Cooperative Learning

Learning Strategies:

Reporting based on personal information, describing, organizing ideas, narrating in the past and present times

Critical Thinking Strategy:

Comparing and contrasting

//·//·//·//·//·//·//·//·//

Learning Strategies:

Reporting based on personal information, describing, organizing ideas in paragraphs, narrating in the past

EJERCICIO ORAL

H. *Mis deportes y juegos favoritos*   Talk with a classmate and (1) tell each other what sports and board games you generally like to play. Then think back to the last time you participated in a holiday gathering with some of your extended family (aunts, uncles, cousins, grandparents) where you played various sports and/or games. (2) Describe that event and (3) tell who was there. (4) Identify two things you and your partner can find in common and (5) one element that is different about the experiences you are describing.

EJERCICIO ESCRITO

I. *Una narración*   Write about an interesting, dramatic, or funny incident that you remember from a trip you took at some point in the past. Use the preterite throughout your narration.

Vocabulario

Temas y contextos

Las vacaciones

correr en la playa
los clavadistas
el concierto de rock
la discoteca
los mariscos
la música de mariachi
la naturaleza
el volcán

Las diversiones y los deportes

jugar...
  al ajedrez
  al boliche
  a las damas
  al dominó
  a los naipes

Vocabulario general

Verbos

caer(se)   dividir
clavar(se)   traer
dar

Adjetivos

contento(a)
costoso(a)
feroz
furioso(a)
inolvidable
nervioso(a)
triste

Adverbios

al principio
por fin

Lectura CULTURAL

LOS LLANOS VENEZOLANOS

Learning Strategy:

Previewing

Antes de leer

1. Look at the photos, map, and the title of the reading to form some impressions about its content.
2. If you were to take a trip to a rain forest in Latin America, what would you expect to see there?

Guía para la lectura

Learning Strategies:

Reading for cultural information, reading for main ideas, identifying, reading for details

Critical Thinking Strategy:

Categorizing

A. The following narrative by a young boy about his trip to Venezuela describes a series of sights and experiences that were memorable for him. Read the first sentence of each paragraph to get an idea of what he did. On a separate sheet of paper, summarize in your own words what the main idea is in each paragraph.

B. Now read the passage carefully and answer the following questions.

1. Make a list of all of the people identified in the reading. Who are they?
2. Make a list of all the animals identified in the reading. What are they?

C. Look over the following questions. Read the passage again and answer them.

1. ¿De dónde son los tíos de Miguel y adónde fueron de vacaciones?
2. En general, ¿cómo es la región del río Orinoco?
3. ¿Por qué no pudo nadar Miguel cuando hacía mucho calor?
4. ¿Qué pasó cuando Miguel y sus tíos trataron de comprar unas canastas?
5. ¿Qué recibían los indios a cambio de sus canastas?

Los llanos venezolanos

En septiembre mis tíos, que viven en Caracas, me invitaron a pasar unas semanas con ellos antes de empezar el colegio. Visité muchos lugares pero el fin de semana que fuimos a los llanos del Orinoco me pareció fantástico. Esta zona de prados que tiene 1.000 km de largo y 320 km de ancho, se extiende entre los Andes y el río Orinoco. Es una región muy plana, donde hay algunas pequeñas elevaciones. Tiene muchos ríos que fluyen del Orinoco.

Cruzamos varios de estos ríos durante el viaje. Tenía muchas ganas de nadar, porque hacía mucho calor, ¡pero había pirañas! Mis tíos me dijeron que también hay caimanes *(crocodiles)*, pero no vimos ninguno. Vi muchos pájaros rojos, blancos, rosados. En un árbol vi una iguana enorme.

Algo que nunca voy a olvidar de este viaje fue nuestro encuentro con una tribu de indios. Buscábamos un lugar para acampar y pasar la noche cuando vimos humo que salía de entre unos árboles. Nos acercamos. Y allí encontramos un pequeño pueblo indio. Aunque no hablábamos la misma lengua, inmediatamente pudimos entendernos. Coromoto, un chico de mi edad, me enseñó como hacían canastas, collares y pulseras. Yo quería tener una canasta de recuerdo y mi tía quería canastas para decorar la casa. No pudimos comprarlas porque los indios no usan el dinero. Finalmente las cambiamos por naranjas, una fruta que ellos no conocían.

Abajo: una iguana
Derecha: Un termitero inmenso en Venezuela

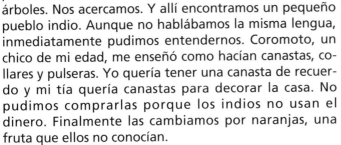

14

AL AIRE LIBRE

El ciclismo es un deporte de gran popularidad. Los ciclistas de países hispanos tienen mucho éxito en los campeonatos del mundo.

Objectives:

》》 **U**nderstanding short descriptions of outdoor sports

》》 **D**escribing places and events in the past

Strategies:

》》 **P**ersuading

》》 **S**upporting an opinion

》》 **D**rawing inferences

PRIMERA ETAPA

Preparación

>> **D**o you like to ride a bicycle? Why or why not?

>> **D**o you have a bicycle?

>> **D**id you have a bicycle when you were younger?

>> **I**s the bicycle that you have now different from the one you had as a child? in what ways?

El ciclismo

Cargarás con todo el equipo

Headphones
Ideal para hacer deporte sin perder el ritmo.

Atleta urbano
Hombre o mujer que, sin castigarse el cuerpo, vive en la ciudad deportivamente.

Mochila
Para que te eches todo, incluso tus problemas, a las espaldas.

Camiseta
Imprescindible para el atleta urbano, porque con ella puedes hacer de todo: ir en mountain bike, correr, caminar y pasear.

Cámara fotográfica
Demuestra a tus amistades que eres un verdadero atleta urbano. Enséñales la foto.

Botella de Trinaranjus
Todo atleta urbano se refresca de una manera natural y Trinaranjus sin burbujas es el refresco más natural e imprescindible para conseguir, entre otras cosas, el equipo del atleta urbano.

Mountain bike
Hay muchas maneras de practicar el atletismo urbano, pero hacerlo con una mountain bike es de la más cómodas.

Ahora, Trinaranjus te regala miles de camisetas, mochilas, headphones y cámaras de fotos. Y, además, sortea 50 mountain bikes. Todo, para que puedas tener el equipo de atleta urbano al completo. Las instrucciones las encontrarás en las botellas de Trinaranjus.

imprescindible: indispensable / *mountain bike: bicicleta de montaña* / *headphones: auriculares* / *sortea:* raffles off

¡Aquí te toca a ti!

A. *Un anuncio*   Completa las oraciones con la opción que se corresponda mejor con el contenido del anuncio de la página 371.

1. Un atleta urbano es un hombre o una mujer que…
    a. vive en la ciudad deportivamente.
    b. vive en una ciudad.
2. La cámara es para demostrar a tus amigos que…
    a. eres un(a) buen(a) atleta.
    b. vas a pasear.
3. La manera más cómoda de practicar el atletismo urbano es
    a. con una bicicleta de montaña.
    b. caminando.
4. La camiseta es necesaria para…
    a. no tener frío.
    b. ir en bicicleta de montaña, correr, caminar y pasear.
5. Todo atleta urbano se refresca con…
    a. tres naranjas.
    b. Trinaranjus.
6. Trinaranjus te regala…
    a. cientos de camisetas, mochilas y cámaras de fotos.
    b. miles de camisetas, mochilas, auriculares y cámaras de fotos.
7. Trinaranjus es un refresco natural…
    a. con gas.
    b. sin gas.
8. Trinaranjus también…
    a. sortea cincuenta bicicletas de montaña.
    b. da cincuenta bicicletas de montaña.
9. En la mochila pones…
    a. de todo.
    b. tus problemas.
10. Las instrucciones para el sorteo están en…
    a. las tiendas donde compras Trinaranjus.
    b. las botellas de Trinaranjus.

Repaso

B. Cambia los verbos en cursiva, abajo y en la página 373, al pretérito.

1. En la escuela mi hermano y yo *leemos* sobre los volcanes de Centroamérica.
2. Poco después, *oímos* en la televisión de un accidente en un parque nacional costarricense.

3. Según las noticias, un turista *se cae* en un cráter.
4. *Sabemos* que un hombre *puede* ayudar al turista.
5. Lo *pone* sobre los hombros para salvarlo.
6. Yo *creo* que ese hombre *es* muy valiente.

C. Nuestras vacaciones en Costa Rica   Cambia los verbos subrayados *(underlined)* al pretérito.

1. Nosotros <u>pasamos</u> una semana de vacaciones en Costa Rica. *(Begin with **El año pasado...**)*
2. Nuestro viaje <u>comienza</u> en San José, donde mi padre <u>hace</u> reservaciones en el famoso Hotel Cariari.
3. El primer día, <u>damos</u> un paseo por el mercado, donde <u>compramos</u> mucho café para llevar a nuestros amigos. También <u>visitamos</u> el Museo de Arte Costarricense, una fábrica de joyas *(jewel factory)* y el enorme Monumento a la Guerra de 1856.
4. El segundo día, <u>salimos</u> para Puntarenas. <u>Conducimos</u> a la costa en un coche que mi padre <u>alquila</u> para el viaje. En camino *(On the way)*, <u>conocemos</u> varios pueblos interesantes.
5. Por fin, <u>llegamos</u> a una hermosa playa de arenas *(sands)* blancas en el Pacífico. <u>Pedimos</u> ceviche *(marinated fish)* fresco y mariscos. Yo <u>como</u> un pescado grande.
6. Después de pasar unos días en la playa, toda la familia <u>va</u> a visitar el Parque Nacional Volcán Poás. A pesar de que *(Even though)* <u>empieza</u> a llover, <u>podemos</u> subir al enorme cráter de un volcán activo. Por suerte *(Luckily)*, <u>vemos</u> una pequeña erupción de vapores y gases.
7. Después, <u>volvemos</u> a San José, donde <u>vamos</u> a un concierto en el famoso Teatro Nacional en el centro de la ciudad.
8. Al día siguiente, <u>salimos</u> para los EE.UU. Todos <u>estamos</u> de acuerdo que el viaje a Costa Rica <u>es</u> muy interesante y que <u>aprendemos</u> mucho.

ESTRUCTURA

The imperfect and the preterite: Past actions

Antes, yo **iba** a México cada año. Pero el año pasado, yo **fui** a Costa Rica.	In the past, I *used to go* to Mexico every year. But last year, I *went* to Costa Rica.

In previous units you learned two past tenses, the preterite and the imperfect. When narrating or describing in the past, think of all actions as having a beginning, a middle, and an end. The preterite is used to report only *the beginning and the ending* of an action in the past. The middle stage or *continued process of an action*—and nothing more—is always described by the imperfect.

The main distinction between the use of the preterite and the imperfect has to do with certain *aspects* of actions in the past:

1. If an action is viewed as having been either begun or completed within any definite time period, occurs only once, or is repeated a specific number of times, the verb will be in the *preterite.*

La semana pasada, yo **fui** a la casa de mis abuelos. *(single occurrence)*

El sábado y el domingo pasado **fuimos** al cine juntos. *(specified number of repetitions)*

Mi abuelo **jugó** al tenis tres veces en su vida. *(specified number of repetitions in a definite time period)*

2. If a past action is habitual, repeated an unspecified number of times, or performed in an indefinite time period, the verb will be in the *imperfect.*

De joven, **iba** a la casa de mis abuelos todos los fines de semana. *(habitual occurrence)*

Íbamos al cine juntos. *(unspecified number of repetitions)*

Mi abuelo **jugaba** a menudo al tenis. *(indefinite time period)*

3. If an action is considered ongoing, or already in progress, the verb will be in the imperfect, whether or not the action takes place in either a definite or an indefinite period of time.

Mi abuelo **jugaba** a las 5:00. *(in progress at definite time)*

4. As a general rule, the preterite moves a story's action forward in past time while the imperfect tends to be more descriptive.

Aquí practicamos

D. Cuando era niño(a)...   Alternando con otro(a) estudiante, hagan las siguientes preguntas. Presten atención *(Pay attention to)* al uso del imperfecto.

1. Cuando eras niño(a), ¿te gustaba montar en bicicleta? ¿Por qué sí o por qué no?
2. ¿Cuál era tu actividad favorita?
3. ¿Tenías una bicicleta? ¿Cómo era la bicicleta?
4. ¿Adónde ibas cuando montabas en bicicleta?
5. ¿Con quién montabas en bicicleta?
6. Cuando paseabas en bicicleta ¿de qué distancia eran tus recorridos?
7. ¿Ibas en bicicleta a la escuela cuando eras más joven?
8. ¿Jugabas algún tipo de juego con tu bicicleta? ¿Qué hacías?

E. ¿Tú lo hiciste?   Each time your parent asks you if you've done something you were supposed to do, you answer *Not yet* (**Todavía no**).

Then you say what you *were doing* instead. Use both the preterite and the imperfect to give your excuses.

Modelo: ¿Lavaste la ropa? (hablar por teléfono)
Todavía no. No lavé la ropa porque hablaba por teléfono.

1. ¿Hiciste tu tarea? (jugar al tenis)
2. ¿Hablaste con tu padre? (estar en casa de mis amigos)
3. ¿Comiste? (escuchar cintas)
4. ¿Te duchaste? (mirar la televisión)
5. ¿Hiciste los mandados? (tocar la guitarra)
6. ¿Acompañaste a tu hermana al centro? (escribir una carta)
7. ¿Compraste el pan? (dar un paseo)
8. ¿Arreglaste tu cuarto? (echar una siesta)

¿Fuiste al centro con un(a) amigo(a)?

Aquí escuchamos:
"Una excursión en bicicleta"

Antes de escuchar

Before listening to the conversation about a bicycle excursion, look at the following questions to get an idea of which information to focus on as you listen.

Después de escuchar

1. ¿Cuántos kilómetros viajaron?
2. ¿Cuántos días duró el viaje?
3. ¿Dónde pasaron la noche?
4. ¿A qué hora comenzaban en camino cada día?
5. ¿A qué hora terminaban cada día?

¡Aquí te toca a ti!

F. *Un fin de semana típico*   Work with a classmate and ask and answer each other's questions about what four activities you used to do on a typical weekend when you were in elementary school. Remember to use the *imperfect* tense in your questions and answers since you are talking about what you *used to do* on a regular basis (as part of a routine).

G. *El año pasado*   Now ask and answer questions about four things you did last year that are memorable. Remember to use the *preterite* tense since you are talking about specific, one-time events that happened in the past.

¡Adelante!

EJERCICIO ORAL

Learning Strategies:

Providing information, organizing information, persuading

H. *El club de ciclismo*   Try to convince your partner to join the same bicycle club that you joined a year ago. In order to get him or her interested in the club, tell (1) what you did last year with the club, (2) how many excursions you took, (3) where you went, (4) with whom you went, and (5) what you usually did as opposed to what you did on one trip in particular. (Use the preterite and imperfect tenses appropriately.)

EJERCICIO ESCRITO

Learning Strategies:

Organizing ideas in a paragraph, providing information

I. *Un viaje en bicicleta*   You are still trying to convince your partner to join your bicycle club. At the end of a bicycle trip, send your partner a postcard in which you describe the trip. Give several details about the excursion, such as (1) where you went, (2) how far, (3) when you left and returned, (4) how many bikers there were, (5) what the weather was like, (6) three interesting things that you saw, and (7) two exciting experiences. (8) Be sure to date and sign your card.

SEGUNDA ETAPA

Preparación

>> **H**ave you ever gone hiking? If so, when and where?

>> **I**s white-water rafting an activity that interests you or would interest you? Why, or why not?

El senderismo y el rafting

El senderismo es muy saludable y es una buena manera para apreciar la naturaleza.

El senderismo también se conoce como el andinismo y el alpinismo, nombres que vienen de las montañas llamadas los Andes en Sudamérica y los Alpes en Europa.

el senderismo: hiking

EL SENDERISMO

El senderismo, o el montañismo, es una actividad muy de moda. También es divertido y saludable. Practicarlo significa caminar por un espacio natural generalmente montañoso. Se puede caminar hasta llegar a la **cima** de la montaña. Desde allí se ven **paisajes** maravillosos. Por medio del senderismo podemos **aumentar** nuestros **conocimientos** sobre la geografía, los animales, la vegetación, la historia y las costumbres de las zonas rurales.

the top (of mountain)
landscapes

increase
knowledge

   El **equipo** necesario es muy simple. Los zapatos son muy importantes y deben ser **cómodos, ligeros** y apropiados al tipo del **terreno** en que se va a caminar. Otros elementos esenciales son una mochila fuerte, una **cantimplo-ra,** un pequeño **botiquín** y un **bastón.**

equipment
comfortable / light / terrain, land surface / canteen / first-aid kit / walking stick, cane

   En España hay más de 8.000 kilómetros de **senderos.** Algunos son muy largos, como el que va desde Valencia hasta Lisboa en Portugal. Otros **atraviesan** los hermosos paisajes montañosos de los Pirineos en la frontera con Francia. Si te gusta caminar por las montañas y te interesa la naturaleza, ¿qué mejor manera de conocer España durante las vacaciones?

paths

go across

El rafting es un deporte muy divertido y muy popular en España.

EL RAFTING

Si tienes interés en la aventura y en **disfrutar del** aire libre, deportes como el rafting, el **descenso de cañones** y el esquí acuático son los que te van a gustar. El rafting es un deporte muy popular en España. En Cataluña hay **campeonatos mundiales** de canookayak. Para practicarlo, sólo necesitas tener doce años, saber nadar y tener un espíritu muy **aventurero**.

El raft es una **balsa neumática** en la que pueden ir entre ocho y doce personas. Hay expediciones organizadas que duran cinco días. Tres días se hacen descensos de rafting. Otro día hay una excursión por un cañón y el otro hay práctica de esquí acuático.

disfrutar de: enjoy / *descenso de cañones:* climbing down canyons / *campeonatos mundiales:* world championships / *aventurero:* adventurous / *balsa neumática:* inflatable raft

¡Aquí te toca a ti!

A. ¿Qué va con qué? Decide which items go with which sport. Are there some that don't apply to either sport?

	El senderismo	El rafting
un río		
un esquí		
un bastón		
una canasta		
una bicicleta		
una mochila		
una cima		
un botiquín		
una raqueta		
una montaña		
una pelota		
una cantimplora		
unos animales		
unos zapatos		
un barco		

B. Verdad o falso Indica si los comentarios son verdaderos o falsos según la información sobre el senderismo y el rafting en las páginas 377 y 378. Si es falso el comentario, explica por qué.

1. Es necesario tener mucho equipo para hacer senderismo.
2. Es importante saber nadar si vas a practicar el rafting.
3. En España hay muy pocos senderos para la persona que hace senderismo.
4. Normalmente hay expediciones de rafting que duran cincuenta días.
5. Es importante llevar una cantimplora cuando haces senderismo.
6. Los zapatos son importantes cuando estás en una balsa.
7. Aprendemos mucho sobre la naturaleza al hacer senderismo.
8. Para hacer rafting debemos llevar un buen bastón.
9. El rafting es para las personas que tienen un espíritu aventurero.

Repaso

C. El descubrimiento (discovery) **de América** Put the following sentences into the past, changing the underlined verbs to the imperfect or the preterite, according to the context and intended meaning.

1. Cristóbal Colón <u>sale</u> del puerto español de Palos el 3 de agosto de 1492.
2. En esa época, mucha gente <u>cree</u> que el mundo <u>es</u> plano *(flat)*.
3. Colón <u>quiere</u> probar *(to prove)* que <u>es</u> redondo y encontrar una ruta a las Indias.
4. Colón <u>cruza</u> el Atlántico en tres pequeñas carabelas *(sailing ships)*.
5. Muchos de sus hombres <u>tienen</u> miedo y <u>quieren</u> volver a España.
6. Pero Colón <u>insiste</u> en seguir adelante.
7. Por fin, después de diez semanas de viaje, <u>desembarcan</u> *(they step ashore)* en una isla del Caribe el 12 de octubre.
8. Colón ahora <u>está</u> en América, pero todavía <u>piensa</u> que el territorio <u>es</u> las Indias.
9. <u>Hace</u> otros tres viajes a América.
10. En su último viaje (1502–1504), Colón <u>explora</u> la costa de Centroamérica.
11. <u>Vuelve</u> a España donde <u>se enferma</u>, muriendo *(dying)* dos años después sin saber que América <u>es</u> un nuevo continente.

ESTRUCTURA

The imperfect and the preterite: Descriptions

Ayer **fui** al centro. Allí **me encontré** con Juan y **fuimos** al Café Topo en la Avenida Central. **Conversamos** por tres horas. **Estábamos** muy contentos de estar juntos. **Hacía** mucho sol y yo **llevaba** un vestido ligero *(light)* y unas sandalias. Juan **llevaba** un sombrero amarillo y una chaqueta marrón muy bonita. **Estábamos** muy a la moda *(fashionable)* los dos.

Note that the preceding paragraph contains verbs in both the preterite and the imperfect. The first four verbs are in the preterite because they indicate actions that occurred at a very specific time in the past (yesterday). The remaining verbs are in the imperfect because they describe a state or a condition in the past.

The imperfect is generally used in four types of descriptions in the past:

1. Physical
2. Feelings
3. Attitudes and beliefs
4. State of health

La casa **era** grande. Nuestra casa **era** blanca.
Nosotros **estábamos** contentos. Él **estaba** triste.
Yo **creía** que ustedes **tenían razón.**
Mi hermano **estaba** enfermo.

Aquí practicamos

D. Los testigos (Witnesses)   You and your classmates were witnesses to a crime. You're now asked by the police to describe what you saw. Change the sentences into the imperfect tense.

 Dos hombres y una mujer están en el banco.
Dos hombres y una mujer estaban en el banco.

1. Un hombre es muy alto, tiene el pelo negro, tiene barba, lleva una camisa verde, es delgado, habla en voz *(voice)* muy alta, parece fuerte y lleva una pistola grande.
2. El segundo hombre no es tan alto, es gordo, tiene bigote, lleva una camiseta sucia, no habla, tiene el pelo rojo, lleva una mochila y camina muy rápido.
3. La mujer es alta y es delgada, tiene el pelo rubio, tiene la cara redonda *(round)*, lleva pantalones y una camiseta, también lleva sandalias amarillas, tiene una bolsa y es la conductora *(driver)* del coche.
4. El coche es un Fiat, es gris y es bastante nuevo.
5. Nosotros estamos muy nerviosos y tenemos miedo.
6. Los empleados del banco son muy valientes. Están bastante tranquilos.

Nota gramatical

The imperfect and the preterite: Interrupted actions

El Sr. Sosa trabajaba en
Panamá cuando **nació** su hijo.
Estaba en su oficina cuando su
esposa **llamó** por teléfono.
Hablaba con un amigo cuando
supo la noticia.

Mr. Sosa was working in Panamá
when his son *was born.*
He was in his office when his
wife *called.*
He was talking with a friend
when *he found out* the news.

Each model sentence contains a verb in the imperfect and another in the
preterite. The imperfect describes what *was going on* when something else
happened. The preterite is used to tell what *happened* to interrupt an action.
Note that in Spanish the imperfect often corresponds to the progressive forms
was doing or *were doing* in English.

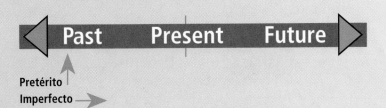

Past   Present   Future

Pretérito
Imperfecto

E. *Las interrupciones*   The following people didn't get anything done because something always happened to interrupt them. Describe what happened in each case by putting together the elements provided to create a sentence in the past. Remember that the action in progress must be in the imperfect and the interrupting action must be in the preterite.

> *Modelo:*   yo / hacer / mi tarea / cuando / oír el teléfono
> *Yo hacía mi tarea cuando oí el teléfono.*

1. mi mamá / desayunarse / cuando / llegar la carta
2. nosotros / dar una vuelta en el coche / cuando / ella / tener el accidente
3. cuando / Jorge / llegar / yo / quitar la mesa
4. Pablo y Marcos / jugar al vólibol / cuando / comenzar a llover
5. cuando / Luis / ponerse mal / Sergio / preparar la comida
6. nosotros / mirar / la televisión / cuando / llegar mis tíos
7. yo / hacer / los mandados / cuando / yo / ver a mis amigos
8. cuando / tú / saber / la noticia / tus padres / estar en el teatro

F. *Una fiesta*   Describe a las personas en el dibujo. Usa el imperfecto.

> *Modelo:*   *El muchacho tenía el pelo castaño, era delgado y llevaba una camiseta.*

G. *¿Qué hacían ellos cuando... ?*   Use the preterite and the imperfect to describe what the people in the drawings on page 383 were doing when something else happened. Follow the model.

> *Modelo:*   *María Luisa tocaba la guitarra cuando Pedro se cayó.*

María Luisa

Pedro

tocar / caerse

1. comer / llegar

2. jugar / empezar a llover

3. empezar a bailar / charlar

4. hablar / decir

5. jugar / llegar

6. dar un paseo / encontrarse con

Aquí escuchamos:
"Entrevista con un ciclista"

Antes de escuchar

Before listening to a short interview with a cyclist, think about some of the questions you might ask if you were doing the interview for your school paper. Then look at the following questions to get an idea of the content of the interview you'll hear between a **periodista** (*journalist*) and a student who is a member of a bicycle club.

START

Después de escuchar

Escucha la entrevista una vez más y después contesta las siguientes preguntas.

1. ¿Cómo se llama el club de ciclismo de los jóvenes?
2. ¿Cuántos miembros hay en el club ahora?
3. En general, ¿qué hacen los miembros del club los fines de semana?
4. ¿Qué hace el grupo durante las vacaciones?
5. ¿Qué dice el ciclista sobre el equipaje que lleva en una excursión?
6. ¿Cuesta mucho dinero el ciclismo? ¿Por qué?

¡Aquí te toca a ti!

H. Nuestra aventura excelente Work with a partner and make up a description of a bike trip you took last summer. Imagine that you took the trip together and include details from real life as well as your imagination about what happened during this trip to make it an unforgettable or unbelievable adventure. Use the preterite and imperfect tenses appropriately.

///-///-///-///-///-///-///

Learning Strategies:

Organizing details in a sequence, describing, providing information, reporting based on personal knowledge, making an oral presetation

Critical Thinking Strategies:

Making associations, imagining

EJERCICIO ORAL

I. Mis fotos You've just returned from either a hiking trip or a bicycle trip in a national park and have lots of photos to show your friends. Imagine the scene on each photo (use the photo above as an example, but invent other scenes), and tell your classmates what they are seeing and what you did in each place. Follow the model.

 Modelo: *Aquí me ven con Mario en el Parque Nacional en _____.*
Estamos en una montaña muy grande. Caminamos por muchas horas. Llegamos a la cima de la montaña. Allí vimos un paisaje muy bonito.

EJERCICIO ESCRITO

J. ¿Cuál prefieres? You have been selected to attend a camp next summer. Now you must choose which of the activities (**el ciclismo, el senderismo, el rafting**) you prefer as your "specialty," the one on which you will spend most of your time. Write a letter to the camp director explaining which activity you prefer over the others. Describe (1) what that activity involves; (2) when, where, and with whom you last participated in the activity; and (3) why you like it better than the other two. Give at last four reasons for your preference. Remember to date and sign your letter.

///-///-///-///-///-///-///

Learning Strategies:

Describing, expressing preferences, organizing information, supporting an opinion

Critical Thinking Strategies:

Analyzing, comparing and contrasting, determining preferences

385

Vocabulario

Para charlar

Para hablar del ciclismo

la bicicleta
la bicicleta de montaña

Para hablar del senderismo

atravesar
el bastón
el botiquín
la cantimplora
la cima
cómodo(a)
ligero(a)
la montaña
el montañismo
el paisaje
el sendero
el terreno

Para hablar del rafting

aventurero(a)
la balsa neumática
el barco
el canookayak
el descenso de cañones
el esquí acuático
el río

Vocabulario general

Verbos

refrescarse

Sustantivos

los auriculares
el (la) atleta
la cámara fotográfica
la camiseta
el campeonato mundial
la canasta
el equipo
la excursión
la mochila

Otras expresiones

con gas (sin gas)

Lectura CULTURAL

///-/-/-/-/-/-/-/-/-/
Learning Strategies:

*Brainstorming,
previewing*

EN BICICLETA

Antes de leer

1. Look at the photos and the title of the reading to determine its content.
2. Think about what you know about bicycles. Do we use them for recreation, exercise, transportation?
3. Do you own a bicycle? Has the bicycle become more popular in recent years? Why, or why not?

Guía para la lectura

A. Read the first sentence of each paragraph and, on a separate sheet of paper, note the main idea of each one.

B. Look over the following questions. Read the passage again and then answer the questions.

1. Según el artículo, ¿cuántos años cumple la bicicleta este año?
2. ¿Cómo son las bicicletas de hoy en día?
3. ¿Qué tipos de bicicleta de los EE.UU. tienen mucha popularidad?
4. ¿Quiénes usan mucho la bicicleta en su vida diaria?
5. ¿Cuáles son algunos de los beneficios *(benefits)* de la bicicleta?
6. ¿Cuál es uno de los peligros *(dangers)* de montar en bicicleta?
7. ¿Quiénes tienen mucho éxito en los campeonatos de ciclismo?

En bicicleta

a bicicleta, que se usó por primera vez en el año 1840, perdió popularidad con la llegada de los primeros automóviles. Pero su nueva vida es una realidad, no sólo porque es un vehículo ecologista sino porque las bicicletas de hoy son ligeras y también rápidas.

El uso de la bicicleta de montaña, una especialidad importada de los Estados Unidos, y el peligro de las calles cambiaron las preferencias de los ciclistas. La bicicleta todo terreno también es preferida por montañeros y ecologistas. Es un deporte que, según sus aficionados, resulta menos aburrido y peligroso que pedalear en la ciudad.

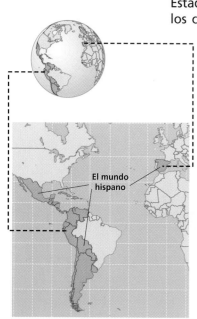

El mundo hispano

Aunque las carreteras no son el lugar ideal para los ciclistas, los aficionados a este deporte crecen cada día en los países de habla española.

Son cada vez más los jóvenes que van al colegio o a la universidad en bicicleta, a pesar de que no hay carriles-bici en las ciudades. Cada fin de semana, chicos y chicas cambian los libros y los bolígrafos por el manillar y los pedales.

La llegada del buen tiempo y los éxitos de los ciclistas del mundo hispano en los campeonatos de ciclismo hacen de la bicicleta el vehículo de moda. Además, no contamina, no hace ruido, no gasta combustible y ayuda a estar en forma. ¡Viva la bicicleta!

15 DOS DEPORTES POPULARES

El baloncesto es muy popular porque todo el mundo puede practicarlo.

Objectives:

>>> **U**nderstanding short descriptions of team sports

>>> **D**escribing places and events in the past

>>> **T**alking about the recent past

Strategies:

>>> **D**rawing meaning from context

>>> **S**ummarizing

>>> **S**equencing

PRIMERA ETAPA

Learning Strategies:

Brainstorming, preview-
ing, reporting based on
personal knowledge

Learning Strategies:

Reading for cultural
information, reading
for main ideas

Preparación

>> **D**o you like soccer?

>> **D**o you know what "The World Cup" is?

>> **H**ave you played soccer yourself? Have you watched a game?

>> **W**hat are some of the differences between soccer and football, as they are called in the U.S.?

El fútbol

Los cinco principales jugadores hispanos de fútbol

aficionados: fans

La copa Mundial de fútbol tiene lugar cada cuatro años. Es el evento deportivo más grande del mundo, con millones y millones de aficionados. El fútbol es, sin duda, el deporte más popular en todos los países de habla española. "El Mundial" de 1994 tuvo lugar en los Estados Unidos y fue un gran éxito con el público norteamericano.

Cinco de los veinticuatro países que se clasificaron para el campeonato (después de la eliminación de casi 140 países que participaron en la competencia) eran hispanohablantes: Argentina, Bolivia, Colombia, España y México. Su país vecino, Brasil, ganó la prestigiosa Copa Mundial por cuarta vez, ahora el único equipo de fútbol en la historia con ese récord.

Hugo Sánchez (México)

No digas Hugo, di gol. Los años no pasan por él. Jugó en el Mundial de 1994 a la edad de 35 años. Todavía da mucho que hablar por su talento.

Faustino Asprilla (Colombia)

La velocidad es su arma. Tiene mucha habilidad para anotar goles. En muchos partidos del Mundial fue la estrella de su equipo.

Andoni Zubizarreta (España)

Éste es uno de los mejores arqueros del mundo. Defiende con agilidad y fuerza. Los goles contra él son pocos.

arqueros: goalies
anotar: to make

Marco Antonio Etcheverry (Bolivia)

Sólo tiene 23 años. En ataque siempre es rápido. Su equipo cuenta con su entusiasmo y con sus goles.

Tab Ramos (Estados Unidos)

Es el mejor jugador estadounidense técnicamente hablando. Controla y avanza el balón con gran agilidad. Es fuerte y muy competitivo.

balón: pelota

¡Aquí te toca a ti!

A. _Su nacionalidad_ Di de dónde son los equipos de estas estrellas de fútbol.

1. Zubizarreta 2. Ramos 3. Sánchez 4. Etcheverry 5. Asprilla

B. *Su talento individual*   Indica una de las cosas que cada jugador hace mejor cuando juega con su equipo, basándote en las páginas 390 y 391.

1. Etcheverry   2. Sánchez   3. Asprilla   4. Ramos   5. Zubizarreta

C. *La copa mundial*   Contesta las preguntas sobre el Mundial basándote en la página 390.

1. ¿Qué importancia tiene el fútbol en los países de habla española?
2. ¿Con qué frecuencia juegan los países del mundo para el campeonato de fútbol?
3. ¿Dónde jugaron los equipos para el Mundial en 1994?
4. ¿Cuántos países hispanohablantes participaron en este campeonato?
5. ¿Quién ganó La Copa Mundial en 1994?

Repaso

D. *La historia de un crimen*   Read the following account of a bank holdup. As you read, change the underlined present tense verbs to the imperfect or the preterite, according to the context.

Hay dos hombres y una mujer en un banco. Llegan a las 14:00. Yo estoy a la ventanilla. Uno de los hombres es muy alto, tiene el pelo negro, tiene barba y es muy delgado. Habla en una voz muy alta y parece impaciente. Lleva una pistola.

El otro hombre no es alto. Es gordo y tiene bigote. Lleva una camiseta con "Malibu" escrito en la espalda. Les pide a los clientes las carteras. Toma también nuestros relojes.

La mujer es alta. Tiene el pelo rubio. Lleva unos pantalones y una camiseta. Tiene una bolsa de mano. Pone nuestras cosas en una bolsa blanca. En seguida sale del banco. Es la conductora del coche.

El coche es un Fiat. Es gris y es bastante nuevo.

Hay muchos clientes en el banco. Nosotros estamos muy nerviosos. Tenemos miedo.

Los empleados del banco son muy valientes. Están tranquilos. Un empleado toca la alarma y los hombres corren del banco rápidamente. Afortunadamente, la policía llega unos pocos minutos después, pero los ladrones (robbers) ya no están allí.

ESTRUCTURA

The imperfect and the preterite: Changes of meaning and translation

As you have already learned, the decision to use one of the two past tenses with certain verbs in Spanish sometimes has a distinct effect on the overall message conveyed.

Carlos **estuvo** enfermo ayer.	Carlos *was* sick yesterday. *(He got sick and has recovered by now.)*
Carlos **estaba** enfermo ayer.	Carlos *was* sick yesterday. *(That was his condition at the time with no indication of the outcome.)*

Some verbs have different meanings in the preterite and the imperfect.

querer

Mi papá **quería** ayudarnos.	My dad *wanted* to help us. *(mental state; intention)*
Mi papá **quiso** ayudarnos.	My dad *tried* to help us. *(He actually did something.)*

no querer

Alicia **no quería** ver la película.	Alicia *didn't want* to see the movie. *(mental state; lack of desire)*
Alicia **no quiso** ver la película.	Alicia *refused* to see the movie. *(She truly refused.)*

poder

Él **podía** arreglar el coche.	He *was capable* of fixing the car.
Él **pudo** arreglar el coche.	He *succeeded* in fixing the car.

tener (que)

El diplomático **tenía** que aceptar la invitación a la ceremonia.	The diplomat *had* to accept the invitation to the ceremony. *(He was under obligation to do so but may not have done it.)*
El diplomático **tuvo** que aceptar la invitación a la ceremonia.	The diplomat *was compelled* to accept the invitation to the ceremony. *(He was compelled and he accepted it.)*

saber

¿**Sabías** que el avión llegaba tarde?	*Were you aware* that the plane was arriving late? *(Did you already know this?)*
Supe esta mañana que llegaba tarde.	*I found out* this morning that it was arriving late. *(first knowledge of this fact)*

conocer

¿**Conocías** a Carolina cuando eras niño?	*Did you know* Carolina when you were a child? *(Were you acquainted with her back then?)*
No, la **conocí** el año pasado.	No, *I met* her last year. *(I became acquainted with her for the first time.)*

Aquí practicamos

E. *¿Qué pasó? ¿Qué pasaba?* Choose one of the verb forms in italics, either the imperfect or the preterite tense, according to the meaning provided by the context in parentheses. Follow the model.

 Ramón y yo *nos conocimos / nos conocíamos* / en Montevideo. (for the first time)
Ramón y yo nos conocimos en Montevideo.

1. ¿Cómo *supiste / sabías* lo que pasó en el aeropuerto? (you found out right away)
2. Sus hermanas *decían / dijeron* que no les gustaban las películas de horror. (they would always say this)
3. El padre de Carlos no *quería / quiso* prestarle su coche. (that's why Carlos had to take a taxi)
4. ¿Cuándo *conociste / conocías* a Emilio Estévez? (for the first time)
5. *Tenía que ir / Tuve que ir* a la reunión porque soy presidente del grupo. (and that's why I finally went after all)
6. Ustedes no *supieron / sabían* cuánto dinero llevaron del banco los criminales. (you weren't able to get this information)
7. El profesor de matemáticas *pudo / podía* resolver el problema. (but he didn't do it because it was my homework assignment)
8. El perro *quería / quiso* salir de la casa mientras tú dormías. (he tried three times)
9. Roberto y yo nos *conocimos / conocíamos* en la escuela secundaria. (we were already friends back then)
10. La abuela *quiso / quería* besar al niño, pero él se fue corriendo. (so she didn't get to kiss him)

F. *Entre amigos* Using the cues in parentheses, answer your friend's questions with the appropriate use of the imperfect or the preterite. Use the verb(s) in each question in your response. Follow the model.

Modelo: ¿Tú me llamaste por teléfono? (sí / hace media hora)
Sí, te llamé hace media hora.

1. ¿Me viste esta mañana? (sí / en el centro)
2. ¿Dónde estaba yo cuando me viste? (en una librería)
3. ¿Me buscabas? (no)
4. ¿Querías hablar conmigo? (sí / para invitarte al Café Topo)
5. ¿Por qué no entraste en la librería? (estar en el autobús)
6. ¿Me llamaste anoche? (sí / a las 8:00)
7. ¿Sabías que hoy es el cumpleaños de Eduardo Bolaños? (sí / ayer)
8. ¿Le compraste un regalo? (sí / esta mañana)
9. ¿Ya se lo diste? (no)

10. ¿Cuándo pensabas dárselo? (esta noche / en el Café Topo)
11. ¿Dijo Eduardo que podía salir esta noche? (sí / después de las 7:30)
12. ¿Pudiste reservar una mesa en el Café Topo? (sí / para las 8:00)
13. ¿A quién más invitaste? (Silvia y Marisol)
14. ¿Ah sí? ¿Dónde conociste a Marisol? (en la fiesta de Eduardo / el año pasado)
15. ¿A quién le pediste el coche? (a mi papá)
16. ¿Tuviste suerte? (sí / mucha)

G. **Las noticias del día** Working with two classmates, take turns adding some information to the part of the sentence that is provided. Invent the necessary details. Follow the model.

Learning Strategy:

Expressing past time

Critical Thinking Strategies:

Seeing cause-and-effect relationships, imagining, creating

  Ayer, a las 10:00 de la mañana, un criminal…
Ayer, a las 10:00 de la mañana, un criminal entró en el banco. Afortunadamente, la policía llegó inmediatamente…

1. El presidente dice que cuando era niño, siempre…
2. La semana pasada, el actor Emilio Estévez…
3. Hoy supimos por primera vez que…
4. El representante de Nueva York dijo que él no era responsable, que él no…
5. El embajador *(ambassador)* conoció a la reina *(queen)* de Gran Bretaña cuando…
6. El sábado pasado, el equipo de fútbol de Colombia…
7. Ayer hizo tanto calor que todos nosotros…
8. En el último minuto del partido de fútbol, el equipo boliviano…
9. Cuando oyeron las noticias, los pobres muchachos…
10. Nadie sabe por qué, pero el sábado pasado, dos hombres…

Aquí escuchamos:
"Los resultados de dos partidos de fútbol"

Antes de escuchar

What information do you usually expect when you listen to a brief report on two soccer games? Read the following questions so that you will know what details to listen for as you listen to the sportscaster.

Después de escuchar

Escucha al reporte otra vez y luego contesta en español las siguientes preguntas.

1. ¿Quién ganó el partido entre Argentina y Bolivia?
2. ¿Qué pasaba cuando cada equipo trataba de anotar un gol?
3. ¿Quién anotó al final el gol para la victoria?
4. ¿Cómo anotó el gol este jugador?
5. ¿Cuál equipo ganó el partido entre los Estados Unidos y Colombia?
6. ¿Cómo jugó la defensa de los Estados Unidos?
7. ¿Qué pasaba cada vez que los colombianos se acercaban al arco?
8. ¿Quién anotó el gol para la victoria a los 40 minutos de la segunda mitad?

¡Aquí te toca a ti!

H. Un buen partido Work with a classmate and take turns telling each other about an exciting soccer or football game you have seen recently. You can base your description on a real event or make up details about an imaginary one. Tell (1) who played, (2) when, (3) where, and (4) who won, including some information about (5) how specific players helped to win or lose the game.

A algunos minutos del final del partido, el equipo local anotó el gol de la victoria.

¡Adelante!

EJERCICIO ORAL

I. El fútbol y La Copa Mundial   With your partner, discuss in Spanish the importance of soccer as a sport, particularly in the Spanish-speaking world. Based on the information in this chapter, mention (1) its popularity, (2) the World Cup, (3) how often this international competition takes place, (4) where it was held in 1994, and (5) who some of the stars of the game are. (6) Add any other details that you may know.

Learning Strategies:

Describing, organizing information, summarizing

EJERCICO ESCRITO

J. ¿Quién ganó?   Write about a soccer game to a Spanish-speaking pen pal. Indicate (1) who played, (2) when, (3) what the outcome was, (4) who scored, and (5) a detail or two about the game. You can base it on a real game or make up the information for this exercise. Use the preterite and imperfect tenses appropriately.

Learning Strategies:

Describing, identifying, reporting in the past

397

SEGUNDA ETAPA

Preparación

>> **D**o you play basketball? If so, when do you play?

>> **W**ho are some of the famous basketball players that you like to watch?

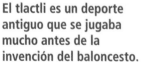

El tlactli es un deporte antiguo que se jugaba mucho antes de la invención del baloncesto.

"TLACTLI", UN DEPORTE AMERICANO ORIGINAL

El primer partido de baloncesto tuvo su origen en 1891 en los Estados Unidos, hace más de cien años. Pero ya existía un deporte similar que se jugaba entre las civilizaciones que vivían en México antes de la llegada de Cristobal Colón al continente americano. Se llamaba el juego de pelota, o "tlactli" en la lengua de los mayas.

Se jugaba en campos rectangulares que tenían paredes de una altura de unos 13 metros. En las paredes laterales había dos anillos de piedra. Cada anillo estaba colocado verticalmente a 10 metros de altura, uno frente al otro. El campo estaba dividido en dos partes y cada uno de los dos equipos ocupaba una parte del campo de juego.

Los jugadores tenían que pasar la pelota por uno de los anillos del campo del otro equipo. El equipo que podía hacerlo primero ganaba el juego. Esto era muy difícil porque los jugadores sólo podían tocar la pelota con las rodillas o con las caderas. No podían usar las manos ni los pies. Además la pelota era muy dura.

Todavía se pueden ver muchos campos para el juego de pelota en las ruinas de las antiguas ciudades mayas.

¡Aquí te toca a ti!

A. ¿Verdad o falso? Según el texto, decide si los comentarios son verdaderos o falsos. Si son falsos, da la información correcta.

1. "Tlactli" es un juego parecido al baloncesto.
2. El campo en el que se jugaba tenía paredes bajas y un anillo grande en cada una.
3. La pelota con la que se jugaba era dura.
4. Los jugadores podían tocar la pelota con los pies.
5. Ya no es posible ver los campos de este juego.

B. ¿Cómo era el juego? Completa las oraciones con la información apropiada basándote en el texto en las páginas 398–399.

1. "Tlactli" era un juego…
   a. fácil. **b.** aburrido. **c.** difícil.

2. El campo tenía la forma de un…
   a. rectángulo. **b.** triángulo. **c.** círculo.

3. Para ganar el juego los jugadores tenían que…
   a. correr con la pelota en la mano por 100 metros.
   b. pasar la pelota por el anillo en la pared.
   c. jugar por cuatro horas sin parar.

4. El campo en el que se jugaba estaba dividido en…
   a. dos partes. **b.** tres partes. **c.** cuatro partes.

Repaso

C. Una aventura en la naturaleza Pair up with a classmate and tell him or her about something interesting that happened to you when you were younger while on a camping trip with your family. You may base this outdoor adventure on a real experience or make up the details for this exercise. Tell how old you were, where you went, with whom, for how long, and do your best to describe what happened that is so memorable. Use the preterite and imperfect tenses as accurately as you can.

ESTRUCTURA

The preterite and the imperfect: Summary

The following table outlines the various uses of the preterite and the imperfect. As you study it, keep in mind the following basic principles:

1. Both the preterite and the imperfect are past tenses.
2. Most Spanish verbs can be put into either tense, depending upon the aspect of the activity that is reported and the meaning that is to be conveyed.
3. As a general rule, the preterite narrates and moves a story's action forward in past time: **Me levanté, tomé** un café y **salí** de la casa.
4. As a general rule, the imperfect tends to be more descriptive: **Hacía** buen tiempo, los niños **jugaban** en el parque mientras yo **descansaba** tranquilamente sobre un banco.

Preterite	Imperfect
Actions that are begun or completed as single events	
	Actions repeated habitually
Ella **corrió** hacia el parque.	Ella **desayunaba** conmigo todos los días.
Ellos **llegaron** a las 7:00.	Siempre **salíamos** a bailar.
Actions that are repeated a specified number of times or that have a time limit	*Actions that occur simultaneously over an indefinite period of time*
Ayer **jugamos** al tenis tres veces.	Todas las noches papá **leía** el periódico
Vivió allí por diez años.	mientras mamá **preparaba** la cena.
	Ongoing activities, scenes, and conditions not regarding length of time involved or outcome
Actions that describe a chain of events	
Compré una limonada, **me senté** en un banco en el parque y **descansé** un poco.	**Corría** por el parque central de la ciudad.
	La noche de la fiesta, **llevaba** un traje elegante.
	Hacía buen tiempo.
	Telling time and age
	Eran las 5:00 de la tarde.
	El actor **tenía** diez años.

Preterite	Imperfect
Sudden changes in mental states or conditions seen as completed (moods, feelings, opinions, illnesses, or other physical complaints)	*General mental states*
En ese momento, **tuve** miedo de subir al avión. Hasta ese día, **creí** que podía hacerlo. **Estuve** preparado para subir hasta que **me puse** tan nervioso que **fue** imposible seguir.	En esos días, **tenía** miedo de subir al avión. **Creía** que podía hacerlo. **Estaba** tan preparado para subir que **me sentía** valiente.
	Descriptions of characteristics of people, things, or physical conditions
	Era un muchacho fuerte y sano. El jardín **estaba** lleno de flores. Las sillas **estaban** pintadas de amarillo.

Aquí practicamos

D. *Un mal día* Basándote en los dibujos y las pistas en esta página y la página 402, describe el día de Catalina. Usa el imperfecto o el pretérito según el contexto. Sigue el modelo.

Modelo: despertarse
Catalina se despertó a las 7:00.

1. despertarse a las 7:00
quedarse en cama quince minutos

2. levantarse
estar cansada
vestirse
no estar bien vestida

3. salir de la casa
llover
darse prisa para llegar a la escuela

4. esperar
subir
no poder sentarse

5. entrar en
llegar tarde
no saber las respuestas
recibir una mala nota
estar descontenta

6. regresar a su casa
acostarse temprano

E. Ayer...   Now tell a partner the story of your day yesterday. Use appropriate verbs from the following list or any other verbs you've learned. Use the imperfect or the preterite according to the context. Then your partner will tell you about his or her day.

despertarse	estar contento(a)	estar cansado(a)
levantarse	estar de mal humor	tener mucho trabajo
tener hambre	salir	comer
preparar	reunirse	practicar deportes
llegar	tener sed	acostarse
ir	llegar a tiempo / tarde	hablar con
hacer buen tiempo, etc.		
vestirse		

F. *Otro descubridor* (discoverer)

Read the following historical passage, changing the underlined present tense verbs into either the preterite or the imperfect, according to the context.

En 1513, Vasco Núñez de Balboa <u>es</u> el primer europeo que <u>ve</u> el Océano Pacífico desde el este. Muchas personas creen que el escudo (coat of arms) *de su familia representa el descubrimiento del Océano Pacífico, pero en realidad es mucho más antiguo. La historia dice que un señor de la familia de Balboa, que <u>está</u> perdido* (lost) *en las montañas de Francia, <u>ve</u> allí un león que <u>lucha</u> contra una serpiente muy grande. Después de que el hombre <u>ayuda</u> al león, éste <u>es</u> su amigo hasta la muerte. El hombre le <u>da</u> el león al rey de Francia, pero el noble animal <u>está</u> triste y no <u>puede</u> olvidar a su amigo. Un día, <u>sale</u> del palacio para buscarlo. <u>Va</u> al mar, al mismo punto donde había llegado con el hombre a la costa de Francia, y <u>entra</u> en el agua, donde <u>muere</u>. Después de esto, la familia Balboa <u>manda</u> hacer un escudo con el cuadro de un león entrando en el mar.*

Aquí escuchamos:
"El campamento de básquetbol"

Antes de escuchar

You will hear Mario and Mark talk about an experience at basketball camp.

Have you ever been to a basketball camp? If so, what was it like? If not, what do you think it might be like?

Después de escuchar

Según la información que escuchaste, decide si los comentarios son verdaderos o falsos. Si uno es falso, da la información correcta.

1. Mark dijo que después de los primeros días practicaba cinco horas cada día.
2. En el campamento hay unos veinte jugadores.
3. Mario quería ir al campamento para jugar en uno de los equipos.
4. Mark dijo que Mario podía quedarse en el dormitorio con él.

¡Aquí te toca a ti!

G. *Un partido de básquetbol* Work with a classmate and talk about a basketball game you have either played in or watched live or on television. You may base your information on a real event or make one up. Mention such details as (1) who played, (2) when and where the game took place, (3) the score, (4) why it was exciting, and (5) which player or players played well.

¡Adelante!

EJERCICIO ORAL

H. El básquetbol   Discuss the sport of basketball with your partner, mentioning (1) what equipment you need, (2) where you can play, (3) whether you like to play or not, and (4) who some of the better known players are. Then (5) agree on who you think are the best five players (current and/or past)—the five that you would name to your "Dream Team."

EJERCICIO ESCRITO

I. Un deporte antiguo   Using the information you have learned about "tlactli" on pages 398–399, write a paragraph describing it. Remember to use the imperfect tense.

Para charlar

Para hablar de los deportes

el (la) aficionado(a)
anotar goles
el (la) arquero(a)
el balón
el básquetbol / el baloncesto
el campo de juego
el éxito
el partido
el récord

Lectura CULTURAL

TODOS LOS DEPORTES

Antes de leer

1. Look at the photos and the title of the reading. What is the article about?
2. In which of the sports shown in the photos have you participated?
3. List in Spanish as many sports as you can.

Learning Strategies:

Drawing meaning from key words, brainstorming

Guía para la lectura

A. Now scan the article to see which sports are mentioned. Compare these words to the ones on your list, adding the sports from the article that are not already on your list.

Learning Strategies:

Reading for main ideas, reading for details

B. Read the first sentence of each paragraph to get an idea of its content. On a separate sheet of paper, write down your ideas for each paragraph.

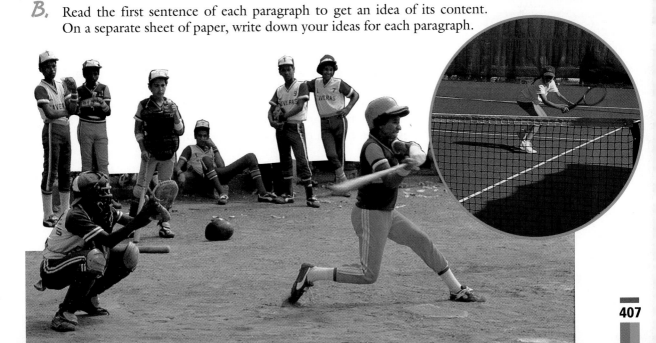

El mundo hispano

C. Look over these questions. Read the passage again and answer them.

1. ¿Cuál es el deporte más popular en los países de habla española?
2. ¿Cuáles son dos deportes que se juegan a caballo?
3. ¿Qué deporte se jugaba hace siglos en México que se parece al básquetbol?
4. ¿En qué países hispanos se juega mucho el béisbol?
5. ¿Qué deporte que se juega en otros países es de origen español?
6. ¿Cómo se llaman algunas de las campeonas hispanas de tenis?

Todos los deportes

En el mundo hispano se practican todos los deportes más conocidos, junto con otros originarios de algunas de sus culturas. Entre éstos algunos han atravesado las fronteras, como *el jai-alai* o "pelota", un deporte de origen español que hoy se juega en otros países, especialmente en los Estados Unidos.

Los deportes ecuestres, o a caballo, tienen mucha difusión en el mundo hispano y los caballos españoles. Cada cultura fue adaptando los caballos y la equitación a sus propios usos y costumbres. *Las charreadas* son un evento ecuestre característico de México, mientras *el pato* se practica en Argentina desde principios del siglo XVII. *El polo*, originario de la India y difundido por los británicos, cuenta con excelentes jugadores en América Latina.

El fútbol es el deporte más popular en varios países latinoamericanos: Brasil, Argentina, Uruguay, Chile, Perú y México. Y en España, desde luego, es el deporte número uno. Pero también es cada vez mayor la popularidad del baloncesto, que tuvo su origen el siglo pasado en los Estados Unidos. En América Latina, donde se lo llama *básquetbol*, o *basket*, es también uno de los deportes más populares. Un juego muy similar existía ya en México antes de la conquista. En las ruinas de las antiguas ciudades hay canchas para el "juego de pelota", que consistía en pasar una pelota por un arco de piedra.

Otro juego estadounidense, el béisbol, es importante en varios países de Latinoamérica. Es el deporte nacional en Cuba y en la República Dominicana. También Puerto Rico, México, Nicaragua, Panamá y Venezuela cuentan con equipos excelentes.

Otro juego de pelota es el tenis. Son varios los campeones hispanos de tenis, y sobre todo, las campeonas: las españolas, Arantxa Sánchez Vicario y Conchita Martínez, la argentina Gabriela Sabatini y la estadounidense de origen dominicano Mary Joe Fernández.

Aquí leemos

Estrategia para la lectura

When reading interviews, keep the setting in mind: one person is there to ask questions, and the other to answer them. When reading an interview, concentrate on the questions first, then go to the answers. This particular interview is between a journalist and María Peláez, a 16-year-old Olympic swimmer. Notice that each person has a different style of speaking. The journalist is very direct, whereas María often says **"pues…"** to give herself time to think of an answer. María's language is also more informal than the journalist's. As you read what each person says, keep a mental picture of the speaker in mind.

Antes de leer

Before reading the interview with a swimmer, think about the kinds of questions you would ask if you were writing an article for your school paper. Then scan the text and read only the questions that the journalist asks. Think about likely answers to these questions.

Entrevista con María Peláez, una chica extraordinaria

Introducción

María, excelente nadadora de 16 años, es campeona de España y de Europa en 200 m mariposa. Fue finalista en los Juegos Olímpicos de Barcelona. Su colegio es miembro de la Federación Española de Natación, donde los mejores entrenadores preparan a los nadadores jóvenes españoles para la competencia internacional. Hablamos con ella cuando salía de la piscina.

Periodista: ¿Cuándo descubriste que te gustaba nadar?
María: Pues, cuando tenía cinco años, cuando empezaron mis hermanas y empecé yo también, en unos cursos de natación.
Periodista: ¿Y cuándo empezaste a practicar?
María: Pues… así más fuerte hace unos tres o cuatro años.
Periodista: ¿Cuántas horas al día practicas?
María: Ahora mismo como cuatro o cinco.
Periodista: ¿Qué es lo que encuentras más difícil de la natación?
María: Pues, depende… eso de ir a practicar todos los días es lo más duro.

Periodista: ¿Y el deporte te ayuda a estudiar?

María: Hombre... hay que combinarlo. El deporte y los estudios son difíciles de llevar a la vez, pero sí que los llevo bien.

Periodista: ¿Practicas otros deportes?

María: No, así en serio la natación nada más.

Periodista: Tú fuiste a las Olimpiadas de Barcelona en el 92. Cuéntanos un poco cómo fue.

María: Pues... fue algo muy especial, super emocionante. Eso de estar allí con los deportistas que nada más ves por la tele, y a lo mejor son tus ídolos...

Periodista: ¿Hiciste amistades con deportistas de otros países?

María: Sí, con un argentino, con un estadounidense...

Periodista: ¿Piensas ir a Atlanta, para las próximas Olimpiadas?

María: Sí, por supuesto, si es posible.

Actividad

A. Escoge la información correcta sobre María.

1. María empezó a practicar la natación cuando tenía...
   a. quince años.   **b.** ocho años.   **c.** cinco años.

2. La nadadora dijo que lo más difícil para ella era...
   a. no poder comer lo que quería.
   b. tener que ir a practicar cada día.
   c. la competencia con otros nadadores.

3. Según María, es importante...
   a. estudiar más que practicar.
   b. combinar la práctica con los estudios.
   c. practicar más que estudiar.

4. Cuando fue a las Olimpiadas de Barcelona, María conoció a...
   a. su novio.
   b. muchos deportistas famosos.
   c. actores de televisión.

Ya llegamos

Actividades orales

A. Hablamos de nuestra niñez (childhood). Imagine that you are a counselor-in-training at a summer camp. You and your fellow counselors are sitting around the campfire on a night off reminiscing about your childhood. Tell about (1) the sports you used to play in elementary school, mentioning your age when you played them; and (2) the sports and games you used to play in the summertime, including where you spent your summers. Then (3) recount one incident that happened to you or a close friend or family member while playing some game or sport.

Finally, determine experiences that some of you have in common, selecting (1) the most unexpected thing you have in common, (2) the experience(s) shared by the greatest number of you, and (3) the most unique experience mentioned. Be prepared to report these results to the class.

B. Mi deporte favorito Pair up with a classmate and tell each other about your favorite sport, why you like it, how often you play it, where and with whom.

C. En mi tiempo libre Talk to a classmate about the leisure-time activities you enjoyed last summer.

Actividades escritas

D. Una aventura Write about an interesting, strange, funny, or terrible experience you had in the past.

E. Intercambio deportivo Write a brief letter to a Spanish-speaking exchange student in which you describe two sports that are popular in the United States. Inquire about the sports that are most popular in his or her country.

F. Mis vacaciones You've just returned from an awesome vacation. Write a brief letter to a friend who lives in a Spanish-speaking country and tell him or her what you did.

Cooperative Learning

Learning Strategies:

Selecting and reporting personal information, narrating in the past, organizing ideas

Critical Thinking Strategy:

Categorizing, evaluating

Critical Thinking Strategies:

Expressing preferences, evaluating

Learning Strategies:

Selecting and reporting personal information, describing, narrating in the past, organizing ideas in paragraphs

Conexión

Las estadísticas de béisbol

AL EMPEZAR

How do baseball fans decide which players on the All-Star ballot they should vote for? One way is to compare the players' statistics. What statistics do you think are important for measuring a batter's performance? Look at the following chart to see what statistics you will be learning about.

LOS SUPER-ESTRELLAS DE BÉISBOL

ESTADÍSTICAS

Nombre	Posición	TB	H	B	2B	3B	J	CI	PROM
Fielder, Cecil	1era base	624	163	78	25	0	44	133	0,261
Peña, Tony	Receptor	464	107	37	23	2	5	48	
Canseco, José	Jardín	572	152	78	32	1	44	122	
Carter, Joe	Jardín	638	174	49	42	3	33	108	
Griffey, Ken Jr.	Jardín	548	179	71	42	1	22	100	
Eisenreich, Jim	Jardín	375	113	20	22	3	2	47	
González, Juan	Jardín	545	144	42	34	1	27	102	

Clave

TB	= turnos de batear (**at bats**)	3B	= triples
H	= hits	J	= jonrones (**homeruns**)
B	= boletos (**walks**)	CI	= carreras impulsadas (**runs batted in**)
2B	= dobles	PROM	= promedio (**batting average**)

figures

Una de las **cifras** más importantes es el número de hits que pega un jugador en relación con el número de turnos de batear que ha tenido. Esto se llama su promedio. Se considera bueno un promedio de 0,300 o más.

¿CÓMO SE CALCULA EL PROMEDIO?

Se divide el número de hits por el número de turnos de batear y se redondea el número a tres dígitos después de la coma decimal.

Según el gráfico, Cecil Fielder tuvo 624 turnos de batear y pegó 163 hits. Para calcular su promedio, se divide 163 por 624.

$$\frac{\text{hits}}{\text{turnos de batear}} = \text{promedio}$$

$$\frac{163}{624} = 0{,}261217 = 0{,}261$$

ACTIVIDAD A

You will notice that in the chart, the writers forgot to fill in the averages for each player. Can you figure out what their averages should be?

1. El promedio de Tony Peña $107 \div 464 =$ _____
2. El promedio de José Canseco
3. El promedio de Joe Carter
4. El promedio de Ken Griffey, Jr.
5. El promedio de Jim Eisenreich
6. El promedio de Juan González

ACTIVIDAD B

Imagine that the season went just one week longer. Prepare the new chart in your notebook based on the information about the players' performance for the week.

Cecil Fielder pegó 4 hits en 24 turnos de batear.
José Canseco pegó 6 hits en 20 turnos de batear.
Joe Carter pegó 6 hits en 23 turnos de batear.
Ken Griffey, Jr. pegó 3 hits en 18 turnos de batear.
Jim Eisenreich pegó 8 hits en 20 turnos de batear.
Juan González pegó 5 hits en 22 turnos de batear.

	Nombre	TB	H	PROM
	Fielder, Cecil	648	167	0.258
1.	Canseco, José			
2.	Carter, Joe			
3.	Griffey, Jr., Ken			
4.	Eisenreich, Jim			
5.	González, Juan			

Critical Thinking Strategies

The numbers in parentheses on pages 415–418 refer to the chapter in which the strategy may be found.

Analysis

The separation of a whole into its identifiable parts

Analyzing

Examining an object or an idea, studying it from every angle to see what it is, how it works, how many similarities and differences it has from other objects or ideas, and how its parts relate or fit together
> Analyzing (2, 4, 5, 8, 11, 12, 14, 15)
> Analyzing time relationships (15)

Categorizing

Organizing information into groups with similar qualities or attributes
> Categorizing (PC, 1, 4, 13, 14, 15)

Comparing and contrasting

Looking for similarities and/or differences between ideas, people, places, objects, and situations
> Comparing and contrasting (PA, PC, 1, 2, 3, 4, 5, 6, 7, 8, 9, 10, 13, 14, 15)
> Comparing (PA, 4, 7)
> Contrasting (2, 7)

Creating

Producing an original product of human invention or imagination; originating; bringing about; dreaming up
> Creating (6, 8, 10, 12, 13, 15)
> Imagining (6, 8, 13, 15)

Making associations

Using an idea, person, event, or object to trigger the memory of another, seeing relationships between two or more things
> Making associations (PA, PB, 1, 2, 3, 4, 5, 6, 7, 8, 9, 10, 11, 12, 13, 14)

Sequencing

Arranging details in order according to specified criteria
> Ranking (4)
> Sequencing (2, 3, 7, 8, 9, 12, 15)

Synthesis

The combining of separate elements to form a unified, coherent whole

Drawing inferences

Guessing logical explanations or reasons for choices, actions, events, or situations
> Drawing inferences (PA, PC, 1, 12, 13, 14)

Hypothesizing

Making an assertion as a basis for reasoning or argument
> Hypothesizing (5, 12)

Predicting

Expecting behavior, actions, or events based on prior experience and/or available facts
> Predicting (1, 5, 6, 10, 11)

Seeing cause-and-effect relationships

Anticipating a logical result from an action or event
> Drawing conclusions (PA, PB)
> Problem solving (4)
> Seeing cause-and-effect relationships (1, 8, 9, 12, 13, 15)
> Solving problems (5)

Synthesizing

Pulling together pieces of information and ideas to create a new whole
> Generalizing (10, 13)

Evaluation

Determination of worth; judgment; appraisal

Determining preferences

Making personal value judgments
> Determining preferences (8, 14, 15)

Evaluating

Determining worth; judging
> Evaluating (PA, PB, PC, 1, 3, 9, 10, 12, 15)

Prioritizing

Establishing precedence in order of importance or urgency; determining relative value
> Prioritizing (6, 11)

Learning Strategies

Receptive Strategies

Active listening (PB, 5, 9, 12)
Asking for information (PC, 1, 4, 5, 10, 12, 14)
    Asking for personal information (PA, 1, 4, 7, 9, 11, 12)
    Asking questions (1, 2, 4, 5, 6, 7, 10, 12)
    Asking questions based on context (PC)
    Making requests (10)
    Requesting information (13)
    Requesting personal information (7)
Drawing meaning from context (14, 15)
    Drawing meaning from key words (15)
    Selecting appropriate meaning from context (7)
    Using cognates for meaning (2, 6)
Listening for details (PA, PB, 1, 2, 3, 4, 6, 7, 8, 9, 10, 11, 12, 13, 14, 15)
Listening for main ideas (6, 14)
Previewing (1, 2, 3, 4, 5, 6, 7, 8, 9, 10, 11, 12, 13, 14, 15)
Reading a calendar (PC)
Reading a chart (12)
Reading a map (PB, 4)
    Reading a weather map (1)
Reading a schedule (PB)
Reading a timetable (5)
Reading for cultural information (1, 2, 4, 5, 6, 7, 8, 9, 10, 11, 12, 13, 14, 15)
Reading for details (3, 4, 5, 6, 7, 8, 9, 10, 11, 12, 13, 14, 15)
    Reading for ideas (PC, 1, 8)
    Reading for information (7, 8, 12)
    Reading for relevant information (12)
    Reading for specific details (PC)
    Scanning for cognates (1, 3, 7, 8, 9)
    Scanning for details (8, 15)
Reading for main ideas (2, 7, 9, 10, 13, 14, 15)
    Reading for gist (2, 8)

Productive Strategies

Describing (PA, 1, 2, 3, 4, 6, 7, 8, 9, 10, 11, 13, 15)
    Describing and interpreting spatial relationships based on personal information (5)
    Describing based on personal information (1)
    Describing based on visual information (1, 5, 7, 10)
    Describing spatial relationships (PB)
Expressing past time (10, 11, 12, 13, 14, 15)
    Expressing future time (9)
    Expressing past and future time (5)
    Expressing present and future time (8)
    Expressing present and past time (10, 11, 12)
    Narrating in the past (4, 5, 10, 13, 15)
    Narrating in the past and present times (13)
    Narrating in the present, past, and future (5)
    Reporting in the past (10, 13)
    Reporting in the past based on visual cues (13)
    Reporting in the past, present, and immediate future based on visual cues (13)
Expressing preferences (4)
    Commenting on preferences (9, 10)
    Expressing opinion (1, 2, 12)
    Stating preferences (1)
Giving directions (PB)
Identifying (7, 13, 15)
    Identifying based on visual cues (10)
Listing (PB, PC, 1, 2, 3, 6, 7, 8, 9, 10, 11, 12, 15)
Providing information (8, 10, 11, 13, 14)
    Answering questions (4, 6, 7)
    Answering questions based on personal information (7)
    Answering questions based on visual cues (4)
    Giving details (2)
Giving information (2, 5)
    Giving information based on personal experience (13)
    Giving personal information (7)
    Inferring information based on visual cues (4)
    Making suggestions (3)
    Providing personal information (PB, PC, 3, 7, 10, 14)
    Responding to questions (1)
Reporting (PA, 1, 2, 3, 7, 15)
    Reporting based on personal experience (12)
    Reporting based on personal knowledge (PA, PC, 1, 7, 8, 9, 11, 12, 13, 14, 15)
    Reporting based on visual information (PB, PC, 1, 5, 7, 9, 10, 11, 14, 15)
Selecting information (PA, 2, 3, 10)

Organizational Strategies

Brainstorming (8, 9, 10, 11, 12, 13, 14, 15)
Collecting information (PA)
    Collecting information in an article (1)
    Completing a chart (7)
    Creating a graph (12)
    Organizing notes in a chart (PB)
    Recording information on a chart (PB, 10, 13)
    Taking notes (PA, 1, 3, 9)
    Taking notes in a chart (7, 8, 10, 12)
    Taking notes on a calendar (7, 12)
    Tallying results in a poll (PB)
Determining time frame (4)
Interviewing (PA, 3, 4, 7, 10)
Making plans (PC)
Organizing (1, 3, 7, 8)
    Organizing a survey (12)
    Organizing details (3, 4, 5, 12, 13)
    Organizing details in a sequence (7, 10, 15)
    Organizing ideas (7, 10, 11, 13, 15)
    Organizing ideas in a paragraph (13, 14, 15)

Organizing information (PA, 1, 3, 4, 9, 14, 15)
Organizing information in a chart (4)
Scheduling (PB)

Multitasking Strategies

Calculating (5)
Calculating time conversions (6)
Making calculations (4)
Correcting (8)
Negotiating (1, 2, 4, 6, 8, 9, 10, 13)

Persuading (14)
Reaching an agreement (PB, PC)
Paraphrasing (1, 2, 3, 6)
Polling (PB, 4, 13)
Recommending (11)
Selecting and giving personal information (1, 7, 15)
Selecting and organizing information (PA, PB, 1)
Selecting and providing information (10)
Summarizing (6, 15)

Supporting choices (PB, 15)
Making decisions (4)
Supporting an opinion (PA, 1, 2, 3, 6, 8, 9, 14)
Supporting assertions (PC)
Supporting decisions (PC)
Using culturally appropriate language (PA)
Applying appropriate expressions (6)
Using appropriate journalistic tone (10)
Verifying (PB, PC)
Writing an invitation (8)

Reading Strategies

Predicting

When you predict, you use what you already know about a topic, person, or event. Using what you already know helps you make a logical prediction which, in turn, helps you to focus on the material you are reading. You make a prediction and then you read to check if your prediction is correct. (Unit 1)

Previewing

By looking over the whole reading before you start to read it, you begin to get a sense of what it may be about. There are several ways to do this.

Using the title to predict meaning

Look at the title and ask yourself questions about it. Then predict answers to your questions. (2, 3, 6, 7, 8, 9, 10, 11, 12, 13, 14, 15, Unit 2)

Activating background knowledge

Recall what you already know about the topic. (1, 2, 4, 5, 6, 7, 9, 10, 11, 12, 13, 14, 15, Unit 1)

Using photos, art work, and illustrations to predict meaning

Look at the pictures and predict what the reading is about. (2, 3, 4, 5, 6, 7, 8, 9, 10, 11, 12, 13, 14, 15)

Skimming

Look quickly at the reading to get the gist of its content, determining what kind of text it is. It may be a description, a narration, a comparison, a characterization, etc. (2, 3, 8, Unit 4)

Scanning

Look quickly for specific information, letting your eyes move quickly down the page. Don't worry about every word. Slow down when you see words or phrases that might be important to you. Look for clues in the text, such as names, dates, numbers, to help you see what kind of information is being presented. (1, 3, 4, 5, 6, 7, 8, 9, 10, 11, 12, 13, 14, 15; Units 2, 3, 5)

Cognate recognition

*Cognates are words that look alike in two languages, for example, **hospital, universidad, moderno,** etc., shared by Spanish and English. There are cognates, however, whose meaning is not what it at first appears to be, for example **lectura** does not mean lecture but reading. (1, Unit 2)*

Finding main ideas

Main ideas are the central or most important ideas contained in a reading. It may have many related ideas, but one or two ideas are usually the most important of all. (2, 10, 13, 14, 15; Units 2, 3)

Using context to guess meaning

Sometimes you can figure out the meaning of a difficult word by looking at the context—the other words and expressions in the sentence or nearby sentences. Look at these cues to help you. (Unit 2)

Paraphrasing

When you paraphrase, you put information and ideas into your own words. If you stop and paraphrase while you are reading, you can check your comprehension as you go along. Paraphrasing after you finish reading is a good way to check your understanding and help you to remember ideas and information. (3, 13)

Taking notes in a chart

Taking notes as you read helps you organize and remember important information. When you take notes, write down the most important information only. One type of chart you might use may have the main ideas in one column and the details in another column. (3, 8, 9)

Glossary of Functions

The numbers in parentheses refer to the chapter in which the word or phrase may be found.

Describing weather / climate

¿Qué tiempo hace?   *(1)*
Hace   buen tiempo.   *(1)*
    mal tiempo.   *(1)*
    sol.   *(1)*
    calor.   *(1)*
    frío.   *(1)*
    viento.   *(1)*
    fresco.   *(1)*
Está despejado.   *(1)*
    nublado.   *(1)*
    resbaloso.   *(1)*
Llueve.   *(1)*
Llovizna.   *(1)*
Nieva.   *(1)*
Truena.   *(1)*
Hay nubes.   *(1)*
    niebla.   *(1)*
    neblina.   *(1)*
    hielo.   *(1)*
    tormenta.   *(1)*
La temperatura está
  en cinco grados.   *(1)*

Talking about the date

¿Cuál es la fecha de hoy?   *(1)*
¿Cuál es la fecha de… ?   *(1)*
¿Qué fecha es hoy?   *(1)*
¿A cuántos estamos?   *(1)*
Hoy es el 5 de octubre.   *(1)*
Yo nací el 5 de febrero.   *(1)*

Describing people

Él / Ella tiene el pelo moreno.   *(3)*
        los ojos azules.   *(3)*
        la nariz pequeña.   *(3)*
Él tiene bigote y barba.   *(3)*
Él / Ella es fuerte.   *(3)*
      alto(a).   *(3)*
      alegre.   *(3)*
      simpático(a).   *(3)*
      impaciente.   *(3)*
      serio(a).   *(3)*
      generoso(a).   *(3)*
      independiente.   *(3)*
      optimista.   *(3)*
      perezoso(a).   *(3)*
      trabajador(a).   *(3)*
¿Cuánto mides?   *(12)*
Mido un metro.   *(12)*
¿Cuánto pesas?   *(12)*
Peso… kilos.   *(12)*
Él / Ella se guarda la línea.   *(12)*

Getting / Paying for a hotel room

Yo quisiera…   *(4)*
Buscamos…   *(4)*
Necesitamos una habitación…
    para dos personas.   *(4)*
    por tres noches.   *(4)*
    con una cama matrimonial.   *(4)*
    con dos camas sencillas.   *(4)*
    con (sin) baño.   *(4)*
    en el primer piso.   *(4)*
    con televisor.   *(4)*
    con teléfono.   *(4)*
Tenemos una reservación.   *(4)*
¿Puede usted arreglar la cuenta?   *(4)*
¿Tiene usted la cuenta
  para la habitación… ?   *(4)*
Voy a pagar en efectivo.   *(4)*
        con cheques de viajero.   *(4)*
        con una tarjeta de crédito.   *(4)*

Expressing time relationships

Yo llego a tiempo.   *(5)*
      tarde.   *(5)*
      temprano.   *(5)*
En (veinte minutos, etc.)   *(5)*
Por (una hora, etc.)   *(5)*
Hace (un año, dos días, etc.).   *(5)*

To talk about missing someone

Te extraño.   *(5)*
Me extrañas.   *(5)*

Los extrañan. *(5)*

Thanking someone

*Les agradezco con todo el corazón
   su hospitalidad.* *(5)*
Mil gracias por… *(5)*
Muchas gracias por… *(5)*

Asking for and making clarifications

¿Cómo se dice… ? *(6)*
¿Qué quiere decir… ? *(6)*
¿Qué dijiste? *(6)*
No sé como se dice… *(6)*

Finding an apartment

Yo prefiero un apartamento…
   pequeño. *(6)*
   amueblado. *(6)*
   cerca de la universidad. *(6)*
   con dos dormitorios. *(6)*

Talking about daily routines

Yo me despierto a… *(7)*
   me levanto a… *(7)*
   me baño a… *(7)*
   me cepillo los dientes. *(7)*
   me lavo (el pelo, las manos, etc.). *(7)*
   me maquillo. *(7)*
   me peino. *(7)*
   me afeito. *(7)*
   me ducho. *(7)*
   me acuesto a… *(7)*
   me duermo. *(7)*
   me visto. *(7)*

Inviting someone

Nos daría mucho gusto… *(8)*
Tenga la bondad de… *(8)*
Nos vemos a / en… *(8)*
¿Te parece bien? *(8)*
Contéstame cuanto antes. *(8)*

Talking about films

Es una comedia. *(8)*
   un drama psicológico. *(8)*
   un documental. *(8)*
   una película policíaca. *(8)*
      de terror. *(8)*
      de ciencia-ficción. *(8)*
      de aventura. *(8)*

¿A qué hora dan la película?
Dan la película a… *(8)*

Preparing for a party

Yo compro las bebidas. *(7)*
Yo lavo los platos. *(7)*
Yo pongo la mesa. *(7)*
Yo traigo los discos. *(8)*
Yo me encargo de la comida. *(8)*
                  los refrescos. *(8)*
                  las invitaciones. *(8)*
Yo invito a los amigos. *(8)*
La fiesta comienza a… *(8)*
Vamos a echar la casa por la ventana. *(9)*

Making plans for vacation

¿Qué vamos a hacer para las vacaciones? *(9)*
Vamos a visitar… *(9)*
         acampar. *(9)*
         esquiar. *(9)*
Vamos de viaje a… *(9)*
¿Por qué no acampamos? *(9)*
         dormimos en una tienda de campaña? *(9)*
         pasamos las vacaciones en… ? *(9)*
         tomamos el sol? *(9)*
         vamos a la costa? *(9)*
            a la orilla del mar? *(9)*
            a las montañas? *(9)*
         visitamos un centro ecuestre? *(9)*

Talking about health and fitness

Quiero bajar (subir) de peso. *(10)*
Ella se cayó. *(10)*
   se lastimó. *(10)*
   se cortó. *(10)*
Él se rompió (el brazo, la pierna, etc.). *(10)*
   se torció (la muñeca, el tobillo, etc.). *(10)*
   se lastimó (la mano, el dedo, etc.). *(10)*
   se cortó (la frente, el pie, etc.). *(10)*
¿Estás en forma? *(10)*
Yo me pongo en forma. *(10)*
Nosotros (no) nos sentimos bien (mal). *(10)*
Tengo dolor de cabeza. *(10)*
                  garganta. *(10)*
                  estómago. *(10)*
Él tuvo un accidente. *(10)*
¿Cómo te sientes? *(10)*
¿Te sientes bien (mal)? *(10)*
No te ves muy bien. *(10)*

¿Qué te pasa?   (10)
¿Qué te pasó?   (10)
¿Te lastimaste?   (10)
¿Tuviste un accidente?   (10)
Él tiene fiebre.   (10)
     escalofríos.   (10)
     catarro.   (10)
Ella tiene la gripe.   (10)
     una alergia.   (10)
     un virus.   (10)
     la tos.   (10)
     una infección.   (10)
Él tose.   (11)
Ella estornuda.   (11)
Me duele la cabeza.   (11)
     la garganta.   (11)
     el brazo.   (11)
     el estómago.   (11)
Estoy mareado(a).   (11)
¿Cuánto tiempo hace que te sientes así?   (11)

Identifying medicines

Quisiera algo para la garganta.   (11)
     los ojos.   (11)
     la tos.   (11)
     la alergia.   (11)
     la fiebre.   (11)
     la gripe.   (11)

Quisiera unas aspirinas.   (11)
     un antihistamínico.   (11)
     un antibiótico.   (11)
     unas pastillas para la garganta.   (11)
     unas gotas para los ojos.   (11)
     un jarabe para la tos.   (11)
El médico me dio la receta.   (11)
Tengo la medicina.   (11)

Talking about the past

¿Desde cuándo?   (12)
¿Cuánto tiempo hace?   (12)
Desde (que)…   (12)
Hace…   (12)

Verb Charts

SIMPLE TENSES

Infinitive	Present Indicative	Imperfect	Preterite	Commands	
hablar to speak	hablo	hablaba	hablé	habla	(no hables)
	hablas	hablabas	hablaste	hable	
	habla	hablaba	habló	hablad	(no habléis)
	hablamos	hablábamos	hablamos	hablen	
	habláis	hablabais	hablasteis		
	hablan	hablaban	hablaron		
aprender to learn	aprendo	aprendía	aprendí	aprende	(no aprendas)
	aprendes	aprendías	aprendiste	aprenda	
	aprende	aprendía	aprendió	aprended	(no aprendáis)
	aprendemos	aprendíamos	aprendimos	aprendan	
	aprendéis	aprendíais	aprendisteis		
	aprenden	aprendían	aprendieron		
vivir to live	vivo	vivía	viví	vive	(no vivas)
	vives	vivías	viviste	viva	
	vive	vivía	vivió	vivid	(no viváis)
	vivimos	vivíamos	vivimos	vivan	
	vivís	vivíais	vivisteis		
	viven	vivían	vivieron		

COMPOUND TENSES

Present progressive	estoy estamos estás estáis está están	hablando aprendiendo viviendo

SIMPLE TENSES

Infinitive Present Participle Past Participle	Present Indicative	Imperfect	Preterite	Commands
pensar *to think* **e → ie** pensando pensado	**pienso** **piensas** **piensa** pensamos pensáis **piensan**	pensaba pensabas pensaba pensábamos pensabais pensaban	pensé pensaste pensó pensamos pensasteis pensaron	**piensa** **no pienses** **piense** pensad **no penséis** **piensen**
doler *to hurt* **o → ue** doliendo dolido	**duelo** **dueles** **duele** dolemos doléis **duelen**	dolía dolías dolía dolíamos dolíais dolían	dolí doliste dolió dolimos dolisteis dolieron	
pedir *to ask for* **e → i, i** **pidiendo** pedido	**pido** **pides** **pide** pedimos pedís **piden**	pedía pedías pedía pedíamos pedíais pedían	pedí pediste **pidió** pedimos pedisteis **pidieron**	**pide** **no pidas** **pida** pedid **no pidáis** **pidan**
dormir *to sleep* **o → ue, u** **durmiendo** dormido	**duermo** **duermes** **duerme** dormimos dormís **duermen**	dormía dormías dormía dormíamos dormíais dormían	dormí dormiste **durmió** dormimos dormisteis **durmieron**	**duerme** **no duermas** **duerma** dormid **no durmáis** **duerman**

SIMPLE TENSES

Infinitive / Present Participle / Past Participle	Present Indicative	Imperfect	Preterite	Commands
comenzar *to begin* (e → ie) **z → c before e** comenzando comenzado	comienzo comienzas comienza comenzamos comenzáis comienzan	comenzaba comenzabas comenzaba comenzábamos comenzabais comenzaban	**comencé** comenzaste comenzó comenzamos comenzasteis comenzaron	comienza **(no comiences)** **comience** comenzad **(no comencéis)** **comiencen**
conocer *to know* **c → zc before a, o** conociendo conocido	**conozco** conoces conoce conocemos conocéis conocen	conocía conocías conocía conocíamos conocíais conocían	conocí conociste conoció conocimos conocisteis conocieron	conoce **(no conozcas)** **conozca** conoced **(no conozcáis)** **conozcan**
pagar *to pay* **g → gu before e** pagando pagado	pago pagas paga pagamos pagáis pagan	pagaba pagabas pagaba pagábamos pagabais pagaban	**pagué** pagaste pagó pagamos pagasteis pagaron	paga **(no pagues)** **pague** pagad **(no paguéis)** **paguen**
tocar *to play* **c → qu before e** tocando tocado	toco tocas toca tocamos tocáis tocan	tocaba tocabas tocaba tocábamos tocabais tocaban	**toqué** tocaste tocó tocamos tocasteis tocaron	toca **(no toques)** **toque** tocad **(no toquéis)** **toquen**

*Verbs with irregular **yo** forms in the present indicative

SIMPLE TENSES

Infinitive Present Participle Past Participle	Present Indicative	Imperfect	Preterite	Commands
andar	ando	andaba	**anduve**	anda (no andes)
to walk	andas	andabas	**anduviste**	ande
andando	anda	andaba	**anduvo**	andad (no andéis)
andado	andamos	andábamos	**anduvimos**	anden
	andáis	andabais	**anduvisteis**	
	andan	andaban	**anduvieron**	
*caer(se)	**caigo**	caía	caí	cae (no caigas)
to fall	caes	caías	**caíste**	**caiga**
cayendo	cae	caía	**cayó**	caed (**no caigáis)**
caído	caemos	caíamos	**caímos**	**caigan**
	caéis	caíais	**caísteis**	
	caen	caían	**cayeron**	
*conducir	**conduzco**	conducía	**conduje**	conduce (**no**
to drive	conduces	conducías	**condujiste**	**conduzcas)**
conduciendo	conduce	conducía	**condujo**	**conduzca**
conducido	conducimos	conducíamos	**condujimos**	conducid (**no**
	conducís	conducíais	**condujisteis**	**conduzcáis)**
	conducen	conducían	**condujeron**	**conduzcan**
creer	creo	creía	creí	cree (no creas)
to believe	crees	creías	creíste	crea
creyendo	cree	creía	**creyó**	creed (no creáis)
creído	creemos	creíamos	creímos	crean
	creéis	creíais	creísteis	
	creen	creían	**creyeron**	

*Verbs with irregular **yo** forms in the present indicative

SIMPLE TENSES

Infinitive Present Participle Past Participle	Present Indicative	Imperfect	Preterite	Commands
*dar to give dando dado	**doy** das da damos dais dan	daba dabas daba dábamos dabais daban	**di** **diste** **dio** **dimos** **disteis** **dieron**	da (**no des**) **dé** dad (**no deis**) den
*decir to say, tell **diciendo** **dicho**	**digo** **dices** **dice** decimos decís **dicen**	decía decías decía decíamos decíais decían	**dije** **dijiste** **dijo** **dijimos** **dijisteis** **dijeron**	**di** (**no digas**) **diga** decid (**no digáis**) **digan**
*estar to be estando estado	**estoy** **estás** **está** estamos estáis **están**	estaba estabas estaba estábamos estabais estaban	**estuve** **estuviste** **estuvo** **estuvimos** **estuvisteis** **estuvieron**	**está** (**no estés**) **esté** estad (**no estéis**) **estén**
*hacer to make, do haciendo **hecho**	**hago** haces hace hacemos hacéis hacen	hacía hacías hacía hacíamos hacíais hacían	**hice** **hiciste** **hizo** **hicimos** **hicisteis** **hicieron**	**haz** (**no hagas**) **haga** haced (**no hagáis**) **hagan**

*Verbs with irregular **yo** forms in the present indicative

SIMPLE TENSES

Infinitive Present Participle Past Participle	Present Indicative	Imperfect	Preterite	Commands
ir *to go* **yendo** ido	**voy** **vas** **va** **vamos** **vais** **van**	**iba** **ibas** **iba** **íbamos** **ibais** **iban**	**fui** **fuiste** **fue** **fuimos** **fuisteis** **fueron**	**ve (no vayas)** **vaya** id **(no vayáis)** **vayan**
leer *to read* **leyendo** **leído**	leo lees lee leemos leéis leen	leía leías leía leíamos leíais leían	leí leíste **leyó** leímos leísteis **leyeron**	lee (no leas) lea leed (no leáis) lean
*oír *to hear* **oyendo** **oído**	**oigo** **oyes** **oye** **oímos** **oís** **oyen**	oía oías oía oíamos oíais oían	oí **oíste** **oyó** **oímos** **oísteis** **oyeron**	**oye (no oigas)** **oiga** oíd **no oigáis** **oigan**
poder *can, to be able* **pudiendo** podido	**puedo** **puedes** **puede** podemos podéis **pueden**	podía podías podía podíamos podíais podían	**pude** **pudiste** **pudo** **pudimos** **pudisteis** **pudieron**	

*Verbs with irregular **yo** forms in the present indicative

SIMPLE TENSES

Infinitive Present Participle Past Participle	Present Indicative	Imperfect	Preterite	Commands
*poner *to place, put* poniendo **puesto**	**pongo** pones pone ponemos ponéis ponen	ponía ponías ponía poníamos poníais ponían	**puse** **pusiste** **puso** **pusimos** **pusisteis** **pusieron**	**pon (no pongas) ponga** poned **(no pongáis) pongan**
*saber *to know* sabiendo sabido	**sé** sabes sabe sabemos sabéis saben	sabía sabías sabía sabíamos sabíais sabían	**supe** **supiste** **supo** **supimos** **supisteis** **supieron**	sabe **(no sepas) sepa** sabed **(no sepáis) sepan**
*salir *to go out* saliendo salido	**salgo** sales sale salimos salís salen	salía salías salía salíamos salíais salían	salí saliste salió salimos salisteis salieron	**sal (no salgas) salga** salid **(no salgáis) salgan**
ser *to be* siendo sido	**soy** **eres** **es** **somos** **sois** **son**	era eras era éramos erais eran	**fui** **fuiste** **fue** **fuimos** **fuisteis** **fueron**	**sé (no seas) sea** sed **(no seáis) sean**

*Verbs with irregular **yo** forms in the present indicative

SIMPLE TENSES

Infinitive Present Participle Past Participle	Present Indicative	Imperfect	Preterite	Commands
*tener to have teniendo tenido	**tengo** **tienes** **tiene** tenemos tenéis tienen	tenía tenías tenía teníamos teníais tenían	**tuve** **tuviste** **tuvo** **tuvimos** **tuvisteis** **tuvieron**	**ten (no tengas)** **tenga** tened (**no** **tengáis)** **tengan**
traer to bring **trayendo** **traído**	**traigo** traes trae traemos traéis traen	traía traías traía traíamos traíais traían	**traje** **trajiste** **trajo** **trajimos** **trajisteis** **trajeron**	trae (**no traigas)** **traiga** traed (**no** **traigáis)** **traigan**
ver to see viendo **visto**	**veo** ves ve vemos veis ven	**veía** **veías** **veía** **veíamos** **veíais** **veían**	**vi** **viste** **vio** **vimos** **visteis** **vieron**	ve (**no veas)** **vea** ved (**no veáis)** vean

Spanish-English

The numbers in parentheses refer to the chapters in which active vocabulary words or phrases may be found.

a to, at (A)
abajo down, downwards
abogado(a) *m.(f.)* lawyer
abrazo *m.* hug (5)
abrigo *m.* coat
abril April (1)
¡No, en absoluto! Absolutely not!
abuela *f.* grandmother (A)
abuelo *m.* grandfather (A)
aburrido(a) bored, boring (2)
acabar de... to have just . . .
acampar to camp (9)
accidente *m.* accident (10)
acción *f.* action
aceite *m.* oil
aceituna *f.* olive (C)
acequia *f.* irrigation ditch
acerca de about
acercarse to approach
acostarse (ue) to go to bed (7)
activo(a) active (3)
además besides
adicional additional (12)
adiós good-bye (A)
admitir to admit (12)
¿adónde? where?
adorar to adore
aeropuerto *m.* airport (B)
afeitarse to shave (7)
aficionado(a) *m.(f.)* (sports) fan 15
afortunadamente fortunately
agilidad *f.* agility 15
agosto August (1)
agradable pleasant (10)
Les agradezco. I thank you. (5)
el agua *f.* water
   agua mineral (sin gas) mineral water (without carbonation) (C)
ahora now
   ahora mismo right now
ahorrar to save
aire acondicionado air-conditioned (6)

ajedrez *m.* chess 13
al to the
al aire libre in the open air
alboroto *m.* disturbance
alcanzar to reach, achieve (11)
alegre happy (2)
alemán(ana) German (A)
Alemania Germany
alentar to encourage
alergia *f.* allergy (11)
alfombra *f.* rug, carpet (A)
algo something
algodón *m.* cotton
algún día someday
alimento *m.* food
alma *f.* soul
almacén *m.* department store
almidón *m.* starch (12)
alquilar to rent
   alquilar un vídeo to rent a video
alquiler *m.* rent (6)
alrededor around
alto(a) tall
alumno(a) *m.(f.)* student
allá over there
allí there
amable friendly
amar to love
amarillo(a) yellow (2)
ambicioso(a) ambitious (3)
americano(a) American (A)
amigo(a) *m.(f.)* friend (A)
amistad *f.* friendship
(completamente) amueblado (fully) furnished (6)
anaranjado(a) orange (color) (2)
andar to go along, walk
anillo *m.* ring
animal *m.* animal (A)
ancho(a) wide
anoche last night (C)
anotar un gol make a goal, score (15)
ansiedad *f.* anxiety (12)
anterior previous (9)
antes before

antibiótico *m.* antibiotic (11)
antiguo(a) old
antihistamínico *m.* antihistamine (11)
antipático(a) disagreeable
anual annual (11)
anunciar to announce
año *m.* year (C)
aparentemente apparently (12)
apartamento *m.* apartment (A)
apellido *m.* last name (A)
aprender to learn (A)
aprovechar to take advantage of (8)
aquel(la) that
aquél(la) *m.(f.)* that one
aquí here
   Aquí tiene... Here you have . . . (C)
árbol *m.* tree
área de acampar *f.* campground (9)
Argentina Argentina
argentino(a) Argentine (A)
aro *m.* hoop
arquero(a) *m.(f.)* goaltender (15)
arquitecto(a) *m.(f.)* architect
arreglar to arrange, fix (6)
arriba up, above
arroz *m.* rice
arte *m.* or *f.* art (A)
artículo *m.* article (12)
ascensor *m.* elevator (4)
asegurar to assure (10)
¿Así es? Is that it?
asistir a to attend (A)
aspirina *f.* aspirin (11)
un atado de a bunch of (C)
ataque *m.* attack, offense (15)
atleta *m.(f.)* athlete (14)
atlético(a) athletic (3)
atún *m.* tuna
atravesar to cross (14)
atrever to dare
atrevido(a) *m.(f.)* daring
aunque although
auriculares *m.* headphones (14)
ausencia *f.* absence

autobús *m.* bus (B)
  estación de autobuses *f.* bus terminal
avanzar to advance (15)
¡Ave María! Good heavens!
avenida *f.* avenue (B)
aventurero(a) adventurous (14)
avión *m.* airplane
ayer yesterday
ayudar to help
azúcar *m.* sugar
azul blue (2)

bailar to dance (A)
baile *m.* dance
  baile folklórico folk dance
  baile popular popular dance
bajar to go down, lower
  bajar de peso to lose weight (10)
bajo(a) short (height)
balanceado(a) balanced (12)
balón *m.* ball (15)
baloncesto *m.* basketball (13)
balsa neumática *f.* inflatable raft
banana *f.* banana (C)
banco *m.* bank (B)
bañarse to bathe oneself (7)
baño *m.* bath (4)
bar de tapas *m.* tapas restaurant (C)
barato(a) cheap
barba *f.* beard (3)
barco *m.* boat (14)
barrio *m.* neighborhood
básquetbol *m.* basketball
bastante rather, enough (B)
bastón *m.* walking stick (14)
bebé *m.* or *f.* baby (12)
bebida *f.* drink
béisbol *m.* baseball
Belice Belize
belleza *f.* beauty
beneficiarse to benefit (5)
beso *m.* kiss
biblioteca *f.* library (B)
bicicleta *f.* bicycle (A)
  bicicleta de montaña *f.* mountain bike (14)
bidé *m.* bidet (4)
bien well, fine, very (A)
bigote *m.* mustache (3)
billete *m.* ticket
  billete de diez viajes ten-trip ticket

billete de ida y vuelta roundtrip ticket
billete sencillo one-way ticket
biología *f.* biology
blanco(a) white (2)
blusa *f.* blouse
boca *f.* mouth (10)
bocadillo *m.* sandwich (French bread) (C)
boda *f.* wedding (8)
boliche *m.* bowling (13)
bolígrafo *m.* ball-point pen (A)
Bolivia Bolivia
boliviano(a) Bolivian
bolsa *f.* purse
bomba *f.* pump
bonito(a) pretty (2)
borrador *m.* eraser (A)
bosque *m.* forest
bota *f.* boot
una botella de a bottle of (C)
botiquín *m.* first aid kid (14)
boutique *f.* boutique
Brasil Brazil
brazo *m.* arm (10)
brindis *m.* toast (salutation) (8)
bronceado(a) tan (3)
brusco(a) gruff
bucear to snorkel, dive
buceo *m.* snorkeling, diving
bueno(a) good (2)
  ¡Bueno! Hello! (telephone)
  Buenos días. Good morning. (A)
  Buenas noches. Good evening., Good night.
  Buenas tardes. Good afternoon.
buscar to look for (4)

caballo *m.* horse
cabeza *f.* head (10)
cabina de teléfono *f.* telephone booth (4)
cacahuete *m.* peanut
cada every, each (10)
cadera *f.* hip
caerse to fall (10)
café *m.* café, coffee
  café *adj.* dark brown (2)
  café (con leche) coffee (with milk) (C)
caimán *m.* alligator
cajón *m.* drawer (5)

calamares *m.* squid (C)
calcetín *m.* sock
calcio *m.* calcium (12)
calculadora *f.* calculator (A)
calidad *f.* quality (4)
caliente warm, hot (7)
calle *f.* street (B)
¡Cálmate! Calm down! (9)
calor *m.* heat (1)
caloría *f.* calorie (12)
cama *f.* bed (A)
  cama (matrimonial / sencilla) (double / single) bed
cámara *f.* camera
camarero(a) *m.(f.)* waiter (waitress)
cambiar to change
cambio *m.* change, alteration
caminar to walk
camino *m.* road
camisa *f.* shirt
camiseta *f.* T-shirt
campeonato mundial *m.* world championship (14)
campo de juego *m.* field (sports) (15)
Canadá Canada (13)
canadiense Canadian
canasta *f.* basket (14)
cancha *f.* field (sports) (15)
canookayak canoe, kayak (14)
cansado(a) tired
cantar to sing (A)
cantidad *f.* quantity
cantimplora *f.* canteen (14)
cañón *m.* canyon (14)
capacidad *f.* capacity (10)
capital *f.* capital city (13)
cara *f.* face (10)
cariñoso(a) loving, affectionate
carne *f.* meat, beef (C)
carnicería *f.* butcher shop
caro(a) expensive (2)
carretera *f.* highway, road
carril-bici *m.* bike path
carrito *m.* shopping cart
cartel *m.* poster
cartera *f.* wallet (A)
casa *f.* house (A)
casado(a) married (A)
casi almost (7)
castaño(a) hazel (eyes), medium-brown (hair) (3)
castillo *m.* castle
catarro *m.* a cold (11)
catedral *f.* cathedral (B)

categoría *f.* category (4)
causa *f.* cause (12)
cebolla *f.* onion (C)
celebrar to celebrate
cenar to have supper
ceniza *f.* ash (14)
centenar *m.* hundred
centro *m.* downtown, the center (A)
  centro comercial shopping center
cepillarse (el pelo / los dientes) to brush (one's hair / teeth) (7)
cera *f.* wax
cerca de near (B)
cereal *m.* cereal (12)
cerrar(ie) to close
Chao. Good-bye. (A)
chaqueta *f.* jacket
charlar to chat (7)
cheque de viajero *m.* traveler's check (4)
chica *f.* girl
chico *m.* boy
chile *m.* hot pepper
Chile Chile
chileno(a) Chilean
China China
chino(a) Chinese (A)
chocolate *m.* chocolate (C)
chorizo *m.* Spanish sausage (C)
ciclismo *m.* cycling
cien(to) one hundred
ciencia *f.* science (A)
cima *f.* top (of a mountain) (14)
cincuenta fifty
cine *m.* movie theater (C)
cinta *f.* tape (recording) (A)
cinturón *m.* belt
cita *f.* date, appointment
cirugía *f.* surgery
ciudad *f.* city (A)
¡Claro! Of course!
  ¡Claro que no! Of course not! (4)
  ¡Claro que sí! Of course! (reaffirmed)
clásico(a) classic(al) (2)
clasificar to classify (4)
clavadista *m.* or *f.* diver
clavarse to dive (Mexico) (13)
clóset *m.* closet (5)
club *m.* club
cocina *f.* kitchen (6)
cocinar to cook (6)
coche *m.* car (A)
coche-caravana *m.* camper (9)

codo *m.* elbow (10)
colegio *m.* school
colina *f.* hill
collar *m.* necklace
Colombia Colombia
colombiano(a) Colombian
color *m.* color
  ¿De qué color es... ? What color is . . . ? (2)
combustible *m.* fuel
comedor *m.* dining room (6)
comentar to comment
comenzar (ie) to begin (7)
comer to eat (C)
cómico(a) comical, funny (3)
comida *f.* meal, food
  comida mexicana Mexican food
como how, as, like
  como a around, about
  como de costumbre as usual
¿cómo? how?, what? (A)
  ¿Cómo se dice... ? How do you say . . . ? (6)
  ¿Cómo es / son? How is it / are they?
  ¿Cómo está(s)? How are you?
  ¿Cómo te llamas? What's your name? (A)
  ¿Cómo te sientes? How do you feel? (10)
cómoda *f.* dresser (A)
cómodo(a) comfortable
compañía *f.* company
comparación *f.* comparison
compartir to share
competencia *f.* competition (15)
completo(a) complete (2)
comportamiento *m.* behavior
comprar to buy (A)
comprender to understand
comprensivo(a) understanding
comprobar(ue) to check
computadora *f.* computer (A)
con with (A)
  con frecuencia frequently (10)
  con regularidad regularly (10)
  con todo el corazón with all my heart (5)
concierto *m.* concert
concurso de poesía *m.* poetry contest
conducir to drive (13)
confort *m.* comfort (4)
confortable comfortable (4)
congelado(a) frozen

conjunto *m.* group, unit
conmigo with me
conocer to know (person, place) (3), met (15)
conocimiento *m.* knowledge
consecutivo(a) consecutive (10)
consejo *m.* advice
conserva *f.* preserve
constantemente constantly (11)
construir to build
contador(a) *m.(f.)* accountant
contar (ue) to count
  contar con count on, rely on
contento(a) content (13)
contestar to answer, respond
  Contéstame cuanto antes. Answer me as soon as possible. (8)
continuar to continue
continuo(a) continuous (10)
contra la pared against the wall
conveniente convenient (7)
conversación telefónica *f.* telephone conversation
convertirse en to become
corazón *m.* heart (5)
cordillera *f.* mountain range
corredor *m.* corridor, hallway (4)
correr to run
cortar(se) to cut (oneself) (10)
cortina *f.* curtain (6)
corto(a) short (length) (3)
cosa *f.* thing
cosechar to harvest
costa *f.* coast (9)
Costa Rica Costa Rica
costar (ue) to cost (9)
costarricense Costa Rican
costoso(a) costly (13)
de costumbre customarily (C)
coyuntura *f.* joint (10)
crecer to grow
creer to believe (13)
crema *f.* cream
croissant *m.* croissant
crónica *f.* news chronicle
cruzar to cross (B)
cuaderno *m.* notebook (A)
cuadra *f.* city block
cuadro *m.* painting (2)
¿cuál? which?
  ¿Cuál es la fecha de hoy? What is the date today? (1)
cualquier any, whichever
cuando when (A)

¿cuánto(a)? how much / many?

  ¿Cuánto cuesta? How much does it cost? (C)

  ¿Cuánto tiempo hace? How long ago? (12)

  ¿Cuánto tiempo hace que te sientes así? How long have you felt this way?

  ¿Cuántos años tienes? How old are you? (A)

  ¿A cuántos estamos? What is the date? (1)

  ¿Cuántos hay? How many are there?

cuarenta forty

cuarto *m.* room (A), quarter (B)

  ... cuarto(s) de hora ... quarter(s) of an hour (5)

cuarto(a) fourth (4)

cuatrocientos(as) four hundred

Cuba Cuba

cubano(a) Cuban

cubierto(a) covered

cuchara *f.* spoon (6)

cuchillo *m.* knife (6)

cuello *m.* neck (10)

cuenta *f.* bill (4)

cuento contigo I'm counting on you (8)

cuero *m.* leather

cuesta it costs (C)

¡Cuidado! Careful! Watch out!

cuidar to care for (11)

  Cuídese. (Cuídate.) Take care of yourself. (A)

culpa *f.* fault (7)

cultivar to cultivate

cumbre *f.* summit

cumpleaños *m.* birthday (C)

curso de verano *m.* summer course

dar to give (11)

  dar una caminata to take a hike

  dar un paseo to take a walk (A)

  dar una película to show a movie (8)

  dar una vuelta to turn over (2)

  darles la despedida to say good-bye, give a going-away party (8)

  darse por satisfecho to have reason to feel satisfied with oneself

  darse prisa to hurry (7)

  Nos daría mucho gusto... It would give us great pleasure... (8)

de of (B)

  de acuerdo okay (C)

  de la / del of the

  de nada you're welcome

  ¿De qué color es...? What color is...? (2)

  ¿De veras? Really?

deber to owe, must, should

débil weak (3)

décimo(a) tenth (4)

decir to say, tell (6)

  ¿Cómo se dice...? How do you say...? (6)

  decir que sí (no) to say yes (no) (6)

  es decir that is to say

  lo que dice... what ... says (4)

  para decir la verdad to tell the truth (6)

  querer decir to mean (6)

  dedicarse a to devote oneself to (9)

dedo (de la mano) *m.* finger (10)

  dedo del pie toe (10)

defensa *f.* defense (15)

delante de in front of (B)

delgado(a) thin

delicioso(a) delicious (2)

demandar to demand (10)

demasiado too (much) (1)

¡Dense prisa! Hurry up! (7)

dentista *m.* or *f.* dentist

dentro de within (8)

depender de to depend on (1)

deporte *m.* sport (A)

derecha right (B)

  a la derecha to the right (B)

desafío *m.* challenge

desarrollar to develop (12)

desayunarse to eat breakfast (7)

desayuno *m.* breakfast (4)

descansar to rest (A)

descenso *m.* descent, the climb down (14)

desconocido(a) unknown

describir to describe

  le describe describes to him, her, you

Descríbeme... Describe ... for me. (2)

desde (que) since (12)

  ¿Desde cuándo? Since when? (12)

desear to want, wish for

desearles to wish them (8)

desfile *m.* parade

deshonesto(a) dishonest (3)

desierto *m.* desert

despacio slowly, slow

despedirse (i, i) de to say good-bye to

despejado cloudy (1)

despertarse (ie) to wake up (7)

después after

detrás de behind, in back of (B)

día *m.* day (B)

  el Día de la Independencia Independence Day

  el Día de la Madre Mother's Day (C)

  el Día del Padre Father's Day (C)

diciembre December (1)

diente *m.* tooth (10)

dificultad *f.* difficulty (12)

difundir to spread

¡Diga / Dígame! Hello! (answering the phone)

¡No me digas! You don't say!

digestión *f.* digestion (12)

Dime. Tell me.

dinero *m.* money

¿en qué dirección? in which direction?

directamente directly (7)

disco compacto compact disc

discoteca *f.* discotheque (B)

discreto(a) discreet (3)

disculparse to apologize

discutir to argue

disfrutar de to enjoy (8)

divertido(a) enjoyable (2)

divertirse (ie,i) to have a good time (7)

dividir to divide (13)

divorciado(a) divorced (A)

doblar to turn (B)

una docena de a dozen (C)

doctor(a) *m.(f.)* doctor

doler (ue) to hurt (11)

dolor de (cabeza / espalda / estómago) *m.* (head / back / stomach)ache (11)

domingo *m.* Sunday (B)

dominicano(a) Dominican

dominó *m.* dominoes (13)

¿dónde? where?

  ¿De dónde es / eres? Where are you from?

  ¿Dónde está...? Where is...?

  ¿Dónde hay...? Where is / are there...?

dormilón(ona) *m.(f.)* sleepyhead (7)

dormir (ue, u) (la siesta) to sleep (take a nap) (4)

  dormirse to fall asleep (7)

dormitorio *m.* bedroom (6)

dos two (C)

   los(las) dos the two, both

doscientos(as) two hundred

dosis *f.* dose (10)

ducha *f.* shower (4)

ducharse to take a shower (7)

duda *f.* doubt (12)

Me duele(n)… My . . . hurt(s). (11)

dueño(a) *m.(f.)* owner

dulce *m.* sweet, candy

durante during (5)

durar to last (7)

duro(a) hard

E

echar una siesta to take a nap (1)

económico(a) economical (2)

Ecuador Ecuador (13)

ecuatoriano(a) Ecuadoran

edad *f.* age (5)

edificio *m.* building

en efectivo in cash (4)

eficiente efficient (10)

ejemplo *m.* example (7)

el *m.* the (A)

él he

El Salvador El Salvador

elegante elegant (2)

ella she

ellos(as) *m.(f.)* they

empacar to pack

empezar (ie) to begin

empleado(a) *m.(f.)* employee

empuje *m.* push

en in, on (A)

   En (el mes de)… In (the month of) . . . (1)

   en… minutos in . . . minutes (5)

ecabezar to head

Encantado(a). Delighted. (A)

encargarse de to take charge of (7)

encender (ie) to light

encerrarse (ie) to lock oneself in

enchilada *f.* enchilada (C)

encontrar (ue) to find

encuesta *f.* survey

energía *f.* energy (12)

enero January (1)

enfermero(a) *m.(f.)* nurse

enfermo(a) sick

enojado(a) angry, mad

ensalada *f.* salad (C)

   ensalada de frutas fruit salad

ensalada de guacamole guacamole (C)

ensalada de vegetales (verduras) vegetable salad

enseñar to teach

entender to understand

entero(a) whole

entonces then

entrada *f.* entrance ticket

entre… y… between . . . and . . . (B)

entrenador coach, trainer

entrevista *f.* interview

envolverse to become involved

epidemia *f.* epidemic (11)

equipo *m.* equipment (14); team

equitación *f.* horseback riding (9)

es is

   Es de… Is from . . ., It belongs to . . .

   Es la una. It's one o'clock. (B)

escalofríos *m.* chills (11)

escaparate *m.* shop window

escribir to write

   escribir a máquina to type (C)

escritorio *m.* desk (A)

escuchar to listen (to)

escuela *f.* school (A)

   escuela secundaria high school

escultura *f.* sculpture (A)

ese(a) that

ése(a) *m.(f.)* that one

a eso de at about, around (7)

espacio *m.* space

espalda *f.* back (10)

España Spain

español(a) Spanish (A)

especial special

espectáculo *m.* spectacle, show

espejo *m.* mirror (4)

esperar to wait, hope (5)

   los espera waits for them (7)

   espero que Uds. puedan visitar I hope that you can visit (5)

   Espero que no sea… I hope it's not . . . (8)

esposa *f.* wife

esposo *m.* husband

esquí *m.* ski

   esquí acuático *m.* waterskiing

esquiar to ski (C)

   esquiar en agua to waterski (9)

en la esquina de… y… on the corner of . . . and . . . (B)

establecer to establish

estación *f.* station

estación de autobuses bus terminal

estación de metro subway station

estación de trenes railroad station

estacionamiento parking (6)

estacionar to park

estadio *m.* stadium (B)

estado *m.* state

los Estados Unidos United States (B)

estadounidense American, from the United States

estante *m.* bookshelf (5)

estar to be (A)

   estar de mal humor to be in a bad mood

   estar de visita to be visiting (12)

   Está bien. Okay.

   Está (despejado / nublado / resbaloso). It's a (clear / cloudy / slippery) day. (1)

   ¿Estás en forma? Are you in shape? (10)

   ¿Cómo está(s)? How are you? (A)

este *m.* east (B)

este(a) (mes / tarde) this (month / afternoon) (C)

éste(a) *m.(f.)* this one

estéreo *m.* stereo (A)

estilo *m.* style

estómago *m.* stomach (10)

estornudar to sneeze (11)

estrella *f.* star

estudiante *m.* or *f.* student

estudiar to study (A)

estufa *f.* stove (6)

evento social *m.* social event (10)

evitar to avoid

exactamente exactly (12)

Exacto. Exactly. (8)

exagerar to exaggerate

¡No te excites! Don't get excited!

excursión tour (14)

exigir to demand

éxito *m.* success (15)

experto(a) expert (10)

expresar to express

expresión *f.* expression

extrañar to miss (5)

   Te (Los) extraño. I miss you (plural). (5)

extraño(a) strange

F

fácil easy

facilitar to facilitate (12)
falda *f.* skirt
falta *f.* lack (12)
familia *f.* family (A)
familiar *m.* relative, family member
famoso(a) famous
farmacia *f.* pharmacy, drugstore (B)
favorito(a) favorite
febrero February (1)
fecha *f.* date
    ¿Cuál es la fecha de hoy? What is the date today? (1)
felicidad *f.* happiness
feo(a) ugly (2)
feria *f.* fair
feroz ferocious (13)
fibra *f.* fiber (12)
fiebre *f.* fever (11)
    fiebre del heno hay fever (11)
fiesta *f.* party
    fiesta del pueblo religious festival honoring a town's patron saint
fin de semana *m.* weekend
al final de at the end of (B)
finalmente finally
finca *f.* farm
flan *m.* caramel custard
flauta *f.* flute (A)
florería *f.* flower shop
flotar to float (10)
al fondo de at the end of
formal formal (2)
formar to form (12)
formidable wonderful (2)
francés(esa) French (A)
Francia France
con frecuencia frequently (10)
frecuentemente frequently (B)
frente *f.* forehead (10)
frente a across from, facing
en frente de across from, facing (B)
fresa *f.* strawberry (C)
fresco(a) cool (1)
frijoles *m.* beans (C)
frío(a) cold (1)
frontera *f.* border (11)
fruta *f.* fruit (12)
fuego *m.* fire
fuegos artificiales *m.* fireworks
fuente *f.* fountain
fuera de outside of
fuerte strong (3)
fuerza *f.* force, strength
funcionar to function, work

furioso(a) furious (13)
fusilar to shoot
fútbol *m.* soccer
    fútbol americano football
futuro *m.* future

galleta *f.* biscuit, cookie
ganar to earn
garaje (para dos coches) *m.* (two-car) garage (6)
garganta *f.* throat (10)
gas
    con gas carbonated (14)
    sin gas not carbonated (14)
gastar to spend
gato *m.* cat
por lo general in general (C)
generoso(a) generous (3)
genial pleasant
gente *f.* people
geografía *f.* geography
gimnasio *m.* gym(nasium)
globo *m.* globe, sphere, balloon
gobierno *m.* government
gol *m.* goal (sports) (15)
golf *m.* golf (9)
gordo(a) fat
gotas para los ojos *f.* eyedrops (11)
grabadora *f.* tape recorder (A)
gracias thank you (A)
    mil gracias por... thanks a million for ... (5)
    muchas gracias por... thank you very much (many thanks) for ... (5)
grado *m.* degree (1)
(50) gramos de (50) grams of (C)
Gran Bretaña Great Britain
granadina *f.* grenadine
grande big, large (A)
grano *m.* bean
grasa *f.* fat (12)
grave grievous, grave (10)
gripe *f.* flu (11)
gris gray (2)
grupo *m.* group
guapo(a) handsome
guardar la línea to watch one's weight
Guatemala Guatemala
guatemalteco(a) Guatemalan
guisante *m.* pea (C)
guitarra *f.* guitar (A)
gustar to like (A)

(No) (Me) gusta(n) (mucho)... (I) (don't) like . . . (very much). (A)
gusto *m.* taste
    con mucho gusto with pleasure
    Mucho gusto. Nice to meet you. (A)

habilidad *f.* ability (15)
habitación *f.* room (4)
hablar to talk
hacer to do, make
    hacer alpinismo to go mountain climbing
    hacer la cama to make the bed
    hacer ciclismo to bicycle (13)
    hacer ejercicio to exercise
    hacer ejercicios aeróbicos to do aerobics (10)
    hacer la equitación to go horse-back riding (9)
    hacer gimnasia to do exercises, gymnastics (10)
    hacer las maletas to pack suitcases
    hacer un mandado to do an errand (4)
    hacer un viaje to take a trip
    hacer windsurfing to windsurf (13)
    hace... . . . ago, it has been . . . (C)
    Hace (buen tiempo / calor / sol / viento). It's (nice / hot / sunny / windy) out. (1)
    ¿Cuánto tiempo hace? How long ago? (12)
    ¿Cuánto tiempo hace que te sientes así? How long have you felt this way? (11)
hamburguesa (con queso) *f.* hamburger (cheeseburger) (C)
harina *f.* flour
hasta until
    Hasta luego. See you later. (A)
hay there is / are (B)
    Hay (hielo / niebla / tormenta). It's (icy / foggy / stormy). (1)
    hay que pasar por... one must go through . . . (4)
    Hay que ser razonables. Let's be reasonable.
helado *m.* ice cream
hermana *f.* sister (A)
hermano *m.* brother (A)

hermoso(a) beautiful
hielo *m.* ice (1)
hierro *m.* iron (12)
hija *f.* daughter (A)
hijo *m.* son (A)
hijo(a) único(a) *m.(f.)* only child (A)
hispano(a) Hispanic
historia *f.* history (A)
histórico(a) historical (2)
hockey sobre hierba *m.* field hockey (13)
hoguera *f.* campfire, bonfire
hoja (de papel) *f.* sheet (of paper) (C)
Hola. Hello. (A)
hombre *m.* man
hombro *m.* shoulder (10)
Honduras Honduras
hondureño(a) Honduran
honesto(a) honest (3)
hora *f.* hour (B)
horario *m.* schedule
horno (de microondas) *m.* (microwave) oven (6)
horóscopo *m.* horoscope (2)
horrible horrible
hospital *m.* hospital (B)
hospitalidad *f.* hospitality (5)
hotel *m.* hotel (B)
hoy today (B)
    Hoy es el (día) de (mes). Today is the (day) of (month). (1)
hueso *m.* bone (12)
humo *m.* smoke

idealista idealist(ic) (3)
idioma *m.* language
iglesia *f.* church (B)
igualdad *f.* equality
Igualmente. Same here. (A)
impaciente impatient (3)
impermeable *m.* raincoat
incluido(a) included (4)
increíble incredible (6)
independiente independent (3)
indicación *f.* indication (12)
indígena *m. or f.* native
indiscreto(a) indiscreet (3)
infantil infantile, childish (2)
infección *f.* infection (11)
ingeniero(a) *m.(f.)* engineer
Inglaterra England
inglés(esa) English (A)

inolvidable unforgettable (13)
intelectual intellectual (3)
inteligente intelligent
interesante interesting (2)
invierno *m.* winter (1)
invitación *f.* invitation
ir to go (A)
    ir a… to be going to . . .
    ir de camping to go camping
    ir de compras to go shopping
    ir de pesca to go fishing
    irse to leave, go away (7)
Italia Italy
italiano(a) Italian (A)
izquierda left (B)
    a la izquierda to the left (B)

jabón *m.* soap (5)
jamón *m.* ham (C)
Japón Japan
japonés(esa) Japanese (A)
jarabe *m.* cough syrup (11)
jardín *m.* garden (6)
jazz *m.* jazz (A)
jinete *m.* rider, horseman
joven young
juego *m.* game
jueves *m.* Thursday (B)
jugador(a) *m.(f.)* player (15)
jugar (ue) to play (1)
    jugar a las damas to play checkers (13)
    jugar a los naipes to play cards (13)
    jugar al baloncesto to play basketball
    jugar al golf to play golf
    jugar al hockey to play hockey
    jugar al hockey sobre hierba to play field hockey
    jugar al (tenis / vólibol) to play (tennis / volleyball) (9)
jugo *m.* juice
julio July (1)
junio June (1)
junto(a) together

un kilo de a kilo(gram) of (C)
    medio kilo de half a kilo(gram) of (C)

kilómetro *m.* kilometer

la *f.* the (A)
lácteo dairy (12)
    producto lácteo *m.* dairy product (12)
lado *m.* side
    al lado de beside (B)
    del lado de mi padre (madre) on my father's (mother's) side (A)
lámpara *f.* lamp (4)
lancha *f.* (nav.) launch
lápiz *m.* pencil (A)
largo(a) long (2)
las *f. pl.* the (A)
lastimarse to hurt oneself (10)
    ¿Te lastimaste? Did you hurt yourself? (10)
una lata de a can of (C)
latido *m.* (heart) beat
latín *m.* Latin (7)
lavabo *m.* sink (4)
lavadora *f.* washing machine
lavar to wash (5)
    lavar la ropa to wash clothes (7)
    lavar los platos to wash dishes (7)
    lavarse (las manos, el pelo, los dientes) to wash (one's hands, hair, brush one's teeth) (7)
leche *f.* milk (C)
lechuga *f.* lettuce (C)
leer to read (A)
lejos de far from (B)
lengua *f.* language, tongue (A)
lesión *f.* injury
levantarse to get up (7)
    levantar pesas to lift weights
una libra de a pound of (C)
librería *f.* bookstore (B)
libro *m.* book (A)
licuado (de mango) *m.* (mango) milkshake (C)
ligero(a) light (2)
limón *m.* lemon (C)
limonada *f.* lemonade (C)
lindo(a) pretty
línea *f.* line
lípidos *m.* lipids (12)
listo(a) ready
literatura *f.* literature (A)
un litro de a liter of (C)

logro *m.* attainment, success
llamarse to be named (A)
   (Yo) me llamo… My name is . . .
llano *m.* plain (land)
llave *f.* key (A)
llegar (a / de) to arrive (at / from) (4)
lleno(a) full
llevar to carry, take (A)
   llevar a cabo to carry out
   lo lleva takes him
llorar to cry
llover (ue) a cántaros to·rain cats and dogs (1)
Llovizna. It's drizzling. (1)
Llueve. It's raining. (1)
los *m. pl.* the (A)
luego later, afterwards
lugar *m.* place, location
   en primer lugar in the first place
lujo *m.* luxury (4)
luna *f.* moon
lunes *m.* Monday (B)

M

m² (metros cuadrados) square meters (6)
madrastra *f.* stepmother (A)
madre *f.* mother (A)
¡Magnífico! Magnificent! (9)
maíz *m.* corn (C)
mal poorly
maleta *f.* suitcase
malo(a) bad (2)
mandado *m.* errand (C)
mandar to give an order (11)
manejo *m.* management, handling
manera *f.* way, manner (10)
   de esa manera in that way
manija *f.* handle, clamp
manillar *m.* handle bar
mano *f.* hand (10)
mantenerse en condiciones óptimas to stay in top condition (10)
mantequilla *f.* butter
manzana *f.* apple (C)
mañana tomorrow (C)
   mañana (por la mañana / noche) tomorrow (morning / night) (C)
mañana *f.* morning (B)
   de la mañana in the morning
   por la mañana in the morning (C)
maquillarse to put on makeup (7)
máquina *f.* machine

máquina de escribir typewriter (A)
mar *m.* sea (1)
marcar un gol make a goal, score (15)
mariposa *f.* butterfly
marisco *m.* shellfish (13)
mármol *m.* marble
marrón maroon
martes *m.* Tuesday (B)
marzo March (1)
más more
   más o menos so-so
   más… que more . . . than
matemáticas *f.* mathematics (A)
máximo(a) maximum (10)
mayo May (1)
mayonesa *f.* mayonnaise
mayor older
mayoría *f.* majority (12)
mecánico(a) *m.(f.)* mechanic
media *f.* stocking
medianoche *f.* midnight
médico *m.* or *f.* doctor
medio *m.* middle, means
   medio de transporte means of transportation
medio(a) half
   media hora half hour (5)
   medio kilo de half a kilo of (C)
mediodía *m.* noon
medir (i, i) to measure (12)
mejor better
mejorar to improve (12)
melocotón *m.* peach
melón *m.* melon (C)
menor younger
menos less
   al menos at least (4)
   menos… que… less . . . than
   por lo menos at least (1)
a menudo often (10)
mercado *m.* market (C)
   mercado al aire libre open-air market
merienda *f.* snack
mermelada *f.* jam, jelly
mes *m.* month (C)
meseta *f.* high plain
mesita de noche *f.* night table (4)
meta *f.* goal
metro *m.* subway (B)
mexicano(a) Mexican (A)
México Mexico
mezcla *f.* mixture
mi my (A)
mí me

microbio *m.* microbe (11)
Mido… I am . . . tall. (12)
miedo *m.* fear (15)
miércoles *m.* Wednesday (B)
mil thousand
milla *f.* mile
millón million
mineral *m.* mineral (12)
minuto *m.* minute (B)
mirar to look at, watch
   mirar la televisión to watch television (A)
   mirarse to look at oneself (7)
   ¡Mira! Look!
misa de Acción de Gracias *f.* Thanksgiving mass
mismo(a) same (7)
   lo mismo the same (12)
mitad *f.* half; (5) middle
mochila *f.* backpack (A)
moda *f.* style
moderno(a) modern (2)
de todos modos at any rate (11)
en este momento at this moment
montaña *f.* mountain (1)
montañismo *m.* hiking (14)
montar a caballo to ride a horse (9)
montar en bicicleta to ride a bicycle
montículo *m.* mound
morado(a) purple (2)
moreno(a) dark-haired, brunet(te)
morir to die
motocicleta *f.* motorcycle, moped (A)
moverse (ue) to move (7)
movimiento *m.* movement (10)
   movimiento muscular muscle movement (12)
muchísimo very much
mucho(a) a lot
   muchas veces a lot of, many times (10)
muerto(a) dead (A)
lo muestra shows it (5)
mujer *f.* woman
mundo *m.* world
muñeca *f.* wrist (10)
músculo *m.* muscle (12)
museo *m.* museum (B)
música *f.* music
   música clásica classical music (A)
   música de mariachi mariachi music (13)
muslo *m.* thigh (10)
muy very (A)

Muy bien, gracias. Very well, thank you.

nacer to be born
(Él / Ella) nació… (He / She) was born . . . (1)
nacionalidad *f.* nationality
nada nothing
nadar to swim
naranja *f.* orange (C)
nariz *f.* nose (10)
natación *f.* swimming
naturaleza *f.* nature (A)
navegación a vela *f.* sailing (9)
navegar en velero (una tabla vela) to sail (to sailboard) (9)
neblina *f.* fog (1)
necesitar to need (4)
negocio *m.* business
   hombre (mujer) de negocios *m.(f.)* businessman(woman)
negro(a) black (2)
nervio *m.* nerve (12)
nervioso(a) nervous (13)
Nicaragua Nicaragua
nicaragüense Nicaraguan
nido *m.* nest
niebla *f.* fog (1)
nieto(a) *m.(f.)* grandson(daughter) (3)
Nieva. It's snowing. (1)
nieve *f.* snow (1)
niño(a) *m.(f.)* child
nivel *m.* level
no no
noche *f.* night (B)
   de la noche at night (B)
   por la noche at night (C)
nombre *m.* name (A)
normalmente normally (C)
norte *m.* north (B)
norteamericano(a) North American
nosotros(as) *m.(f.)* we
novato(a) *m.(f.)* beginner
novecientos(as) nine hundred
noveno(a) ninth (4)
noventa ninety
noviembre November (1)
novio(a) *m.(f.)* boy(girl)friend, fiance(é)
nube *f.* cloud (1)
nublado cloudy (1)
nuestro(a) our

nuevo(a) new
   de nuevo again (7)
número *m.* number
nunca never (B)

o or
ochenta eighty
ochocientos(as) eight hundred
octavo(a) eighth (4)
octubre October (1)
ocuparse de to take care of (7)
odiar to hate
oeste *m.* west (B)
oferta *f.* sale
   ¿No está en oferta? It's not on sale?
oficina de correos post office
ofrecer to offer
oír to hear (13)
ojo *m.* eye (3)
optimista optimist(ic) (2)
oración *f.* sentence
orden *m.* order
   a sus órdenes at your service
oreja *f.* ear (10)
orgulloso(a) proud
orilla del mar *f.* seashore
oscuro(a) dark
otoño *m.* autumn, fall (1)
otro(a) other
   otra cosa another thing
   en otra oportunidad at some other time
oxígeno *m.* oxygen (10)

paciente patient (3)
padrastro *m.* stepfather (A)
padre *m.* father (A)
   padres *m. pl.* parents
pagar to pay (4)
país *m.* country (A)
paisaje *m.* countryside, landscape (14)
pájaro *m.* bird
palabra *f.* word
pálido(a) pale (3)
pan *m.* bread (C)
   pan dulce any sweet roll
   pan tostado toast
panadería *f.* bakery
Panamá Panama
panameño(a) Panamanian

pantalones *m.* pants, slacks
   pantalones de campana bell-bottom pants
papa *f.* potato (C)
papel *m.* paper (C)
   papel de avión air mail stationery (C)
   papel para escribir a máquina typing paper
papelería *f.* stationery store (C)
un paquete de a package of (C)
par *m.* pair
para for, in order to (B)
Paraguay Paraguay
paraguayo(a) Paraguayan
sin parar without stopping
pardo(a) brown (2)
parece it appears
   ¿Te parece bien? Is that okay with you? (8)
pared *f.* wall
parque *m.* park (B)
parque zoológico *m.* zoo
parte *f.* part
   en parte al menos at least in part (12)
   parte del cuerpo body part (11)
partido *m.* game (15)
(el lunes / la semana) pasado(a) last (Monday / week) (C)
pasar to pass (9)
   pasar tiempo to spend time (A)
   Lo pasamos bien. We have / had a good time.
paseo *m.* walk (A)
   dar un paseo to take a walk (A)
pasta *f.* pasta
pastel *m.* pastry, pie
pastilla *f.* pill (11)
patata *f.* potato (Spain) (C)
   patatas bravas potatoes in a spicy sauce (C)
patinar to skate
   patinar sobre ruedas to rollerskate
pecho *m.* chest (10)
un pedazo de a piece of (C)
pedir (i) to ask for, request (C)
peinarse to comb (7)
película *f.* movie (A)
   película de aventura adventure movie
   película de ciencia ficción science fiction movie
   película cómica comedy movie

película de horror   horror movie
peligro   m.   danger
peligroso(a)   dangerous
pelirrojo(a)   redheaded
pelo   m.   hair   (3)
pelota   f.   ball
   pelota de tenis   tennis ball
pensar (ie)   to think
peor   worse, worst
pepino   m.   cucumber   (C)
pequeño(a)   small   (A)
pera   f.   pear   (C)
perder (ie)   to lose
Perdón.   Excuse me.   (C)
perezoso(a)   lazy   (3)
perfeccionar   to perfect   (5)
perfecto(a)   perfect   (3)
periódico   m.   newspaper   (6)
periodista   m. or f.   journalist
período   m.   period (of time)   (2)
no permiten   do not permit, do not
   allow   (4)
pero   but
perro   m.   dog
persona   f.   person   (4)
Perú   Peru
peruano(a)   Peruvian
pesadilla   f.   nightmare   (12)
pesado(a)   heavy   (2)
pesar   to weigh   (12)
   Peso… kilos.   I weigh . . . kilos.
a pesar de   in spite of
pescado   m.   fish
pesimista   pessimist(ic)   (2)
piano   m.   piano   (A)
picante   spicy   (C)
pie   m.   foot   (B)
   a pie   on foot   (B)
pierna   f.   leg   (10)
pimienta   f.   pepper (spice)
pintor(a)   m.(f.)   painter
pintura   f.   painting   (A)
piscina   f.   swimming pool
piso   m.   floor   (4)
   (en el primer) piso   (on the first)
   floor   (4)
pizza   f.   pizza   (C)
plan   m.   floor plan   (6)
planear   to plan
plano(a)   flat
plano del metro   m.   subway map
planta   f.   floor, plant   (A)
   planta baja   ground floor   (4)
plátano   m.   banana

plata   f.   silver, money
plato   m.   dish, plate   (6)
playa   f.   beach
playa de estacionamiento   f.   parking
   lot
plaza   f.   square   (B)
pluma   f.   fountain pen
poco(a)   few, a little
poder   to be able (to)   (13), (preterite)
   made an attempt   (15)
   No puedo dormir.   I can't sleep.
   (11)
   ¿Puede Ud. arreglar la cuenta?
   Can you make up the bill?   (4)
policía   f.   police, m.   police
   officer
   estación de policía   f.   police station
política   f.   politics   (A)
pollo   m.   chicken   (C)
poner   to put   (6)
   poner la mesa   to set the table   (7)
   ponerse   to put on   (7)
   ponerse en forma   to get in shape
   (10)
por   for, during   (4)
   por eso   that is why
   por eso mismo   for that very reason
   por favor   please   (C)
   por fin   finally   (13)
   por … horas   for … hours   (5)
   por lo general   in general   (C)
   por lo menos   at least
   por supuesto   of course
¿por qué?   why?   (C)
   ¿por qué no?   why not?   (C)
porque   because
portafolio   m.   briefcase   (A)
portero(a)   m.(f.)   goaltender   (15)
posesión   f.   possession
poste   m.   post
póster   m.   poster   (A)
practicar   to practice   (9)
   practicar el surfing   to surf
   practicar la vela   to sail
práctico(a)   practical   (2)
prado   m.   pasture
precio   m.   price   (4)
preferencia   f.   preference
preferir (ie, i)   to prefer
preguntar   to ask (a question)
premio   m.   prize
preocupado(a)   worried, preoccupied
preocupar   to worry
   No se preocupen.   Don't worry.   (8)

preparar   to prepare
   les voy a preparar…   I'm going to
   prepare, make . . . for you.
   prepararse   to get ready, prepare
   oneself   (7)
presentación   f.   presentation, introduction
presentar   to present, introduce   (12)
   Le (Te) presento a…   This is . . .
   (introduction)   (A)
presión   f.   pressure   (10)
prestar atención   to pay attention   (5)
primavera   f.   spring   (1)
primer(o/a)   first   (4)
primo(a)   m.(f.)   cousin   (A)
al principio   in, at the beginning   (13)
producto lácteo   m.   dairy product
   (12)
profesión   f.   profession
profesor(a)   m.(f.)   professor, teacher
programa de intercambio   m.
   exchange program   (5)
pronóstico   m.   forecast
propina   f.   tip
proteína   f.   protein   (12)
(el año / la semana) próximo(a)   next
   (year / week)   (C)
prueba   f.   test, quiz
pudo   he / she / it could   (2)
pueblo   m.   town   (9)
puente   m.   bridge
puerco   m.   pork   (C)
puerta   f.   door
Puerto Rico   Puerto Rico
puertorriqueño(a)   Puerto Rican
pues   then, well then
pulmón   m.   lung   (10)
pulsera   f.   bracelete
punto   m.   point   (11)

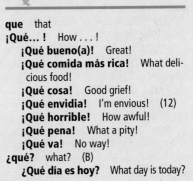

que   that
¡Qué… !   How . . . !
   ¡Qué bueno(a)!   Great!
   ¡Qué comida más rica!   What deli-
   cious food!
   ¡Qué cosa!   Good grief!
   ¡Qué envidia!   I'm envious!   (12)
   ¡Qué horrible!   How awful!
   ¡Qué pena!   What a pity!
   ¡Qué va!   No way!
¿qué?   what?   (B)
   ¿Qué día es hoy?   What day is today?

¿Qué dijiste? What did you say? (6)

¿Qué fecha es hoy? What is the date today? (1)

¿Qué hay? What's new?

¿Qué hora es? What time is it? (B)

¿A qué hora… ? What time . . . ? (B)

¿Qué pasó? What's going on?

¿Qué te pasa? What's the matter with you? (10)

¿Qué te pasó? What happened to you? (10)

¿Qué tal? How are you? (A)

¿Qué tiempo hace? What's the weather like? (1)

quedarse en cama to stay in bed (7)

querer (ie) to want (C), tried (15)

no querer (preterite) refused (15)

querer decir to mean (6)

querido(a) dear (5)

quesadilla *f.* quesadilla, Mexican cheese turnover (C)

queso *m.* cheese (C)

¿quién? who?

¿De quién es? Whose is it?

Quiero presentarle(te) a… I want to introduce you to . . . (A)

química *f.* chemistry

quinceañera *f.* fifteenth birthday party (8)

quinientos(as) five hundred

quinto(a) fifth (4)

quiosco de periódicos *m.* newspaper kiosk

… quisiera… … would like . . . (C)

Quisiera algo (alguna cosa) para… I would like something for . . . (11)

Quisiera presentarle(te) a… I would like to introduce you to . . . (A)

(nosotros) quisiéramos… we would like . . . (C)

quitar la mesa to clear the table (7)

radio despertador *m.* clock radio (A)

raqueta *f.* racquet

rara vez rarely (B)

un buen rato a good while (7)

reacción *f.* reaction (2)

realista realist(ic) (3)

rebanada de pan *f.* slice of bread

recepción *f.* reception desk (4)

recibir to receive

recoger to pick up, harvest

lo recoge pick him / it up

reconocer to recognize

récord *m.* record (sports) (15)

recuerdo *m.* memory

recuperar to recuperate (12)

red *f.* network

refresco *m.* soft drink

refrigerador *m.* refrigerator (6)

regalo *m.* gift

regatear to bargain

regresar to return (7)

regular okay, regular, average (2); to regulate (12)

con regularidad regularly (10)

reírse (i, i) to laugh

remedio *m.* remedy (11)

renovar (ue) to renew (12)

de repente suddenly

repetir (i, i) to repeat (12)

la República Dominicana the Dominican Republic

res *m.* beef (C)

resbaloso(a) slippery (1)

reservación *f.* reservation (4)

resfrío *m.* a cold

respuesta *f.* answer, response (8)

restaurante *m.* restaurant (B)

resultado *m.* result (12)

reunirse to meet, get together (7)

revisar to review, check, look over

riesgo *m.* risk

río *m.* river (14)

riquísimo very delicious

ritmo cardíaco *m.* heart rate (12)

rock *m.* rock music (A)

rodilla *f.* knee (10)

rojo(a) red (2)

romántico(a) romantic (2)

romper(se) to break (a body part) (10)

roncar to snore (12)

ropa *f.* clothing (5)

rosado(a) pink (2)

rubio(a) blond(e) (3)

ruido *m.* noise

Rusia Russia

ruso(a) Russian (A)

sabroso(a) tasty (A)

sacapuntas *m.* pencil sharpener (A)

sacar to get out something, obtain

sal *f.* salt

sala *f.* room

sala de baño bathroom (4)

sala de estar living room (6)

salida *f.* exit (5)

salir (con / de / para) to leave (with / from / for) (4)

salir con to go out with

salsa *f.* type of music

salsa picante hot, spicy sauce (C)

saltamontes *m.* grasshopper

salud *f.* health (12)

saludar to greet

saludo *m.* greeting

salvadoreño(a) Salvadoran

sandalia *f.* sandal

sandía *f.* watermelon (C)

sándwich (de jamón con queso) *m.* (ham and cheese) sandwich (C)

seco(a) dry (12)

secretario(a) *m.(f.)* secretary

en seguida right away, at once (9)

seguir (i, i) to continue, follow (B)

según according to

segundo(a) second (4)

seguro(a) sure

seiscientos(as) six hundred

semana *f.* week (C)

sencillo(a) simple (10)

sendero *m.* path (14)

senderismo *m.* hiking (14)

sensacional sensational (2)

sentarse (ie) to sit down (7)

sentido *m.* sense

sentirse (ie, i) bien (mal) to feel good (bad) (10)

señal *f.* signal, sign (12)

señor *m.* Mr., sir (A)

señora *f.* Mrs., ma'am (A)

señorita *f.* Miss (A)

septiembre September (1)

séptimo(a) seventh (4)

ser to be (A)

Será una sorpresa; no les digas nada. It will be a surprise; don't say anything to them. (8)

ser humano *m.* human being

serie *f.* series, sequence

serio(a) serious (2)

servicios sanitarios *m.* rest rooms

sábado *m.* Saturday (B)

saber to know (a fact) (1); found out (15)

sabor *m.* flavor, taste

servilleta *f.* napkin (6)

servirse (i, i) to prepare for oneself, to serve oneself (7)

    ¿En qué puedo servirle(s)? How can I help you?

sesenta sixty

setecientos(as) seven hundred

setenta seventy

sexto(a) sixth (4)

si if

sí yes

siempre always (C)

    ¡Siempre lo hacemos! We always do it!

¿Cómo te sientes? How do you feel? (10)

¿Te sientes bien (mal)? Do you feel well (bad)? (10)

Lo siento. I'm sorry.

siglo *m.* century

significado *m.* meaning

lo siguiente the following (4)

silla *f.* chair (A)

sillón *m.* armchair (5)

simpático(a) nice

simple simple (4)

sin without (4)

    sin embargo nevertheless

    sin límite unlimited

    sin parar without stopping (11)

sistema *m.* system

    sistema cardiovascular cardiovascular system (10)

    sistema de clasificación classification system (4)

sitio *m.* place

situado(a) situated, located (B)

sobre *m.* envelope (C)

soda *f.* soda

sofá *m.* sofa, couch (6)

sol *m.* sun (1)

soledad *f.* solitude

sólo only (7)

soltero(a) single (3)

solución *f.* solution (10)

Son de… They are from . . . , They belong to . . .

Son las… It's . . . o'clock. (B)

sonreírse (i, i) to smile (12)

soñar to dream

sorpresa *f.* surprise (8)

sorteo *m.* raffle (14)

(Yo) (no) soy de… I am (not) from . . . (A)

(Yo) soy de origen… I am of . . . origin. (A)

su his, her, your, their (5)

subir to go up, climb, rise

    subir de peso to gain weight (12)

sucio(a) dirty (5)

sudar to sweat (10)

suéter *m.* sweater

suficiente sufficient, enough

sufrir to suffer (11)

¡Super! Super!

sur *m.* south (B)

T

taco (de carne) *m.* (beef) taco (C)

talento *m.* talent (15)

tal vez perhaps (8)

también also, too (A)

tampoco neither

tan so

    tan(to)… como… as much . . . as

tapa *f.* Spanish snack (C)

taquería *f.* taco stand (C)

taquilla *f.* booth

tardarse to take a long time (7)

    tarda… minutos it takes . . . minutes (B)

tarde late (5)

tarde *f.* afternoon

    por la tarde in the afternoon (C)

tarea *f.* homework (7)

tarjeta *f.* card (C)

    tarjeta de abono transportes commuter pass

    tarjeta de crédito credit card (4)

    tarjeta de cumpleaños birthday card (C)

    tarjeta del Día de la Madre Mother's Day card (C)

taxi *m.* taxi

taza *f.* cup (6)

té (helado) *m.* (iced) tea (C)

teatral theatrical (2)

teatro *m.* theater (A)

teléfono *m.* telephone (4)

televisor *m.* television set (A)

    televisor a colores color television set

temer to fear

temperatura *f.* temperature (1)

    La temperatura está en… grados (bajo cero). It's . . . degrees (below zero). (1)

temprano early (5)

tenedor *m.* fork (6)

tener to have (A)

    tener… años to be . . . years old (A)

    tener dolor de… to have a . . . ache (10)

    tener ganas de… to feel like…

    tener hambre to be hungry

    tener miedo to be afraid (15)

    tener que to be obligated, was compelled to (15)

    tener razón to be right (10)

    tener sed to be thirsty

    tener suerte to be lucky

Tenga la bondad de responder tan pronto como sea posible. Please be kind enough to respond as soon as possible. (8)

tenis *m.* tennis

tercer(o/a) third (4)

terraza *f.* terrace, porch (6)

terreno *m.* terrain, land surface (14)

territorio *m.* territory

tía *f.* aunt (A)

tiempo *m.* time, weather

    a tiempo on time (5)

    buen (mal) tiempo good (bad) weather (1)

    ¿Cuánto tiempo hace? How long ago? (12)

    ¿Cuánto tiempo hace que te sientes así? How long have you felt this way? (11)

tienda *f.* store

    tienda de campaña tent (9)

    tienda de deportes sporting goods store

    tienda de música music store

    tienda de ropa clothing store

tiene he / she / it has

    ¿Tiene Ud… ? Do you have . . . ? (C)

    ¿Tiene Ud. cambio de… pesetas? Do you have change for . . . pesetas? (C)

    ¿Tiene Ud. la cuenta para… ? Do you have the bill for . . . ? (4)

    ¿Cuántos años tienes? How old are you? (A)

tierra *f.* land

tímido(a) timid (3)

tío *m.* uncle (A)

tirarse to dive, throw oneself (10)
toalla *f.* towel (5)
tobillo *m.* ankle (10)
tocar to touch, play (instrument) (A)
todavía still, yet
todo(a) all
  en todo caso in any event
  Es todo. That's all. (C)
  todos los días every day (C)
  de todos modos at any rate
tomar to take (B)
  tomar el sol to sunbathe
  tomar la temperatura to take a temperature (11)
tomate *m.* tomato (C)
tonificar to tone up (10)
tono muscular *m.* muscle tone (12)
tonto(a) silly, stupid, foolish
torcerse to twist (a body part) (10)
tormenta *f.* storm (1)
torneo *m.* tournament
torpe clumsy
tortilla *f.* cornmeal pancake (Mexico)
  tortilla de patatas Spanish omelette (C)
tos *f.* cough (11)
toser to cough (11)
pan tostado *m.* toast
tostador *m.* toaster (6)
trabajador(a) *m.(f.)* worker, hard-working
trabajar to work (A)
tradicional traditional (A)
traer to bring (8)
tráigame… bring me . . . (C)
tratar de to try to (12)
trato *m.* treatment
tren *m.* train (B)
trepar to climb
tres three (C)
trescientos(as) three hundred
triste sad (2)
trompeta *f.* trumpet (A)
trotar to jog (10)
Truena. There's thunder. (1)
tu your (1)
tú you (familiar) (A)
turista *m.* or *f.* tourist
¿Tuviste algún accidente? Did you have an accident? (10)

ubicar to locate

ubicado(a) located
un(a) *m.(f.)* a, an (A)
  Un(a)… , por favor. One . . . , please. (C)
único(a) only
universidad *f.* university (B)
uno one (C)
unos(as) some (C)
Uruguay Uruguay
uruguayo(a) Uruguayan
usted/Ud. you (formal) (A)
usualmente usually
útil useful (4)
uva *f.* grape (C)

va a haber there is going to be
vacaciones *f.* vacation (9)
vacío(a) vacant, empty (6)
valiente brave (3)
¡Vamos! Let's go! (C)
  Vamos a… Let's go . . .
  Vamos a ver. Let's see.
  nos vamos we're leaving
variado(a) varied (2)
varios(as) various, several
vaso *m.* glass (6)
a veces sometimes (B)
vecino(a) *m.(f.)* neighbor (3)
vegetales *m.* vegetables (12)
veinte twenty
velocidad *f.* speed (15)
vendedor(a) *m.(f.)* salesman(woman)
vender to sell
venezolano(a) Venezuelan
Venezuela Venezuela
venir to come (B)
ventaja *f.* advantage (10)
ventana *f.* window (6)
ver to see (C)
  A ver. Let's see.
  nos vemos we'll see each other
verano *m.* summer (1)
¿De veras? Really? (12)
verdad *f.* truth
  ¿verdad? right?
verdaderamente truly
verde green (2)
No te ves muy bien. You don't look very well. (10)
vestido *m.* dress
vestirse (i, i) to get dressed (7)
vez *f.* time, instance

de vez en cuando from time to time (B)
una vez once
una vez al año once a year
viajar to travel (A)
viaje *m.* trip
  agencia de viajes *f.* travel agency
viajero(a) traveler
vida *f.* life
vídeo *m.* videocassette, VCR (A)
viejo(a) old (2)
viento *m.* wind (1)
viernes *m.* Friday (B)
violeta violet (2)
violín *m.* violin (A)
virus *m.* virus (11)
visitar to visit (5)
vista nocturna *f.* night vision (12)
vitamina *f.* vitamin (12)
vivir to live
  (Yo) vivo en… I live in . . . (A)
volcán *m.* volcano
vólibol *m.* volleyball
volver (ue) to return (1)
vosotros(as) *m.(f.)* you (familiar plural)
voy I go (A)
  (Yo) voy a hacerlo. I'm going to do it.

WC *m.* toilet (4)
waterpolo *m.* waterpolo
windsur *m.* windsurfing

Y

y and (A)
ya already (7)
  ya en casa once home (7)
  ¡Ya es hora! It's about time!
yo I (A)
yogur *m.* yogurt

Z

zanahoria *f.* carrot (C)
zapatería *f.* shoe store
zapato *m.* shoe
  zapato de tacón high-heeled shoe
  zapato de tenis tennis shoe

English-Spanish

The numbers in parentheses refer to the chapters in which active vocabulary words or phrases may be found.

a / an **un(a)** *m.(f.)* (A)
ability **habilidad** *f.* (15)
according to **según**
(to) be able to **poder** (13, 15)
about **como a**; (with regard to) **acerca de**
absence **ausencia** *f.*
Absolutely not! **¡No, en absoluto!** (9)
accident **accidente** *m.* (10)
   Did you have an accident? **¿Tuviste algún accidente?** (10)
accountant **contador(a)** *m.(f.)*
(head / back / stomach)ache **dolor de (cabeza / espalda / estómago)** *m.* (11)
(to) achieve **alcanzar** (11)
across from **frente a, en frente de** (B)
action **acción** *f.*
active **activo(a)** (3)
additional **adicional** (12)
(to) admit **admitir** (12)
(to) adore **adorar**
(to) advance **avanzar** (15)
advantage **ventaja** *f.* (10)
(to) take advantage of **aprovechar** (8)
adventure movie **película de aventura** *f.*
adventurous **aventurero(a)** (14)
advice **consejo** *m.* (3)
(to) do aerobics **hacer ejercicios aeróbicos** (10)
(to) be afraid **tener miedo** (15)
after **después**
afternoon **tarde** *f.*
   in the afternoon **por la tarde** (C)
afterwards **luego**
again **de nuevo** (7)
against the wall **contra la pared**
age **edad** *f.* (5)
agility **agilidad** *f.* (15)
... ago **hace...** (C)
air-conditioned **aire acondicionado** (6)
airplane **avión** *m.*

airport **aeropuerto** *m.* (B)
all **todo(a)**
allergy **alergia** *f.* (11)
alligator **caimán** *m.*
do not allow **no permiten** (4)
almost **casi** (7)
already **ya** (7)
also **también** (A)
alteration **cambio** *m.*
although **aunque**
always **siempre** (C)
ambitious **ambicioso(a)** (3)
American **americano(a)** (A)
   American, from the United States **estadounidense**
and **y** (A)
angry **enojado(a)**
animal **animal** *m.* (A)
ankle **tobillo** *m.* (10)
(to) announce **anunciar**
annual **anual** (11)
another thing **otra cosa**
(to) answer **contestar**
answer **respuesta** *f.* (8)
   Answer me as soon as possible. **Contéstame cuanto antes.** (8)
antibiotic **antibiótico** *m.* (11)
antihistamine **antihistamínico** *m.* (11)
any **cualquier**
apartment **apartamento** *m.* (A)
(to) apologize **disculparse**
apparently **aparentemente** (12)
it appears **parece** (3)
apple **manzana** *f.* (C)
appointment **cita** *f.*
(to) approach **acercarse**
April **abril** (1)
architect **arquitecto(a)** *m.(f.)*
area **superficie** *f.*
Argentina **Argentina**
Argentine **argentino(a)** (A)
(to) argue **discutir**
arm **brazo** *m.* (10)
armchair **sillón** *m.* (5)

around **a eso de** (7); **alrededor** *adv.*
(to) arrange **arreglar** (6)
(to) arrive (at / from) **llegar (a / de)** (4)
art **arte** *m.* or *f.* (A)
article **artículo** *m.* (12)
as **como**
ash **ceniza** *f.*
(to) ask (a question) **preguntar**
(to) ask for **pedir (i)** (C)
(to) fall asleep **dormirse (ue)** (7)
aspirin **aspirina** *f.* (11)
(to) assure **asegurar** (10)
at **a** (A)
at about **a eso de** (7)
athlete **atleta** *m.(f.)* (14)
athletic **atlético(a)** (3)
attack **ataque** *m.* (15)
attainment **logro** *m.*
(to) attend **asistir a** (A)
August **agosto** (1)
aunt **tía** *f.* (A)
autumn **otoño** *m.* (1)
avenue **avenida** *f.* (B)
average **regular** (2)
(to) avoid **evitar**

baby **bebé** *m.* or *f.* (12)
back **espalda** *f.* (10)
   in back of **detrás de** (B)
backpack **mochila** *f.* (A)
bad **malo(a)** (2)
bakery **panadería** *f.*
balanced **balanceado(a)** (12)
ball **pelota** *f.;* **balón** *m.* (15)
balloon **globo** *m.*
ball-point pen **bolígrafo** *m.* (A)
banana **banana** *f.* (C); **plátano** *m.*
bank **banco** *m.* (B)
(to) bargain **regatear**
baseball **béisbol** *m.*
basket **canasta** *f.* (14)
basketball **básquetbol** *m.;* **baloncesto** *m.* (13)

bath **baño** *m.* (4)
(to) bathe oneself **bañarse** (7)
bathroom **sala de baño** *f.* (4)
(to) be **estar** (A); **ser** (A)
  (to) be in a bad mood **estar de mal humor**
  (to) be ... years old **tener... años** (A)
beach **playa** *f.*
bean **grano** *m.*
beans **frijoles** *m.* (C)
beard **barba** *f.* (3)
beat (heart) **latido** *m.*
beautiful **hermoso(a)**
beauty **belleza** *f.*
because **porque**
(to) become **convertirse en**
  (to) become involved **envolverse**
bed **cama** *f.* (A)
  (double / single) bed **cama (matrimonial / sencilla)**
bedroom **dormitorio** *m.* (6)
beef **carne de res, carne** *f.* (C)
before **antes**
(to) begin **comenzar (ie)** (7); **empezar(ie)**
beginner **novato(a)** *m.(f.)*
in / at the beginning **al principio** (13)
behavior **comportamiento** *m.*
behind **detrás de** (B)
(to) believe **creer** (13)
Belize **Belice**
It belongs to ... **Es de...**
  They belong to ... **Son de...**
belt **cinturón** *m.*
(to) benefit **beneficiarse** (5)
beside **al lado de** (B)
besides **además**
better **mejor**
between ... and ... **entre... y...** (B)
bicycle **bicicleta** *f.* (A)
(to) bicycle **hacer ciclismo** (13)
bidet **bidé** *m.* (4)
big **grande** (A)
bike path **carril-bici** *m.*
bill **cuenta** *f.* (4)
  Can you make up the bill? **¿Puede Ud. arreglar la cuenta?** (4)
  Do you have the bill for ...? **¿Tiene Ud. la cuenta para...?** (4)
biology **biología** *f.*
bird **pájaro** *m.*
birthday **cumpleaños** *m.* (C)
  birthday card **tarjeta de cumpleaños** *f.* (C)

biscuit **galleta** *f.*
black **negro(a)** (2)
block (city) **cuadra** *f.*
blond(e) **rubio(a)** (3)
blouse **blusa** *f.*
blue **azul** (2)
boat **banco** *m.* (14)
body part **parte del cuerpo** *f.* (11)
Bolivia **Bolivia**
Bolivian **boliviano(a)**
bone **hueso** *m.* (12)
book **libro** *m.* (A)
bookshelf **estante** *m.* (5)
bookstore **librería** *f.* (B)
boot **bota** *f.*
booth **taquilla** *f.*
border **frontera** *f.* (11)
bored, boring **aburrido(a)** (2)
(to) be born **nacer**
  (He / She) was born ... **(Él / Ella) nació...** (1)
both **los (las) dos**
a bottle of **una botella de** (C)
boutique **boutique** *f.*
bowling **boliche** *m.* (13)
boy **chico** *m.*
boyfriend **novio** *m.* (3)
brave **valiente** (3)
Brazil **Brasil**
bread **pan** *m.* (C)
(to) break (a body part) **romper(se)** (10)
breakfast **desayuno** *m.* (4)
bridge **puente** *m.*
briefcase **portafolio** *m.* (A)
(to) bring **traer** (8)
bring me ... **tráigame...** (C)
brother **hermano** *m.* (A)
brown **pardo(a)** (2)
  brown, dark **café** (2)
  medium-brown hair **castaño(a)** (3)
brunet(te) **moreno(a)**
(to) brush (one's hair / teeth) **cepillarse (el pelo / los dientes)** (7)
build **construir**
building **edificio** *m.*
a bunch of **un atado de** (C)
bus **autobús** *m.* (B)
  bus terminal **estación de autobuses** *f.*
business **negocio** *m.*
businessman(woman) **hombre (mujer) de negocios** *m.(f.)*
but **pero**
butcher shop **carnicería** *f.*

butter **mantequilla** *f.*
butterfly **mariposa** *f.*
(to) buy **comprar** (A)

café **café** *m.* (2)
calcium **calcio** *m.* (12)
calculator **calculadora** *f.* (A)
Calm down! **¡Cálmate!**
calorie **caloría** *f.* (12)
camera **cámara** *f.*
(to) camp **acampar** (9)
camper **coche-caravana** *m.* (9)
campfire **hoguera** *f.*
campground **área de acampar** *f.* (9)
a can of **una lata de** (C)
Canada **Canadá**
Canadian **canadiense**
candy **dulce** *m.*
canoe/kayak **canookayak** (14)
canteen **cantimplora** *f.* (14)
canyon **cañón** *m.*
capacity **capacidad** *f.* (10)
capital city **capital** *f.*
car **coche** *m.* (A)
caramel custard **flan** *m.*
carbonated **con gas** (14)
  not carbonated **sin gas** (14)
card **tarjeta** *f.* (C)
cardiovascular system **sistema cardiovascular** (10)
(to) care for **cuidar** (11)
  (to) take care of **ocuparse de** (7)
  Take care of yourself. **Cuídese. (Cuídate.)** (A)
Careful! **¡Cuidado!**
carpet **alfombra** *f.* (A)
carrot **zanahoria** *f.* (C)
(to) carry **llevar** (A)
  (to) carry out **llevar a cabo**
in cash **en efectivo** (4)
castle **castillo** *m.*
cat **gato** *m.*
category **categoría** *f.* (4)
cathedral **catedral** *f.* (B)
cause **causa** *f.* (12)
(to) celebrate **celebrar**
center **centro** *m.* (A)
century **siglo** *m.*
cereal **cereal** *m.* (12)
chair **silla** *f.* (A)
  armchair **sillón** *m.* (5)
challenge **desafío** *m.*

(to) change **cambiar**

change **cambio** *m.*

    Do you have change for . . . pesetas?
¿Tiene Ud. cambio de… pesetas? (C)

(to) take charge of **encargarse de** (7)

(to) chat **charlar** (7)

cheap **barato(a)**

(to) check (go over) **revisar**; (verify) **comprobar**

cheese **queso** *m.* (C)

    cheeseburger **hamburguesa con queso** *f.* (C)

chemistry **química** *f.*

chess **ajedrez** *m.* (13)

chest **pecho** *m.* (10)

chicken **pollo** *m.* (C)

child **niño(a)** *m.(f.)*

childish **infantil** (2)

Chile **Chile**

Chilean **chileno(a)**

chills **escalofríos** *m.* (11)

China **China** (13)

Chinese **chino(a)** (A)

chocolate **chocolate** *m.* (C)

church **iglesia** *f.* (B)

city **ciudad** *f.* (A)

classic(al) **clásico(a)** (2)

classification system **sistema de clasificación** (4)

(to) classify **clasificar** (4)

(to) clear the table **quitar la mesa** (7)

It's a clear day. **Está despejado.** (1)

(to) climb **subir; trepar**

clock radio **radio despertador** *m.* (A)

(to) close **cerrar (ie)**

closet **clóset** *m.* (5)

clothing **ropa** *f.* (5)

    clothing store **tienda de ropa** *f.*

cloud **nube** *f.* (1)

cloudy **despejado, nublado** (1)

    It's a cloudy day. **Está nublado.** (1)

club **club** *m.*

clumsy **torpe**

coach **entrenador**

coast **costa** *f.* (9)

coat **abrigo** *m.*

coffee (with milk) **café (con leche)** *m.* (C)

a cold **catarro** *m.* (11); **resfrío** *m.*

cold **frío(a)** (1)

Colombia **Colombia**

Colombian **colombiano(a)**

color **color** *m.*

What color is . . . ? **¿De qué color es… ?** (2)

(to) comb **peinarse** (7)

(to) come **venir** (B)

comedy movie **película cómica** *f.*

comfort **confort** *m.* (4)

comfortable **cómodo(a)**, (14); **confortable**

comical **cómico(a)** (3)

(to) comment **comentar**

commuter pass **tarjeta de abono transportes** *m.*

compact disc **disco compacto** *m.*

company **compañía** *f.*

comparison **comparación** *f.*

competition **competencia** *f.* (15)

complete **completo(a)** (2)

computer **computadora** *f.* (A)

concert **concierto** *m.*

consecutive **consecutivo(a)** (10)

constantly **constantemente** (11)

content **contento(a)** (13)

contest **concurso** *m.*

(to) continue **continuar, seguir (i, i)** (B)

continuous **continuo(a)** (10)

convenient **conveniente** (7)

(to) cook **cocinar** (6)

cookie **galleta** *f.*

cool **fresco(a)** (1)

(to) cool off **refrescarse** (14)

corn **maíz** *m.* (C)

on the corner of . . . and . . . **en la esquina de… y…** (B)

cornmeal pancake (Mexico) **tortilla** *f.*

corridor **corredor** *m.* (4)

(to) cost **costar (ue)** (9)

Costa Rica **Costa Rica**

Costa Rican **costarricense**

costly **costoso(a)** (13)

(it) costs **cuesta** (C)

cotton **algodón** *m.*

couch **sofá** *m.* (6)

cough **tos** *f.* (11)

    cough syrup **jarabe** *m.* (11)

(to) cough **toser** (11)

(he / she / it) could **pudo** (2)

(to) count **contar (ue)**

    (to) count on **contar con**

    I'm counting on you **cuento contigo** (8)

country **país** *m.* (A)

countryside **paisaje** *m.* (14)

cousin **primo(a)** *m.(f.)* (A)

covered **cubierto(a)**

cream **crema** *f.*

credit card **tarjeta de crédito** *f.* (4)

croissant **croissant** *m.*

cross **cruz** *f.*

(to) cross **cruzar** (B); **atravesar** (14)

(to) cry **llorar**

Cuba **Cuba**

Cuban **cubano(a)**

cucumber **pepino** *m.* (C)

cup **taza** *f.* (6)

curtain **cortina** *f.* (6)

customarily **de costumbre** (C)

(to) cut (oneself) **cortar(se)** (10)

cycling **ciclismo**

dairy **lácteo** (12)

    dairy product **producto lácteo** *m.* (12)

dance **baile** *m.*

    popular dance **baile popular**

(to) dance **bailar** (A)

danger **peligro** *m.*

dangerous **peligroso(a)**

(to) dare **atrever**

daring **atrevido(a)**

dark **oscuro(a)**

dark-haired **moreno(a)**

date **fecha** *f.*; (appointment) **cita** *f.*

    What is the date? **¿A cuántos estamos?** (1)

    What is the date today? **¿Qué fecha es hoy?, ¿Cuál es la fecha de hoy?** (1)

daughter **hija** *f.* (A)

day **día** *m.* (B)

    What day is today? **¿Qué día es hoy?**

dead **muerto(a)** (A)

dear **querido(a)** (5)

December **diciembre** (1)

defense **defensa** *f.* (15)

degree **grado** *m.* (1)

    It's . . . degrees (below zero). **La temperatura está en… grados (bajo cero).** (1)

delicious **delicioso(a)** (2)

    very delicious **riquísimo**

    What delicious food! **¡Qué comida más rica!**

Delighted. **Encantado(a).** (A)

(to) demand **demandar** (10); **exigir**

dentist **dentista** *m.* or *f.*

deparment store **almacén** *m.*
(to) depend on **depender de** (1)
descent **decenso** *m.* (14)
(to) describe **describir**
　Describe . . . for me. **Descríbeme…**
　describes to him, her, you **le describe** (3)
desert **desierto** *m.*
desk **escritorio** *m.* (A)
(to) develop **desarrollar** (12)
(to) devote oneself to **dedicarse** (9)
(to) die **morir**
difficulty **dificultad** *f.* (12)
digestion **digestión** *f.* (12)
dining room **comedor** *m.* (6)
in which direction? **¿en qué dirección?**
directly **directamente** (7)
dirty **sucio(a)** (5)
disagreeable **antipático(a)**
discotheque **discoteca** *f.* (B)
discreet **discreto(a)** (3)
dish **plato** *m.* (6)
dishonest **deshonesto(a)** (3)
disturbance **alboroto** *m.*
(to) dive **tirarse** (10), **clavarse** (Mexico) (13)
diver **clavadista** *m. or f.* (13)
(to) divide **dividir** (13)
divorced **divorciado(a)** (A)
(to) do **hacer**
　I'm going to do it. **(Yo) voy a hacerlo.**
　We always do it! **¡Siempre lo hacemos!**
doctor **doctor(a)** *m.(f.);* **médico(a)** *m.(f.)*
dog **perro** *m.*
Dominican **dominicano(a)**
the Dominican Republic **la República Dominicana**
dominoes **dominó** *m.* (13)
door **puerta** *f.*
dose **dosis** *f.* (10)
doubt **duda** *f.* (12)
down **abajo**
(to) go down **bajar**
downtown **centro** *m.* (A)
a dozen **una docena de** (C)
drawer **cajón** *m.* (5)
(to) dream **soñar**
dress **vestido** *m.*
(to) get dressed **vestirse (i, i)** (7)
dresser **cómoda** *f.* (A)
drink **bebida** *f.*
(to) drive **conducir** (13)
It's drizzling. **Llovizna.** (1)
drugstore **farmacia** *f.* (B)

dry **seco(a)** (12)
during **durante** (5), **por** (4)

each **cada** (10)
ear **oreja** *f.* (10)
early **temprano** (5)
(to) earn **ganar**
east **este** *m.* (B)
(to) eat **comer** (C)
　(to) eat breakfast **desayunarse** (7)
　(to) eat supper **cenar**
easy **fácil**
economical **económico(a)** (2)
Ecuador **Ecuador**
Ecuadoran **ecuatoriano(a)**
efficient **eficiente** (10)
eight hundred **ochocientos(as)**
eighth **octavo(a)** (4)
eighty **ochenta**
El Salvador **El Salvador**
elbow **codo** *m.* (10)
elegant **elegante** (2)
elevator **ascensor** *m.* (4)
employee **empleado(a)** *m.(f.)*
empty **vacío(a)** (6)
enchilada **enchilada** *f.* (C)
(to) encourage **alentar**
at the end of **al final de** (B); **al fondo de**
energy **energía** *f.* (12)
engineer **ingeniero(a)** *m.(f.)*
England **Inglaterra**
English **inglés(esa)** (A)
(to) enjoy **disfrutar de** (8)
enjoyable **divertido(a)** (2)
enough **bastante, suficiente** (B)
entrance ticket **entrada** *f.*
envelope **sobre** *m.* (C)
I'm envious! **¡Qué envidia!** (12)
epidemic **epidemia** *f.* (11)
equality **igualdad** *f.*
equipment **equipo** *m.* (14)
eraser **borrador** *m.* (A)
errand **mandado** *m.* (C)
　(to) do an errand **hacer un mandado** (C)
(to) establish **establecer**
in any event **en todo caso**
every **cada** (10)
　every day **todos los días** (C)
exactly **exactamente** (12); **exacto** (8)
(to) exaggerate **exagerar**
example **ejemplo** *m.* (7)

exchange program **programa de intercambio** *m.* (5)
Don't get excited! **¡No te excites!**
Excuse me. **Perdón.** (C)
(to) do exercises **hacer gimnasia** (10)
(to) exercise **hacer ejercicio**
exit **salida** *f.* (5)
expensive **caro(a)** (2)
expert **experto(a)** (10)
(to) express **expresar**
expression **expresión** *f.*
eye **ojo** *m.* (3)
eyedrops **gotas para los ojos** *f.* (11)

face **cara** *f.* (10)
(to) facilitate **facilitar** (12)
facing **frente a, en frente de** (B)
fair **feria** *f.*
fall **otoño** *m.* (1)
(to) fall **caerse** (10)
family **familia** *f.* (A)
famous **famoso(a)**
fan (of sports) **aficionado(a)** *m.(f.)* (15)
far from **lejos de** (B)
farm **finca** *f.*
fat **gordo(a)** *adj.*
fat **grasa** *f.* (12)
father **padre** *m.* (A)
Father's Day **el Día del Padre** (C)
fault **culpa** *f.* (7)
favorite **favorito(a)**
fear **miedo** *m.* (15)
(to) fear **temer**
February **febrero** (1)
(to) feel good (bad) **sentirse (ie, i) bien (mal)** (10)
　Do you feel well (bad)? **¿Te sientes bien (mal)?** (10)
(to) feel like . . . **tener ganas de…**
ferocious **feroz** (13)
festival (religious) honoring a town's patron saint **fiesta del pueblo**
fever **fiebre** *f.* (11)
few **poco(a)**
fiance(é) **novio(a)** *m.(f.)* (3)
fiber **fibra** *f.* (12)
field (sports) **campo de juego** *m.;* **cancha** *f.* (15)
field hockey **hockey sobre hierba** *m.* (13)
fifteenth birthday party **quinceañera** *f.* (8)

fifth **quinto(a)** (4)
fifty **cincuenta**
finally **finalmente, por fin** (13)
(to) find **encontrar (ue)**
fine **bien** (A)
finger **dedo (de la mano)** *m.* (10)
fire **fuego** *m.*
fireworks **fuegos artificiales** *m.*
first **primer(o/a)** (4)
   in the first place **en primer lugar**
first aid kit **botiquín** *m.* (14)
fish **pescado** *m.*
five hundred **quinientos(as)**
(to) fix **arreglar** (6)
flat **plano(a)**
flavor **sabor** *m.*
(to) float **flotar** (10)
floor **planta** *f.* (A); **piso** *m.* (4)
   (on the first) floor **(en el primer) piso** (4)
   floor plan **plan** *m.* (6)
   ground floor **planta baja** (4)
flour **harina** *f.*
flower shop **florería** *f.*
flu **gripe** *f.* (11)
flute **flauta** *f.* (A)
fog **neblina** *f.*; **niebla** *f.* (1)
   It's foggy. **Hay niebla.** (1)
folk dance **baile folklórico** *m.*
(to) follow **seguir (i, i)** (B)
the following **lo siguiente** (4)
food **alimento** *m.*; **comida** *f.*
foolish **tonto(a)**
foot **pie** *m.* (B)
   on foot **a pie** (B)
football **fútbol americano** *m.*
for **por** (4); **para** (B)
   for . . . hours **por... horas** (5)
forecast **pronóstico** *m.*
force **fuerza** *f.*
forehead **frente** *f.* (10)
forest **bosque** *m.*
fork **tenedor** *m.* (6)
(to) form **formar** (12)
formal **formal** (2)
fortunately **afortunadamente**
forty **cuarenta**
found out **saber** (preterite) (15)
fountain **fuente** *f.*
fountain pen **pluma** *f.*
four hundred **cuatrocientos(as)**
fourth **cuarto(a)** (4)
France **Francia**
French **francés(esa)** (A)

frequently **con frecuencia** (10); **fre-cuentemente** (B)
Friday **viernes** *m.* (B)
friend **amigo(a)** *m.(f.)* (A)
friendly **amable**
friendship **amistad** *f.*
Is from . . . **Es de...**
in front of **delante de** (B)
frozen **congelado(a)**
fruit **fruta** *f.* (12)
   fruit salad **ensalada de frutas** *f.*
full **lleno(a)**
(to) function **funcionar** (2)
funny **cómico(a)** (3)
furious **furioso(a)** (13)
(fully) furnished **(completamente) amue-blado** (6)
future **futuro** *m.*

(to) gain weight **subir de peso** (12)
game **partido** *m.* (15); **juego** *m.*
(two-car) garage **garaje (para dos coches)** *m.* (6)
garden **jardín** *m.* (6)
in general **por lo general** (C)
generous **generoso(a)** (3)
geography **geografía** *f.*
German **alemán(ana)** (A)
Germany **Alemania**
(to) get out something **sacar**
(to) get together **reunirse** (7)
(to) get up **levantarse** (7)
gift **regalo** *m.*
girl **chica** *f.*
girlfriend **novia** *f.* (3)
(to) give **dar** (11)
   (to) give a going-away party **darles la despedida** (8)
(drinking) glass **vaso** *m.* (6)
globe **globo** *m.*
(to) go **ir** (A)
   I go **voy** (A)
   (to) go along **andar**
   (to) go away **irse** (7)
   (to) go to bed **acostarse (ue)** (7)
   (to) go camping **ir de camping**
   (to) go down **bajar**
   (to) go fishing **ir de pesca**
   (to) go up **subir** (4)
   (to) be going to . . . **ir a...**
goal (sport) **gol** *m.* (15); (objective) **meta** *f.*

goaltender **arquero(a)** *m.(f.);* **portero(a)** *m. (f.)* (15)
golf **golf** *m.* (9)
good **bueno(a)** (2)
   Good afternoon. **Buenas tardes.**
   Good evening. **Buenas noches.**
   Good grief! **¡Qué cosa!**
   Good heavens! **¡Ave María!**
   Good morning. **Buenos días.** (A)
   Good night. **Buenas noches.**
good-bye **adiós, chao**
   (to) say good-bye **darles la despedida** (8)
   (to) say good-bye to **despedirse (i, i) de**
(50) grams of **(50) gramos de** (C)
granddaughter **nieta** *f.* (3)
grandfather **abuelo** *m.* (A)
grandmother **abuela** *f.* (A)
grandson **nieto** *m.* (3)
grape **uva** *f.* (C)
grasshopper **saltamontes** *m.*
grave **grave** *adj.* (10)
gray **gris** (2)
Great! **¡Qué bueno(a)!**
Great Britain **Gran Bretaña**
green **verde** (2)
(to) greet **saludar**
greeting **saludo** *m.*
grenadine **granadina** *f.*
grievous **grave** (10)
ground floor **planta baja** (4)
group **grupo** *m.;* (unit) **conjunto** *m.*
(to) grow **crecer**
guacamole **ensalada de guacamole** *f.* (C)
Guatemala **Guatemala**
Guatemalan **guatemalteco(a)**
guitar **guitarra** *f.* (A)
gym(nasium) **gimnasio** *m.* (10)

hair **pelo** *m.* (3)
half **medio(a); mitad** *f.*
hallway **corredor** *m.* (4)
ham **jamón** *m.* (C)
hamburger **hamburguesa** *f.* (C)
hand **mano** *f.* (10)
handle **manija** *f.*
handlebar **manillar** *m.*
handling **manejo** *m.*
handsome **guapo(a)**

What happened to you? **¿Qué te pasó?** (10)

happiness **felicidad** f.

happy **alegre** (2)

hard **duro(a)** f. (C)

hard-working **trabajador(a)** (3)

(to) harvest **cosechar**

(he / she / it) has **tiene**

it has been . . . **hace...** (C)

(to) hate **odiar**

(to) have **tener** (A)

(to) have a . . . ache **tener dolor de...** (10)

(to) have a good time **divertirse (ie, i)** (7)

(to) have just . . . **acabar de...**

Do you have . . . ? **¿Tiene Ud... ?** (C)

We have / had a good time. **Lo pasamos bien.** (9)

hay fever **fiebre del heno** (11)

hazel (eyes) **castaño(a)** (3)

he **él**

head **cabeza** f. (10)

headphones **auriculares** m. (14)

health **salud** f. (12)

(to) hear **oír** (13)

heart **corazón** m. (5)

heart rate **ritmo cardíaco** m. (12)

with all my heart **con todo el corazón** (5)

heat **calor** m. (1)

heavy **pesado(a)** (2)

Hello. **Hola.** (A)

Hello! (answering the phone) **¡Bueno!, ¡Diga / Dígame!**

(to) help **ayudar**

her **su** (5)

here **aquí**

Here you have . . . **Aquí tiene...** (C)

high school **escuela secundaria**

high-heeled shoe **zapato de tacón**

highway **carretera** f.

(to) take a hike **dar una caminata**

hiking **montañismo** m. (14); **senderismo** m. (14)

hill **colina** f.

hip **cadera** f.

his **su** (5)

Hispanic **hispano(a)**

historical **histórico(a)** (2)

history **historia** f. (A)

homework **tarea** f. (7)

Honduran **hondureño(a)**

Honduras **Honduras**

honest **honesto(a)** (3)

hoop **aro** m.

(to) hope **esperar** (5)

I hope it's not . . . **Espero que no sea...** (8)

I hope that you can visit **espero que Uds. puedan visitar** (5)

horoscope **horóscopo** m. (2)

horrible **horrible**

horror movie **película de horror**

horse **caballo** m.

horseback riding **equitación** f. (9)

(to) go horseback riding **hacer la equitación** (9)

horseman **jinete** m.

hospital **hospital** m. (B)

hospitality **hospitalidad** f. (5)

hot **caliente** (7)

It's hot out. **Hace calor.** (1)

hot, spicy sauce **salsa picante** f. (C)

hotel **hotel** m. (B)

hour **hora** f. (B)

half hour **media hora** (5)

house **casa** f. (A)

how **como**

how? **¿cómo?**

How . . . ! **¡Qué... !**

How are you? **¿Cómo está(s)?, ¿Qué tal?** (A)

How awful! **¡Qué horrible!**

How can I help you? **¿En qué puedo servirle(s)?**

How do you feel? **¿Cómo te sientes?** (10)

How do you say . . . ? **¿Cómo se dice... ?** (6)

How is it / are they? **¿Cómo es / son?**

How long ago? **¿Cuánto tiempo hace?** (12)

How long have you felt this way? **¿Cuánto tiempo hace que te sientes así?**

how much / many? **¿cuánto(a)?**

How many are there? **¿Cuántos hay?**

How much does it cost? **¿Cuánto cuesta?** (C)

How old are you? **¿Cuántos años tienes?** (A)

hug **abrazo** m. (5)

human being **ser humano** m.

(to) be hungry **tener hambre**

(to) hurry **darse prisa** (7)

Hurry up! **¡Dense prisa!** (7)

(to) hurt **doler (ue)** (11)

(to) hurt oneself **lastimarse** (10)

Did you hurt yourself? **¿Te lastimaste?** (10)

My . . . hurt(s). **Me duele(n)...** (11)

husband **esposo** m.

I **yo** (A)

I am (not) from . . . **(Yo) (no) soy de...** (A)

I am of . . . origin. **(Yo) soy de origen...** (A)

I am . . . tall. **Mido...** (12)

ice **hielo** m. (1)

ice cream **helado** m.

It's icy. **Hay hielo.** (1)

idealist(ic) **idealista** (3)

if **si**

impatient **impaciente** (3)

impossible **imposible**

(to) improve **mejorar** (12)

in **en** (A)

iIn (the month of) . . . **en (el mes de)...** (1)

included **incluido(a)** (4)

incredible **increíble** (6)

Independence Day **el Día de la Independencia**

independent **independiente** (3)

indication **indicación** f. (12)

indiscreet **indiscreto(a)** (3)

infantile **infantil** (2)

infection **infección** f. (11)

inflatable raft **barco neumático** m. (14)

injury **lesión** f.

instance **vez** f.

intellectual **intelectual** (3)

intelligent **inteligente**

interesting **interesante** (2)

interview **entrevista** f.

(to) introduce **presentar** (12)

I want to introduce you to . . . **Quiero presentarle(te) a...** (A)

I would like to introduce you to . . . **Quisiera presentarle(te) a...** (A)

introduction **presentación** f.

invitation **invitación** f.

iron **hierro** m. (12)

irrigation ditch **acequia** f.

is **es**

Italian **italiano(a)** (A)

Italy **Italia**

jacket **chaqueta** *f.*
jam **mermelada** *f.*
January **enero** (1)
Japan **Japón**
Japanese **japonés(esa)** (A)
jazz **jazz** *m.* (A)
jeans **vaqueros** *m.*
jelly **mermelada** *f.*
(to) jog **trotar** (10)
joint **coyuntura** *f.* (10)
journalist **periodista** *m.* or *f.*
juice **jugo** *m.*
July **julio** (1)
June **junio** (1)
(to) have just . . . **acabar de...**

key **llave** *f.* (A)
a kilo(gram) of **un kilo de** (C)
    half a kilo(gram) of **medio kilo de** (C)
kilometer **kilómetro** *m.*
kiss **beso** *m.*
kitchen **cocina** *f.* (6)
knee **rodilla** *f.* (10)
knife **cuchillo** *m.* (6)
(to) know (a fact) **saber** (1); (a person,
    place) **conocer** (3)
knowledge (understanding) **conocimiento**
    m.

lack **falta** *f.* (12)
lamp **lámpara** *f.* (4)
land **tierra** *f.*
landscape **paisaje** *m.*
language **lengua** *f.* (A); **idioma** *m.*
large **grande** (A)
(to) last **durar** (7)
last (Monday / week) **(el lunes / la se-
    mana) pasado(a)** (C)
last night **anoche** (C)
late **tarde** (5)
later **luego**
Latin **latín** *m.* (7)
(to) laugh **reírse (i, i)**
lawyer **abogado(a)** *m.(f.)*
lazy **perezoso(a)** (3)
(to) learn **aprender** (A)
at least **al menos** (4); **por lo menos**

at least in part **en parte al menos**
    (12)
leather **cuero** *m.*
(to) leave **irse** (7)
    (to) leave (with / from / for) **salir (con /
    de / para)** (4)
    we're leaving **nos vamos**
left **izquierda** (B)
    to the left **a la izquierda** (B)
leg **pierna** *f.* (10)
lemon **limón** *m.* (C)
lemonade **limonada** *f.* (C)
less **menos**
    less . . . than **menos... que...**
Let's be reasonable. **Hay que ser razon-
    ables.**
Let's go! **¡Vamos!** (C)
    Let's go . . . **Vamos a...**
Let's see. **Vamos a ver.** (4), **A ver.**
lettuce **lechuga** *f.* (C)
level **nivel** *m.*
library **biblioteca** *f.* (B)
life **vida** *f.*
(to) lift weights **levantar pesas**
light **ligero(a)** (2)
(to) light **encender (ie)**
like **como**
(to) like **gustar** (A)
    (I) (don't) like . . . (very much). **(No)
    (Me) gusta(n) (mucho)...** (A)
line **línea** *f.*
lipids **lípidos** *m.* (12)
(to) listen (to) **escuchar**
a liter of **un litro de** (C)
literature **literatura** *f.* (A)
a little **poco(a)**
(to) live **vivir**
I live in . . . **(Yo) vivo en...** (A)
living room **sala de estar** *f.* (6)
located **situado(a)** (B); **ubicado(a)**
location **lugar** *m.*
(to) lock oneself in **encerrarse (ie)**
long **largo(a)** (2)
(to) look at **mirar**
    (to) look at oneself **mirarse** (7)
    Look! **¡Mira!**
    You don't look very well. **No te ves
    muy bien.** (10)
(to) look for **buscar** (4)
(to) look over **revisar**
(to) lose **perder (ie)**
(to) lose weight **bajar de peso** (10)
a lot **mucho(a)**
    a lot of times **muchas veces** (10)

(to) love **amar**
loving **cariñoso(a)**
(to) lower **bajar**
(to) be lucky **tener suerte**
lung **pulmón** *m.* (10)
luxury **lujo** *m.* (4)

ma'am **señora** *f.* (A)
machine **máquina** *f.*
mad **enojado(a)**
Magnificent! **¡Magnífico!** (9)
majority **mayoría** *f.* (12)
(to) make **hacer**
    I'm going to make . . . for you. **Les voy
    a preparar...**
    (to) make the bed **hacer la cama**
    (to) make a goal **anotar un gol, mar-
    car un gol** (15)
man **hombre** *m.*
manner **manera** *f.* (10)
marble **mármol** *m.*
March **marzo** (1)
market **mercado** *m.* (C)
maroon **marrón**
married **casado(a)** (A)
mathematics **matemáticas** *f.* (A)
What's the matter with you? **¿Qué te
    pasa?** (10)
maximum **máximo(a)** (10)
May **mayo** (1)
mayonnaise **mayonesa** *f.*
me **mí**
meal **comida** *f.*
(to) mean **querer decir** (6)
meaning **significado** *m.*
means **medio** *m.*
    means of transportation **medio de
    transporte**
(to) measure **medir (i, i)** (12)
meat **carne** *f.* (C)
mechanic **mecánico(a)** *m.(f.)*
(to) meet **reunirse** (7)
melon **melón** *m.* (C)
memory **recuerdo** *m.*
square meters **m² (metros cuadrados)**
    (6)
Mexican **mexicano(a)** (A)
    Mexican food **comida mexicana** *f.*
Mexico **México**
microbe **microbio** *m.* (11)
microwave oven **horno de microondas**
    m. (6)

middle **medio** *m.*

midnight **medianoche** *f.*

mile **milla** *f.*

milk **leche** *f.* (C)

(mango) milkshake **licuado (de mango)** *m.* (C)

million **millón**

mineral **mineral** *m.* (12)

mineral water (without carbonation) **agua mineral (sin gas)** *f.* (C)

minute **minuto** *m.* (B)

in . . . minutes **en... minutos** (5)

mirror **espejo** *m.* (4)

Miss **señorita** *f.* (A)

(to) miss **extrañar** (5)

I miss you (plural). **Te (Los) extraño.** (5)

mixture **mezcla** *f.*

modern **moderno(a)** (2)

at this moment **en este momento**

Monday **lunes** *m.* (B)

money **dinero** *m.*

month **mes** *m.* (C)

moon **luna** *f.*

moped **motocicleta** *f.* (A)

more **más**

more . . . than **más... que**

morning **mañana** *f.* (B)

in the morning **de la mañana** (B); **por la mañana** (C)

mother **madre** *f.* (A)

Mother's Day **el Día de la Madre** *m.* (C)

Mothers' Day card **tarjeta del Día de la Madre** *f.* (C)

motorcycle **motocicleta** *f.* (A)

mound **montículo** *m.*

mountain **montaña** *f.* (1)

mountain range **cordillera** *f.*

mountain bike **bicicleta de montaña** *m.* (14)

mountain climbing **alpinismo** *m.*

(to) go mountain climbing **hacer alpinismo**

mouth **boca** *f.* (10)

(to) move **moverse (ue)** (7)

movement **movimiento** *m.* (10)

movie **película** *f.* (A)

movie theater **cine** *m.* (C)

Mr. **señor** *m.* (A)

Mrs. **señora** *f.* (A)

much **mucho(a)**

as much . . . as . . . **tan(to)... como...**

very much **muchísimo**

muscle **músculo** *m.* (12)

muscle movement **movimiento muscular** *m.* (12)

muscle tone **tono muscular** *m.* (12)

museum **museo** *m.* (B)

music **música** *f.*

classical music **música clásica** (A)

mariachi music **música de mariachi** (13)

music store **tienda de música** *f.*

must **deber**

mustache **bigote** *m.* (3)

my **mi** (A)

name **nombre** *m.* (A)

last name **apellido** *m.* (A)

My name is . . . **(Yo) me llamo...** (A)

What's your name? **¿Cómo te llamas?** (A)

(to) be named **llamarse** (A)

(to) take a nap **dormir la siesta** (4)

napkin **servilleta** *f.* (6)

nationality **nacionalidad** *f.*

native **indígena** *m.* or *f.*

nature **naturaleza** *f.* (A)

near **cerca de** (B)

neck **cuello** *m.* (10)

necklace **collar** *m.*

(to) need **necesitar** (4)

neighbor **vecino(a)** *m.(f.)* (3)

neighborhood **barrio** *m.*

neither **tampoco**

nerve **nervio** *m.* (12)

nervous **nervioso(a)** (13)

nest **nido** *m.*

network **red** *f.*

never **nunca** (B)

nevertheless **sin embargo**

new **nuevo(a)**

newspaper **periódico** *m.* (6)

newspaper kiosk **quiosco de periódicos** *m.*

next (year / week) **(el año / la semana) próximo(a)** (C)

Nicaragua **Nicaragua**

Nicaraguan **nicaragüense**

nice **simpático(a)**

Nice to meet you. **Mucho gusto.** (A)

It's nice out. **Hace buen tiempo.** (1)

night **noche** *f.* (B)

at night **de la noche** (B); **por la noche** (C)

last night **anoche** (C)

night table **mesita de noche** *f.* (4)

night vision **vista nocturna** *f.* (12)

nightmare **pesadilla** *f.* (12)

nine hundred **novecientos(as)**

ninety **noventa**

ninth **noveno(a)** (4)

no **no**

No way! **¡Qué va!**

noise **ruido** *m.*

noon **mediodía** *m.*

normally **normalmente** (C)

north **norte** *m.* (B)

North American **norteamericano(a)**

nose **nariz** *f.* (10)

notebook **cuaderno** *m.* (A)

nothing **nada**

November **noviembre** (1)

now **ahora**

right now **ahora mismo**

number **número** *m.*

nurse **enfermero(a)** *m.(f.)*

(to) be obligated **tener que** (15)

(to) obtain **sacar**

It's . . . o'clock. **Son las...** (B)

It's one o'clock. **Es la una.** (B)

October **octubre** (1)

of **de** (B)

of course **por supuesto**

Of course! **¡Claro!**

Of course!! (reaffirmed) **¡Claro que sí!**

Of course not! **¡Claro que no!** (4)

of the **de la / del**

(to) offer **ofrecer**

often **a menudo** (10)

oil **aceite** *m.*

okay **de acuerdo** (C); **regular** (2)

Okay. **Está bien.**

Is that okay with you? **¿Te parece bien?** (8)

old **viejo(a); antiguo(a)**

older **mayor**

olive **aceituna** *f.* (C)

Spanish omelette **tortilla de patatas** (C)

on **en** (A)

on foot **a pie** (B)

on time **a tiempo** (5)

once **una vez**

at once **en seguida** (9)

once home **ya en casa** (7)

once a year **una vez al año**
one **uno** (C)
    One . . . , please. **Un(a)…, por favor.**
    (C)
one hundred **cien(to)**
one-way ticket **billete sencillo**
onion **cebolla** *f.* (C)
only **sólo** (7); *adj.* **único(a)**
only child **hijo(a) único(a)** *m.(f.)* (A)
open-air market **mercado al aire libre**
optimist(ic) **optimista** (2)
or **o**
orange (color) **anaranjado(a)** (2)
orange (fruit) **naranja** *f.* (C)
order **orden** *m.*
    (to) give an order **mandar** (11)
    in order to **para** (B)
other **otro(a)**
our **nuestro(a)**
(microwave) oven **horno (de microondas)**
    m. (6)
outside of **fuera de**
(to) owe **deber**
owner **dueño(a)** *m.(f.)*
oxygen **oxígeno** *m.* (10)

P

(to) pack **empacar** (14)
    (to) pack suitcases **hacer las maletas**
a package of **un paquete de** (C)
painter **pintor(a)** *m.(f.)* (2)
painting **cuadro** *m.* (2);
    pintura *f.* (A)
pair **par** *m.*
pale **pálido(a)** (3)
Panama **Panamá**
Panamanian **panameño(a)**
pants **pantalones** *m.*
paper **papel** *m.* (C)
    air mail stationery **papel de**
    avión (C)
    typing paper **papel para escribir a**
    máquina *m.*
parade **desfile** *m.*
Paraguay **Paraguay**
Paraguayan **paraguayo(a)**
parents **padres** *m. (pl.)*
park **parque** *m.* (B)
to park **estacionar**
parking **estacionamiento** *m.* (6)
    parking lot **playa de estaciona-**
    miento *f.*
part **parte** *f.*

party **fiesta** *f.*
(to) pass **pasar** (9)
pasta **pasta** *f.*
pastry **pastel** *m.*
pasture **prado** *m.*
path **sendero** *m.* (14)
patient **paciente** (3)
(to) pay **pagar** (4)
    (to) pay attention **prestar atención** (5)
pea **guisante** *m.* (C)
peach **melocotón** *m.*
peanut **cacahuete** *m.*
pear **pera** *f.* (C)
pen, ball-point **bolígrafo** *m.;* fountain
    pluma *f.*
pencil **lápiz** *m.* (A)
    pencil sharpener **sacapuntas** *m.* (A)
people **gente** *f.*
pepper (spice) **pimienta** *f.*
    hot pepper **chile** *m.*
perfect **perfecto(a)** (3)
(to) perfect **perfeccionar** (5)
perhaps **tal vez** (8)
period (of time) **período** *m.* (2)
do not permit **no permiten** (4)
person **persona** *f.* (4)
Peru **Perú**
Peruvian **peruano(a)**
pessimist(ic) **pesimista** (2)
pharmacy **farmacia** *f.* (B)
piano **piano** *m.* (A)
(to) pick up **recoger**
pie **pastel** *m.*
a piece of **un pedazo de** (C)
pill **pastilla** *f.* (11)
pink **rosado(a)** (2)
pizza **pizza** *f.* (C)
place **lugar** *m.;* **sitio** *m.*
high plain **meseta** *f.*
(to) plan **planear**
plant **planta** *f.* (A)
plate **plato** *m.* (6)
(to) play **jugar (ue)** (1)
    (to) play (golf / tennis / volleyball) **jugar**
    al (golf / tenis / vólibol) (9)
    (to) play cards **jugar a los naipes** (13)
    (to) play checkers **jugar a las damas**
    (13)
    (to) play (instrument) **tocar** (A)
player **jugador(a)** *m.(f.)* (15)
pleasant **agradable** (10); **genial**
please **por favor** (C)
    Please be kind enough to respond as soon
    as possible. **Tenga la bondad de**

    responder tan pronto como sea
    posible. (8)
with pleasure **con mucho gusto**
    It would give us great pleasure . . . **Nos**
    daría mucho gusto… (8)
poetry contest **concurso de poesía** *m.*
point **punto** *m.* (11)
police **policía** *f.*
    police officer **policía** *m.*
    police station **estación de policía** *f.*
politics **política** *f.* (A)
poorly **mal**
porch **terraza** *f.* (6)
pork **carne de puerco** *m.* (C)
possession **posesión** *f.*
post **poste** *m.*
post office **oficina de correos** *f.*
poster **póster** *m.* (A); **cartel** *m.*
potato **papa** *f.;* **patata** (Spain) *f.* (C)
    potatoes in a spicy sauce **patatas**
    bravas (C)
a pound of **una libra de** (C)
practical **práctico(a)** (2)
(to) practice **practicar** (9)
(to) prefer **preferir (ie, i)**
preference **preferencia** *f.*
preoccupied **preocupado(a)**
(to) prepare **preparar**
    (to) prepare oneself **prepararse** (7)
    (to) prepare for oneself **servirse (i, i)**
    (7)
    I'm going to prepare… **les voy a**
    preparar…
(to) present **presentar** (12)
presentation **presentación** *f.*
preserve **conserva** *f.*
pressure **presión** *f.* (10)
pretty **bonito(a)** (2); **lindo(a)**
previous **anterior** (9)
price **precio** *m.* (4)
prize **premio** *m.*
profession **profesión** *f.*
professor **profesor(a)** *m.(f.)*
protein **proteína** *f.* (12)
proud **orgulloso(a)**
Puerto Rican **puertorriqueño(a)**
Puerto Rico **Puerto Rico**
pump **bomba** *f.*
purple **morado(a)** (2)
purse **bolsa** *f.*
push **empuje** *m.*
(to) put **poner** (6)
(to) put on **ponerse** (7)
(to) put on makeup **maquillarse** (7)

Q

quality **calidad** *f.* (4)
quantity **cantidad** *f.*
quarter **cuarto** *m.* (B)
   . . . quarter(s) of an hour   . . . **cuarto(s)**
   de hora (5)
quesadilla **quesadilla** *f.* (C)

R

racquet **raqueta** *f.*
raffle **sorteo** *m.* (14)
railroad station **estación de trenes**
(to) rain cats and dogs **llover (ue) a cán-**
   taros (1)
raincoat **impermeable** *m.*
It's raining. **Llueve.** (1)
rarely **rara vez** (B)
at any rate **de todos modos**
rather **bastante** (B)
(to) reach **alcanzar** (11)
reaction **reacción** *f.* (2)
(to) read **leer** (A)
ready **listo(a)**
   (to) get ready **prepararse** (7)
realist(ic) **realista** (3)
Really? **¿De veras?**
for that very reason **por eso mismo**
Let's be reasonable **Hay que ser**
   razonables. (1)
(to) receive **recibir**
reception desk **recepción** *f.* (4)
(to) recognize **reconocer**
record (sports) **récord** *m.* (15)
(to) recuperate **recuperar** (12)
red **rojo(a)** (2)
redheaded **pelirrojo(a)**
refrigerator **refrigerador** *m.* (6)
(to) refuse **no querer** (preterite) (15)
regular **regular** (2)
regularly **con regularidad** (10)
(to) regulate **regular** (12)
relative (family) **familiar** *m.*
remedy **remedio** *m.* (11)
(to) renew **renovar (ue)** (12)
rent **alquiler** *m.* (6)
(to) rent **alquilar**
   (to) rent a video **alquilar un vídeo**
(to) repeat **repetir (i, i)** (12)
(to) request **pedir (i)** (C)
reservation **reservación** *f.* (4)
(to) respond **contestar**

response **respuesta** *f.* (8)
(to) rest **descansar** (A)
rest rooms **servicios sanitarios** *m.*
restaurant **restaurante** *m.* (B)
result **resultado** *m.* (12)
(to) return **regresar** (7); **volver (ue)**
   (1)
(to) review **revisar**
rice **arroz** *m.*
(to) ride a bicycle **montar en bicicleta**
(to) ride a horse **montar a caballo** (9)
right **derecha** (B)
   right? **¿verdad?**
   (to) be right **tener razón** (10)
   to the right **a la derecha** (B)
   right away **en seguida** (9)
   right now **ahora mismo**
ring **anillo** *m.*
(to) rise **subir** (14)
risk **riesgo** *m.*
river **río** *m.* (14)
road **camino** *m.*
rock music **rock** *m.* (A)
(to) rollerskate **patinar sobre ruedas**
romantic **romántico(a)** (2)
room **cuarto** *m.* (A);, **habitación** *f.*
   (4); **sala** *f.*
roundtrip ticket **billete de ida y vuelta**
rug **alfombra** *f.* (A)
(to) run **correr** (A)
Russia **Rusia**
Russian **ruso(a)** (A)

sad **triste** (2)
(to) sail (to sailboard) **navegar en velero**
   (una tabla vela) (9); **practicar la**
   vela
sailing **navegación a vela** *f.* (9)
salad **ensalada** *f.* (C)
   vegetable salad **ensalada de vege-**
   tales (verduras) *f.*
sale **oferta** *f.*
   It's not on sale? **¿No está en oferta?**
salesman(woman) **vendedor(a)** *m.(f.)*
salsa (type of music) **salsa** *f.*
salt **sal** *f.*
Salvadoran **salvadoreño(a)**
same **mismo(a)** (7)
   Same here. **Igualmente.** (A)
   the same **lo mismo** (12)
sandal **sandalia** *f.*
sandwich (French bread) **bocadillo** *m.* (C)

(ham and cheese) sandwich **sándwich**
   (de jamón con queso) *m.* (C)
(to) have reason to feel satisfied with oneself
   darse por satisfecho
Saturday **sábado** *m.* (B)
sauce **salsa** *f.* (C)
Spanish sausage **chorizo** *m.* (C)
(to) save **ahorrar**
(to) say **decir** (6)
   (to) say yes (no) **decir que sí (no)** (6)
   what . . . says **lo que dice. . .** (4)
   What did you say? **¿Qué dijiste?** (6)
   You don't say! **¡No me digas!**
schedule **horario** *m.*
school **colegio** *m.;* **escuela** *f.* (A)
science **ciencia** *f.* (A)
   science fiction movie **película de**
   ciencia-ficción *f.*
(to) score (soccer) **anotar un gol, marcar**
   un gol (15)
sculpture **escultura** *f.* (A)
sea **mar** *m.* (1)
seashore **orilla del mar** *f.*
second **segundo(a)** (4)
secretary **secretario(a)** *m.(f.)*
(to) see **ver** (C)
   See you later. **Hasta luego.** (A)
   we'll see each other **nos vemos**
(to) sell **vender**
sensational **sensacional** (2)
sense **sentido** *m.*
sentence **oración** *f.*
September **septiembre** (1)
sequence, series **serie** *f.*
serious **serio(a)** (2)
(to) serve oneself **servirse (i, i)** (7)
at your service **a sus órdenes**
(to) set the table **poner la mesa** (7)
seven hundred **setecientos(as)**
seventh **séptimo(a)** (4)
seventy **setenta**
several **varios(as)**
(to) get in shape **ponerse en forma**
   (10)
   Are you in shape? **¿Estás en forma?**
   (10)
(to) share **compartir**
(to) shave **afeitarse** (7)
she **ella**
sheet (of paper) **hoja (de papel)** *f.* (C)
shellfish **marisco** *m.*
shirt **camisa** *f.*
shoe **zapato** *m.*
   shoe store **zapatería** *f.*

(to) shoot **fusilar**

(to) go shopping **ir de compras** (A)

   shopping cart **carrito** *m.*

   shopping center **centro comercial**

short (height) **bajo(a)**; (length) **corto(a)** (3)

should **deber**

shoulder **hombro** *m.* (10)

show **espectáculo** *m.*

(to) show a movie **dar una película** (8)

shower **ducha** *f.* (4)

   (to) take a shower **ducharse** (7)

shows it **lo muestra** (5)

sick **enfermo(a)**

side **lado** *m.*

   on my father's (mother's) side **del lado de mi padre (madre)** (A)

sign, signal **señal** *f.* (12)

silly **tonto(a)**

silver **plata** *f.*

simple **sencillo(a)** (10); **simple** (4)

since **desde (que)** (12)

   Since when? **¿Desde cuándo?** (12)

(to) sing **cantar** (A)

single **soltero(a)** (3)

sink **lavabo** *m.* (4)

sir **señor** *m.* (A)

sister **hermana** *f.* (A)

(to) sit down **sentarse (ie)** (7)

situated **situado(a)** (B)

six hundred **seiscientos(as)**

sixth **sexto(a)** (4)

sixty **sesenta**

(to) skate **patinar**

ski **esquí** *m.*

(to) ski **esquiar** (A)

skirt **falda** *f.*

slacks **pantalones** *m.*

(to) sleep **dormir (ue, u)** (4)}

   I can't sleep. **No puedo dormir.** (11)

sleepyhead **dormilón(ona)** *m.(f.)* (7)

slice of bread **rebanada de pan** *f.*

slippery **resbaloso(a)** (1)

   It's a slippery day. **Está resbaloso.** (1)

slow, slowly **despacio**

small **pequeño(a)** (A)

(to) smile **sonreírse (i, i)** (12)

smoke **humo** *m.*

snack **merienda** *f.*

   Spanish snack **tapa** *f.* (C)

(to) sneeze **estornudar** (11)

(to) snore **roncar** (12)

(to) snorkel **bucear**

snorkeling **buceo** *m.*

snow **nieve** *f.* (1)

It's snowing. **Nieva.** (1)

so **tan**

   so-so **más o menos**

soap **jabón** *m.* (5)

soccer **fútbol** *m.*

social event **evento social** *m.* (10)

sock **calcetín** *m.*

soda **soda** *f.*

sofa **sofá** *m.* (6)

soft drink **refresco** *m.*

solitude **soledad** *f.*

solution **solución** *f.* (10)

some **unos(as)** (C)

someday **algún día**

something **algo**

sometimes **a veces** (B)

son **hijo** *m.* (A)

I'm sorry. **Lo siento.**

soul **alma** *f.*

south **sur** *m.* (B)

space **espacio** *m.*

Spain **España**

Spanish **español(a)** (A)

special **especial**

speed **velocidad** *f.* (15)

spectacle **espectáculo** *m.* (13)

(to) spend **gastar**

   (to) spend time **pasar tiempo** (A)

sphere **globo** *m.*

spicy **picante** (C)

   spicy sauce **salsa picante** *f.* (C)

spoon **cuchara** *f.* (6)

sport **deporte** *m.* (A)

sporting goods store **tienda de deportes**

(to) spread **difundir**

spring **primavera** *f.* (1)

square **plaza** *f.* (B)

   square meters **m² (metros cuadrados)** (6)

squid **calamares** *m.* v

stadium **estadio** *m.* (B)

star **estrella** *f.*

starch **almidón** *m.* (12)

state **estado** *m.*

station **estación** *f.*

stationery store **papelería** *f.* (C)

(to) stay in bed **quedarse en cama** (7)

(to) stay in top condition **mantenerse en condiciones óptimas** (10)

stepfather **padrastro** *m.* (A)

stepmother **madrastra** *f.* (A)

stereo **estéreo** *m.* (A)

still **todavía**

stocking **media** *f.*

stomach **estómago** *m.* (10)

without stopping **sin parar** (11)

store **tienda** *f.*

storm **tormenta** *f.* (1)

   It's stormy. **Hay tormenta.** (1)

stove **estufa** *f.* (6)

strange **extraño(a)**

strawberry **fresa** *f.* (C)

street **calle** *f.* (B)

strong **fuerte** (3)

student **alumno(a)** *m.(f.);* **estudiante** *m.* or *f.*

(to) study **estudiar** (A)

stupid **tonto(a)**

style **estilo** *m.;* **moda** *f.*

subway **metro** *m.* (B)

   subway map **plano del metro** *m.*

   subway station **estación de metro**

success **éxito** *m.* (15)

suddenly **de repente**

(to) suffer **sufrir** (11)

sufficient **suficiente**

sugar **azúcar** *m.*

(to) suggest **sugerir (ie, i)**

suitcase **maleta** *f.*

summer **verano** *m.* (1)

summit **cumbre** *f.*

sun **sol** *m.* (1)

(to) sunbathe **tomar el sol**

Sunday **domingo** *m.* (B)

It's sunny out. **Hace sol.** (1)

Super! **¡Super!**

sure **seguro(a)**

(to) surf **practicar el surfing**

surgery **cirugía** *f.*

It will be a surprise; don't say anything to them. **Será una sorpresa; no les digas nada.** (8)

survey **encuesta** *f.*

(to) sweat **sudar** (10)

sweater **suéter** *m.*

sweet **dulce** *m.*

   sweet roll, any **pan dulce**

(to) swim **nadar**

swimming **natación** *f.*

swimming pool **piscina** *f.*

system **sistema** *m.*

T-shirt **camiseta** *f.*

(beef) taco **taco (de carne)** *m.* (C)

   taco stand **taquería** *f.* (C)

(to) take **tomar** (B)
    (to) take a long time **tardarse** (7)
    takes him **lo lleva**
    (it) takes … minutes **tarda… minutos** (B)
talent **talento** *m.* (15)
(to) talk **hablar**
tall **alto(a)**
tan **bronceado(a)** (3)
tapas restaurant **bar de tapas** *m.* (C)
tape (recording) **cinta** *f.* (A)
    tape recorder **grabadora** *f.* (A)
taste **gusto** *m.*
tasty **sabroso(a)**
taxi **taxi** *m.*
(iced) tea **té (helado)** *m.* (C)
(to) teach **enseñar**
teacher **profesor(a)** *m.(f.)*
team **equipo** *m.*
telephone **teléfono** *m.* (4)
    telephone booth **cabina de teléfono** *f.* (4)
    telephone conversation **conversación telefónica** *f.*
television set **televisor** *m.* (A)
    color television set **televisor a colores** *m.*
(to) tell **decir** (6)
    (to) tell the truth **para decir la verdad** (6)
    Tell me. **Dime.**
temperature **temperatura** *f.* (1)
    (to) take a temperature **tomar la temperatura** (11)
ten-trip ticket **billete de diez viajes**
tennis **tenis** *m.*
    tennis ball **pelota de tenis**
    tennis shoe **zapato de tenis**
tent **tienda de campaña** (9)
tenth **décimo(a)** (4)
terrace **terraza** *f.* (6)
terrain **terreno** *m.* (14)
territory **territorio** *m.*
test **prueba** *f.;* **examen** *m.*
thank you **gracias** (A)
    thank you very much (many thanks) for . . . **muchas gracias por…** (5)
    I thank you. **Les agradezco.** (5)
    thanks a million for . . . **mil gracias por…** (5)
Thanksgiving mass **misa de Acción de Gracias** *f.*
that **aquel(la), ese(a), que**
    Is that it? **¿Así es?**
    that is to say **es decir**

that is why **por eso**
that one **aquél(la)** *m.(f.),* **ése(a)** *m.(f.)*
That's all. **Es todo.** (C)
the **el** *m.,* **la** *f.,* **las** *f. pl.,* **los** *m. pl.* (A)
theater **teatro** *m.* (A)
theatrical **teatral** (2)
their **su** (5)
then **entonces, pues**
there **allí**
    there is / are **hay** (B)
    there is going to be **va a haber**
    over there **allá**
they **ellos(as)** *m.(f.)*
    They are from . . . **Son de…**
thigh **muslo** *m.* (10)
thin **delgado(a)**
thing **cosa** *f.*
(to) think **pensar (ie)**
third **tercer(o/a)** (4)
(to) be thirsty **tener sed**
this (month / afternoon) **este(a) (mes / tarde)** (C)
This is… (introduction) **Le (Te) presento a…** (A)
    this one **éste(a)** *m.(f.)*
thousand **mil**
three **tres** (C)
three hundred **trescientos(as)**
throat **garganta** *f.* (10)
one must go through . . . **hay que pasar por…** (4)
(to) throw oneself **tirarse** (10)
There's thunder. **Truena.** (1)
Thursday **jueves** *m.* (B)
ticket **billete** *m.*
time **tiempo** *m.,* **vez** *f.*
    at some other time **en otra oportunidad**
    on time **a tiempo** (5)
    from time to time **de vez en cuando** (B)
    It's about time! **¡Ya es hora!**
What time . . .? **¿A qué hora… ?** (B)
    What time is it? **¿Qué hora es?** (B)
    many times **muchas veces** (10)
timid **tímido(a)** (3)
tip **propina** *f.*
tired **cansado(a)**
to **a** (A)
    to the **al**
toast (salutation) **brindis** *m.* (8)
toast (food) **pan tostado** *m.*
toaster **tostador** *m.* (6)

today **hoy** (B)
    Today is the (day) of (month). **Hoy es el (día) de (mes).** (1)
toe **dedo del pie** *m.* (10)
together **junto(a)**
toilet **WC** *m.* (4)
tomato **tomate** *m.* (C)
tomorrow **mañana** (C)
tomorrow (morning / night) **mañana (por la mañana / noche)** (C)
(to) tone up **tonificar** (10)
tongue **lengua** *f.* (A)
too **también** (A)
    too (much) **demasiado** (1)
tooth **diente** *m.* (10)
top (of a mountain) **cima** *f.* (14)
(to) touch **tocar** (A)
tour **excursión** *f.* (14)
tourist **turista** *m.* or *f.*
tournament **torneo** *m.*
towel **toalla** *f.* (5)
town **pueblo** *m.* (9)
traditional **tradicional** (A)
train **tren** *m.* (B)
(to) travel **viajar** (A)
    travel agency **agencia de viajes** *f.*
traveler **viajero(a)**
    traveler's check **cheque de viajero** *m.* (4)
treatment **trato** *m.*
tree **árbol** *m.*
trip **viaje** *m.*
    (to) take a trip **hacer un viaje**
truly **verdaderamente**
trumpet **trompeta** *f.* (A)
truth **verdad** *f.*
(to) try to **tratar de** (12)
Tuesday **martes** *m.* (B)
tuna **atún** *m.*
(to) turn **doblar** (B)
(to) turn over **dar una vuelta** (2)
twenty **veinte**
(to) twist (a body part) **torcerse** (10)
two **dos** (C)
    the two **los(las) dos**
two hundred **doscientos(as)**
(to) type **escribir a máquina** (C)
typewriter **máquina de escribir** *f.* (A)

ugly **feo(a)** (2)
uncle **tío** *m.* (A)
(to) understand **comprender; entender**
understanding **comprensivo(a)**

unforgettable **inolvidable** (13)
United States **los Estados Unidos** (B)
university **universidad** f. (B)
unknown **desconocido(a)**
unlimited **sin límite**
until **hasta**
up **arriba** m. (1)
(to) go up **subir**
Uruguay **Uruguay** (13)
Uruguayan **uruguayo(a)**
useful **útil** (4)
as usual **como de costumbre**
usually **usualmente**

VCR **vídeo** m. (A)
vacant **vacío(a)** (6)
vacation **vacaciones** f. (9)
varied **variado(a)** (2)
various **varios(as)**
vegetable **vegetal** m. (12)
Venezuela **Venezuela**
Venezuelan **venezolano(a)**
very **muy, bien** (A)
   Very well, thank you. **Muy bien,
   gracias.**
videocassette **vídeo** m. (A)
violet **violeta** (2)
violin **violín** m. (A)
virus **virus** m. (11)
(to) visit **visitar** (5)
   (to) be visiting **estar de visita** (12)
vitamin **vitamina** f. (12)
volcano **volcán** m.
volleyball **vólibol** m.

(to) wait **esperar** (5)
   waits for them **los espera** (7)
waiter (waitress) **camarero(a)** m.(f.)
(to) wake up **despertarse (ie)** (7)
walk **paseo** m.
   (to) take a walk **dar un paseo** (A)
(to) walk **caminar**
walking stick **bastón** m. (14)
wall **pared** f.
wallet **cartera** f. (A)
(to) want **desear, querer(ie)** (C, 15)
warm **caliente** (7)
(to) wash **lavar** (5)
   (to) wash (one's hands, hair, brush one's
   teeth) **lavarse (las manos, el pelo,
   los dientes)** (7)

(to) wash clothes **lavar la ropa** (7)
(to) wash dishes **lavar los platos** (7)
washing machine **lavadora** f.
(to) watch **mirar**
   (to) watch one's weight **guardar la
   línea**
   Watch out! **¡Cuidado!** (3)
   (to) watch television **mirar la televisión** (A)
water **el agua** f.
watermelon **sandía** f. (C)
(to) waterski **esquiar en agua** (9)
waterskiing **esquí acuático** m.
way **manera** f. (10)
in that way **de esa manera**
wax **cera** f.
we **nosotros(as)** m.(f.)
weak **débil** (3)
weather **tiempo** (1)
   What's the weather like? **¿Qué tiempo
   hace?** (1)
wedding **boda** f. (8)
Wednesday **miércoles** m. (B)
week **semana** f. (C)
weekend **fin de semana** m.
(to) weigh **pesar** (12)
   I weigh . . . kilos. **Peso... kilos.** (12)
you're welcome **de nada**
well **bien** (A)
   well then **pues**
west **oeste** m. (B)
what? **¿qué?, ¿cómo?** (B)
   What a pity! **¡Qué pena!**
   What's going on? **¿Qué pasó?**
   What's new? **¿Qué hay?**
when **cuando** (A)
where? **¿adónde?, ¿dónde?**
   Where are you from? **¿De dónde es /
   eres?**
   Where is . . .? **¿Dónde está... ?**
   Where is / are there . . . ? **¿Dónde
   hay... ?**
which? **¿cuál?**
whichever **cualquier**
a good while **un buen rato** (7)
white **blanco(a)** (2)
who? **¿quién?**
whole **entero(a)**
Whose is it? **¿De quién es?**
why? **¿por qué?** (C)
   why not? **¿por qué no?** (C)
wide **ancho(a)**
wife **esposa** f.
wind **viento** m. (1)
window **ventana** f. (6)

shop window **escaparate** m.
(to) windsurf **hacer windsurfing** (13)
It's windy out. **Hace viento.** (1)
winter **invierno** m. (1)
(to) wish for **desear**
   (to) wish them **desearles** (8)
with **con** (A)
   with all my heart **con todo el
   corazón** (5)
   with me **conmigo**
   with pleasure **con mucho gusto**
within **dentro de** (8)
without **sin** (4)
   without stopping **sin parar**
woman **mujer** f.
wonderful **formidable** (2)
word **palabra** f.
(to) work **trabajar, funcionar** (A)
worker **trabajador(a)** m.(f.)
world **mundo** m.)
world championship **campeonato mundial** m. (14)
(to) worry **preocupar**
   worried **preocupado(a)**
   Don't worry. **No se preocupen.** (8)
worse, worst **peor**
. . . would like… **quisiera…** (C)
   I would like something for . . . **Quisiera
   algo (alguna cosa) para...** (11)
   we would like . . . **(nosotros)
   quisiéramos...** (C)
wrist **muñeca** f. (10)
(to) write **escribir**

year **año** m. (C)
yellow **amarillo(a)** (2)
yes **sí**
yesterday **ayer**
yogurt **yogur** m.
you (familiar) **tú** (A), (familiar plural)
   vosotros(as) m.(f.), (formal)
   usted/Ud., (formal plural)
   ustedes/Uds. (A)
young **joven**
younger **menor**
your **tu, su** (5)

zoo **parque zoológico** m.

Text Permissions

We wish to thank the authors, publishers, and holders of copyright for their permission to reprint the following:

p. 24 , 139, 140, 142 and 149 © MICHELIN from Michelin Green/Red Guide, 1995, permission No. 95–270;   **p. 29 and 37** El Corte Inglés maps and brochures;   **p. 92** adapted from "Del tiempo y otros temas" by José Juan Arrom in *Hispanoamérica: Panorama contemporáneo de su cultura,* New York, HarperCollins, 1969;   **p. 110, 127, 161, 232, 251, 268, 369, 377, 388, and 408** EL SOL 1991, 1992, 1993, 1994 issues, copyright © 1991, 1992, 1993, 1994 by Scholastic Inc., reprinted by permission of Scholastic Inc.;   **p. 185–186** "Programación" from *Diario 16,* Información y prensa, S.A., © 1990 INPRESA;   **p. 211** Names, likenesses and biographical information of active major league baseball players used by permission of Major League Baseball Players Association;   **p. 260** brochure from El Parque Nacional Volcán Poás, Costa Rica;   **p. 270–271** map, article adapted from "Alpamayo: En la cima" by Diana Zileri, CARETAS, 1987;   **p. 338** illustration, article adapted from "Acerca de los dolores musculares" by Robert P. Sheldon, *El Regional,* 1990.

Photo Credits

Unless specified below, all photos in this text were selected from the *Heinle & Heinle Image Resource Bank*. The *Image Resource Bank* is Heinle & Heinle's proprietary collection of tens of thousands of photographs related to the study of foreign language and culture.

Photographers who have contributed to the resource bank include:

Angela Coppola
Carolyn Ross
Jonathan Stark
Kathy Tarantola

p. 19 (bottom, right) Peter Menzel / Stock, Boston,   **p. 28** (bottom, left) Odyssey / Frerck / Chicago,   **p. 64** (left) J. Hammerstrom / DDB Stock Photo,   **p. 65** Antipodes / Gamma-Liaison,   **p. 72** (bottom left) Roberto Bunge / DDB Stock Photo,   **p. 72** (bottom right) Peter d'Angelo / Tony Stone Worldwide,   **p. 73** Lawrence Migdale / Tony Stone Worldwide,   **p. 85** Bob Daemmrich / Stock, Boston,   **p. 92** Ulrike Welsch,   **p. 104** (top right) Robert Fried / DDB Stock Photo,   **p. 110** (top left) Frederic De LaFosse / SYGMA,   **p. 110** (top, right) George Rose / Gamma-Liaison,   **p. 110** (bottom) The Kobal Collection,   **p. 125** Bill Wisser / Gamma-Liaison,   **p. 198** (top) Stuart Franklin / MAGNUM Photo,   **p. 198** (bottom) Robert Fried / DDB Stock Photo,   **p. 208** Chip and Rosa María de la Cueva Peterson,   **p. 233** Rafael Wollmann / Gamma-Liaison,   **p. 253** Bea Hunn / DDB Stock Photo,   **p. 255** Frank Siteman / Stock, Boston,   **p. 267** © Douglas Richardson,   **p. 279** Esbin-Anderson / The Image Works,   **p. 288** Mark Antman / The Image Works,   **p. 302** Photonews / Gamma-Liaison,   **p. 319** (left) Odyssey / Frerck / Chicago,   **p. 352** Byron Augustin / DDB Stock Photo,   **p. 353** Odyssey / Frerck / Chicago,   **p. 369** (left) Thierry Orban / SYGMA,   **p. 369** (right) David R. Austen / Stock, Boston,   **p. 370** Larry Mangino / The Image Works,   **p. 377** Odyssey / Frerck / Chicago,   **p. 378** Rob Crandall / Stock, Boston,   **p. 385** Rob Crandall / The Image Works,   **p. 390** Reuters / Bettmann,   **p. 391** (top, left) Reuters / Bettmann,   **p. 391** (top, right) Reuters / Bettmann,   **p. 391** (bottom, left) Reuters / Bettmann,   **p. 391** (bottom, right) Rick Rickman / Duomo,   **p. 397** T. Arruza / The Image Works